D0938815

Guilt
and
Children

Guilt

and

Children

Edited by

JANE BYBEE

Department of Psychology
Northeastern University
Boston, Massachusetts

ACADEMIC PRESS

San Diego   London   Boston   New York   Sydney   Tokyo   Toronto

This book is printed on acid-free paper. ∞

Copyright © 1998 by ACADEMIC PRESS

All Rights Reserved.
No part of this publication may be reproduced or transmitted in any form or by any
means, electronic or mechanical, including photocopy, recording, or any information
storage and retrieval system, without permission in writing from the publisher.

Academic Press
a division of Harcourt Brace & Company
525 B Street, Suite 1900, San Diego, California 92101-4495, USA
http://www.apnet.com

Academic Press Limited
24-28 Oval Road, London NW1 7DX, UK
http://www.hbuk.co.uk/ap/

Library of Congress Card Catalog Number: 97-80321

International Standard Book Number: 0-12-148610-9

PRINTED IN THE UNITED STATES OF AMERICA
97 98 99 00 01 02 QW 9 8 7 6 5 4 3 2 1

Contents

PART I

What Is Guilt?

1   *How Does Guilt Differ from Shame?*

June Price Tangney

PART II

How Does Guilt Develop?

5 The Emergence of Gender Differences in Guilt during Adolescence

Jane Bybee

PART III

Inducing, Instilling, and Alleviating Guilt

6 Inducing Guilt

Roy F. Baumeister

7 Religion and Guilt in Childhood

Lane Fischer and P. Scott Richards

8 *Guilt and Sexuality in Adolescents*

Donald L. Mosher

9 *The Development of Reactions to Guilt-Producing Events*

Jane Bybee, Rolande Merisca, and Rashid Velasco

P A R T   IV

Guilt and Adjustment

10 *Avoiding and Alleviating Guilt through Prosocial Behavior*

Mica Estrada-Hollenbeck and Todd F. Heatherton

11 *Guilt in the Classroom*

Christopher Williams

12 *Guilt and Abnormal Aspects of Parent–Child Interactions*

Geri R. Donenberg and John R. Weisz

13 *Guilt and Mental Health*

Jane Bybee and Zandra N. Quiles

Contributors

Numbers in parentheses indicate the pages on which the authors' contributions begin.

Karen Caplovitz Barrett (75)
Department of Psychology
Colorado State University
Ft. Collins, Colorado 80525

Roy Baumeister (127)
Department of Psychology
Case Western Reserve University
Cleveland, Ohio 44106

Jane Bybee (113, 185, 269)
Department of Psychology
Northeastern University
Boston, Massachusetts 02115

Geri R. Donenberg (245)
Northwestern University Medical
　School
Chicago, Illinois 60611

Mica Estrada-Hollenbeck (215)[1]
Department of Psychology
Harvard University
Cambridge, Massachusetts 02138

Tamara J. Ferguson (19)
Department of Psychology
Utah State University
Logan, Utah 84322

Lane Fischer (139)
Department of Educational Psychology
Brigham Young University
Provo, Utah 84602

Todd Heatherton (215)
Department of Psychology
Dartmouth College
Hanover, New Hampshire 03755

Martin L. Hoffman (91)
Department of Psychology
New York University
New York, New York 10012

Rolande Merisca (185)
Department of Psychology
Northeastern University
Boston, Massachusetts 02115

[1]Current address: 2430 Ovieda Place, Carlsbad, California 92009

Donald L. Mosher (157)
Department of Psychology
University of Connecticut
Storrs, Connecticut 06268

Zandra N. Quiles (269)
Department of Psychology
Northeastern University
Boston, Massachusetts 02115

P. Scott Richards (139
Department of Educational Psychology
Brigham Young University
Provo, Utah 84602

Hedde Stegge (19)
Department of Children and Youth
  Psychology
Free University of Amsterdam
Amsterdam, The Netherlands

June Price Tangney (1)
Department of Psychology
George Mason University
Fairfax, Virginia 22030

Rashid Velasco (185)
Department of Psychology
Northeastern University
Boston, Massachusetts 02115

John R. Weisz (245)
Department of Psychology
University of California, Los Angeles
Los Angeles, California 90032

Christopher Williams (233)
Institute for Prevention Research
Department of Public Health
Cornell University Medical School
New York, New York 10021

Preface

Guilt has long been viewed by members of the psychological and psychiatric communities as a harmful and debilitating emotion—a wellspring of neuroses, psychoses, and depression. This viewpoint fit well with the zeitgeist of the late 1960s and 1970s. Guilt over sexual behavior declined as stigmas surrounding casual, premarital, and extramarital sex and sex with multiple partners eased. Sin and virtue became quaint anachronisms. "Guilt trips" foisted upon children were seen as contributing to nothing but hang-ups. Self-help books portrayed guilt as a toxic and unnecessary emotion. Yet, over the years, as teen pregnancy rates soared, as crime rates climbed, and as the spector of AIDS loomed ever larger, the viewpoint that guilt is unnecessary has been challenged.

After a decade of neglect in the 1980s, current research findings from psychological research underscore positive aspects of guilt. Individuals more prone to the emotion are more likely to engage in volunteer charity work. Peers report that high-guilt individuals are more caring, considerate, honest, and trustworthy. Higher guilt is related to less racism. High-guilt students receive better grades in school and have better study skills. Students higher on guilt are also less aggressive and have fewer conduct problems in school. Guilt may even be a lifesaver. Adolescents with a greater proclivity for the emotion are more likely to delay sexual intercourse until they are older and, as young adults, those higher on guilt have sex less frequently and with fewer partners, putting them at lower risk for AIDS. Moreover, adolescents who are more predisposed to guilt are more likely to adhere to prescribed medical regimes. Guilt, in fact, relates to a wide array of behaviors that have historically correlated with few, if any, personality or individual difference variables.

This volume contains contributions from such eminent founding fathers in the field of guilt research as Martin Hoffman and Donald Mosher as well as contributions from rising young investigators and well-regarded scholars in other areas who have recently turned a portion of their talents and interest to guilt. In the following chapters, this gifted cast of contributors explores the origins and development of guilt and its relationship to adaptive behavior and mental illness in children.

How is guilt different from shame? The two emotions are often confused, and as Tangney (Chapter 1) points out, long-held views in the academic and broader community on how the emotions differ have proved wrong as often as not. Traditional wisdom, for example, holds that the emotions are associated with different types of situations, with shame resulting from "competitive defeat, a sexual rebuff, a social snub, invasion of privacy, or being ridiculed" (H. B. Lewis, 1979, p. 382) and guilt resulting from failure to meet responsibilities. Empirical studies, however, show few differences in the types of situations that evoke the two emotions. Another common misconception is that shame arises from public exposure and censure, whereas guilt is a private experience between the person and his or her conscience. Analyses of narratives of shame- and guilt-evoking incidents, however, indicate no differences between events occurring in the presence of an observing audience and those in which the emotion was experienced when the person was alone.

Tangney identifies the characteristics that do differentiate guilt from shame, drawing in part from her own groundbreaking research. In shame, the individual's focus of attention is on the self and its deficiencies; the self serves as both judge and accused, and the ashamed individual experiences global devaluation. The concern is with the real or imagined perceptions of others. The emotion is phenomenologically experienced as acutely painful, with a sense of shrinking and feeling awkward, small, helpless, and worthless. The ashamed individual reacts to the emotion by wanting to hide, disappear, or retaliate. Remediation is difficult because it involves recasting or remaking the self. In guilt, the focus is on the victim or the misbehavior and, hence, is more circumscribed. Concerns are with the victim's sufferings and ramifications of the act. The emotion is experienced as an unpleasant sense of remorse and tension accompanied by an urgent need to expiate or relieve the emotion. Reactions include making reparation, confessing, and apologizing.

Once key differences between the two emotions are established, the stage is set for an examination of the effects of development. The remainder of Chapter 1 is devoted to identifying and discussing developmental milestones and accompanying changes that enable the individual to experience shame and guilt as increasingly discrete emotions. According to Tangney, a sense of self and a set of standards that one fails to meet are prerequisites for both emotions. As one's self-image and internalized standards become more complex and abstract, the events eliciting the emotions of shame and guilt may likewise evolve. According to Tangney, to experience guilt and shame as distinct emotions, childen must have the ability to make clear distinctions between self and behavior and be capable of making complex attributional appraisals of situations and determinations of blame. Tangney points out that children cannot distinguish between "enduring characteristics of the self and more transient types of behaviors" until around age 8. She reviews evidence that children are not able to articulate differences between guilt and shame until this time. Afterward, there is ample evidence that the emotions may be readily distinguished. This viewpoint differs markedly from that of Barrett (Chapter 3) and others who argue that guilt emerges as an emotion distinct from shame as early as age 2.

How can guilt be assessed in children? At what age may guilt be reliably measured? Ferguson and Stegge (Chapter 2) begin their review of guilt measures appropriate for use with children by presenting their theoretical conceptualization of key defining elements of guilt. They review the most recently devised measures of guilt designed for adults and then turn their attention to measures constructed for children. In a summary table, they present information on the internal consistency of each measure and the relationship of the guilt indices to internalizing and externalizing symptoms. Additional information on scale construction, psychometric properties, and appropriate age range for each measure is contained in the text. The authors' review, in turn, self-report scenario-based measures, self-report forced-choice measures, semiprojective measures, and observational measures. Next, Ferguson and Stegge discuss the advantages and disadvantages of using hypothetical versus real-life eliciting situations to assess guilt and problems with findings that may be confounded by the willingness of the participant to take the perspective of or empathize with the main character. Concerns with social desirability effects and discriminant validity are also discussed. The authors express their views on the currently popular practice of partialling out the effects of one emotion (such as shame) to examine the "pure" effects of another (as in investigations of "shame-free" guilt). The chapter closes with recommendations and thoughts on assessing maladaptive aspects of guilt. Sample items from reviewed instruments and information on ordering the complete questionnaire are contained in the Appendix.

When in development does guilt first appear? This is a central question of Barrett's chapter (Chapter 3) on the early origins of guilt. According to psychoanalytic theory, guilt cannot be present in young children because it does not arise until after the resolution of the Oedipal conflict and establishment of the superego. Recent research contradicts this viewpoint and suggests that guilt is present much earlier and is evident in children as young as 2. What cognitive prerequisites, if any, are required for guilt to be experienced? Barrett presents perspectives from several major theories on this question. She also reviews results of studies conducted with toddlers in which they exhibit an unexpected amount of interpersonal concern and reparative behavior. Further findings indicate that guilt-relevant behaviors such as reparation, confession, and apologies are evident during the second year of life, much earlier than was previously thought.

Hoffman originally advanced the position that guilt develops from empathy early in development when the child realizes that he or she is the cause of another's distress. Hoffman's work on guilt and empathy has garnered widespread attention, admiration, and acceptance. In Chapter 4, he presents a comprehensive model of empathy-based guilt and its development. He explores five types of moral encounters that may give rise to empathic distress and guilt: (a) innocent bystander, where one observes another person in pain or need and feels guilt over not acting to alleviate the person's distress; (b) transgressor, where the individual has committed or is contemplating the commission of a transgression and feels guilty over the act or the thought; (c) virtual transgressor, where no transgression or act of omission is involved, but guilt arises anyway because a relationship partner is suffering; (d) multiple claimants, where the individual is forced to choose which victim to help and which to ignore; and (e) caring versus justice, where the individual must choose between helping an individual or following a moral principle.

Each variety of empathy-based guilt is presented in turn, subtypes are reviewed, and effects of development are discussed. In the section on virtual transgressions, for example, Hoffman discusses relationship guilt, which arises in ambiguous situations where one's relationship partner is feeling sad or down and one feels somehow to blame. Separation guilt is said to result when children feel guilty about growing up and leaving home. Guilt over achievement may result from succeeding or accomplishing things that peers or family members do not. Guilt over affluence occurs when individuals engage in lifestyle comparisons. The chapter provides a rich overview of the types of events that evoke guilt in children.

Who is more prone to guilt—males or females—and why? Do individuals become more prone to guilt with development or less? What are the differences in the types of situations that females and males feel guilty about? These questions are addressed by Bybee in Chapter 5. Answers emerging from empirical research may be surprising to many readers, as they fall in a direction opposite to that predicted by traditional wisdom in psychology and psychoanalytic thought. From a Freudian perspective, for example, males would be expected to develop the stronger superego and hence to experience the most intense guilt. Yet studies indicate that from adolescence onward, females are more prone than males to guilt. Further, whereas most models of moral and prosocial development posit an increase in moral thought, affect, and action with development, recent findings indicate that feelings of guilt plummet. Theoretical and empirical work on gender differences is surprisingly sparse. In the absence of an existing framework within which to interpret empirical findings, Bybee offers a rudimentary model. Bybee points out that, during childhood, males are more likely than females to mention aggression as a source of guilt. Aggression is, however, a part of the male sex-role stereotype and appears to be tolerated by parents and peers alike. Males may become inured to feelings of guilt over aggression, and as aggressive acts become fewer in number with development, guilt may decrease in frequency and intensity as well. Females, in contrast, are more likely than males to mention guilt over inconsiderate and disingenuous behavior in the context of close interpersonal relationships. Inconsiderateness runs counter to the female sex-role stereotype, and misbehavior in general is not well tolerated by parents and friends of females. Moreover, rather than diminishing, inconsiderateness becomes a greater source of guilt during adolescence. For females, the decline in guilt intensity during adolescence is less marked and appears to reverse itself sooner. The author reviews gender and developmental differences in guilt intensity, in what adolescents feel guilty about, and in who makes them feel guilty. Finally, Bybee discusses the findings that many of the strongest correlates of guilt—

internalizing disorders, aggression, criminality, empathy, nurturing behaviors, and so on—also differ strongly across sex.

How do parents make their child feel guilty? Should they? According to Baumeister (Chapter 6), guilt often originates in close interpersonal relationships. Guilt may grow from empathy when an individual realizes he or she has hurt or injured another person. Guilt may be rooted as well in feelings of anxiety over exclusion or rejection that may result from hurting another person. The closer the emotional bond between the parties, the greater the concern over the other's feelings and with preserving the relationship, and hence, the greater the potential that guilt will arise. Baumeister repeatedly finds in empirical study that interpersonal neglect is the most common source of guilt. Guilt induction may help adults not only in guiding children's behavior in day-to-day interactions but in the larger task of socialization. Guilt induction may also help the parent–child and other close, communal relationships from weakening and deteriorating. Can guilt induction backfire? In a word, yes. The inducer may feel guilty over manipulating the other person, and the recipient of an attempt at guilt induction may feel angry and resentful. Baumeister closes by noting that parents may be reluctant to instill guilt in children because of fears of damaging the child's sense of self-esteem. Baumeister is a highly regarded expert in the fields of both self-esteem and guilt. He observes that inordinately high self-esteem (and accompanying feelings of superiority and entitlement) can present its own set of problems and recommends instilling an equitable mixture of guilt and self-esteem.

Who feels the most guilt? In a friendly exchange to which I was party, a rabbi argued that Jews are the group most prone to guilt and, indeed, invented the emotion. To this, a priest responded that although Jews may have invented guilt, Catholics have perfected it. In casual conversation, the important role that religious faith, texts, and leaders play in inculcating guilt is widely acknowledged, yet the research literature on guilt and religion is quite sparse. Fischer and Richards (Chapter 7) explore reasons for this neglect. They point out that both religion and guilt have been unfairly maligned as sources and symptoms of poor mental health. The authors argue that to meaningfully assess the relationship of religion to mental health, refined conceptualizations of both religiosity and guilt are necessary. An intrinsic religious orientation, that is, being involved in religion and internally committed to it because one truly believes in it, is associated with socioemotional competence and freedom from pathological guilt. In contrast, an extrinsic religious orientation, that is, being involved in religion to obtain social and personal benefits, is associated with both poor socioemotional competence and unhealthy guilt. Further, greater participation in religious activities is *positively* correlated with a healthy proclivity for guilt and is *negatively* correlated with chronic, maladaptive guilt (perhaps because religion provides children with the principles and sense of responsibility that engender guilt, but offers means such as confession and prayer to relieve the emotion). Beyond distinguishing types of guilt and dimensions of religiosity, Fischer and Richards offer insights into the beliefs of specific religions and religious denominations (e.g., Sikhism, Judaism, Catholicism, Episcopalianism, Presbyterianism, and Mormonism). In interviews conducted with religious leaders and representatives, they explore precipitators of guilt as well as ritualistic and personal means of alleviating the emotion. The authors close with a review of several models of religious development and thoughts on how guilt may develop alongside religious beliefs.

Mosher's essay on guilt and sexuality in adolescents (Chapter 8) presents a fresh, theoretically rich examination of the inhibitory or interruptive aspects of guilt in sexual behavior using Tomkin's script theory as a conceptual model. The chapter is intellectually challenging, densely packed, and filled with such a wealth of complex, varied, and novel ideas that it is impossible to do it justice in a brief summary. Among the highlights are Mosher's discussion of how emotions may permutate and change in intensity well after the precipitating event. Upon reflection, for example, a sexual event that first resulted in excitement and joy may turn to guilt, and feelings of guilt may, upon further reflection, become magnified or amplified so that over time the affect accompanying an event may in no way resemble the original emotion. Another chapter highlight is Mosher's discussion of the differential role of disgust, guilt, and shame in the interruption and discouragement of sexual activities. Mosher sees disgust as a more toxic emotion than guilt, more contaminating, and more likely to evoke responses involving purification. Sexual acts that are viewed by observers as sexually disgusting rather than evocative of guilt are more likely to be met with contempt and distain. Under what precipitating conditions does guilt inhibit sexual enjoyment and activities? What role do parents play in the socialization of sexual guilt? What are appropriate guidelines for the sex education of adolescents? Mosher, who is also a leading expert in sexual behavior, offers his perspectives.

How do children react to guilt-producing events and how do these responses change over the course of development? Bybee, Merisca, and Velasco (Chapter 9) provide an extensive review of the literature and the results of two original empirical investigations. They group guilt reactions into the following categories: reconciliation and action tendencies (e.g., victim-oriented concern, confession, apologies, renunciation, restitution); self-blame and intropunitive responses (e.g., recognition of wrongdoing, intensifiers, rumination); rationalizations (e.g., justifications, excuses); avoidance; concern with detection and punishment; hedonistic reactions; and unresponsiveness. Content analyses of self-described reactions to guilt-producing incidents are used to identify the most and least common reactions among 205 5th, 8th, and 11th graders and to examine effects of development. Excerpts from adolescents' narratives provide examples of each type of response. The authors report that renunciation and attempts to reestablish the relationship (in the absence of apology or reparation), which have received little attention in past work on guilt, were very common guilt responses among adolescents in their sample. In contrast, self-hatred, which has received much attention, was very infrequently mentioned. With development, preoccupation with punishment lessened. In contrast, remorse, renunciation, use of intensifiers, and efforts to reestablish the damaged relationship doubled and tripled in frequency from the 5th to the 11th grades.

Intellectualizations may serve to extinguish feelings of guilt and eliminate its potential for motivating positive social behaviors. In the second study reported in Chapter 9, Bybee et al. find that students ($N = 109$) who used rationalizations more in reaction to guilt-producing incidents experienced less guilt. Greater use of rationalizations was associated with less prosocial behavior and greater aggression as reported by peers as well as greater self-reported racism.

Guilt has long been considered to be one of the "social" or "moral" emotions. In Chapter 10, Estrada-Hollenbeck and Heatherton develop their conceptualization of the interpersonal functions of guilt. They begin by arguing that, unlike shame, guilt is associated with action tendencies that are reconciliatory in nature (apologies rather than cover-up), arises from specific events that are amenable to change or repair (transgressions rather than an ongoing condition), and prompts concern with the victim rather than the observer's perceptions. These differences may explain, in part, why guilt is associated more strongly than shame with prosocial behavior. The authors then turn briefly to the social roots of guilt, pointing to the origins of the emotion in empathy and highlighting the important influences of parental warmth and the social environment in its development. They then define prosocial behavior, describing two major categories of prosocial behavior: relationship-mending behaviors, which repair or restore relationships; and relationship-enhancing behaviors, which promote or sustain relationships. They review empirical evidence that individuals engage in relationship-mending actions such as concessions, apologies, and restitutions to reduce guilt and engage in relationship-enhancing actions such as helping and volunteerism to avoid experiencing guilt. In an original, exploratory study included at the end of the chapter, the authors examine processes of forgiveness that arise in the aftermath of guilt-producing events. Few past studies have examined forgiveness despite its importance in the repair and maintenance of interpersonal bonds. One key finding of the authors' investigation is that perpetrators continue to feel guilt over the transgression even when they are forgiven. Continued feelings of guilt may help the perpetrator learn lessons from the transgression. Unexpectedly, victims who did not forgive the perpetrator (versus those who did forgive) experienced very high levels of guilt—levels as high as those reported by the perpetrator. Perhaps victims felt guilty because rebuffing the perpetrator (by refusing forgiveness) caused pain. The results suggest that forgiveness may be as important for the victim as it is for the instigator.

Williams (Chapter 11) explores the useful functions that guilt may serve in the classroom. He notes that guilt may operate as a self-imposed sanction for substandard behavior, a function that may be especially important when formal punishment is inappropriate (such as when students have tried, but not put forth their best). Guilt may prevent the individual from thinking about, and hence planning to commit, prohibited acts. Guilt may help students remember and learn from past transgressions. The emotion may also be so arresting that it stops a behavior midstream and redirects it. Guilt may provide an important social signal to others that the experiencing individual is a sensitive and contrite person and may convince observers that the guilty party is deserving of forgiveness. In addition, guilt is associated with action tendencies (such as apologies and desires for reparation) that are inherently prosocial in nature.

Williams acknowledges that guilt is a social emotion that may originate in empathy and needs for social acceptance. He notes the emotion is related to less aggressiveness and greater prosocial behavior. The author also argues that guilt develops alongside conscience and may give rise to individualistic strivings. He provides evidence that guilt is linked not only to positive social behaviors, but to a wide spectrum of goal-directed behaviors such as assertiveness, frustration tolerance, and academic achievement. Williams reports that outside the classroom, guilt is related to less sexually promiscuous and coercive behavior and less illegal drug use. Williams explores the reasons that children in higher academic tracks are more prone to guilt. He closes with a discussion of the use of guilt induction by teachers as a discipline technique in the classroom.

Although guilt may serve positive functions in interpersonal relationships and may promote individualistic strivings and achievement, it has a darker side as well. Donenberg and Weisz (Chapter 12) explore the relationship of guilt to psychopathology in children and the origins of unhealthy manifestations of guilt in abnormal parent–child interactions. The authors point out that just as deficiencies in guilt may result in sociopathy, conduct problems, and antisocial behavior, an excess of guilt and exaggerated feelings of responsibility may result in depression, overinvolvement in dysfunctional relationships with the parent, and concern with others to the point of neglecting one's own needs. At either extreme, according to this view, guilt may become maladaptive. How is guilt inculcated in children from normal families? The authors review general child-rearing styles and disciplinary responses to children's transgressions. For example, induction (i.e., providing explanations for rules, explaining consequences) is associated with high levels of guilt and reparation in children, whereas power assertive techniques (i.e., threats, force, punishment) are associated with less guilt. What specifically can individuals say to make others feel guilty? They may state relationship obligations ("A daughter is supposed to help her mother around the house"), make comparisons ("Your sister always cleans her room without my asking"), interrogate the other ("Why didn't you clean your room? You had enough time this weekend to go out with your friends, didn't you? Didn't you remember that I asked you to clean up?"), or acquiesce ("Okay. Fine. I will clean your room myself. Dad and I wanted to go to a movie, but we'll stay home so I can clean your room for you").

How do patterns of guilt induction become dysfunctional? Donenberg and Weisz review ways in which depressed mothers may induce an exaggerated sense of responsibility and guilt in their children. They also review factors such as parental lack of responsibility taking and abusive parenting styles that may result in deficiencies in guilt. Finally, they present the results of an original empirical investigation of guilt induction in parent–child interactions of clinic-referred youngsters. The authors asked 82 parent–child dyads to discuss a real-life conflict. The conversation was video- and audiotaped and guilt-inducing communications were coded. Contrary to expectations that guilt-induction attempts by the parent might lower aggressiveness by the child (and hence be negatively correlated with hostility), a positive correlation was found. Perhaps parents of highly aggressive children were forced to use induction more often in an attempt to control the child's behavior. Also unexpectedly (given the hypothesized link between excessive guilt and internalizing disorders), parent-initiated guilt was unrelated to depression among their children. This finding does, however, fit well with the view (expressed in chapters written by Tangney and Baumeister) that greater guilt and guilt induction are generally adaptive and not sources of psychopathy. In other findings, parents used more guilt induction with older than with younger children, younger parents used guilt induction more frequently than older parents, and both ethnicity and religion affected use of guilt induction in the parent–child interaction.

Researchers have been in sharp disagreement on the role of guilt in psychopathology. Some prominent researchers in the field have argued that guilt does not and, from a theoretical perspective, should not relate to mental illness, as guilt attributions are likely to be unstable, specific, external, and hence unlikely to have long-term ramifications on overall mental well-being. Other researchers have argued that guilt is integrally related to poor mental health. Considerable empirical evidence has been amassed for both positions. The authors' research has provided empirical support for a two-factor model of guilt. In Chapter 13, Bybee and Quiles argue that predispositional guilt (a personality readiness or proclivity for guilt) may be distinguished from chronic guilt (an ongoing condition of guiltiness unattached to immediate or circumscribed triggering events). They maintain that chronic feelings of guilt, undischarged, unresolved, and unalleviated, hold the potential for destructiveness. They review findings that indicate that chronic measures of guilt show significantly stronger relationships than measures of predispositional guilt with poor mental health. Negative feelings, unfocused and unresolved, may contribute to emotional distress by providing an endless reminder of the failing that evoked the guilt. Chronic guilt is also associated with hostility and antisocial behavior. In contrast, predispositional guilt is correlated with prosocial behavior and is not associated with intropunitive symptoms. Is chronic guilt indistinguishable from shame, as some have suggested? Original analyses suggest that each relates independently to indices of psychopathology.

Bybee and Quiles further argue that when characteristics of the individual, guilt reaction, or eliciting situation prevent guilt from being discharged, the emotion may become virulent. Characteristics of the individual such as depression and low self-efficacy interfere with the ability to cope with emotion and put intent into action. Individuals who are incapacitated by depression and accompanying symptoms of indecisiveness, fatigue and helplessness may be unable to act upon feelings of guilt and, for them, the emotion may become dysfunctional. They maintain that reactions to guilt-producing events such as rumination and self-hatred that need-lessly prolong and aggravate feelings of guilt may result from and give rise to inter-nalizing disorders (such as depression and eating disorders). They point out that when guilt arises from insoluble situations such as existential conditions or death of the other party, it may become chronic and hence maladaptive.

Jane Bybee

Reference

Lewis, H. B. (1979). Guilt in obsession and paranoia. In C. E. Izard (Ed.), *Emotions in personality and psychopathology* (pp. 399–414). New York: Plenum.

PART I

What Is Guilt?

CHAPTER 1

How Does Guilt Differ from Shame?

June Price Tangney

George Mason University, Fairfax, Virginia

INTRODUCTION

Parents, teachers, and psychologists alike often use the terms *shame* and *guilt* interchangeably. Shame and guilt are frequently mentioned in the same breath, as moral emotions that regulate social behavior (e.g., "feelings of shame and guilt help a child resist temptation"), or as potentially problematic affective experiences that lie at the heart of many psychological symptoms (e.g., "she was plagued by excessive feelings of shame and guilt, and eventually became depressed"). Recent theory and research, however, has identified important differences between these two closely related emotions—differences that appear to have rather profound implications both for psychological adjustment and for social behavior.

In this chapter,[1] I describe several theoretical distinctions between shame and guilt that have been suggested by social scientists over the years. I begin with a review of earlier attempts to differentiate shame and guilt, including those based on psychoanalytic and anthropological theories. For example, a common basis for

[1]Portions of this chapter were adapted from Tangney, J. P. (1995). Recent empirical advances in the study of shame and guilt. *American Behavioral Scientist, 38,* 1132–1145.

Guilt and Children
Copyright © 1998 by Academic Press. All rights of reproduction in any form reserved.

distinguishing between shame and guilt focuses on presumed differences in the types of situations that elicit these emotions. I summarize recent empirical results that seriously challenge this assumption and describe the breadth of empirical support for Lewis's (1971) reconceptualization, which downplays the objective content of eliciting events and instead highlights differences in the individual's *interpretation* of the role of the self in shame and guilt situations. Consistent with Lewis (1971), a range of studies confirm that distinct phenomenological experiences are associated with shame's focus on the self, and guilt's focus on specific behaviors. This research also indicates that shame and guilt typically lead to very different motivations in interpersonal contexts, with guilt on balance emerging as the more adaptive response to transgressions. I close with a discussion of possible developmental changes in the experience and meaning of these moral emotions.

EARLY DISTINCTIONS BETWEEN SHAME AND GUILT

Historically, scientists and laypersons alike have not made a clear distinction between shame and guilt. In everyday discourse, guilt is typically the favored term, used as a "catch-all" phrase to refer to experiences of both shame and guilt. The average person rarely speaks of his or her own "shame." (In fact, one could easily argue that today's American society is rather "shame-phobic.") Instead, people often use the word "guilt" (e.g., "I felt so *guilty* when I realized how thoughtless I was") when they mean they felt shame, guilt, or some combination of the two. In the clinical and scientific literature, too, the terms "shame" and "guilt" are often used rather loosely, sometimes interchangeably, leading to considerable conceptual confusion.

The Psychoanalytic Perspective

Over the years, psychoanalytically oriented theories have paid the most attention to shame and guilt. But the father of psychoanalysis, Sigmund Freud, too, largely neglected the distinction between these two emotions. In his earlier work, Freud (1905/ 1953) briefly discussed shame as a reaction formation against sexually exhibitionistic impulses, but in his later writings (Freud, 1914/1957; 1923/1961; 1924/1961; 1925/ 1961) he essentially ignored the construct of shame, focusing instead on a rather cognitive concept of guilt in relation to ego–superego conflicts (see Lewis, 1971; Morrison, 1987; and Tangney, 1994, for a more detailed analysis of Freud's approach to shame and guilt). Lewis (1971) has argued that in developing a theory that focused almost exclusively on guilt, Freud (like many contemporary psychologists) may have mislabeled his patients' shame experiences as guilt experiences.

In years following, a number of post-Freudian theorists made explicit attempts to distinguish between shame and guilt within a neo-Freudian structural framework (e.g., Hartmann & Lowenstein, 1962; Jacobson, 1954; Piers & Singer, 1953). Fairly early in his writings, Freud (1914/1957) introduced the notion of an "ego-ideal." Although Freud largely abandoned this construct in his later work, subsequent ego psychologists picked up on this theme and elaborated on the distinction between ego-ideal and superego (or conscience) proper. A number of theorists applied this distinction to their conceptualization of shame and guilt. For example, Piers and Singer (1953) viewed guilt as a reaction to clashes between the ego and superego (with its roots in fears of castration, similar to Freud's own notions). In contrast, shame was conceptualized as a reaction to clashes between the ego and the ego-ideal (with its roots in feelings of inferiority, and consequent fears of loss of love and abandonment). This neo-Freudian distinction between shame and guilt can be seen as a precursor to Lewis's (1971) later distinction between self versus behavior concerns, and it is consistent with Erikson's (1950) descriptions of shame as global exposed self-doubt versus guilt over misguided behavior (initiative). But the neo-Freudian structural distinction is not without its problems. For example, Hartmann and Loewenstein (1962) questioned the practical utility of such a structural distinction. And more recently, Lindsay-Hartz (1984) provided evidence apparently contradicting Piers and Singer (1953), showing that shame typically results from a *negative* ideal (e.g., the recognition that "we are who we do not want to be"), rather than from a recognition that we have failed to live up to some *positive* ego-ideal.

With the emergence of self psychology, shame gained an even more prominent place in psychodynamic theory. Quite a number of psychoanalytically oriented theorists have cited shame as a key component of a range of psychological disorders (Kohut, 1971; A. P. Morrison, 1989; N. K. Morrison, 1987; Nathanson, 1987). But in their new focus on shame, these theories tended to give short shrift to guilt. Ironically, in many cases, the construct of guilt (distinct from shame) is largely neglected and, as in traditional Freudian theory, the distinction between these two emotions is lost.

The Anthropological Perspective

Outside of psychoanalytic circles, when people make a distinction between shame and guilt, they often refer to differences in the content and/or structure of events eliciting these emotions. The assumption here, popularized by midcentury anthropologists (e.g., Benedict, 1946), is that certain *kinds of situations* lead to shame, whereas other *kinds of situations* lead to guilt. For example, there is a long-standing notion that shame is a more "public" emotion than guilt. Shame is seen as arising from public exposure and disapproval of some shortcoming or transgression, whereas guilt is seen as a more "private" experience arising from self-generated pangs of conscience. This public/private distinction remains a frequently cited basis for distinguishing between shame and guilt. Gehm and Scherer (1988), for example, recently speculated that "shame is usually dependent on the public exposure of one's frailty or failing, whereas guilt may be something that remains a secret with us, no one else knowing of our breach of social norms or of our responsibility for an immoral act" (p. 74).

Surprisingly, it appears that for decades no one conducted any empirical research to evaluate this public/private distinction, even though it's a relatively easy proposition to assess. In fact, to our knowledge, our study of children and adults' shame, guilt, and pride experiences represents the first systematic analysis of "audiences" to these emotion-eliciting events (Tangney, Marschall, Rosenberg, Barlow, & Wagner, 1994). In this study, we asked several hundred children and adults to describe recent events in which they had experienced shame, guilt, and pride, and we then analyzed these narrative accounts of real-life emotion episodes to evaluate, among other things, just how public or private these events really were. Our results clearly challenge the anthropologists' public versus private distinction. Although shame and guilt were *each* most often experienced in the presence of others (among both children and adults), a substantial number of respondents (17.2% of children and 16.5% of adults) reported shame experiences occurring alone—when *not* in the presence of others. More importantly, "solitary" shame was equally prevalent as "solitary" guilt. In addition, although adults reported that on average somewhat more people were *present* during shame than guilt-eliciting situations, the number of people *involved* in these events and (most to the point) the frequency with which others were *aware* of the respondents' behavior did not vary as a function of shame and guilt. Similarly, in an independent study of adults' narrative accounts of personal shame, guilt, and embarrassment experiences (Tangney, Miller, Flicker, & Barlow, 1996), there was no evidence that shame was the more "public" emotion. In fact, in this latter study, shame was somewhat *more* likely (18.2%) than guilt (10.4%) to occur outside of the presence of an observing audience.

If shame and guilt do not differ in terms of the degree of public exposure, do they differ in terms of the *types* of the transgressions or failures that elicit them? Not very much, as it turns out. Our analyses of narrative accounts of personal shame and guilt experiences provided by both children and adults indicate that there are very few, if any, "classic" shame-inducing or guilt-inducing situations (Tangney, 1992; Tangney et al., 1994). Most types of events (e.g., lying, cheating, stealing, failing to help another, disobeying parents, etc.) were cited by some people in connection with feelings of shame and by other people in connection with guilt. Unlike moral transgressions, which are equally likely to elicit shame or guilt, there was some evidence that nonmoral failures and shortcomings (e.g., socially inappropriate behavior or dress) may be more likely to elicit shame. Even so, failures in work, school, or sport settings and violations of social conventions were cited by a significant number of children and adults in connection with guilt (Tangney et al., 1994).

LEWIS'S (1971) RECONCEPTUALIZATION: SHAME AND GUILT DIFFER IN FOCUS ON SELF VERSUS BEHAVIOR

How do shame and guilt differ, if not in terms of the types of situations that elicit them? Drawing on a mix of psychoanalytic theory and ego psychology, coupled with a background in cognitive psychology, Helen Block Lewis (1971) developed a new approach to distinguishing between shame and guilt, focusing on differences in the role of the self in these experiences. She wrote:

> The experience of shame is directly about the *self,* which is the focus of evaluation. In guilt, the self is not the central object of negative evaluation, but rather the *thing* done or undone is the focus. In guilt, the self is negatively evaluated in connection with something but is not itself the focus of the experience. (p. 30).

According to Lewis (1971), this differential emphasis on self ("*I* did that horrible thing") vs. behavior ("I *did* that horrible *thing*") leads to very different phenomenological experiences. Shame is an acutely painful emotion that is typically accompanied by a sense of shrinking or of "being small," and by a sense of worthlessness and powerlessness. Shamed people also feel exposed. Although shame doesn't necessarily involve an actual observing audience, present to witness one's shortcomings, there is often the imagery of how one's defective self would appear to others. Lewis (1971) described a split in self-functioning in which the self is both agent and object of observation and disapproval. An observing self witnesses and denigrates the focal self as unworthy and reprehensible. Finally, shame often leads to a desire to escape or to hide—to sink into the floor and disappear.

In contrast, guilt, according to Lewis (1971), is generally a less painful and devastating experience than shame because, in guilt, our primary concern is with a particular behavior, somewhat apart from the self. So guilt doesn't affect one's core identity. Feelings of guilt can be painful, nonetheless. Guilt involves a sense of tension, remorse, and regret over the "bad thing done." People in the midst of a guilt experience often report a nagging focus or preoccupation with the transgression—thinking of it over and over, wishing they had behaved differently or could somehow undo the deed.

There is now considerable empirical support for this distinction between shame and guilt from both quantitative and qualitative studies (Ferguson & Stegge, 1995; Ferguson, Stegge, & Damhuis, 1990a,b, 1991; Lindsay-Hartz, 1984; Lindsay-Hartz, DeRivera, & Mascolo, 1995; Tangney, 1993; Tangney et al., 1994; Tangney, Miller, Flicker, & Barlow, 1996; Wicker, Payne, & Morgan, 1983). For example, in two independent studies, we asked young adults to describe a personal shame experience and a personal guilt experience, and then rate these experiences along a number of phenomenological dimensions (Tangney, 1993; Tangney et al., 1996). The results across the two studies were remarkably consistent. Compared to guilt, shame experiences were rated as significantly more painful and intense. When shamed, people felt physically smaller and more inferior to others. Shame experiences were more likely to involve a sense of exposure and a preoccupation with others' opinions. And when feeling shame, people were more compelled to hide and less inclined to admit what they had done.

Our analyses of phenomenological ratings strongly supported Lewis's (1971) distinction between shame and guilt—with the exception of one key dimension: the focus on self versus behavior. Participants' responses to a single relevant item (i.e., "blamed my *actions* and behavior" vs. "blamed my personality and my *self*") did not differ across shame and guilt experiences. Secondary analyses and anecdotal reports indicated that these lay participants (college undergraduates with little background in psychology) did not really understand the dimension we were attempting to assess (Tangney et al., 1996). The item itself was apparently too abstract and difficult to understand.

Subsequently, we adopted an entirely different approach that did not require participants themselves to rate and evaluate this rather abstract concept. Instead, we coded participants' counterfactual thinking associated with shame and guilt to explore the self versus behavior distinction (Niedenthal, Tangney, & Gavanski, 1994). Four independent studies provided very strong support for Lewis's (1971) conceptualization. For example, in one study, participants described a personal shame or guilt experience and were then asked to "counterfactualize" the event (e.g., list factors that might have caused the event to end differently). Analysis of the counterfactual responses indicated that shame descriptions were more often followed by statements undoing aspects of the self; guilt descriptions were more often followed by statements undoing aspects of behavior. Parallel results were obtained in the three other counterfactual studies, each employing a somewhat different paradigm.

In sum, there is now an impressive body of research—including qualitative case study analyses (Lewis, 1971; Lindsay-Hartz, 1984; Lindsay-Hartz et al., 1995), content analyses of shame and guilt narratives (Ferguson et al., 1990a; Tangney, 1992; Tangney et al., 1994), participants' quantitative ratings of personal shame and guilt experiences (e.g., Ferguson et al., 1991; Tangney, 1993; Tangney et al., 1996; Wicker, Payne, & Morgan, 1983; Wallbott & Scherer, 1988), and analyses of participants' counterfactual thinking (Niedenthal, Tangney, & Gavanski, 1994)—which converge to underscore that shame and guilt are distinct emotional experiences that differ substantially along cognitive, affective, and motivational dimensions, as described by Lewis (1971). These differences are summarized in Table I.

GUILT APPEARS TO BE THE MORE "MORAL" EMOTION

One of the many consistent themes emerging from these diverse studies is that shame and guilt lead to very different motivations for subsequent behavior in interpersonal contexts. A consistent finding is that shame often motivates an avoidance

TABLE I   Key Dimensions on Which Shame and Guilt Differ

	Shame	Guilt
Focus of evaluation	Global self "*I* did that horrible thing."	Specific behavior "I *did* that horrible *thing*."
Degree of distress	Generally more painful than guilt	Generally less painful than shame
Phenomenological experience	Shrinking, feeling small, feeling worthless, powerless	Tension, remorse, regret
Operation of "self"	Self "split" into observing and observed "selves"	Unified self intact
Impact on "self"	Self impaired by global devaluation	Self unimpaired by global devaluation
Concern vis-à-vis, the "other"	Concern with others' evaluation of self	Concern with one's effect on others
Counterfactual processes	Mentally undoing some aspect of the self	Mentally undoing some aspect of behavior
Motivational features	Desire to hide, escape, or desire to strike back	Desire to confess, apologize, or repair

response. Perhaps because shame is generally more painful than guilt, and because shame involves a sense of exposure before a real or imagined audience, people feeling shame often report a desire to flee from the shame-inducing situation, to "sink into the floor and disappear" (Lewis, 1971; Lindsay-Hartz, 1984; Tangney, 1993; Tangney et al., 1996).

Alternately, shamed individuals frequently become angry and blame others for the shame-inducing event (Lewis, 1971; Tangney, Wagner, Fletcher, & Gramzow, 1992; Tangney, 1995; Tangney, Wagner, Barlow, Marschall, & Gramzow, 1996; Wicker et al., 1983). In a shame experience, hostility is initially directed toward the self. Shamed individuals feel like a *bad person* because of some transgression or error. But because shame is typically a very painful, often devastating experience, people in the midst of this experience often feel trapped and overwhelmed. As a result, they are often motivated to engage in all sorts of defensive maneuvers. One way to protect the self, and to regain a sense of control and agency, is to redirect that hostility and blame outward. Here, the shamed person essentially "turns the tables" in a sequence that sounds something like, "Oh, what a horrible person I am . . . and damn it, how could you make me feel that way!" This dynamic is very similar to the one recently described by Baumeister, Smart, and Boden (1996) where ego threats coupled with a shaky self-esteem often result in aggression. In fact, many of the scenarios described by Baumeister et al. (1996) appear to involve substantial feelings of shame.

In any event, either route—shamed withdrawal or shamed rage—centers on behaviors that are unlikely to rectify or remedy the negative effects of one's transgressions. Rather, these behaviors are actually more likely to sever or interfere with interpersonal relationships.

In sharp contrast, guilt appears to motivate us in a more "moral" direction. Guilt keeps people constructively engaged in interpersonal situations at hand. Numerous studies have shown a special link between guilt and empathy (Baumeister, Stillwell & Heatherton, 1994; Leith & Baumeister, in press; Tangney, 1991, 1995; Tangney et al., 1994). People in the midst of a guilt experience are apt to exhibit other-oriented empathy, especially for victims of their transgressions. (In contrast, the self-focused experience of shame actually seems to interfere with feelings of empathy, Leith & Baumeister, in press; Tangney, 1991, 1995.) Even more important, rather than motivating an avoidance response, guilt appears to motivate corrective action (Lewis, 1971; Lindsay-Hartz, 1984; Tangney, 1993; Tangney et al., 1996; Wicker et al., 1983). That is, the tension and regret of guilt is more likely to lead to a desire to confess, apologize, and/or repair the damage that was done, without engendering all the defensive and retaliative responses that are the hallmark of shame. This motivation for reparation may stem from the fact that guilt involves a fairly persistent focus on the offending behavior—and therefore, presumably, on its harmful consequences to others. In addition, in guilt, the self remains relatively intact, unimpaired by shame-related global devaluations. Thus, the self is more mobile and ready to take reparative action. Finally, guilt may foster more constructive, reparative behavior because it essentially poses people with a doable task. Bottom line, what is at issue is not a bad, defective self, but a bad, defective behavior—and, as anyone knows, it is easier to change a bad behavior than to change a worthless, despicable self.

In sum, then, a range of research studies suggest that guilt is, on balance, the more "moral" or adaptive emotion, at least when considering social behavior and interpersonal adjustment. But is there a trade-off vis-à-vis individual psychological adjustment? Might the tendency to experience guilt over one's transgressions, to feel empathy for one's victims, and to set aside one's own needs and desires in favor of the needs of others, ultimately lead to increases in anxiety and depression, or decreases in self-esteem?

The answer is a clear "no." When measures are used that are sensitive to Lewis's (1971) self versus behavior distinction (e.g., scenario-based methods assessing shame proneness and guilt proneness with respect to specific situations).[2] Across studies of

---

[2]There remains some debate on the adaptive or maladaptive nature of guilt, with some differences of opinion stemming from minor variations in the definition of shame and guilt, and far greater disagreements centering on how best to assess these emotion styles (see Harder, 1995 and Tangney, Burggraf, & Wagner, 1995, for good summary of this debate). More recently, researchers in the field are coming to the conclusion that although guilt clearly serves a broad range of adaptive functions (e.g., Baumeister, Stillwell, & Heatherton, 1994; Tangney, 1991, 1994, 1995), there may be a darker side to guilt as well. Of special interest is the chronic, ruminative, unresolved guilt described in the clinical literature. I've suggested that guilt is especially likely to "take a turn for the worse" when it becomes fused with shame (Tangney et al., 1995). And in effect, it is the shame component of a shame–guilt sequence that sets the stage for psychological symptoms. More recently, however, I've joined Jane Bybee, Sue Crowley, Tamara Ferguson, and David Harder in speculating about additional factors that may render some forms of "shame-free" guilt maladaptive (Bybee & Tangney, 1996). These caveats notwithstanding, the weight of the evidence still clearly points to guilt as an emotion with much more positive potential, and far fewer liabilities than the ugly feeling of shame.

both children and adults, the tendency to experience "shame-free" guilt is essentially unrelated to psychological symptoms, whereas people prone to experience shame appear vulnerable to a range of psychological problems (Burggraf & Tangney, 1990; Gramzow & Tangney, 1992; Tangney, 1994; Tangney, Burggraf & Wagner, 1995; Tangney, Wagner, Burggraf, Gramzow & Fletcher, 1991; Tangney, Wagner, & Gramzow, 1992). So across the board, whether considering individual psychological adjustment or adaptive interpersonal behavior, guilt appears to be the "moral affect" of choice.

DEVELOPMENTAL SHIFTS IN THE EXPERIENCE AND FUNCTION OF SHAME AND GUILT

Most of the studies on shame and guilt that I've summarized so far in this chapter were conducted on samples of college students and adults. In other words, most of what we know about these "moral" emotions—the phenomenology of shame and guilt, the differences between these emotions, and their apparent functions in motivating behavior—is drawn from an adult perspective. How far can these results be generalized to younger individuals? Do children and adolescents experience shame and guilt in much the same way as their parents and grandparents? Do these emotions play the same role in regulating children's behavior in interpersonal settings, shaping them into "moral" children, and later in the same way into "moral" adults?

Most developmental psychologists would agree: it is extremely unlikely that the nature and functions of "self-conscious" emotions, such as shame and guilt, remain static across the life span. In contrast to the "basic" emotions (e.g., anger, fear, joy), which emerge very early in life, shame and guilt are among the more developmentally advanced "secondary" or "derived" emotions that emerge later and that hinge on several key cognitive abilities. Most notably, together with other self-evaluative or self-conscious emotions like pride and embarrassment, shame and guilt require (a) a clear recognition of the self as separate from others, and (b) the development of standards against which the self and/or one's behavior is evaluated (M. Lewis, Sullivan, Stanger, & Weiss, 1989; Fischer & Tangney, 1995). When bad things happen, we may feel any one of a number of negative emotions—sadness, disappointment, frustration, or anger. But feelings of shame and guilt typically arise from a recognition of one's *own* negative attributes or negative behaviors—attributes and behaviors that fail to match up to some internally or externally imposed standard. Even in those situations when we feel shame over another person's behavior, that person is almost invariably someone with whom we are closely affiliated or identified (e.g., a family member, friend, or colleague closely associated with the self). It is because that person is part of our self-definition that we experience shame.

In short, self-conscious emotions are about the self; they require a concept of self and a set of standards as a point of comparison. In addition, in the special case of guilt and shame, a third ability is required. In order to experience guilt (about specific behaviors) independent of shame (about the self), one needs the ability to make a clear distinction between self and behavior. It goes without saying that none of these cognitive abilities (recognition of the self, standards, distinction between self and behavior) is present at birth. These cognitive milestones emerge in childhood, first as a glimmer of an ability, and later with development, as increasingly complex and elaborated capacities that amost certainly transform our experience of the emotions to which they are intimately linked.

Changes in Conceptions of the Self

An individual's conception of self—of who he or she is—undergoes a number of dramatic shifts from early childhood through to adulthood (Damon & Hart, 1982), and these changes in turn undoubtedly shape and define the nature of "self"-conscious emotions (see Mascolo & Fischer, 1995). For example, in an inventive series of studies, M. Lewis et al. (1989) have shown that very young children first show behavioral signs of embarrassment (smiling coupled with gaze aversion, touching the face, etc.) in apparently embarrassing situations at the same phase of development in which a rudimentary sense of self emerges—between 15 and 24 months. Moreover, within this span of development, those children who show self-recognition (in a "rouge" test, Amsterdam, 1972; Bertenthal & Fischer, 1978) are the very same children who display signs of embarrassment in an unrelated task. Kids who don't yet recognize the self, don't yet show embarrassment. M. Lewis et al.'s (1989) results are consistent with the notion that a recognized self is a *prerequisite* for emotions such as embarrassment, shame, guilt, and pride (M. Lewis, 1992, 1995; Stipek, 1995; Stipek, Recchia, & McClintic, 1992; see Barrett, 1995, however, for an opposing view).

Certainly, one's comprehension of one's self evolves considerably beyond age 15 months (Damon & Hart, 1982). Children move from a self defined by fairly concrete, often observable characteristics (e.g., gender, physical attributes, etc.), to a self defined by current activities and involvements, then to a self constructed by more enduring patterns of behavior, and later to a self forged of ever more abstract, sophisticated personality traits, integrated meaningfully into one's own "identity." Thus, there are dramatic changes in the "self" that one is conscious of, or which one evaluates, in shame or guilt experiences.

Changes in the Structure of Moral Standards and the Nature of Transgressions

Age-related shifts can be seen, too, in the structure of children's moral standards and in the content of children's transgressions. The structure of children's moral standards becomes more sophisticated with age. A rudimentary sense of right and wrong can be seen in toddlers' social interactions with their mothers (Smetana, 1989), but across the preschool years, the domain of moral judgments expands to include more events and take into account more aspects of these events, until by 4 years of age, children have distinct notions about transgressions' seriousness, punishability, and contingency on rules, and they can reliably distinguish between moral and social conventional transgressions (Smetana et al., 1993).

In our study of children's and adults' descriptions of personal shame and guilt experience (Tangney et al., 1994), we examined developmental differences in the content, structure, and interpersonal focus of the emotion-eliciting events. Not surprisingly, the largest age differences were found in the specific content of the emotion-eliciting situations, undoubtedly reflecting differences in the base rates of everyday experiences of children and adults. For example, sex, infidelity, and the breakup of a romance were cited exclusively by adults; children were much more likely to mention disobeying parents, damaging objects, and accomplishments at a hobby or sport. In addition, however, there were developmental differences in the degree to which respondents mentioned concrete vs. abstract themes, consistent with Bybee's (1993) analysis of children's and adolescents' guilt events. In Williams and Bybee's (1994) study of guilt stories provided by 5th, 8th, and 11th graders, there was a clear trend toward more complex and abstract standards and situations with age. Adolescents were more likely than children to mention guilt over inaction, neglect of responsibilities, and failure to attain ideals. In our study (Tangney et al., 1994), children tended to focus on quite concrete types of events (e.g., hurting someone physically, breaking something), whereas adults mentioned both concrete and abstract concepts and events (e.g., disappointment in aspects of the self, attributes of a loved one, identification with a group).

A related issue concerns the internalization of standards. A range of studies indicate that the events that elicit shame and guilt among children become increasingly internalized and self-relevant with age. Harris's (1989) in-depth analysis of children's understanding of emotion suggests that, between the ages of 5 and 8, children move from a narrow focus on the outcome of an action (was it a good or bad event, regardless of whether or not the self was involved), to a consideration of others' reactions to a behavior (e.g., parental approval or disapproval), to yet a more sophisticated consideration of the self's own reaction (approval or disapproval) to the behavior. Although by age 8, children show a capacity for this latter form of "internalized" response (see Harter & Whitesell, 1989), norms and standards become even more internalized through later childhood and into adolescence. For example, Ferguson et al. (1991) have shown that, in characterizing shame and guilt experiences, younger children (about age 8) are more likely to focus on other people's evaluations and reactions than older children (about age 11). Older children seem to rely more on their own standards in evaluating their behavior.

In our study of children (ages 8–12) and adults (Tangney et al., 1994), we too expected developmental differences in the nature of audience concerns expressed by respondents as they described personal shame, guilt, and pride experiences. But we were surprised to find no evidence that the emotion experiences of older respondents were more internalized or "autonomous," in general. Across the three emotions, children were no more likely than adults to refer to an audience in their account of the events. Similarly, there were no *overall* age differences in the number of people present, in the degree to which others were *aware* of the respondent's behavior, nor in the extent to which respondents' were concerned with others' evaluation of the self.

We did, however, observe an intriguing developmental difference in the *interaction* between age and emotion in predicting audience concerns. In general, these audience dimensions varied little across the three emotions for children. But among adults, a much more differentiated picture emerged. The most striking such interaction was observed in connection with the nature of respondents' interpersonal concerns. Adults were differentially more concerned with others' evaluation in shame and pride situations, and differentially more concerned with their effect on others in guilt situations. Children's interpersonal focus was more uniform across the three types of emotions. This pattern suggests that there are significant development changes, beyond middle childhood, in the degree to which shame and guilt become distinct self-conscious emotions.

Changes in the Degree to Which Shame and Guilt Are Distinct Emotions

In fact, results from several lines of research suggest that the capacity to experience guilt and shame as two distinct emotions develops gradually with age. Although Barrett, Zahn-Waxler, and Cole (1993) have shown that toddlers exhibit distinct *behavioral responses* to transgression (hiding vs. amending), which may be precursors of later tendencies to experience shame and guilt, these individual differences in behavior are likely due to a host of factors, including temperament, socialization, and the like. It seems unlikely that, with the rudimentary sense of self shown by 18-month-old children, comes the ability to experience a well-articulated feeling of guilt (about a specific behavior), distinct from shame (about the self). Shame and guilt are perhaps quintessential examples of what Ferguson (Ferguson & Rule, 1983; Ferguson & Stegge, 1995) terms "attribution-dependent emotions." That is, the shape and phenomenological experience of these emotions hinges greatly on "secondary appraisals"—evaluations not only of the valance of the outcome of an event (primary appraisals), but also fairly complex evaluations of the causes of that event. For example, feelings of shame are most likely to arise from internal, stable, and global attributions for negative events (i.e., a bad self). Feelings of guilt are most likely to arise from internal but fairly unstable and specific attributions for negative events (i.e., a bad behavior).

Developmental research has shown that children do not consistently make complex attributional appraisals of situations, or use such appraisals in their determination of blame, until well into middle childhood. For example, Harris (1989) has shown that up through age 8, children remain largely focused on the valance of the outcome of an event, not the cause. Beginning at about age 8, children begin to distinguish between enduring characteristics of the self and more transient types of behaviors. Nicholls (1978), for example, has shown that it is at about this point in development that children begin to make a meaningful distinction between attributions to ability (enduring characteristics) versus attributions to effort (more unstable, volitional factors). Paralleling this, Damon and Hart's review of developmental changes in conceptions of the self indicates that at about age 8, children begin distinguishing between current behaviors or activities as distinct from more fundamental aspects of the self.

Not surprisingly, research specifically on children's understanding and experience of shame and guilt has shown that it is not until middle childhood that children can reliably distinguish between these two "attribution-dependent" emotions. At ages 5 to 6, children are unable to recount pertinent events that would elicit shame and guilt (Harris, Olthof, Meerum Terwogt, & Hardman, 1987). Similarly, Denham and Couchoud (1991) have observed that very young children typically describe a vague sort of feeling "bad" in varying negative situations, including transgressions and failure, but clearly are unable to articulate differentiated shame and guilt experiences. Limitations in language ability no doubt contribute to such imprecise labeling of emotional experience. But this imprecision, too, almost certainly reflects a relatively rudimentary structure of emotion derived from a fairly unsophisticated structure of causal attributions—and of the self.

By age 8, when children begin to distinguish between stable and unstable attributions (e.g., attributions to behavior vs. attributions to character), researchers begin to find notable differences in children's reports of shame and guilt events and experiences. In an inventive series of studies, Ferguson et al. (1990a, 1990b, 1991) found compelling evidence that children ages 8 and 11 have quite sophisticated, distinct conceptions of shame and guilt. The majority of children this age, for example, could cite relevant shame versus guilt-eliciting situations, and most understood the special connection between guilt and reparative behavior and the connection between shame and denial. These results were quite robust both in in-depth interviews with children (Ferguson et al., 1990a, b) and in a sorting task, where children were asked to classify features as characteristic of guilt, shame, both, or neither emotions (Ferguson et al., 1991). In our own research, we found few reliable differences in 8–12-year-old children's phenomenological ratings of personal shame and guilt experiences, but a qualitative analysis of their narrative accounts revealed some important differences between shame- and guilt-eliciting events (Tangney et al., 1994). Like adults, children conveyed more other-oriented empathy and perspective taking in their descriptions of guilt events, and there were some differences in the types of events cited in connection with emotions (although, as in previous studies [e.g., Tangney, 1992], there were clearly more similarities than differences in the types of events that give rise to feelings of shame and guilt). But as noted earlier, adults' narrative accounts showed even more pronounced differences between shame and guilt (e.g., in terms of the audiences present to witness the events, and in terms of respondents' audience concerns), indicating that, beyond childhood, shame and guilt continue to evolve as distinct affective experiences (Tangney et al., 1994), consistent with Damon and Hart's (1982) description of the continuing evolution of the self.

SUMMARY AND CONCLUSIONS

In this chapter, I've tried to underscore the importance of distinguishing between shame and guilt—both theoretically and empirically. Developmental research indicates that, by middle childhood, people experience shame and guilt as distinct emotions, and it seems likely that these emotions continue to develop and differentiate, at least into adolescence. The key difference between shame and guilt does not center merely on a public–private dimension. Indeed, there is little empirical support for the commonly held assumption that shame arises from public exposure of some failure or transgression, whereas guilt arises from the more private pangs of one's internalized conscience. Rather, there is substantial evidence supporting Lewis's (1971) contention that the fundamental difference between shame and guilt centers on the role of the self. Shame involves fairly global, negative evaluations of the self (i.e., "Who *I* am"). Guilt involves a more articulated condemnation of a specific behavior (i.e., "What I *did*"). This difference in focus (self vs. behavior) may seem somewhat subtle at first glance, but it has far-reaching implications for the immediate phenomenological experience of these emotions, for subsequent motivation, and ultimately for behavior. On balance, shame appears to be a more overwhelming, less consistently adaptive emotion, often bringing with it a range of symptoms and defenses. In contrast, feelings of guilt are more apt to orient people in a constructive, proactive, future-oriented direction. Thus, it seems critical to make a clear distinction between shame and guilt—to avoid confounding these two often confused emotions—when considering such diverse domains as "moral" self-regulation (e.g., resistance to temptation), interpersonal behavior, and psychological adjustment.

REFERENCES

Amsterdam, B. (1972). Mirror self-image reactions before age two. *Developmental Psychobiology, 5,* 297–305.

Barrett, K. C. (1995). A functionalist approach to shame and guilt. In J. P. Tangney & K. W. Fischer (Eds.), *Self-conscious emotions: Shame, guilt, embarrassment, and pride* (pp. 25–63). New York: Guilford Press.

Barrett, K. C., Zahn-Waxler, C., & Cole, P. M. (1993). Avoiders versus amenders: Implications for the investigation of shame and guilt during toddlerhood? *Cognition and Emotion, 7,* 481–505.

Baumeister, R. F., Smart, L., & Boden, J. M. (1996). Relation of threatened egotism to violence and aggression: The dark side of high self-esteem. *Psychological Review, 103,* 5–33.

Baumeister, R. F., Stillwell, A. M., & Heatherton, T. F. (1994). Guilt: An interpersonal approach. *Psychological Bulletin, 115,* 243–267.

Benedict, R. (1946). *The chrysanthemum and the sword*. Boston: Houghton Mifflin.

Berthenthal, B. L., & Fischer, K. W. (1978). Development of self-recognition in the infant. *Developmental Psychology, 14,* 44–50.

Burggraf, S. A., & Tangney, J. P. (1990, June). *Shame-proneness, guilt-proneness, and attributional style related to children's depression*. Poster presented at the meetings of the American Psychological Society, Dallas.

Bybee, J. & Tangney, J. P. (chairs) (August, 1996). *Is guilt adaptive? Functions in interpersonal relationships and mental health*. Symposium presented at the meetings of the American Psychological Association, Toronto.

Damon, W., & Hart, D. (1982). Development of self-understanding from infancy through adolescence. *Child Development, 53,* 841–864.

Denham, S. A., & Couchoud, E. A. (1991). Social-emotional predictors of preschoolers' responses to adult negative emotion. *Journal of Child Psychology and Psychiatry, 32,* 595–608.

Erikson, E. H. (1950). *Childhood and society*. New York: W. W. Norton.

Ferguson, T. J., & Rule, B. G. (1983). An attributional perspective on anger and aggression. In R. Geen & E. Donnerstein (Eds.), *Aggression: Theoretical and empirical reviews* (Vol. 1, pp. 41–74). New York: Academic Press.

Ferguson, T. J., & Stegge, H. (1995). Emotional states and traits in children: The case of guilt and shame. In J. P. Tangney & K. W. Fischer (Eds.), *Self-conscious emotions: Shame, guilt, embarrassment, and pride* (pp. 174–197). New York: Guilford Press.

Ferguson, T. J., Stegge, H., & Damhuis, I. (1990a). Guilt and shame experiences in elementary school-age children. In R. J. Takens (Ed.), *European perspectives in psychology* (Vol. 1, pp. 195–218). New York: Wiley.

Ferguson, T. J., Stegge, H., & Damhuis, I. (1990b, March). *Spontaneous and elicited guilt and shame experiences in elementary school-age children*. Poster presented at the Southwestern Society for Research in Human Development, Dallas, TX.

Ferguson, T. J., Stegge, H., & Damhuis, I. (1991). Children's understanding of guilt and shame. *Child Development, 62,* 827–839.

Fischer, K. W., & Tangney, J. P. (1995). Self-conscious emotions and the affect revolution: Framework and overview. In J. P. Tangney & K. W. Fischer (Eds.), *Self-conscious emotions: Shame, guilt, embarrassment, and pride* (pp. 3–22). New York: Guilford Press.

Freud, S. (1953). Three essays on the theory of sexuality. In J. Strachey (Ed. and Trans.), *The standard edition of the complete psychological works of Sigmund Freud* (Vol. 7, pp. 153–243). London: Hogarth Press. (Original work published 1905).

Freud, S. (1957). On narcissism: An introduction. In J. Strachey (Ed. and Trans.), *The standard edition of the complete psychological works of Sigmund Freud* (Vol. 14, pp. 73–102). London: Hogarth Press. (Original work published 1914).

Freud, S. (1961). The id and the ego. In J. Strachey (Ed. and Trans.), *The standard edition of the complete psychological works of Sigmund Freud* (Vol. 19, pp. 12–66). London: Hogarth Press. (Original work published 1923).

Freud, S. (1961). The dissolution of the Oedipus Complex. In J. Strachey (Ed. and Trans.), *The standard edition of the complete psychological works of Sigmund Freud* (Vol. 19, pp. 173–182). London: Hogarth Press. (Original work published 1924).

Freud, S. (1961). Some psychical consequences of the anatomical distinction between the sexes. In J. Strachey (Ed. and Trans.), *The standard edition of the complete psychological works of Sigmund Freud* (Vol. 19, pp. 248–258). London: Hogarth Press. (Original work published 1925).

Gehm, T. L., & Scherer, K. R. (1988). Relating situation evaluation to emotion differentiation: Nonmetric analysis of cross-cultural questionnaire data. In K. R. Scherer (Ed.), *Facets of emotion: Recent research* (pp. 61–77). Hillsdale, NJ: Erlbaum.

Gramzow, R., & Tangney, J. P. (1992). Proneness to shame and the narcissistic personality. *Personality and Social Psychology Bulletin, 18,* 369–376.

Harder, D. W. (1995). Shame and guilt assessment and relationships of shame and guilt proneness to psychopathology. In J. P. Tangney & K. W. Fischer (Eds.), *Self-conscious emotions: Shame, guilt, embarrassment, and pride* (pp. 368–392). New York: Guilford Press.

Harris, P. L. (1989). *Children and emotion: The development of psychological understanding.* New York: Basil Blackwell.

Harris, P. L., Olthof, T., Meerum Terwogt, M., & Hardman, C. E. (1987). Children's knowledge of the situations that provoke emotion. *International Journal of Behavioral Development, 10,* 319–343.

Harter, S., & Whitesell, N. (1989). Developmental changes in children's emotion concepts. In C. Saarni & P. L. Harris (Eds.), *Children's understanding of emotions.* New York: Cambridge University Press.

Hartmann, E., & Loewenstein, R. (1962). Notes on the superego. *The Psychoanalytic Study of the Child, 17,* 42–81.

Jacobson, E. (1954). The self and the object world: Vicissitudes of their infantile cathexis and their influences on ideational and affective development. *The Psychoanalytic Study of the Child, 9,* 75–127.

Kohut, H. (1971). *The analysis of the self.* New York: International Universities Press.

Leith, K. P., & Baumeister, R. F. (in press). Empathy, shame, guilt, and narratives of interpersonal conflicts: Guilt-prone people are better at perspective taking. *Journal of Personality.*

Lewis, H. B. (1971). *Shame and guilt in neurosis.* New York: International Universities Press.

Lewis, M. (1992). *Shame: The exposed self.* New York: Free Press.

Lewis, M. (1995). Embarrassment: The emotion of self-exposure and evaluation. In J. P. Tangney & K. W. Fischer (Eds.), *Self-conscious emotions: Shame, guilt, embarrassment, and pride* (pp. 198–218). New York: Guilford Press.

Lewis, M., Sullivan, M. W., Stanger, C., & Weiss, M. (1989). Self-development and self-conscious emotions. *Child Development, 60,* 146–156.

Lindsay-Hartz, J. (1984). Contrasting experiences of shame and guilt. *American Behavioral Scientist, 27,* 689–704.

Lindsay-Hartz, J., de Rivera, J., & Mascolo, M. (1995). Differentiating shame and guilt and their effects on motivation. In J. P. Tangney & K. W. Fischer (Eds.), *Self-conscious emotions: Shame, guilt, embarrassment, and pride* (pp. 274–300). New York: Guilford Press.

Mascolo, M. F., & Fischer, K. W. Developmental transformation in appraisals for pride, shame, and guilt. In J. P. Tangney & K. W. Fischer (Eds.), *Self-conscious emotions: Shame, guilt, embarrassment, and pride* (pp. 64–113). New York: Guilford Press.

Morrison, A. P. (1989). *Shame: The underside of narcissism.* Hillsdale, NJ: The Analytic Press.

Morrison, N. K. (1987). The role of shame in schizophrenia. In H. B. Lewis (Ed.), *The role of shame in symptom formation* (pp. 51–87). Hillsdale, NJ: Erlbaum.

Nathanson, D. L. (1987). The shame/pride axis. In H. B. Lewis (Ed.), *The role of shame in symptom formation.* Hillsdale, NJ: Erlbaum.

Nicholls, J. G. (1978). The development of concepts of effort and ability, perception of academic attainment, and the understanding that difficult tasks require more ability. *Child Development, 49,* 800–814.

Niedenthal, P., Tangney, J. P., & Gavanski, I. (1994). "If only I weren't" versus "If only I hadn't": Distinguishing shame and guilt in counterfactual thinking. *Journal of Personality and Social Psychology, 67,* 585–595.

Piers, G., & Singer, A. (1953). *Shame and guilt.* Springfield, IL: Thomas.

Smetana, J. G. (1989). Toddlers' social interactions in the context of moral and conventional transgressions in the home. *Developmental Psychology, 25,* 499–508.

Smetana, J. G., Schlagman, N., & Adams, P. W. (1993). Preschool children's judgments about hypothetical and actual transgressions. *Child Development, 64,* 202–214.

Stipek, D. (1995). The development of pride and shame in toddlers. In J. P. Tangney & K. W. Fischer (Eds.), *Self-conscious emotions: Shame, guilt, embarrassment, and pride* (pp. 237–252). New York: Guilford Press.

Stipek, D., Recchia, S., & McClintic, S. (1992). Self-evaluation in young children. *Monographs of the Society for Research in Child Development, 57* (1, Serial No. 226).

Tangney, J. P. (1991). Moral affect: The good, the bad, and the ugly. *Journal of Personality and Social Psychology, 61,* 598–607.

Tangney, J. P. (1992). Situational determinants of shame and guilt in young adulthood. *Personality and Social Psychology Bulletin, 18,* 199–206.

Tangney, J. P. (1993). Shame and guilt. In C. G. Costello (Ed.), *Symptoms of depression.* (pp. 161–180). New York: John Wiley.

Tangney, J. P. (1994). The mixed legacy of the super-ego: Adaptive and maladaptive aspects of shame and guilt. In J. M. Masling, & R. F. Bornstein, (Eds.), *Empirical perspectives on object relations theory* (pp. 1–28). Washington, DC: American Psychological Association.

Tangney, J. P. (1995). Recent empirical advances in the study of shame and guilt. *American Behavioral Scientist, 38,* 1132–1145.

Tangney, J. P. (1995). Shame and guilt in interpersonal relationships. In J. P. Tangney & K. W. Fischer (Eds.), *Self-conscious emotions: Shame, guilt, embarrassment, and pride* (pp. 114–139). New York: Guilford Press.

Tangney, J. P., Burggraf, S. A., & Wagner, P. E. (1995). Shame-proneness, guilt-proneness, and psychological symptoms. In J. P. Tangney & K. W. Fischer (Eds.), *Self-conscious emotions: Shame, guilt, embarrassment, and pride* (pp. 343–367). New York: Guilford Press.

Tangney, J. P., Marschall, D. E., Rosenberg, K., Barlow, D. H., & Wagner, P. E. (1994). *Children's and adults' autobiographical accounts of shame, guilt and pride experiences: An analysis of situational determinants and interpersonal concerns.* Manuscript under review.

Tangney, J. P., Miller, R. S., Flicker, L., & Barlow, D. H. (1996). Are shame, guilt and embarrassment distinct emotions? *Journal of Personality and Social Psychology, 70,* 1256–1269.

Tangney, J. P., Wagner, P. E., Barlow, D. H., Marschall, D. E., & Gramzow, R. (1996). The relation of shame and guilt to constructive vs. destructive responses to anger across the lifespan. *Journal of Personality and Social Psychology, 70,* 797–809.

Tangney, J. P., Wagner, P. E., Burggraf, S. A., Gramzow, R., & Fletcher, C. (1991, June). *Children's shame-proneness, but not guilt-proneness, is related to emotional and behavioral maladjustment.* Poster presented at the meetings of the American Psychological Society, Washington DC.

Tangney, J. P., Wagner, P. E., Fletcher, C., & Gramzow, R. (1992). Shamed into anger? The relation of shame and guilt to anger and self-reported aggression. *Journal of Personality and Social Psychology, 62,* 669–675.

Tangney, J. P., Wagner, P., & Gramzow, R. (1992). Proneness to shame, proneness to guilt, and psychopathology. *Journal of Abnormal Psychology, 103,* 469–478.

Wallbott, H. G., & Scherer, K. R. (1988). How universal and specific is emotional experience? Evidence from 27 countries and five continents. In K. R. Scherer (Ed.), *Facets of emotion: Recent research* (pp. 31–56). Hillsdale, NJ: Lawrence Erlbaum Associates.

Wicker, F. W., Payne, G. C., & Morgan, R. D. (1983). Participant descriptions of guilt and shame. *Motivation and Emotion, 7,* 25–39.

Williams, C., & Bybee, J. (1994). What do children feel guilty about? Developmental and gender differences. *Developmental Psychology, 30,* 617–623.

CHAPTER 2

Measuring Guilt in Children: A Rose by Any Other Name Still Has Thorns

Tamara J. Ferguson
Utah State University, Logan, Utah

Hedde Stegge
Free University Amsterdam, Amsterdam, The Netherlands

A sense of guilt is a man's greatest asset.
—Nadezhda Mandelstam

Guilt is the 'most terrible sickness that has ever raged in man.'
—Friedrich Nietzsche

INTRODUCTION

When asked to contribute a chapter on the measurement of guilt in children, we asked ourselves *why* the field of psychology could benefit from such instruments. Our answer to the question is predicated on one issue that looms largely on the horizon—namely, on what theoretical or empirical grounds should we expect guilt scores to predict the child's immediate and future psychosocial well-being? We were also concerned about how to write a chapter on measuring guilt without discussing the assessment of closely related emotions, such as shame. Thus, before we review the available measures of guilt in children, we need to (a) clearly delineate what *guilt* is and how it differs from its sibling *shame,* (b) address the question of when individuals are thought to be capable of experiencing, understanding, and reporting their feelings of guilt (and shame); and (c) specify the role that guilt plays in the person's daily functioning in comparison to that of other related emotions.

CONCEPTUALIZATIONS OF GUILT AND SHAME

Prior to delineating the differences between guilt and shame that many authors have identified in the literature, it is necessary to represent the view of several theorists

Guilt and Children
Copyright © 1998 by Academic Press. All rights of reproduction in any form reserved.

that guilt is *not* an affective state (most notably, Cook, 1996; Kaufman, 1992; Nathanson, 1987; Potter-Efron, 1989; Tomkins, 1963). These authors contend that emotion be viewed as an affective–cognitive–behavioral triad, that shame is a primary affect, and that guilt is only one manifestation of the cognitive or behavioral components of the shame triad. Nevertheless, several authors have attempted to differentiate guilt from shame in terms of their experiential and expressive components, the situational antecedents that give rise to the emotional experience, appraisals (Barrett, 1995), or concerns (Frijda, 1986), the meaning of the emotional experience for the person, and the action tendencies associated with each emotion that may lead to the inhibition of certain behaviors, but the expression of others.

Although few expressive components have been identified as unique to either emotion, guilt is generally characterized as an agitation-based emotion or painful feeling of regret that is aroused when the actor actually causes, anticipates causing, or is associated with an aversive event. In guilt, the actor accepts responsibility for a behavior that violates internalized standards of religious, moral, or ethical conduct, focuses on condemning the *deed,* desires to make amends or punish the self, wishes to personally exercise control over the situation, and experiences an approach–avoidance conflict toward the others involved. In contrast, diverse authors characterize shame as a dejection-based, passive, or helpless emotion aroused by self-related aversive events. The ashamed person focuses more on devaluing or condemning the entire *self,* experiences the self as fundamentally flawed, feels self-conscious about the visibility of one's actions, fears scorn, and thus avoids or hides from others (cf. Barrett, 1995; Ferguson & Stegge, 1995; Tangney, 1995a,b).

Serious questions have been raised about whether certain aversive events *uniquely* or prototypically arouse guilt as opposed to shame. For example, both M. Lewis (e.g., 1992b, 1993a) and Weiner (1986) assert that any self-related aversive event could potentially lead to guilt or shame as long as it is perceived as violating a standard, rule, or goal (M. Lewis, 1993a). Guilt is presumably aroused when the actor perceives the negative event as being personally controllable (Weiner, 1986) or attributes it to specific actions by the self (M. Lewis, 1992b). The same negative event could lead to shame if attributed to personally uncontrollable factors such as low ability, a character defect, or a global feature of the self (e.g., Brown & Weiner, 1984; M. Lewis, 1993b). In her review of measures of guilt and shame, Tangney (1996) essentially reaches the same conclusion; that is, that different patterns of attribution elicit the two emotions, but there are few situations that uniquely evoke guilt *or* shame in either children or adults (see also Aronfreed, 1968).

Others, in contrast, suggest that certain events arouse one emotion more often than the other. For example, a social blunder or *faux pas* is said to arouse shame but not guilt (e.g., Edelman, 1985; Wurmser, 1981), since these behaviors are clearly discrepant from the actor's ideals or personal standards (e.g., Higgins, 1987). People often perceive "blunders" as personally uncontrollable, however, so it could be this attribution rather than the behavior's discrepancy from an ideal that fuels the shame response. Many authors view moral transgressions as quintessential inducers of guilt, since these are prototypic "ought violations" that presumably form the crux of this emotion (Higgins, 1987; Moretti & Higgins, 1990). Again, we must note that many perceive transgressions as personally controllable, which could mean that the attribution rather than immorality of the act is a more proximate cause of guilty feelings. Thus, it simply is not clear whether the quality of the event or its attributional underpinnings are what differentiate between guilt- versus shame-arousing situations. And, as Ausubel's (1955) discussion of moral and nonmoral shame makes clear, shame can be the result of moral, ethical, or religious transgressions, as well as any action that one would expect a real or imagined "other" to sanction negatively. Despite disagreements about which events provoke guilt and shame, practically all authors agree that the crux of guilt is its focus on one's bad behavior, whereas shame focuses on the self as an "anti-ideal" (e.g., H. B. Lewis, 1971; Lindsay-Hartz, deRivera, & Mascolo, 1995; Tangney, 1992; 1996; Thrane, 1979).

DEVELOPMENTAL CONSIDERATIONS

Hoffman (1983a) states that many young children face conflicts between their egoistic desires and moral motives. When the egoistic motive wins out, children (and adults, for that matter) pay the price with a kind of "moral" guilt, even though people also feel guilty without consciously entertaining a moral conflict (e.g., when they have harmed another during an argument, by accident, or through negligence; McGraw, 1987). Thus, a child or adult can feel guilty for interpersonal reasons that result from a combination of empathy and the knowledge that the perpetrator caused distress to the victim (Hoffman, 1983b).

In Hoffman's seminal analysis of moral internalization, he emphasizes the important connections between guilt and empathy, and depicts guilt as a mediator of conscience, or an outcome of internalization. From about the age of 2 years onward, children begin to differentiate the self from others, show awareness of which behaviors are—or are not—appropriate, begin to evaluate the outcomes in terms of standards, rules, and goals, and also realize that others have feelings that are affected by their behavior (M. Lewis, 1993a). The capacity to experience empathy develops first in response to a victim's distress, whether caused directly, or simply witnessed, by the child. In this view, the experience of guilt results from the conjunction of empathic responses to another's distress, and the juxtaposition of several realizations: (a) that one can be an agent of harm, (b) that one can control behavior and choose to behave in (non)harmful ways, (c) that there are moral prescriptions and prohibitions about how we treat ourselves, others, and property, and (d) that behavior can be discrepant from these moral dictates (Hoffman, 1976; Kochanska, 1993b; M. Lewis, 1993a,b; Zahn-Waxler & Kochanska, 1990).

Empathy, empathic distress, and fear of consequences are clearly observable in children at around the age of 2 years. Thus, the consensus in the literature seems to be that children experience at least rudimentary forms of guilt in early childhood (around the age of 2½–3 years, Barrett, 1995; Kochanska, 1993b; Zahn-Waxler & Kochanska, 1990). M. Lewis (1992b) also proposes that children, from about the age of 3 years onward, experience "self-conscious, self-evaluative emotions" (which would include shame, guilt, and pride), once they become capable of evaluating their behavior against standards of appropriate conduct (e.g., Lewis, Alessandri, & Sullivan, 1992).

Even though observational studies suggest that children experience guilt and shame at about 2–3 years, we must also consider the age at which children provide reliable reports of their experience or understand components of the two emotions (e.g., Graham, Doubleday, & Guarino, 1984; Nunner-Winkler & Sodian, 1988; Stipek & DeCotis, 1988). In this regard, it is important to note that the word "guilt" is not part of children's active lexicon until about 5½–6 years of age (Ridgeway, Waters, & Kuczaj, 1985). Ridgeway and colleagues (1985) also found that the word *ashamed* is known to 63.3% of 5- to 5½-year-old children, but only a small percentage of the same children (23.3%) actively use the term. Wiggers and van Lieshout (1985) found that fewer than half of the 8-year-old girls tested could freely describe shame as the emotion shown in a videotape, and only 59% of them correctly chose shame from an array of emotions as the one depicted. The same 8-year-old girls easily described and accurately chose depictions of happiness (88%, 94%) and fear (84%, 69%). Ferguson, Stegge, and Damhuis (1991) have shown, nevertheless, that many 7- to 8-year-olds reliably differentiate guilt from shame in tasks that rely less heavily on productive verbal skills.

All things considered, researchers in this area seem to assume that observational or other-report procedures most "safely" measure the experience of guilt and shame in children younger than 7 years. Only after about age 7 can we even *hope* to be confident that children will reliably report on their experiences of the two emotions. However, as M. Lewis (1992b) cautions, we must not be overzealous in our belief that children will reliably or accurately report on their emotional experiences. Even in adults, there are differing degrees to which emotions are accessible—adults go to great lengths to control or mask their feelings of guilt and shame (e.g., Wallbott & Scherer, 1989). Moreover, what actually causes us to feel a particular emotion may be very different from what we believe caused it (M. Lewis, 1993a, 1995; Nisbett & Wilson, 1977).

ON THE FUNCTIONS OF GUILT AND SHAME IN CHILDREN AND ADULTS

In this section, we address the question of *why* we should be interested in developing psychometrically sound measures of guilt, shame, or for that matter, any emotion in children. As Lutz (1988) points out, emotions "serve as the medium of all exchange or conflict" (p. 212) in interaction, and each emotion ideally functions to maximize the value of relationships (deRivera, 1984). Thus, emotions function as signals of one's state in relation to the environment, and are sensitive barometers of the extent to which the relationship impacts a significant concern or belief (Epstein, 1990; Magai & McFadden, 1995). Emotions signal us to act, often long before we are cognitively aware of the need (e.g., Zajonc, 1980). Even though children do not have the sophisticated cognitive capabilities possessed by many adults, their emotions are windows through which we can glimpse their motivations, defenses, and probable future behaviors. And, in terms of the specific emotions of guilt and shame, M. Lewis (1993a) quite eloquently notes "given the place of self evaluation in adult life, it seems clear that self-conscious, evaluative emotions are likely to stand in the center of our emotional life" (p. 572).

Interest in measuring guilt across the life span thus stems, in part, from the large role it is thought to play in healthy and dysfunctional development. Many authors recognize that guilt and shame can fulfill adaptive purposes in specific situations (e.g., Barrett, 1995; Ferguson, Stegge, & Damhuis, 1991; Malatesta & Wilson, 1988). Shame, for example, serves as a momentary reminder to the individual of standards of propriety and the behaviors necessary to remain a part of the social group (e.g., Scheff, 1988). Momentary responses of guilt serve as checks on interpersonally harmful impulses that promote prosocial and inhibit antisocial behaviors. Many definitions and operationalizations of the construct of guilt draw attention to its prosocial, interpersonal, moral, and existential aspects. This emphasis reflects, in part, views in the developmental and social psychological literatures that guilt is a socially valuable emotion (e.g., Baumeister, Stillwell, & Heatherton, 1994; Bybee & Williams, 1995; Tangney, Burggraf, & Wagner, 1995).

Furthermore, a variety of authors caution against judging the negativity of *any* emotion as a root cause of psychopathology (e.g., Bybee & Williams, 1995; Cole, Michel, & Teti, 1994; Thompson, 1994). They remind us that parents often intentionally try to induce guilt in their children with the goal of socializing appropriate, socially acceptable behaviors, especially in cases where children have intentionally perpetrated a wrongdoing (e.g., Ferguson & Denissen, 1982). Parents often exaggerate or dramatize the negative consequences of young children's behavior as a means of teaching them that their behavior can harmfully impact another (e.g., Kochanska, 1991; Williams & Bybee, 1994; Zahn-Waxler & Chapman, 1982).

Zahn-Waxler and Robinson (1995) reiterate Malatesta and Wilson's (1988) idea that all emotions have adaptive purposes. To them, the moral emotion of empathy maintains attachments with significant others, guilt helps to restore severed bonds, and shame protects the self from being identified as a person prone to impropriety. Barrett (1995) sees guilt as teaching a person about the "self-as-agent," from which the person learns that one can undo wrongs by repairing the damage. Baumeister and associates (1994) take issue with predominantly psychodynamic views of guilt which treat it as a largely private phenomenon of self-condemnation (see also Mosher, 1979). They direct attention to the largely interpersonal functions of guilt, arguing that guilty feelings derive fundamentally from a concern with breaches in interpersonal relationships and involve a consequent desire to avoid disrupting communal bonds. Guilt encourages us to attempt to repair a damaged relationship, engage in equity-restoring behaviors, and reestablish emotional balance by reallocating some of the victim's distress to the perpetrator. Guilt also increases the power held by the less influential member of a relationship, without the person having to resort to explicit attempts at coercion. Expressions of regret, remorse, or suffering help to make the victim feel better and acknowledge commitment to the relationship.

Expressions of guilt are thus social displays, conveying recognition that we have violated a code of conduct and that we accept responsibility for ameliorating our untoward actions (Lindsay-Hartz et al., 1995). Bybee, Williams, and Merisca (1994) point out that the discomfort of guilt may be pain with a purpose, since the anxiety it arouses can operate to direct the person's attention toward eliminating undesirable, anxiety-provoking actions from their behavioral repertoire and can also lead the person to renounce future inappropriate behavior (see also Bybee & Williams, 1995; Campos, Mumme, Kermoian, & Campos, 1994). In short, we do need to recognize the adaptive functions of guilt that arise out of a genuine caring for the injured parties.

Yet we must also remember Hoffman's (1977) observation that the operationalization of guilt in developmental research has been a very circumscribed one, emphasizing the deliberate, behaviorally oriented, self-critical manifestations of self-blame, remorse, and reparation. Although there are notable exceptions in developmental research (e.g., Zahn-Waxler, Kochanska, Krupnick, & McKnew, 1990; Zahn-Waxler, Iannotti, Cummings, & Denham, 1990), few have adequately operationalized guilt within a psychoanalytic framework. Freud (1961/1930) viewed guilt as a special type of anxiety, namely, moral or "conscience" anxiety (Izard, 1977; Cameron & Rychlak, 1985). Traditional psychoanalytic theory views moral guilt as deriving from the development of the superego and concomitant internalization of aggressive impulses. Guilt is seen as self-directed aggression or hostility which can become extremely salient, harsh, threatening, and irrational, leading to various affective disorders such as anxiety and depression. From this perspective, guilt could arise from a variety of painful experiences and be manifested in nightmares, an irrational fear of impending punishment, or self-punishment in the form of "accidents" (see Emde, Johnson, & Easterbrooks, 1987; Hoffman, 1977; Piers & Singer, 1953).

Hoffman (1983a) nicely summarizes the psychoanalytic view of guilt, according to which children develop the ability to punish themselves, much as would their parents, by directing hostility that is meant for parents inwardly on themselves. Guilty feelings are therefore a form of self-punishment and remind children of their fear that the caregivers on whom they are dependent could punish or abandon them. This dependency motivates children to steer clear of guilt-provoking behaviors by conforming to parental prescriptions and prohibitions or by mustering defenses that allow the child to hide inappropriate impulses, even from the self. Also operating within a psychodynamic framework, Modell (1971) and Friedman (1985) view love and caring for others as one precursor to irrational or exaggerated forms of guilt. In this regard, they point to the phenomenon of "survivor guilt" which often involves the irrational belief that another would not have been harmed if the person had not pursued selfish goals or interests.

Cognitive analyses of depression, psychoanalytic treatments of internalizing disorders, clinical accounts, and case studies all illustrate how guilt can serve the individual maladaptively when it involves obsessive, exaggerated self-blame and rumination that focuses on self-condemnation and punishment (e.g., Blatt, Quinlan, Chevron, McDonald, & Zuroff, 1982; Harder, Cutler, & Rockart, 1992; Jones & Kugler, 1993; Jones, Kugler, & Adams, 1995; Leckman et al., 1984). Lindsay-Hartz et al. (1995) note that guilt is maladaptive when motivated out of fear of rejection or when used as a defense against one's inability to control unwanted events. As a defense, guilt can shield individuals from their true, often unconscious, worrisome motives.

Zahn-Waxler (1993) illustrates how young, egocentric and empathic children can come to see themselves as overly responsible for behaviors that they know their parents perceive as disloyal or disturbing. These children often take on too much responsibility or self-blame for the parents' own fate, which can make them vulnerable to depression. Guilt can become exaggerated, especially in depressed individuals, because of a paradoxical, simultaneous tendency to feel powerless yet responsible for anything that goes wrong (cf. Zahn-Waxler & Kochanska, 1990). Zahn-Waxler, Cole, and Barrett (1991) propose that extreme levels of empathy can interfere with children's ability to recognize their own needs as separate from those of another, facilitate codependent behaviors, and also lead to guilt when attempts to make others feel better "fail." Caregivers who themselves have problems are known to use guilt-inducing techniques (Miceli, 1992) that promote extreme levels of empathy in their children by unfairly interpreting actions as representing injury or conflict, holding children overly accountable, withdrawing affection, and essentially perpetuating a "cycle of victimization" (cf. Kochanska, 1991, 1993b; Moulton, Burnstein, Liberty, & Altucher, 1966; Susman, Trickett, Ianotti, Hollenbeck, & Zahn-Waxler, 1985; Tangney, Wagner, Fletcher, & Gramzow, 1991; Zahn-Waxler, Radke-Yarrow, & King, 1979). Zahn-Waxler and her colleagues thus appropriately remind us that some children (especially females) develop pathogenic beliefs and behaviors, including a misplaced sense of responsibility, unrealistic ideas about their own culpability and power in producing a person's plight, as well as heightened levels of empathy and guilt, enmeshment, overregulation, and overcontrol. Harder (1995) has also reviewed literature showing that unresolved feelings of guilt (e.g., when the harm done cannot be repaired) involve a pronounced sense of despair, intropunitive reactions, and are central features to depression and other types of psychopathology.

We think it is clear that guilt or shame, as state reactions, usually (but certainly not always) adaptively serve the individual by signaling important changes that need to take place in the person's internal and/or external environment. Any emotion can become problematic, however, when it results in mood disturbances or intractable patterns of personality, interferes with boundaries, or promotes habitual and inflexible patterns of defense. Chronic exposure to guilt- or shame-inducing messages can lead to what Malatesta and Wilson (1988) label a "surfeit pathology" (too much of an emotion) or affective style that actively guides the person's processing of information, self-evaluation, and self-regulatory behavior across time and situations (Magai & McFadden, 1995). Other individuals can chronically underuse the same emotions to organize and interpret experience. Guilt and shame can thereby become deficit affective styles or traits which may, with time, lead to forms of psychopathology reflecting problems with externalization or deficits in conscience—such as oppositional defiant disorder, conduct disorder, and antisocial personality disorder (cf. Johnson, Kim, & Danko, 1989; Malatesta & Wilson, 1988; Zahn-Waxler & Robinson, 1995).

Importantly, in our view, not even the tendency to persistently organize (or fail to organize) and interpret experiences in terms of a particular emotion is *sufficient* to label it as maladaptive. After all, individuals who consistently feel bad, show signs of remorse, and make amends when they *really* have done something wrong would be considered socially well adjusted. In other words, rather than equating the (mal)adaptiveness of an emotion with its state or trait nature, we would like to encourage researchers to take a different look at this issue. Specifically, we ask the field to contemplate the information perceivers use to make dispositional or trait attributions. Although considerable revisions have been made to early attributional perspectives, such as those contributed by Jones and Davis (1965) or Kelley (1967), we believe that Kelley's original ideas about covariation can serve as a useful analogy in conceptualizing emotion as adaptive or maladaptive. Kelley proposed that people search for three types of covariation information in assessing the causal locus of their own or others' behaviors: consistency, consensus, and distinctiveness. In terms of guilt-relevant behaviors (including the way in which the person experiences, expresses, appraises, and acts upon the emotion), we might ask the following:

1. Does the target person (e.g., Harold) regularly display these behaviors across time in targeted situations (consistency)?
2. Do other people display these behaviors in the same situations (consensus)?
3. In these situations, does Harold display guilt-relevant behaviors only in the presence of a particular other or in the presence of many others (distinctiveness)?

If Harold displays guilt-relevant behaviors with high consistency, low consensus, and low distinctiveness, we might conclude that *something* about Harold is driving his emotional reactions of guilt. In terms of guilt's adaptive value, the consensual status of Harold's emotional behavior is the most diagnostic piece of covariation information (cf. Ferguson & Wells, 1980; Orvis, Cunningham, & Kelley, 1975). We would argue that a person likely has a "real problem" with surfeit guilt (or shame, or happiness, or joy, or *any* emotion), the greater the frequency and intensity of these behaviors in situations in which most comparable others would *not* respond in the same way (low consensus).

Our basic message is thus: *Many* of the situations that researchers use to assess guilt are ones in which the consensual response probably *would* be guilt. The fact that Harold compared to Ned responds more consistently or less distinctively to these consensual guilt-provoking situations probably tells us more about Harold's desire to respond in a socially acceptable manner than it tells us that poor Harold has a problem with guilt. It should therefore not surprise us to find that higher guilt ratings in these "guilt consensual" situations relate to higher scores on indices of social adjustment. Conversely, many of the situations employed in the measurement literature on shame are ones in which shame is *not* the consensual response. We should therefore expect to find that higher shame ratings in these low consensual situations relate to indices of maladaptation. We urge the reader to keep the covariation analogy in mind as we review the diverse literature on measuring guilt (and shame).

MEASURES OF GUILT (AND SHAME) IN ADULTS

Most measures of guilt and shame in children are variations of instruments developed for adults. To appreciate the instruments for children, it is therefore useful to consider several of the available measures for adults. In addition to providing clearer theoretical distinctions between the constructs of guilt and shame, recent research with adults has paid increasing attention to differentiating the two emotion traits at the measurement level (e.g., Tangney, 1990; 1991). Tangney (1996, see also Harder & Lewis, 1987) provides an extensive review of the psychometric properties of measures with adults, arguing that many of them are clearly inadequate on conceptual and methodological grounds. Methodological problems with these instruments vary in nature, ranging from confounding guilt with shame (e.g., Beall, 1972; Evans, Jessup, & Hearn, 1975; Klass, 1987; Mosher, 1966) to assessing guilt and shame using words that challenge even university students' active vocabulary (e.g., Hoblitzelle, 1987).

Tangney (1996) purports that three instruments are the most promising measures of adults' proneness to guilt and/or shame. These are the Test of Self-Conscious Affect (TOSCA; Tangney, Wagner, & Gramzow, 1989), the Personal Feelings Questionnaire-2 (PFQ-2; Harder & Zalma, 1990), and the Guilt Inventory (GI; Kugler & Jones, 1992). The TOSCA is a scenario-based measure in which participants rate on a series of 5-point scales their likelihood of responding to 15 situations in ways that have been precoded to reflect guilt, shame, and other responses (e.g., pride in the self). The measure operationalizes guilt proneness as a cross-situationally consistent tendency to express high degrees of regret, remorse, apology, and reparation, whereas it operationalizes shame proneness as a consistently strong inclination to criticize the self or withdraw across situations. The PFQ-2 is a 16-item checklist in which respondents rate their feelings, precoded for guilt or shame, on a 4-point scale to reflect how often they experience each feeling. The PFQ-2 represents guilt with items such as, "worry about hurting or injuring someone" or "intense guilt," whereas it captures shame with items such as "feel ridiculous," or "feel disgusting to others." Finally, the GI distinguishes among state guilt, trait guilt, and a third construct (moral standards) that Kugler and Jones (1992) consider orthogonal to the affective experience of guilt, at both the state and trait level. The GI consists of 45 statements which participants rated on a 5-point scale (1 = very untrue of me or strongly disagree; 5 = very true of me or strongly agree). It measures state guilt with items such as, "I have recently done something that I deeply regret," trait guilt with statements such as, "Guilt and remorse have been a part of my life for as long as I can recall," and moral standards with phrases such as, "I have always believed strongly in a firm set of moral-ethical principles." Each of the three measures show good internal consistency reliability, but the discriminant validity of the TOSCA and PFQ-2 measures of guilt proneness and shame proneness is questionable, given the high correlations found between the two subscales (e.g., r = .52 for PFQ-2 Guilt and PFQ-2 Shame, Harder & Zalma, 1990; r = .45 for TOSCA Shame and TOSCA Guilt, Tangney, Burggraf, & Wagner, 1995).

Tangney (1996) makes several arguments supporting her conclusion that scenario-based measures (such as the TOSCA), although not without limitations, are nevertheless the best currently available measures of guilt and shame proneness. First, the GI does not contain a scale that measures shame proneness, which prevents us from examining discriminant validity unconfounded from issues concerning method variance. Secondly, the GI Trait Guilt Scale contains items that could indicate shame (e.g., "Frequently, I just hate myself for something I have done."). Third, although she praises the PFQ-2 for its high face validity and ease of administration, Tangney expresses several related concerns about this instrument. She argues that the PFQ-2 may only tap into an overall tendency to report general negative affectivity, since it places heavy demands on respondents' abilities to distinguish terms referring to guilt from those denoting shame—which she views as a task too abstract for even well-educated adults (cf. Tangney, 1989; Tangney, Marshall, Rosenberg, Barlow, & Wagner, 1993). She further contends that global adjective rating tasks, which are devoid of contextual information, may themselves be a shame-inducing experience—only further undermining participants' abilities to clearly distinguish guilt from shame.

If we momentarily accept Tangney's (1996) conclusion that scenario-based measures are the best available assessments of guilt and shame proneness, we can proceed to ask a pressing question regarding relationships between these constructs and indices of psychopathology (e.g., depression or anxiety). Tangney and her associates have repeatedly reported that shame, or guilt "fused" with shame, are primary contributors to the development of maladaptive tendencies (Tangney, 1995a; 1993; Tangney, Wagner, & Gramzow, 1990). As assessed by the TOSCA after partialling out its shared variance with guilt, shame proneness, reliably correlates with a variety of indices of psychopathology, such as anger, low empathy, and depression (Tangney, 1989; Tangney, Wagner, Hill-Barlow, Marschall, & Gramzow, 1996; Tangney et al.,

1995). In contrast, Tangney and her colleagues view guilt proneness itself as an adaptive emotion, since scenario-based measures do not correlate highly with the same indices of psychopathology after its shared variance with shame is removed (Tangney, 1995a; Tangney et al., 1995).

Based on results using the TOSCA or other scenario-based measures (e.g., the Self-Conscious Affect and Attribution Inventory or SCAAI, Burggraf & Tangney, 1989; Tangney, 1990; Tangney, Burggraf, Hamme, & Domingos, 1988a,b) to index guilt and shame proneness, we would therefore conclude that shame, or shame fused with guilt, is the self-conscious emotion most responsible for the development of symptoms of psychopathology. "Shame-free guilt," on the other hand, is an emotional style that may serve to protect the individual from developing symptoms and that may promote the development of socially adaptive behaviors (Tangney, Wagner, Burggraf, Gramzow, & Fletcher, 1991).

There are at least two problems with "ending the story" here, however. First, we would be ignoring the chronic, destructive, or ruminative aspects of guilt to which clinicians so frequently allude and that the literature identifies as symptomatic of anxiety disorders or major depression (Harder, 1995; Kubany et al., 1995; Kubany & Manke, 1995; Kugler & Jones, 1992). For example, one of the criteria for diagnosing a major depressive disorder refers to reported "feelings of worthlessness or excessive or inappropriate guilt . . . nearly every day" (*DSM-IV*, American Psychiatric Association, 1994, p. 327) and/or "guilty preoccupations or ruminations over minor past failings [with] exaggerated sense of responsibility for untoward events" (p. 321). Second, this approach minimizes the known empirical relationships between indices of psychopathology and measures of guilt, as represented by the GI and the PFQ-2. Several findings illustrate this point.

Harder (1995) reviews a series of studies in which he finds that the PFQ-2 guilt scale, when partialed for PFQ-2 shame indices and/or other measures of shame (e.g., Hoblitzelle, 1987), correlates positively with depression, self-derogation, public self-consciousness, the global severity index, and total symptom indices from the Symptom Checklist-90-Revised (SCL-90-R; Derogatis, 1983), as well as more specific indices from the SCL-90-R, such as somaticization, interpersonal sensitivity, hostility–anger, and psychoticism. Brody (1996), using the PFQ-2 (among other measures of emotion) also finds that males' reports of shame, and especially of guilt, are related to negative boundary permeability of the mother–son relationship (see also Olver, Aries, & Batgos, 1989). Although weaker, females' reports of positive boundary permeability in the mother–daughter relationship were negatively correlated with negative symptoms as measured by an Emotion Story task (including references to fear, guilt, and shame). Jones and Kugler (1993) additionally find that the trait scale of the GI correlates consistently positively with college students' reports of various symptoms (e.g., loneliness, shyness, depression, anxiety) and bad feelings (e.g., resentment, suspicion, anger), but that high trait guilt relates inversely to positive feelings (e.g., satisfaction, comfort). Good acquaintances saw target students who were greater in trait guilt as scoring higher on various negative indices (e.g., disenchantment, a tendency towards feeling guilty) but lower on positive ones (e.g., loving, meticulous, involved). Thus, we see that—either when partialed for shame (Harder) or assessed using the trait approach least criticized by Tangney (Jones & Kugler, 1993)—guilt does correlate positively with possible indices of psychopathology in adults.

We also have results indicating that the three top measures of guilt and shame proneness in adults lack convergent validity (Ferguson & Crowley, in press). Using confirmatory factor analyses, we tested for the presence of three latent method factors (the GI, TOSCA-M, and PFQ-2) and assessed the viability of a two-factor model of guilt and shame measurement (with one latent construct representing guilt scales from the three instruments, and the other reflecting the shame scales available in only two of the instruments). We confirmed the presence of a strong method factor and found that the TOSCA and PFQ-2 shame subscales nicely represented the latent factor of shame. Importantly, the guilt subscale from the original TOSCA was essentially unrelated (path value = .009) to any of the other guilt scales that well represented a latent "guilt" factor, including a new scale that we added to the TOSCA representing more ruminative or chronic feelings of guilt (cf. Crowley & Ferguson, 1994, 1995; Ferguson, 1993).

Ferguson and Crowley (in press) point out that the guilt responses in the original TOSCA are situationally appropriate reactions that immediately rectify the wrong done and increase others' trust in the perpetrator's willingness and ability to commit to rules of conduct in relationships (see also Harder, 1995; Jones & Kugler, 1993; Quiles & Bybee, in press). It is therefore not surprising that these guilt responses are so highly related to various indices of adjustment (e.g., Tangney et al., 1995). In contrast, in the checklist measures of guilt, participants are free to call on any of their past experience(s) in offering their ratings. High guilt scores in these measures likely reflect an amalgam of repeated mistakes, hurtful behaviors, and perhaps critical life events or unusually severe incidents retrieved from the individuals' network of rich associations about their life experiences. The same quality of experience may also be captured by the ruminative guilt reactions that we added to the TOSCA. Thus, it is also not surprising that the checklist measures and ruminative guilt scale show an opposing relationship to symptoms and indices of adjustment. Fortunately, researchers have started to recognize that guilt and shame can vary in their adaptive value and are incorporating this awareness into their measurement protocols with adults (Tangney, Ferguson, Wagner, Crowley, & Gramzow, 1996). We will observe the same trend in research concerning the measurement of guilt (and shame) in children.

MEASURES OF GUILT (AND SHAME) IN CHILDREN

There are several measures of guilt and/or shame in children and we have summarized the most widely used ones in Table I in terms of their reliabilities and

TABLE I Measures of Guilt (and Shame) in Children: Reliability and Examples of Range of Relationships Found for Selected Indices of Internalizing, Externalizing, and Adjustment

Instruments and scales (N of items)[a]	Age/grade of participants	Internal consistency reliability[b]	Sample internalizing[c]	Sample externalizing[d]	Sample adjustment[e]
TOSCA-C Guilt (15)	8- to 12-year-olds	.79	−.06 to .06 (d)	−.00 to −.14 (an)	.18 to .24 (em)
			−.09 to .12 (a)	−.04 to .04 (ag)	
TOSCA-C Shame (15)	8- to 12-year-olds	.78	.16 to .28 (d)	.17 to .21 (an)	.14 to .15 (em)
(see Tangney, Wagner, Burggraf, Gramzow, & Fletcher, 1991)					
TOSCA-A Guilt (15)	13- to 18-year-olds	.81	−.07 (ah)	−.18 to −.39 (ag)	.29 to .45 (ad)
TOSCA-A Shame (15)	13- to 18-year-olds	.77	.33 (ah)	.18 to .26 (ag)	.00 to −.05 (ad)
(see Tangney, Wagner, Gavlas, Hill-Barlow, Marschall, & Gramzow, 1992)					
C-CARS-Guilt (8)	5- to 12-year-olds	.86	NA	NA	.29 (ad)
	5- to 7-year-olds		−.13 (i)	−.14 (e)	NA
	10- to 12-year-olds		−.08 (i)	−.36 (e)	NA
C-CARS-Shame (8)	5- to 12-year-olds	.81	NA	NA	.24 (ad)
	5- to 7-year-olds		−.13 (i)	−.22 (e)	NA
	10- to 12-year-olds		−.26 (i)	−.26 (e)	NA
(see Ferguson, Stegge, Miller, & Olsen, 1996)					
Nonconsenual Situations Only					
SCEMAS-Guilt (5)	5- to 12-year-olds	.75	.31 (d)	NA	−.27 (sc)
SCEMAS-Shame (5)	5- to 12-year-olds	.74	.25 (d)	NA	−.26 (sc)
			.24 (a)		
(see Stegge & Ferguson, 1994)					

(continues)

TABLE I (continued)

Instruments and scales (N of items)[a]	Age/grade of participants	Internal consistency reliability[b]	Sample internalizing[c]	Sample externalizing[d]	Sample adjustment[e]
Children's Guilt Inventory (24)	5th to 11th grades				
Guilt over personal lapses (11)		.87			
	5th grade		NS & NR (d)	NS & NR (ao)	.43 (ad)
	11th grade		NS & NR (d)	−.33 (ao)	.31 to .44 (ad)
Guilt when not at fault (5)		.67			
	5th grade		NS & NR (d)	NS & NR (ao)	NS & NR (ad)
	11th grade		NS & NR (d)	−.25 (ao)	.35 (ad)
Guilt over inequity (4)		.61			
	5th grade		NS & NR (d)	NS & NR (ao)	NS & NR (ad)
	11th grade		NS & NR (d)	−.23 (ao)	.26 (ad)
Guilt failure to attain ideals (4)		.61			
	5th grade		NS & NR (d)	NS & NR (ao)	NS & NR (ad)
	11th grade		NS & NR (d)	NS & NR (ao)	.23 (ad)
(see Bybee, Williams, & Merisca, 1996)					
SCEQC Guilt (10)	8- to 12-year-olds	.68 (test−retest = .73)	NS & NR (d)	NS & NR (ag)	−.32 (bp)
			NS & NR (a)	−.44 (ag)	
SCEQC Shame (10)	8- to 12-year-olds	.74 (test−retest = .62)	NS & NR (d)	NS & NR (ag)	NS & NR (bp)
			.27 (a)		
(see Haimowitz, 1996)					

(continues)

TABLE I *(continued)*

Instruments and scales (N of items)[a]	Age/grade of participants	Internal consistency reliability[b]	Sample internalizing[c]	Sample externalizing[d]	Sample adjustment[e]
Trait Affect Measure (40)	5th to 11th graders	.91	.04 (a)	−.26 (ao)	.12 to .21 (ad)
Trait Affect Measure–Short (18)	5th to 11th graders	.83	−.10 (a)	−.20 (ao)	.27 to .29 (ad)
(see Bybee & Williams, 1995)			−.11 (d)		.29 (h)
CIIDC (4 situations)	7–9 year olds	50–95% (kappas)			
		Children of depressed mothers	NA	NS & NR (ag)	Tau = −.13 (e)
		Children of well mothers	NA	NS & NR (ag)	Tau = .27 (e)
(see Zahn-Waxler, Kochanska, Krupnick, & McKnew, 1990)					
My Child (100)	21–70 months old				
Affective discomfort	Girls		.24 (af)	.24 (ii)	
	Boys	*(Split-half)*	.09 (af)	−.03 (ii)	
	(Test–retest)				
Guilt, remorse after wrongdoing (13)	(.55)	(.79)	NA	NA	NA
Concern over good feelings with parent (4)	(.29)	(.62)	NA	NA	NA
Empathy/prosocial (13)	(.55)	(.79)	NA	NA	NA
Apology (4)	(.53)	(.66)	NA	NA	NA
Active moral regulation/vigilance	Girls		−.21 (af)	.30 (ii)	
	Boys		−.06 (af)	.51 (ii)	
Confession (5)	(.79)	(.73)	NA	NA	NA
Reparation/amends (9)	(.62)	(.74)	NA	NA	NA
Concern about others' transgressions (7)	(.53)	(.82)	NA	NA	NA
Internalized conduct (20)	(.69)	(.93)	NA	NA	NA
(see Kochanska, DeVet, Goldman, Murray, & Putnam, 1994)					

(continues)

TABLE I (continued)

Instruments and scales (N of items)[a]	Age/grade of participants	Internal consistency reliability[b]	Sample internalizing[c]	Sample externalizing[d]	Sample adjustment[e]
My Child-Guilt (51)	2–11 year olds				
General guilt behavior (11)		.91	.65 (i)	−.09 (e)	NA
Concern over feelings with parent after wrongdoing (8)		.71	.19 (i)	.30 (e)	NA
Confession (4)		.58	−.58 (i)	−.81 (e)	NA
Apology and/or promise not to do it anymore (5)		.88	.36 (i)	.15 (e)	NA
Reparation/amends (6)		.73	.39 (i)	−.09 (e)	NA
Internalized standards of conduct (6)		.73	.41 (i)	−.08 (e)	NA
Empathic, prosocial response to another's distress (10)		.66	.12 (i)	.16 (e)	NA
My Child-Shame (51)	2–11 year olds				
General shame behaviors (11)		.83	.79 (i)	.39 (e)	NA
Concern over good feelings with parents after failure (6)		.80	.68 (i)	.34 (e)	NA
Excusing/rationalizing (5)		.68	.57 (i)	−.07 (e)	NA
Avoidance behavior (7)		.71	.46 (i)	.38 (e)	NA
Standards of internalized conduct (7)		.77	.67 (i)	.47 (e)	NA
Self-focus (10)		.78	.70 (i)	.57 (e)	NA
Denial of feeling (5)		<.60	NA	NA	NA
(see Ferguson, Stegge, & Barett, 1996)					

[a]TOSCA, Test of Self-Conscious Affect: C, Children, A, Adolescents; C-CARS, Child Version–Child Attribution Inventory; SCEMAS, Self-Conscious Emotions Maladaptive and Adaptive Scales; SCEQC, Self-Conscious Emotions Questionnaire for Children; CIIDC, Children's Interpretations of Interpersonal Distress and Conflict

[b]Cronbach's alpha.

[c] (d) depression, (a) anxiety, (i) internalizing, (ah) anger held in, (af) arousable and fearful. NS and NR denote that the correlation was not significant and therefore was not reported by the author(s) cited.

[d] (an) anger, (ag) aggression, (bp) behavior problems, (e) externalizing problems, (ao) acting-out, (ii) low impulsivity but high inhibitory control.

[e] (ad) adaptive behavior, (em) empathy, (h) honesty, (sc) self-perceived competence.

relationships to liberally selected and at times idiosyncratic indices of problems with internalization (e.g., depression) or externalization (e.g., anger/hostility). The Appendix also contains authors' addresses, brief background information regarding the measures, information regarding samples in which the measures have been tested, and examples of items and/or scenarios.

Self-Report Scenario-Based Measures

Test of Self-Conscious Affect for Children (Adolescents)

Tangney, Wagner, Burggraf, Gramzow, and Fletcher (1991) developed the Test of Self-Conscious Affect for Children (TOSCA-C) intended for use with 8- to 12-year-old children. In this self-report instrument, children read 10 negative and 5 positive scenarios (provided by an independent sample of 140 8- to 12-year-old children) depicting a range of behaviors (e.g., failing after not studying or upholding norms of honesty). For all scenarios, children rate on a 5-point scale the extent to which they would think or feel in ways that reflect precoded representations of guilt (e.g., self-admonitions about trying harder), shame (e.g., trait attributions about being stupid), and externalization (e.g., "It was my friend's fault."). For the five positive scenarios, children also rate the extent to which they would feel pride in the self (alpha pride), pride regarding their behavior (beta pride), or engage in defenses of detachment (e.g., "We do it all the time and we always make up."). The sum of the ratings across the target scenarios represents the child's guilt proneness, shame proneness, or proneness scores on the remaining constructs. Burggraf and Tangney (1989) actually first developed the SCAAI for Children, but Tangney and her colleagues (1990) recommend that the TOSCA-C be used in its place since the former is based on experimenter- rather than child-generated incidents. A version of the TOSCA for adolescents (TOSCA-A) is available (Tangney, Wagner, Gavlas, & Gramzow, 1991), which consists of 15 scenarios and response alternatives appropriate for this age group.

Internal consistency reliability estimates for guilt and shame proneness scores from the TOSCA-C are high in two large samples of 5th-grade or 4th-, 5th-, and 6th-grade boys and girls representing diverse ethnic and socioeconomic backgrounds (see Table 1). Cronbach's alpha for the even larger sample of male and female adolescents who completed the TOSCA-A is also highly satisfactory for the guilt- and shame-proneness scales. Tangney reports that girls score higher than boys on the guilt-proneness scale, although these differences are not consistently statistically significant. It is important to note that the TOSCA indices of guilt and shame proneness are highly correlated in child and adolescent samples (e.g., rs = .48 and .42, cf. Tangney, Wagner, Hill-Barlow, Marschall, & Gramzow, 1996).

Because of the substantial covariation between scores for guilt and shame proneness, these authors consistently use part correlations to factor out shame from guilt (or vice versa) before examining relations of these two scores to various criteria. Tangney and her colleagues invariably find that shame-free guilt in children and adolescents correlates negatively with various indices of antisocial tendencies (e.g., direct or displaced physical, verbal, or symbolic aggressive responses), negatively or negligibly with various symptoms (e.g., a tendency to somaticize, obsess, or show depression and anxiety), positively or negligibly with self-concept, and positively with reports of constructive means of dealing with anger-provoking incidents (e.g., Tangney, 1995b; Tangney et al., 1995; Tangney et al., 1996). Guilt-free shame, in contrast, correlates positively with most of these "maladaptive" cognitive and behavioral reactions to anger arousal, but negatively with symptoms, self-concept, and more constructive ways of coping with anger (cf. Tangney, 1995b; Tangney, Wagner, & Gramzow, 1992; Tangney, Wagner, Burggraf, Gramzow, & Fletcher, 1991; Tangney et al., 1996; Tangney et al., 1995).

Child Version-Child Attribution and Reaction Survey

We developed a scenario-based measure of guilt and shame proneness intended for use with a broader age range (5- to 12-year-old children). The Child Version-Child Attribution and Reaction Survey (C-CARS; Stegge & Ferguson, 1990) is an interview measure based, partly, on Tangney et al.'s SCAAI-C and the TOSCA-C (see Appendix I). We modified Tangney and her colleagues' measures in two ways. First, we suspected that the guilt-prone reactions operationalized by Tangney et al. were limited to responses of a socially desirable nature (e.g., "I should apologize.") when compared to the shame-prone alternatives (e.g., "I would feel stupid."). We based our suspicions on results showing that both children and adults consistently showed a higher average guilt- than shame-prone reaction. For example, using a modified adult version of the original TOSCA (Ferguson & Crowley, 1993), Ferguson and Crowley (1996) found that both male and female college students ($n = 282$) consistently report that one would and should feel the kind of guilt responses represented in the original TOSCA ($Ms = 3.85, 3.97$) much more so than they think one would or should feel ashamed ($Ms = 2.95, 2.43$) or would/should feel more ruminative or obsessive aspects of guilt ($Ms = 3.18, 2.95$). In revising the child version of the instrument, our intent, therefore, was to reduce the social desirability of the reactions by including additional guilt responses such as confession or self-punishment.

Second, because children completing the TOSCA-C (or SCAAI-C) must successively judge several reactions to the same situation, we thought that they would admit to strongly feeling only one of these several emotions (see Ferguson et al., 1991). We based this suspicion on Harter's (Harter, 1983; Harter & Whitesell, 1989) research showing that it is difficult for young children to imagine experiencing two emotions simultaneously. We designed the C-CARS to minimize children's dilemma of admitting to mixtures of emotion by presenting each situation on three different trials and having them rate only one reaction per trial.

As seen in the Appendix, the C-CARS consists of written and pictorial representations of the child involved in four moral transgression and four failure situations. Children respond on a 5-point Likert scale to questions precoded as representing guilt ("I would feel I did something wrong"), shame ("I am a mean kid for not helping"), or defensive externalization ("He should learn to take better care of his things"). Internal consistency reliability of the guilt proneness, shame proneness, and externalization scales are high (cf. Ferguson, Stegge, Miller, & Olsen, 1996). After rating each response, children answer a justification question "Why would you feel that way?", which has been reliably scored as representing interpersonally oriented reasons for the feeling (e.g., citing behavioral standards or showing empathy towards the victim), a tendency to internalize blame, and attempts to ward off anxiety caused by the situation by excusing the self, blaming the environment, denying the action as characteristic of the self, or denying/minimizing the emotional impact of the situation (Olsen, Ferguson, & Knight, 1994).

We find no notable trends with age or sex in the intensity of the responses in a sample of 104 5- to 12-year-old boys and girls (Ferguson, Stegge, Miller, & Olsen, 1996). However, as with others' research with adults and children, the guilt and shame subscale scores correlate substantially ($r = .62$). Part of this sizable correlation obviously reflects shared method variance, but this does not adequately tell the entire story, since guilt proneness negligibly correlates with externalization ($r = .08$), whereas shame proneness shows a higher correlation with externalization ($r = .36, p < .01$).

In terms of construct validity, the C-CARS measure of guilt proneness is virtually unrelated ($r = .07$) to a semiprojective or narrative measure of the same construct (the Children's Interpretations of Interpersonal Distress and Conflict or CIIDC, developed by Zahn-Waxler, Kochanska, Krupnick, & Mayfield, 1988), that we describe in more detail later. We also conducted canonical correlation analyses, treating the three emotion scores (C-CARS guilt, CIIDC guilt, and C-CARS shame) as the predictor variate and children's seven justification answers as the criterion variate. Briefly, we found that the C-CARS measure of guilt loaded on one function and related, among other criteria, to children's tendency to express concern for the victim's welfare and cite standards of behavioral conduct (prototypical guilt concerns in the developmental literature). However, we also found a statistically significant dimension on which only the C-CARS shame and CIIDC guilt themes loaded, and these were related *not* to behavioral standards or showing concern for the victim, but to a contrasting tendency to blame the self and the environment (among other criteria). Finally, we had parents complete the Parent Report Form of the CBCL as an index of internalizing and externalizing problems (Achenbach, McConaughy, & Howell, 1987). Results showed striking differences, within and across ages, in the relationships between scores for guilt proneness, shame proneness, and various symptoms. Briefly, there was an increasingly stronger trend with age for the narrative-derived scores of guilt proneness to correlate positively with symptoms of anxiety, withdrawal/depression, aggression, unpopularity, and family problems. In contrast, the tendency for symptoms to correlate *negatively* with both guilt- *and* shame-proneness scores from the C-CARS also increased with age, as we illustrate in Table 1 by showing comparisons for the youngest and oldest age groups only (cf. Ferguson, Sorenson, Bodrero, & Stegge, 1996).

We clearly have a problem here: Two measures that presumably assess guilt show no correlation whatsoever. Why? Briefly, we submit that the C-CARS presents children with situations in which guilt (and shame) would be, in Kelley's terms, the consensual reaction for most children, since the child is unambiguously responsible for harming another, damaging another's property, or failing at an athletic, school, or social task. When answering questions about their responsibility for the misdeeds or feelings of self-consciousness, it would be difficult for children to claim that they are not at fault or that they do not feel silly. We thus find that many of the children also respond with concern for the victim and are well aware of socially appropriate reasons for why their hypothetical behavior was wrong and even why they might feel stupid in the situation. Given the nonclinical sample of our participants, we would have been surprised if children had denied their responsibility, had failed to express moral concern for the victims, or did not think they looked a little dumb. We are suggesting, therefore, that most of the children actually gave expected consensual high shame, and especially high guilt, responses in these situations because (a) it was almost impossible to deny responsibility for untoward behavior, but (b) it was also psychologically safe to do so. The CIIDC is free of these kinds of problems, since the situations children encounter are ambiguous and do not pretend to place the respondent in the actor's role. Thus, any guilt themes that children express in the CIIDC are likely to be more reflective of their own, ongoing thoughts of unresolved guilt in daily experience. In short, we suspect that the original C-CARS, like all of the measures that involve hypothetical scenarios, is only assessing adaptive types of guilt and perhaps even adaptive forms of shame. The CIIDC, alternatively, allows the child to express concerns that could reflect problems with ruminative, chronic, or unalleviated guilt (Ferguson & Crowley, in press; Quiles & Bybee, in press).

Self-Conscious Emotions: Maladaptive and Adaptive Scales

Stegge, Ferguson, Bokhorst, and Goossens administered an improved version of the C-CARS to Dutch girls and boys attending grade school. The improved version is entitled the SCEMAS (Stegge & Ferguson, 1994) and consists of the original eight situations from the C-CARS plus an additional five situations rated not only for precoded guilt, shame, and externalization, but also pride. The new situations are more ambiguous than the original eight as to whether the expected response would be for the child to react with guilt, shame, or even pride (see the Appendix). The internal consistency reliability of the scales for the original eight situations is good in the Dutch sample, although one of the original situations (wetting one's pants) did not highly correlate with the total scores for the respective guilt, shame, and externalization scales. The five new situations also form homogeneous scales for guilt, shame, and pride but not for externalization.

When we correlate guilt, shame, and pride scores for only these five new situations with indices of symptoms, we find that guilt and shame in the five new situations correlate positively with scores for depression, but negatively with scores for self-perceived competence. Furthermore, shame proneness correlates positively with children's scores on a measure of social anxiety and social desirability as well as peers' ratings of the children's shyness. Importantly, we find that guilt and shame scores from the original eight situations that pull for adaptive responses actually correlate positively with the child's tendency to report pride for the five new situations and with peer ratings of socially adaptive behavior. Parents' ratings of the extent to which their children regularly violated moral norms showed a consistently negative correlation with the youngsters' tendency to answer with high guilt or shame responses in the original eight situations of the C-CARS (rs range from $-.27$ to $-.34$). Alternatively, there were positive relationships between parents' ratings of the extent to which their children adhered to proper norms of conduct and the guilt- and shame-proneness scores from the original eight situations (rs range from .21 to .43). Some of these relationships are summarized in Table 1.

All told, then, results with our own instruments support two tentative conclusions. In the original version of the C-CARS, the shame, and especially the guilt, ratings for children likely represent adaptive, expected, or consensual reactions. However, scores for both guilt and shame proneness from the five new situations (in the SCEMAS) seem to represent more of the maladaptive components of both emotions. These results are important in light of Kelley's model of covariation. It appears that higher ratings of guilt or shame to low consensual situations reveal the more maladaptive potential of both emotions.

Children's Guilt Inventory

Bybee, Williams, and Merisca (1994) developed a scenario-based measure of guilty affect in which children judge on an 8-point scale how guilty a target character would (or should) feel in each of 24 different vignettes. There are six major types of guilt-eliciting situations (transgression, inaction, anticipatory guilt, inequity, failure to attain ideals, and situations in which the target really was not at fault). The scenarios thus represent a wide range of potentially guilt-provoking situations and, like the SCEMAS, some of the situations represent clear moral transgressions or breaches of friendships or equity whereas others are more ambiguous as to whether the target really "should" feel guilty (see the Appendix).

Bybee et al. had 5th-, 8th-, and 11th-grade children rate either how a "target other" should feel in these situations or how they themselves would feel if they were the target. Principal components analysis with varimax rotation for the self-ratings revealed four factors, labeled Guilt over Personal Lapses, Guilt over Not at Fault, Guilt over Inequity, and Failure to Attain Ideals. Although the four factors are orthogonal, the median correlation between factor scores for the four subscales was fairly high (.40).

To examine validity issues, the same children also completed the Children's Depression Inventory (CDI, Kovacs, 1992), a general index of emotionality (assessing their general tendency to experience sadness, happiness, and anger), and they indicated how often their acquaintances and close friends engaged in delinquent activities. The children's teachers used a checklist to summarize their perceptions of children's tendency to act out, show shy or anxious behavior, assertive social skills, good educational performance, high frustration tolerance, and prosocial behavior. In general, self-reports of guilt declined with increasing grade level, especially for children's ratings of how guilty the "other should feel." The intensity of self-ratings of guilt also declined with grade level for lapses and failure to attain ideals, but this drop was greater for males than for females. Guilt continued to decline with age, even after covarying out general emotionality or ratings of peer delinquency. In terms of correlations with criterion variables, guilty affect correlated positively with indices of adjustment and negatively with indices of maladjustment in late adolescence, but not in middle childhood (see Table 1 for results pertinent to 5th- and 11th-grade children).

Self-Conscious Emotions Questionnaire for Children

Haimowitz (1996) modeled her Self-Conscious Emotions Questionnaire for Children (SCEQC) scenario-based measure of guilt and shame after the TOSCA and SCEMAS. The final version of the instrument consists of eight situations that could elicit guilt and/or shame (see the Appendix). Children hear about each incident and then rate on a 5-point scale the extent to which external factors caused their behavior or they would feel shame, guilt, or no emotional involvement. Haimowitz examined the SCEQC's reliability, factor structure, and relationship to several criterion variables in third, fourth, and fifth-grade boys and girls. Internal consistency estimates for the first and second administrations of the revised SCEQC and test–retest reliabilities were acceptable (see Table 1).

Separate factor analyses of scores from each administration of the instrument yielded two factors essentially representing guilt and shame ratings for the moral transgressions (factor 1) or the situations involving public or private self-consciousness (factor 2). Haimowitz argues that the two factors represent "important aspects of guilt and shame" (p. 62) and may be underlying dimensions of the two constructs. We, however, are more skeptical and remind the reader that there have been no unequivocal demonstrations of prototypic guilt- or shame-producing situations in the literature. Moreover, given the high multicollinearity in the data, and the existence of a clear theoretical model that drove creation of the scale, confirmatory factor analyses would have been the recommended technique. The reader should consult Haimowitz's dissertation for the many interesting correlations that she reports between the two factors and a vast array of measures of (mal)adjustment.

Self-Report Forced Choice Measures

Trait Affect Measure

Bybee and Williams (1995) revised the Mosher Forced-Choice Guilt Scale (Mosher, 1966, 1979) for use with children (see the Appendix). The new trait measure of guilt excludes Mosher's original Sex Guilt scale and includes the Hostility and Morality–Conscience subscales, adapted for the language skills of children. To minimize the effects of social desirability and to make the scales more "child-friendly," they used Harter's (1982) structured alternative format procedure. The initial version of the instrument (Study 1) presented children with a series of 40 pairs of alternatives (20 each for Hostility and for Morality–Conscience) and asked them to first choose which alternative of the pair is most like them, and then to rate whether it is "a lot like" or "sort of like" themselves, scored on a 4-point scale. Since the correlation for the two subscales was high ($r = .83$) in their sample of 5th-, 8th-, and 11th-grade girls and boys, both were combined into one measure of guilt, yielding high internal consistency results for the 40-item measure (see Table 1). Because of the high internal consistency results for this measure and the extensive covariation between the two subscales, Bybee and Williams reduced the number of forced-choice alternatives from 40 to 18 for use in their second study for which they also report high internal consistency reliability.

When correlated with scores for teacher reports of classroom weaknesses and strengths, peer nominations of each child's honesty and considerateness, and total scores on the CDI, they find, across grade levels, that the abbreviated trait guilt scores were significantly negatively correlated with internalizing and externalizing symptoms but were positvely correlated with indices of socially and academically skilled behaviors (see Table 1). Few notable differences emerged in the pattern of correlations across grade levels. In contrast to the results from the first study, guilt did decline for males and females from the fifth to eighth grade. Comparing the 8th- to 11th-grade children, guilt significantly increased for females. Females also had higher guilt scores than males.

Bybee and Zigler (1991, Study 2) also assessed the extent to which trait guilt was associated with Katz and Zigler's (1967) measure of self-image disparity in 5th-, 8th-, and 11th-grade boys and girls. Across the three grade levels, they found that trait guilt related to greater self-image disparity. For 5th, but not 8th or 11th graders, they also report that trait guilt related to a greater real self-image. However, the expected positive relationship between trait guilt and self-image disparity did not emerge for the 5th and 8th graders, and only approached significance for the 11th-grade students. They did find that higher educational performance, fewer learning problems, and less acting-out behavior related to a higher ideal self-image and greater guilt. All things considered, it appears from the trait guilt measure that guilt proneness is an adaptive response, although we will temper this conclusion later in the section on social desirability.

Semiprojective Measures

Certain researchers have started to rely more on projective or semiprojective story and play measures of emotion in children (e.g., Buchsbaum & Emde, 1990), in part because of the known biases that even children have in presenting themselves in a positive light (Mood, Johnson, & Shantz, 1978), and because of doubts about children's abilities to emphasize with the characters presented to them in self-report, scenario-based measures of emotion (Feshbach & Roe, 1968). Although questions exist about the predictive validity of projective or fantasy responses for children's actual behavior (e.g., Burton, 1971), some still consider these measures to be better indices of what the child might privately feel, especially when assessments focus on negative affect. Brody and Carter's (1982) study with 7-, 9-, and 11-year-old boys and girls nicely illustrates that children ascribe sadness and fear to a fictional story character more often, and with greater intensity, than they do to themselves. Conversely, children attribute happiness more frequently to themselves than the fictional character. These data suggest that children are likelier to admit to negative emotion in tasks that do not directly portray them as the main character.

Children's Interpretations of Interpersonal Distress and Conflict

Zahn-Waxler, Kochanska, Krupnick, and Mayfield (1988) developed the narrative CIIDC measure, in which children respond to a series of questions after viewing each of four photographs depicting ambiguous situations (see the Appendix). There is no suggestion to child respondents that they should feel guilty, but the procedure does allow considerable leeway for children to express issues of guilt that may be of daily concern to them.

Only 6 of the 78 codes that can be derived from children's answers to the CIIDC (Zahn-Waxler et al., 1988) directly reflect themes of guilt as described by Zahn-Waxler, Kochanska, Krupnick, and McKnew (1990). Zahn-Waxler et al. (1990) examined the relationship between CIIDC guilt scores, guilt scores derived from the psychiatric Childhood Assessment Schedule (13 items pertaining to self-blame or self-attributions of responsibility for negative events, some of which could reflect shame, e.g., "berating self when sad; evidencing feeling ashamed," p. 53, cf. Hodges, McKnew, Cytryn, & McKnew, 1982), and scores also derived from the CIIDC for empathy, relationship concerns, distress, hostility, and prosocial responses. The children in this study were 7- to 9-year-olds, and their mothers had been classified as well or depressed using the Schedule for Affective Disorders and Schizophrenia, Lifetime Version, and scored according to the Research and Diagnostic Criteria (Spitzer & Endicott, 1978). As seen in Table 1, the CIIDC guilt scores for children of well mothers were positively correlated with the CAS psychiatric measure of guilt and with CIIDC indices of empathy/prosocial themes. CIIDC guilt scores were marginally positively correlated with relationship concerns and did not relate to themes of hostility or distress. Looking at this group, we might be tempted to conclude that the semiprojective measure of guilt also assesses adaptive features to guilt. However, for children of depressed mothers, the CIIDC guilt scores were virtually unrelated to CAS guilt or scores for empathy/prosocial, hostility, or distress responses, yielding only a tendency to be related negatively to relationship concerns. There were no differences in the pattern of correlations found for boys and girls. All of these findings underscore the importance of assessing the predictive validity of emotion traits in both clinical and nonclinical samples.

Hoffman (1975)

Hoffman's semiprojective measure of guilt consists of short stories describing wrongful acts (see the Appendix). Hoffman (1975) reports the results of three studies testing male and female seventh graders (Studies 1 and 2) or fifth graders (Study 3). Children responded to two stories in which they pretended to be the protagonist. In one story, the protagonist cheats in a swimming contest and in the other s/he fails to help a lost child who later is killed by a car. Scores for the maximum guilt expressed by children (usually early in the story) and terminal guilt (expressed at the end of the story) were highly correlated ($r = .57$). Hoffman also examined whether these guilt scores were related to internal and external morality (using a Kohlbergian internal moral judgments task; fear of detection or punishment; a second measure of anticipated punishment; an attribution of external morality questionnaire, and ratings of consideration for others). Although the corelations were generally low for the children, Hoffman reports that fear of detection correlated negatively with maximum ($r = -.34$) and terminal ($r = -.19$) guilt, suggesting that the semiprojective measure is a valid measure of moral internalization. Note, however, that the criterion instruments reflecting concern for the other, or an internal sense of morality, did not correlate with the maximum and terminal guilt scores.

Thompson and Hoffman (1980) used a revised version of Hoffman's (1975) semiprojective stories with first-, third-, and fifth-grade girls and boys. Half of these children first received empathy instructions ("think about how the victim would feel at end of the story") before hearing three stories, whereas half received no such instructions. After presenting each story, interviewers asked children how they would feel and why. Thompson and Hoffman report that the empathy group scored higher than controls on all four indices of guilt (guilt intensity; post-wrongdoing feelings and actions: concern for victim; quality of justice principles). Older children showed more story completion guilt, more concern for the victim's welfare, and more frequent use of internal principles of right and wrong. The younger children, in contrast, showed more concern than the older ones with detection and punishment and more hedonistic reactions (pleasure at gaining the other's toy, for example). Using the procedures developed by Thompson and Hoffman, Kochanska (1991) also finds that parents' use of discipline that deemphasizes the use of power during children's toddler years is positively related to their 8- to 10-year-old children's reports of guilt. It thus seems reasonable to conclude that the Hoffman semiprojective measure of guilt is tapping into more adaptive forms of this emotion as reflected in its close association with empathy.

Finally, we should mention the existence of a Narrative Coding Manual, revised by Robinson, Mantz-Simmons, MacFie, and the MacArthur Narrative Working Group (1995), in which they code young children's successive completions of a narrative script for a variety of themes, including those pertinent to guilt and shame. We have not seen results from this project and can therefore not comment on the measure. In addition, results using the IFEEL pictures are also rapidly accumulating but studies using this paradigm have yet to distinguish guilt from shame (e.g., Zahn-Waxler, Ridgeway, Denham, Usher, & Cole, 1993).

Other Report Instruments

Kochanska (1992) has developed an instrument with which parents can report on aspects of young children's conscience. She distinguishes two components of conscience, namely, an ability to experience the guilt, discomfort, or anxiety that society expects people to have in response to an actual or anticipated moral transgression and the ability to self-regulate or refrain from acting on forbidden impulses. In the My Child, Kochanska (1993a) presents parents with 100 items that originally were thought to reflect the two major components of early conscience, expressed as 10 scales (see the Appendix).

My Child

Kochanska (1993a) reports kappas of interparent agreement that range from .49 to .87, with two scales yielding extremely low kappas (Symbolic Reproduction of/ Dealing with Wrongdoing and Sensitivity to Flawed Objects; Themes of Wrongdoing). Principal components analysis (with varimax relation) of the remaining eight scales for parents of children in three different age groups (21–33 months, 34–46 months, and 47–60 months) revealed two conventionally acceptable factors labeled Affective Discomfort (consisting of higher factor loadings for guilt, concern about relationships with parents, empathy, and apology) and Behavioral Control or Active Moral Regulation/Vigilance (consisting of high-factor loadings for confession, internalized moral conduct, reparation, and concern about others' wrongdoing). Girls score higher than boys on the Affective Discomfort factor (Kochanska, 1992). For the individual subscales, all but Confession increased with age, with the difference between the youngest children (21–33 months) and the groups of two older children 34–46 and 47–60 months) obtaining statistical significance. The youngest age group also scored higher than the older ones on the Affective Discomfort factor (Kochanska, 1993a).

In a study relating temperament to the two aspects of conscience, Kochanska and her associates (1994) report that Affective Discomfort in toddler-aged girls related to their being seen as more arousable and fearful, but showing greater inhibitory control and lower impulsivity. Girls and boys with lower impulsivity and higher inhibitory control were much more likely to be seen as actively vigilant and concerned in moral situations. In addition, girls who were more arousable and fearful scored lower on the Active Moral Regulation/Vigilance factor. Generally, these results support Kochanska's view of the important but complex roles played by both anxiety and self-regulation in the internalization of conscience.

My Child-Shame and My Child-Guilt

Thanks to the generous cooperation of G. Kochanska (personal communication, October 1995), we have also been developing two separate versions of the My Child. We intend to use the first to measure parental reports of their children's shame-related affects, cognitions, behaviors, and styles of coping or defense, and the second to measure their reports of components related to guilt (Ferguson, Stegge, & Barrett, 1996). The My Child-Shame and My Child-Guilt instruments each consist of 51 items that parents rate on a 7-point scale, in terms of how true it is of their child. Thus far, we have data from a *very* small sample of 16 parents (4 fathers and 12 mothers) of 8 males and 8 females ranging in age from 2 through 11 years (M = 5.14 and mode = 4 years). As a check on concurrent validity, parents also completed the Parent Report Form of the Child Behavior Checklist (CBCL).

The My Child-Shame consists of seven subscales pertaining to General Shame Behaviors; Concern over Good Feelings with Parents after Failure or Falling Short (representing concern with relationships after the child has failed to meet ideals); Excusing or Rationalizing; Specific Avoidance Behavior; Standards of Internalized Conduct; Self-focus, and a seventh subscale Denial of Feeling that showed poor internal consistency. Patterned after Kochanska's scales, the My Child-Guilt subscales are General Guilt Behaviors; Concern over Good Feelings with Parent after Wrongdoing (representing concern with relationships after the child has been naughty or done something wrong); Confession; Apology and/or Promise Not to Do It Anymore; Reparation/Amends; Internalized Standards of Conduct, and Empathic, Prosocial Response to Another's Distress. The current version of the two shows good, but extremely preliminary, internal consistency reliability for almost all of the scales (see Table 1).

Scores from the My Child-Shame subscales correlated moderately with the broad-band CBCL index of externalizing symptoms and even more highly with that for internalizing symptoms (see Table 1). When we examine the narrower-band internalizing symptoms that have been of interest in the area of guilt and shame, we see that the My Child-Shame subscales consistently correlate with CBCL Withdrawal (rs range from .21 with Internalized Standards of conduct to .78 for the Shame subscale) and CBCL Anxiety/Depression (rs range from .79 for the Shame subscale to .56 for Avoidance). The narrow-band CBCL score for Social Problems is less consistently correlated with the shame scales (rs range from .07 for the Shame subscale to .24 for Self-Focus), as is the narrow-band CBCL score for Aggressive Behavior (rs range from $-.00$ for Internalized Standards of Conduct to .59 for the Parental Concern subscale). All told, in this small sample, parental reports regarding various facets of shame in children correlated more strongly with their tendency to perceive children as having problems with internalization rather than externalization.

Compared to the My Child-Shame version, the My Child-Guilt subscales correlate even less strongly with broad-band indices of externalization compared to internalization (see Table 1). In terms of the narrow-band CBCL indices, we find that CBCL Withdrawal correlated negligibly or negatively with the various My Child-Guilt subscales (rs range from .42 with Guilt to $-.65$ with Confession). However, CBCL Anxiety/Depression scores correlated positively with the Guilt, Apology, and Internalized Standards of Conduct subscales (rs $=$ .82, .35, and .36), but negatively with Confession ($r = -.35$). The only notable correlation for CBCL narrow-band indices is a positive one between Social Problems and Apology ($r = .73$) and a negative one between Aggressive Behavior and Confession ($r = -.73$). All told, tentative evidence suggests that the Guilt version of the My Child is less predictive of problems with either internalization or externalization when compared to its Shame counterpart.

We need to make two final comments regarding the discriminant validity of the Shame and Guilt versions of the My Child. First, there is a nonsurprisingly strong correlation between the General Shame Behaviors and General Guilt Behaviors subscale of each measure ($r = .72$). However, Fisher's z tests reveal that two of the remaining subscales that are unique to the My Child-Guilt measure (Confession, and Empathy, but not Apology) correlated much more highly with the General Guilt Behaviors subscale than with its shame counterpart. Conversely, two of the remaining subscales that are unique to the My Child-Shame measure (Avoidance, Self-Focus, but not Excuses/Rationalization) correlated more highly with the General Shame Behaviors subscale than with the guilt counterpart. These differences notwithstanding, we see that guilt and shame, even in the eyes of parents who were rating fairly circumscribed behaviors, are highly related emotions. However, as is the case with children's self-reports of guilt and shame, the two emotions are nevertheless differentially related to indices of maladjustment.

Situation-Specific or Observational Measures

There are a variety of studies with preadolescent children that index guilt responses using brief, incidental self-reports or observational measures of guilt-like responses (e.g., Chapman, Zahn-Waxler, Cooperman, & Iannotti, 1987; Hoffman & Salzstein, 1967; Kochanska et al., 1994; Kochanska, Aksan, & Koenig, 1995). Because of the situation-specific nature of these measures, we will not review them here.

We will, however, review in this section one observational procedure developed by Barrett, Zahn-Waxler, and Cole (1993) for measuring guilt-relevant, shame-relevant, and nonspecific self-regulatory behaviors in toddlers.

Barrett et al. have developed a coding procedure for classifying toddlers' behavioral reactions to standard violations. They used a broken doll paradigm in the original research, involving 25- to 36-month-old children who were visiting the laboratory with their mother. Children were invited to play with an experimenter's favorite doll (a clown) while the experimenter attended to some tasks in the other room. Unbeknownst to the children, one of the doll's legs was broken, so that as soon as the child picked up the doll, the leg would fall off. The coding procedure focuses on real-time measures of children's behaviors before and after the mishap, and before and after the experimenter returns to display "mild concern" about the broken doll. Behaviors coded as guilt-relevant reflect an amending style that includes discrete behaviors, such as latency to trying to repair the leg or latency to letting the experimenter know that the leg is broken (either through body language or verbalizations directed at the experimenter). Shame-relevant behaviors connote an avoiding style which includes the discrete behaviors of latency to gaze aversion relative to the experimenter, rate of bodily avoidance of the experimenter (movements away from the experimenter, but not toward any other person or object present in the room), and the presence or absence of an embarrassed smile followed, within 5 sec, by gaze aversion from the experimenter. They also coded the child's rate of smiling before the mishap, after the mishap, and the rate of avoidance of the experimenter before the mishap. Coders blind to the purpose of the study achieved high interobserver reliabilities, ranging from .89 to 1.00.

The results showed that avoidance behaviors were more prevalent after the mishap than before. For example, although 79.5% and 26% of the toddlers avoided the experimenter or showed signs of embarrassment after the mishap, only 22.7% and 5% of the toddlers showed the same behaviors before the doll broke. Amending behaviors were also quite frequent, with 79.5% and 77.3% of the children trying to repair the leg or "telling" the experimenter what happened. Barrett et al. independently checked the appearance of shame- and guilt-relevant behaviors in the home situation, by asking mothers to report how frequently their children showed signs of guilt, shame, and sadness as well as how often the children were involved in mishaps similar to the one in the laboratory. Mothers reported a high frequency of shame-relevant (64%) and guilt-relevant (91.7%) behaviors in the home situation.

Barrett et al. also examined whether there were individual differences in toddlers' tendency to express shame- versus guilt-relevant behaviors. Based on both the laboratory and maternal report data, children were classified as "avoiders" versus "amenders" (see Barrett et al. for details on the classification criteria). Subsequent analyses showed that Avoiders indeed displayed less guilt-relevant amending behavior than Nonavoiders, especially males. Avoiders compared to Amenders also displayed more signs of embarrassment following the mishap, but not before. Toddlers high in Amending, in contrast, showed fewer shame-relevant behaviors compared to those high in Avoiding. There thus appear to be distinct individual differences starting at the age of 2 years in children's tendency to manifest shame-versus guilt-prone behavioral styles.

PROBLEMS WITH THE INSTRUMENTS

Hypothetical versus Real Emotion-Provoking Situations

There are several intricately related limitations to current assessments of guilt (and shame) in children. In addition to the limitations cited earlier, the scenario-based measures (our own included) fail to ascertain whether the individual has ever been involved in the depicted situations which, for the most part, are fairly consensual representations of guilt-evoking incidents. Thus, although people may understand how they are expected to react in these situations, we do not know whether they are ever involved in them and how they actually do react when confronted face-to-face with a real instance of moral or social impropriety. Participants can also fairly easily resolve many of the situations by admitting a guilt response rather than other options (e.g., shame). By providing high ratings to questions regarding apology and reparation (all indices of guilt according to the experts), the individual can gain closure on the situation. However, in none of the studies of which we are aware, have participants had to reckon with the victim's rebuff of attempts at reparation or apology. Lindsay-Hartz, De Rivera, and Mascolo (1995) indeed report that the intensity of guilt feelings diminishes when the perpetrator has confessed, offered reparation, or asked for forgiveness. Equally important, however, is their evidence that people seek to "magically undo" a wrong when it was not possible to confess, make repair, or seek forgiveness (see also Kippax, Crawford, Benton, & Gault, 1988). They discuss instances of unresolved guilt, in which the person continually seeks to restore balance by being good, punishing the self, giving up rights, or performing reparative actions that they perceive as symbolic substitutes for situations that they could not resolve (see also Eyre & Ferguson, 1996; Ferguson & Eyre, 1996; Kubany & Manke, 1995). As noted by Thoits (1989), not only are emotions "signals to the self, but they are also signals to others and the objects of others' responses" (p. 332; see also Barrett, 1995; Malatesta & Wilson, 1988; Parkinson, 1995). We need to pay more attention to emotional exchanges between perpetrator and victim, or actor and audience, in terms of how this affects their ability to regulate any emotion—including guilt and its close relative shame.

Perspective Taking and Empathy as Potential Confounds

Scenario-based measures are also susceptible to problems caused by a child's willingness to take the perpetrator's perspective. In this regard, the reader needs to remember Brody and Carter's (1982) finding that children are more likely to admit a negative emotion in tasks that do not directly portray them as the main character. Yet, in this area, practically all of the scenario-based and forced-choice measures request the child to pretend that he or she is the agent of some form of distress. Because the children typically sampled in this line of research are older, there should be no problem with them being able to take the target's perspective (e.g., Feshbach & Roe, 1968). However, we must remember that we are asking children to identify themselves with some fairly (ob)noxious behaviors and painful responses (especially shameful ones). It is thus conceivable that children are not eager to identify with the perpetrator uniformly across the situations, especially when portrayed as the opposite sex. Children's reluctance to consistently adopt the role of perpetrator could thus explain why shame and externalization responses have typically lower mean scores (and variances) than guilt reactions (e.g., Ferguson et al., 1996).

In a related vein, individual differences in a particular type of perspective taking (viz., empathic perspective taking) may contribute to variability in scores on these instruments. Individuals who can empathize with the victim in the various scenarios might respond consistently across situations with high reports of guilt, because they can imagine that someone who hurt a victim in this way *would* feel guilty but *not* because they themselves truly would feel guilty or even would get themselves into this kind of predicament. The person who receives low guilt-proneness scores could simply be incapable of empathizing with the victim, may not be willing to do so, or may truly never be involved in situations of this nature. The greater relationship found between empathy and guilt in the studies we have reviewed earlier is consistent with this observation (e.g., Tangney, 1989; Tangney, Wagner, Burggraf, Gramzow, & Fletcher, 1991). In short, we may well question whether we are measuring the construct of guilt independently of empathic perspective-taking ability and whether this matters.

Social Desirability

The question of how response biases impact the validity of a measure is a general concern in any assessment endeavor. However, developers of instruments to measure guilt (or shame) in children have paid little attention to this issue. It is an issue that we all need to seriously examine, for at least two reasons. First, not only adults, but also children are known to admit less often to experiencing negative than positive emotions (e.g., Walsh, Tomlinson-Keasy, & Klieger, 1974). It goes without saying that admissions to the negative emotions of guilt or shame could be subject to response sets of social desirability. A second, related reason is that guilt may be a more socially desirable response than shame, in part because guilt serves to satisfy a larger community (guilt repairs damaged relationships). A third reason concerns the rapidly accumulating belief (and certain pieces of evidence) that guilt proneness serves adaptive functions for the individual, but that shame proneness puts the individual at more serious risk for the development of symptoms.

Tangney et al. (1996) addressed the question of whether social desirability biases could compromise interpretation of their results. Children in this study completed the Children's Social Desirability-Short Form scale (CSD; Crandall, Crandall, & Katkovsky, 1965). The bivariate and part correlations between scores on the CSD and shame were −.00 and −.15, and for guilt .27 and .31. They argue that the positive relationships between shame and symptoms, or the negative ones between guilt and symptoms, are negligibly impacted by partialling out children's socially desirable response tendencies. We nevertheless later raise concerns with the widespread use of partialling procedures in this literature and question whether this procedure adequately addresses issues of response bias.

Issues of social desirability also apply to the revised measure of trait guilt developed by Bybee and Williams (1995). The first author provided the abbreviated trait guilt instrument to a panel of 10 full-time faculty members (nine Ph.D.'s and one Ed.D.) in clinical psychology, developmental psychology, child–clinical psychology, school psychology, and family and human development. Each of these individuals is actively involved with children and adolescents clinically and/or in one or more of the research areas of assessment of academic, behavioral, and emotional competence or developmental psychopathology. Judges were unaware of the purpose of the instrument, nor did they consult with one another. Each expert made four separate judgments regarding each of the 18 pairs of items that Bybee and Williams had presented to children, identifying which item in each pair (the left-most, right-most, neither, or both) conveyed the response most socially desirable, the most socially adaptive, the most indicative of potential future problems with guilt, and the most indicative of potential future problems with externalization.

Briefly, in the judges' opinions, the large majority of choices being made by children are between portraying themselves as externalizers versus portraying themselves as socially well-adjusted children. There also appears to be a negative relation between judgments of the social desirability and social adaptive nature of each response option and judgments made regarding whether the same response option was indicative of future problems with guilt. For example, one of the response options for 12 of the 18 pairs was rated by 60% or more of the respondents as indicative of future problems with guilt. Of these 12 items, only 3 of them (25%) were also rated as both socially desirable and socially adaptive by 60% or more of the respondents. We are not at all pessimistic about the potential value of the trait guilt scale for children. We instead see these preliminary results as a cautionary note on the difficulties inherent in preventing possible response biases from swaying participants' self-representations.

Discriminant Validity

When we examine the literature on shame- and guilt-proneness, we see repeated indications that guilt and shame highly covary. There are obvious reasons for the overlap between the two constructs, since they both are negative emotions that belong to the same emotion family and, not surprisingly, they often arise in the same situation. The considerable covariation between guilt and shame argues for a hierarchical conceptualization of them, both theoretically and statistically. Watson and Clark (1992) have convincingly demonstrated that there are two nonspecific, broad dimensions of Positive Affect versus Negative Affect (reflecting the strong influence of valence or hedonic tone) that coexist with unique contributions of specific emotions (such as fear, hostility, guilt, etc.). Both levels can contribute independently to relations observed between affect data and other variables (such as personality traits, health complaints, stress, and symptoms of psychopathology, e.g., Wolfe, Finch, Saylor, Blount, Pallmeyer, & Carek, 1987).

Applied to the area of research on guilt and shame, Watson and Clark's argument has some disturbing implications. For example, in the area of self-conscious emotion, we could be interested in predicting how shame proneness impacts variables such as attributional style, dysfunctional cognitions, and parenting styles. However, the specific indices of shame available are not pure measures of this construct, since we know that guilt and shame correlate highly. The shame scale contains both specific variance (shame) and nonspecific variance (negative affect, including guilt, but also others such as anxiety). In order to confidently assess the impact of shame on any criterion, we need to assess other affects and both levels of the structure to determine whether effects are specific, nonspecific, or some combination of the two (cf. Tangney, 1989; Tangney et al., 1993).

Watson and Clark's approach illustrates the problems inherent in a single affect, single-level approach. For example, to study a single affect such as guilt in isolation, it would be natural—but inappropriate—to conclude that this emotion specifically relates to the criterion. Why? Because certain partial correlational analyses could reveal that the significant zero-order relations are almost entirely due to the general Negative Affect factor. By eliminating this nonspecific variance, the relationships could essentially vanish. One cannot demonstrate specific relations in isolation, but must use a multiaffect assessment to tease out the separate contributions of specific and nonspecific factors.

Partialling Procedures or Watch Me Pull a Relationship Out of My Hat!

The seemingly obvious implication of Watson and Clark's argument is that we need to use partialling procedures, either at the bivariate level or in hierarchical multiple regression. Both Harder (1995) and Tangney et al. (1995) report that partialling out guilt from shame minimally affects the relation between shame and various criterion variables in general. However, partialling out shame from guilt results in pronounced changes in the relationship between guilt and criterion variables. Often, removing from guilt the variance due to shame minimizes the bivariate relationship between guilt and indices of psychopathology—even causing the correlations to reverse in direction. The relationship of guilt to measures of adaptive functioning, on the other hand, usually becomes even higher after removing the variance shared with shame.

Unfortunately, psychologists too often take highly correlated variables, partial one for the other in analyzing relationships with yet other variables, and draw statistically and substantively invalid conclusions. The area of research on guilt and shame is replete with these kinds of mistakes, and yet few recognize this. Many believe that guilt proneness is a purely adaptive affective style and that shame proneness is maladaptive. They base this conclusion on the fact that once guilt is partialed for its relationship to shame, it relates negligibly to indices of psychopathology (e.g., depression). On the other hand, shame, after partialed for guilt, moderately relates to the same indices of psychopathology. Using partialling procedures, the weight given to the variable that has a higher bivariate relationship to the predictor (e.g., shame and depression) will increase relative to the weight given to the second criterion (e.g., guilt). This could, however, be an artifact of the multicollinearity between the two criterion variables and is certainly not an unconfounded reflection of the contribution of either shame or guilt to the predictor variable.

Our colleague, Xitao Fan, at Utah State University gives the following example (personal communication, May 1996) of the problem with "bouncing betas": Let's assume that depression bivariately relates to shame at $r = .62$ and guilt at $r = .40$. As the bivariate relation between shame and guilt progressively increases from let's say .10, to .20, to .40, to .60, to .80 (as a function, for example, of the specific measure of guilt and shame used), then shame's partialed relationship to depression will steadily increase (the betas for shame in relationship to depression would be .59, .56, .55, .60, and .83, respectively), while guilt's partialed relationship to depression will steadily decrease, and can even become negative (betas are .34, .29, .18, .05, −.27, respectively)! In fact, the zero-order correlation between shame and indices of psychopathology only has to be .02 higher than the zero-order correlation between guilt and these same indices, for the partialling procedure to artifactually give the weight to shame!

We, too, frequently feel frustrated by the reality of multicollinearity or "bouncing betas," and have yet to find a statistical wand that will magically solve the problems they pose for the assessment of guilt, shame, or their relationship to indices of (mal)adjustment. Although not without limitations of their own, many statisticians point out that canonical correlation, confirmatory factor analyses, and techniques based on generalizability theory are better suited for use situations in which variables share a considerable amount of variance (e.g., Pedhauzer, 1992; Shavelson, Webb, & Rowley, 1989; Thompson, 1984).

Other Problems

There is one additional statistical problem that researchers in this area need to address when relating measures of guilt (or shame) to other criteria. Thus far, researchers have simply assumed that any relationship found would be linear in nature. However, we believe that curvilinear relationships are also quite plausible. That is, up to a point, both guilt and shame proneness may serve adaptive functions. But, when either emotion becomes too extreme, it may well become maladaptive for the individual. Thus, many of the negligible correlations between guilt and maladaptive symptoms, or shame and adaptive ones, could be masking a true nonlinear relationship for both emotion traits.

Moreover, some of the inconsistent results found between guilt or shame and various criteria could reflect the fact that the different measures used in this research are measuring differing parts of the guilt- or shame-proneness distribution. For example, as Quiles and Bybee (1995) note, the PFQ-2 (Harder & Zalma, 1990; Harder, 1990) could be measuring guilt that is chronic or unalleviated. The TOSCAs, on the other hand, could be tapping into the other extreme of the guilt continuum. Thus, it should not surprise us to find that the different measures yield seemingly contradictory relationships with other criteria. Quiles and Bybee (1995) try to resolve the disagreements between researchers promoting the adaptive view of guilt (e.g., Baumeister et al., 1994; Tangney, in press) with those convinced of the maladaptive potential of this emotion (e.g., Harder, 1995; Kugler & Jones, 1992). A factor analytic study that included the PFQ-2, GI, TOSCA, and Mosher scales revealed that the first two loaded on a separate factor from the remaining scales. For both male and female adult respondents, the first factor was related to symptoms of dysfunction as measured using the SCL-90-R (e.g., hostility) Scores on the second factor, which they label "predispositional guilt," did not relate to symptoms of psychopathology but were related to indices of prosocial behavior (e.g., respondents' involvement in volunteer work; see also Merisca & Bybee, 1994, 1996). We have reported similar findings (Ferguson & Crowley, in press; Ferguson et al., 1996).

Related to the distribution issue is researchers' proclivity in this area to sample children (and adults) from nonclinical populations. However, we obviously will never know just how (mal)adaptive any emotion or behavior is without branching into the clinical realm and examining just how large a role guilt and/or shame play in these individuals' pain-filled lives (cf. Kubany & Manke, 1995).

CONCLUDING THOUGHTS

Resolving Disagreements Regarding the (Mal)Adaptive Nature of Emotion

As is obvious from the preceding review, most have taken a criterion or predictive validity approach to address the role of guilt in (mal)adaptive development. Few in the area have actively addressed the question of how we can best conceptualize the (mal)adaptive potential of the emotion of guilt, shame, or related emotions, nor have they asked whether or how we need to incorporate developmental issues in this conceptualization. Averill (1994) asserts that the functions of emotion are difficult to pin down precisely, in part, because emotions have multiple consequences and their functionality is always specific to a particular context (Izard, Blumberg, & Oyster, 1985).

Hermans and Hermans-Jansen (1995) discuss the difficulty of even detecting a dysfunctional value system (within which they subsume emotions), since people often self-select to be in situations that will not overtly threaten their tendency to inflexibly respond with particular emotions (cf. Josephs, 1992). Clark and Watson (1994) note that emotions themselves (including negative ones) are never dysfunctional; they simply "are." Negative relative to positive emotions often possess dysfunctional characteristics of being intensely, frequently, and perennially experienced. In other words, the balance of the person's proclivity to experience positive or negative emotions, the flexibility of the individual's emotional repertoire in processing, integrating, and controlling internal and external inputs (Averill, 1994; Cole, Michel, & Teti, 1994), or what we have labeled one's "emotional resilience," are all important in understanding normative and maladaptive patterns of emotion and its regulation (see also Magai & McFadden, 1995).

Researchers have given little systematic attention to clearly distinguishing the different components of the emotion of guilt (e.g., expressive, experiential/affective, concerns, action tendencies). Kugler and Jones (1992), for example, appropriately note that few make efforts to separate affective aspects of guilt from the moral standards on which this emotion is sometimes based. When it comes to addressing the basis for dysregulation, we therefore do not know whether the maladaptiveness is due to the affective component of an emotion, its cognitive components, styles of coping or defense that have been developed to deal with it, or the person's behavioral manifestation of the emotion. Rutter (1991) points out that there is analogous disagreement regarding the links among emotions, cognitions, and coping in the field of clinically significant depressive disorders, since individuals diagnosed with serious depressive disorder show problems in the domains of extreme negative affect, including the experience of guilt, self-condemnation, and hopelessness. Severely depressed individuals also behave ineffectually and indecisively in coping. Rutter correctly and cogently asks which type of dysfunction constitutes the basic problem:

Is it that such people experience emotions that are so much more extreme than other people's that their cognitions and coping are disrupted and rendered dysfunctional? Or is it that they tend to think in negative ways so the "ordinary" negative comments become intensified and perpetuated? Or is it that their feeling states are unexceptional but that they can cope badly with them or with their negative thoughts or life stressors and challenges? Clearly, poor coping or affect dysregulation cannot be inferred from dysfunctional mood states. That would be merely tautological. Rather, it is necessary to devise some means of measuring the process (regulation) in ways that are independent of outcome (affective dysfunction or maladaptation). (pp. 274–275)

There obviously are ill-understood and complex relationships among emotions, thoughts, and behavior in social interactions that very really serve to regulate and influence each other (Garber, Braafladt, & Zeman, 1991). In the realm of guilt and shame, we will never disentangle these complex interactions by measuring ill-defined and poorly justified admixtures of the components of just these two emotions. The complex problems will also never be solved by focusing attention on *one* of the emotions to the exclusion of a wide range of emotions. Unfortunately, this is exactly what is happening in the area of self-conscious emotion, as testified to by the recent proliferation of measures, studies, and theoretical treatments of either guilt (e.g., Baumeister et al., 1994; Bybee, Williams, & Merisca, 1996) or shame (e.g., M. Lewis, 1992a,b).

We also need to focus more on the entire interpersonal process of guilt across time, asking what children (or adults) feel guilty about and why, what appraisals are and are not adaptive, and what the consequences are of the enacted behavioral tendencies. A person who feels guilt, who has learned to resolve the emotion through apology, reparation, or avoidance of similar situations in the future, *and* whose environment has allowed its resolution in these ways will likely walk away from the situation feeling capable and competent of dealing with an initially uncomfortable feeling. However, obviously, not everybody walks away from a situation having successfully resolved it in these ways. The victims of harm do not always, or cannot, forgive and forget, a person who has learned that one never does wrong or who has been taught that mistakes are always avoidable will likely suffer from guilt far past the proximate circumstance.

Researchers in other areas (e.g., in research on depression and anxiety) have paid dearly for ignoring process aspects of emotion. Compas, Ey, and Grant (1993), for example, discuss inconsistencies in research results on depression, comparing studies that measure depression (a) as a mood state, (b) as a syndrome of interrelated behaviors including depression and anxiety, and (c) as a full-blown clinical disorder. Many of the inconsistencies in results in this literature are more apparent than real, since the measures yielding discrepant findings [represented in (a)–(c)] may simply be tapping into different points in time along the pathway of the development of depression. The same could be true in the area of guilt (and shame). It seems quite plausible that guilt (and shame!) could serve some individuals adaptively and continue to do so throughout the life span. However, biological, social, and coping processes can combine to lessen the adaptive value of either emotion, such that the person—rather than being able to resolve a guilt- or shame-provoking situation—moves to a next level in which s/he ruminates about past mistakes or desires to remake the self. Failure to amend for past wrongs or remake the self, accompanied again by various stressors (e.g., biological or social ones), can then lead to a next level, in which the person succumbs to the full weight or maladaptive guilt and shame.

In this context, it is important to remember Weiner's (1986) attributional perspective on shame and guilt, in which he argues that shame reflects internal attributions of uncontrollability, whereas guilt encompasses internal attributions of control. The person plagued by guilt may be trying to hang onto a view of the self as being in control. At some point in the process, the person may relinquish this belief and take one of two different directions. That is, the person may eventually admit to not being in control of the bad things that "they do," internalize this as a negative self-evaluation, and delve deeper into despair about the self as a controlling agent—all of which could be manifested in maladaptive expressions of both guilt and shame. Alternatively, the person may realize that control simply is not always possible and let the self off the hook. We must not minimize the crucial role that others play during this entire process. The partners in one's relationships (be they specific individuals, smaller groups, or larger institutions) often keep people hooked into believing that they can control the bad things that happen to them or accelerate the target individual's movement from believing in self-control to relinquishing this belief altogether. The literature on victimization, co-dependency, child and spousal abuse, are replete with examples of how much power others can have in affecting our tendency to cling to beliefs about being in control.

Final Thoughts: Harold Revisited

During our seemingly endless expedition throughout the literature on measuring guilt in children, we have been most struck by researchers' failures to measure facets of emotion in terms of their consistent, distinctive, or consensual status. When we reexamine all of the findings keeping the covariation analogy in mind, we believe that it is fair to conclude that (a) shame appears to be a maladaptive emotional orientation in this literature, precisely because this response would be a nonconsensual one in many of the situations tested; (b) shame is, however, not always a low probability response, and in these contexts, could serve the individual adaptively (cf. our own research using the C-CARS versus the SCEMAS); (c) guilt proneness has gotten a "good" rap in this literature primarily because this response would be a highly consensual one in most of the situations examined; but (d) guilt-proneness can also serve the individual maladaptively if expressed intensely in situations that are not likely to elicit guilt as the consensual reaction (cf. measures using semiprojective techniques). We therefore urge researchers in this field to be more diligent about collecting normative data on facets of emotion, against which to compare any one individual's response tendencies.

We also encourage the field to seriously examine an individual's response pattern in terms of its consistency and distinctiveness, which means that measurement needs to involve not only Harold, but all of his regular interaction partners, and the embedded contexts within which he interacts. That is, to really be helpful to Harold, we need to scrutinize how often and with whom he reacts with guilt or shame (in both consensual and nonconsensual situations). We might discover that Harold alone is not the crux of the problem. Rather, we might need to recognize that Harold's life circumstances or routine interaction partners are as much—or even more—a source of his emotional reactions than is "something" about Harold.

ACKNOWLEDGMENTS

We wish to thank several individuals for their input. First, we thank Dr. Xitao Fan for offering sage advice concerning partialling techniques. Second, we appreciate the participation of several faculty members at Utah State University (USU) and Weber State in our small scale validity study—we would thank each of them individually, but that would break our promise of anonymity. Third, we would like to express our sincerest of thanks to several undergraduates at USU, including Corinna Sorenson, Jenifer Byington, and Valarie Frigaard for their help with data collection, data entry, and library work. We are *especially* grateful to Heidi Eyre for her seemingly endless devotion. She assisted in preparing the table, appendix, and reference list. She also collected and entered data for the My Childs and the study involving USU faculty.

APPENDIX: CHILD MEASURES OF GUILT (AND SHAME)

Instrument: Test of Self-Conscious Affect for Children (TOSCA-C) and Test of Self-Conscious Affect for Adolescents (TOSCA-A)
Authors: Tangney, J. P., Wagner, P. E., Burggraf, S. A., Gramzow, R., & Fletcher, C. (TOSCA-C). Tangney, J. P., Wagner, P. E., Gavlas, J., & Gramzow, R. (TOSCA-A).
Designed for: 8–12 year olds (TOSCA-C) and 12–18 year olds (TOSCA-A)

Brief Description

The TOSCA-C is a self-report instrument in which children read 10 negative and 5 positive scenarios depicting a range of behaviors (e.g., failing after not studying or upholding norms of honesty). For all scenarios, children rate on a 5-point scale the extent to which they would think or feel in ways that reflect precoded representations of guilt (e.g., self-admonitions about trying harder), shame (e.g., trait attributions about being stupid), and externalization (e.g., "It was my friend's fault."). For the five positive scenarios, children also rate the extent to which they would feel pride in the self (alpha pride), pride regarding their behavior (beta pride), or engage in defenses of detachment (e.g., "We do it all the time and we always make up"). The sum of the ratings across the target scenarios represents the child's guilt proneness, shame proneness, or proneness scores on the remaining constructs.

Sample Scenario and Rating

Your report card isn't as good as you wanted. You show it to your mother when you get home.

a. Everyone gets bad grades once in a while. (detachment)
b. I really didn't deserve the grades; it wasn't my fault. (externalization)
c. Now that I got a bad report card, I'm worthless. (shame)
d. I should listen to everything the teacher says and study harder. (guilt)

Further information available from: June Price Tangney, Department of Psychology, George Mason University, Fairfax, VA 22030.

Instrument: Child–Child Attribution and Reaction Survey (C-CARS)
Authors: Stegge, H., & Ferguson, T. J.
Designed for: 5–12 year olds

Brief Description

The C-CARS is an interview measure that consists of written and pictorial representations of the child involved in four moral transgressions and four failure situations. Children respond on a 5-point Likert scale to questions precoded as representing guilt (e.g., "I would feel I did something wrong"), shame (e.g., "I am a mean kid for not helping"), or defensive externalization (e.g., "He should learn to take better care of his things"). After rating each response, children answer a justification question "Why would you feel that way?," which has been reliably scored as representing interpersonally oriented reasons for the feeling (e.g., citing behavioral standards or showing empathy towards the victim), a tendency to internalize blame, and attempts to ward off anxiety caused by the situation by excusing the self, blaming the environment, denying the action as characteristic of the self, or denying or minimizing the emotional impact of the situation.

Sample Scenario and Rating

> You are hurrying home one day to watch your favorite television program. You see your little brother/sister outside. S/he is sitting on the sidewalk crying. S/he dropped a bag of marbles and they are rolling all over the place. You don't stop to help him/her. You just keep on walking towards home.

1. How much are you the kind of boy/girl who would feel that you are a mean kid for not helping? (shame)
2. How much are you the kind of boy/girl who would feel that you did something wrong? (guilt)
3. How much are you the kind of boy/girl who would feel that s/he should learn to take better care of his/her things? (externalization)
4. Why would you feel that way?

Further information available from: Tamara J. Ferguson, Department of Psychology, Utah State University, Logan, UT 84322-2810, e-mail address: UF734@cc.usu.edu.

Instrument: Self-Conscious Emotions, Maladaptive and Adaptive Scale (SCEMAS)
Authors: Stegge, H., & Ferguson, T. J.
Designed for: 5–12 year olds

Brief Description

The SCEMAS is an improved version of the C-CARS. It consists of the original eight situations from the C-CARS plus an additional five situations rated not only for precoded guilt, shame, and externalization, but also pride. The new situations are more ambiguous than the original eight as to whether the expected response would be guilt, shame, or even pride. Currently, the five new situations also form homogeneous scales for guilt, shame, and pride but not for externalization. The SCEMAS also seem to represent more of the maladaptive components of both guilt and shame. (SCEMAS is available in both Dutch and English.)

Sample Scenario and Rating

> At school, your teacher says that there'll be a drawing contest. Each kid is allowed to do a drawing at home and then bring it to school the next day. So that afternoon, you and your friend go home and you're both sitting there doing your drawings. You get bored, though, pretty quickly and just want to get the drawing done as fast as you can. But, your friend works on his/her drawing for the whole afternoon, for hours and hours. The next

day, you and your friend give the teacher your drawings. When they announce the winners, you win FIRST PRIZE! The teacher holds up your drawing for everyone to see.

a. You feel guilty, because you didn't really try your best. (guilt)
b. You feel ashamed; and think I wish I hadn't won. (shame)
c. You think: "Oh, I was just lucky." (externalization)
d. You're proud of yourself for having done a good drawing. (pride)

Further information available from: Tamara J. Ferguson, Department of Psychology, Utah State University, Logan, UT 84322-2810 (English version) or Hedy Stegge, Free University Amsterdam, e-mail address: H.Stegge@psy.vu.nl

---

Instrument: Children's Guilt Inventory
Authors: Bybee, J., Williams, C., & Merisca, R.
Designed for: 5th–11th grades

Brief Description

The Children's Guilt Inventory is a scenario-based measure of guilty affect in which children judge on an 8-point scale how guilty a target character would (or should) feel in each of 24 different vignettes. There are six major types of guilt-eliciting situations (transgression, inaction, anticipatory guilt, inequity, failure to attain ideals, and situations in which the target really was not at fault). The scenarios thus represent a wide range of potentially guilt-provoking situations and some of the situations represent clear moral transgressions or breaches of friendship or equity, whereas others are more ambiguous as to whether the target really "should" feel guilty.

Sample Scenario and Rating

Rodney wanted a gold necklace like Tyrone's. One day before gym class, Tyrone left his necklace on the sink in the washroom. Rodney saw the necklace, and almost put it in his pocket to steal it. But then someone walked by, saw the necklace, and gave it back to Tyrone.

How guilty would you feel if you were Rodney?

Further information available from: Jane Bybee, Department of Psychology, 125 Nightingale Hall, Northeastern University, Boston, MA 02115.

Instrument: Self-Conscious Emotions Questionnaire for Children (SCEQC)
Author: Haimowitz, B. R. (1996).
Designed for: 8–12 year olds

Brief Description

The SCEQC is a scenario-based measure of guilt and shame modeled after the TOSCA and SCEMAS. The final version of the instrument consists of eight situations that could elicit guilt and/or shame. Children hear about each incident and then rate on a 5-point scale the extent to which external factors caused their behavior or they would feel shame, guilt, or no emotional involvement.

Sample Scenario and Rating

You are invited for a birthday party of a classmate. Only a few children are invited and you are one of them. You are very excited about this party and you talk about it with your friend in class. You tell about all the nice things you think will happen at the party. Then you ask, "Are you coming, too?" Your friend says, "No, I wasn't invited."

1. You feel like not even going to the party because of what you said and how you acted. (guilt)
2. You feel angry with yourself for talking so much about the party, which your friend was not invited to. (shame)

Further information available from: Barbara Haimowitz, National Trade Publications, 13 Century Hill Drive, Latham, NY 12110-2197.

Instrument: Trait Affect Measure
Authors: Bybee, J., & Williams, C.
Age appropriateness: 5th–11th grades

Brief Description

The Trait Affect Measure is a modification of the Mosher Forced-Choice Guilt Scale for use with children. The new trait measure of guilt excludes Mosher's original Sex Guilt scale and includes the Hostility and Morality—Conscience subscales, adapted for the language skills of children. To minimize the effects of social desirability and to make the scales more "child-friendly," Bybee and Williams used Harter's (1982) structured alternative format procedure. The initial version of the instrument presented children with a series of 40 pairs of alternatives (20 each for Hostility and for Morality—Conscience) and asked them to first choose which alternative of the pair is most like them, and then to rate whether it is "a lot like" or "sort of like" themselves, scored on a 4-point scale. Final version of the instrument consists of 18 items representing an overall guilt scale.

SAMPLE ITEMS (IN BOTH THE 40- AND 18-ITEM VERSIONS):

When some kids do something wrong, they don't feel bothered by it very much	BUT	When other kids do something wrong they feel worse than if they were sick
When some kids get angry and yell at somebody, they feel a lot better afterwards	BUT	When other kids get angry and yell at somebody, they are sorry and apologize
Some kids don't feel bad for very long over failing and being mean	BUT	Other kids try to avoid failing and being mean
Some kids punish themselves by feeling nervous and unhappy	BUT	Other kids never punish themselves.

Further information available from: Jane Bybee, 125 Nightingale Hall, Northeastern University, Boston, MA 02115.

Instrument: Children's Interpretations of Interpersonal Distress and Conflict (CIIDC)
Authors: Zahn-Waxler, C., Kochanska, G., Krupnick, J., & Mayfield, A.
Designed for: 3–9 year olds

Brief Description

Zahn-Waxler and her colleagues developed the narrative CIIDC measure, in which children respond to a series of questions after viewing each of four photographs depicting ambiguous situations. There is no suggestion to child respondents that they should feel guilty, but the procedure does allow considerable leeway for children to express issues of guilt that may be of daily concern to them.

Sample Content

In one situation, the child sees a photograph of an adult female leaving a room with a child onlooking. The respondent is told, "Here the Mommy is looking pretty mad. She says she is leaving for a while because she is very angry. (The rest of the family is in the living room.) Her little girl [or boy] can tell she is mad by the way she looks and her voice sounds angry, too."

The respondent then views a second photograph showing the little girl [boy] looking out a window. The respondent hears, "Now the little girl is watching her Mommy through the window, as she walks away."

1. How is the little girl feeling?
2. What happened to make the Mom angry?

3. What does the little girl think happened to make her Mom angry?
4. Does the little girl think she did something to make her Mom feel that way? (If yes, then what?)
5. Does the little girl think there is anything she could say to make her Mom feel better? (If yes, then what?)
6. Pretend that is your Mom and she is angry. What do you think you would do?

Further information available from: Carolyn Zahn-Waxler, Laboratory of Developmental Psychology, National Institute of Mental Health, Bethesda, MD 20892.

Instrument: Hoffman's semiprojective measure of guilt
Author: Hoffman, M. L. (1975).
Designed for: 5th–7th graders

Brief Description

Hoffman's semiprojective measure of guilt consists of short stories describing wrongful acts. Children respond to two stories in which they pretend to be the protagonist. In one story, the protagonist cheats in a swimming contest and in the other s/he fails to help a lost child who later is killed by a car. Hoffman derived several scores from children's answers, including a 6-point story completion index (post-wrongdoing feelings and actions of wrongdoer), a 7-point guilt intensity score, a 7-point "concern for victim" score (as opposed to worry over detection; or expressions of general concern for the self), and a 6-point score for the quality of justice principles mentioned (referring, for example, to the importance of mutual trust, personal rights).

Sample Stories

> A child, hurrying with a friend to an important sports event, encounters a much younger child who seems lost. He suggests they stop and help, but his friend talks him out of it. The next day he finds out the child ran into the street and was killed by a car. (p. 722)
>
> A child, who has lost many contests at a school picnic and wants desperately to win the underwater swimming race, wins by taking advantage of the muddy condition of the water and swimming only half way and back. (p. 721)

Further information available from: Martin Hoffman, Department of Psychology, New York University, 6 Washington Place, New York, NY 10003.

Instrument: My Child
Author: Kochanska, G.
Designed for: 21 to 70 mos

Brief Description

The My Child is a parental report instrument with which caregivers can report on aspects of young children's conscience. This instrument assesses two aspects of conscience, namely, an ability to experience the guilt, discomfort, or anxiety that society expects people to have in response to an actual or anticipated moral transgression (Affective Discomfort) and the ability to self-regulate or refrain from acting on forbidden impulses (Active Moral Regulation/Vigilance). The My Child consists of 100 items (that originally were throught to reflect the two major components of early conscience), expressed as 10 scales.

Sample Items

1. Guilt or Remorse after Wrongdoing
   "Likely to feel responsible whenever anything goes wrong"
2. Concern over Good Feelings with Parent
   "After having done something naughty, asks to be forgiven"
3. Confession
   "Will spontaneously admit fault or wrongdoing, either verbally or nonverbally"
4. Apology and/or Promise Not to Do It Anymore
   "Will spontaneously say 'sorry' after having done something wrong"
5. Reparation/Amends
   "When s/he has hurt a playmate, s/he will try to make up for it by offering toys or prized possessions to the other child"
6. Concern/Corrections Occasioned by Others' Transgressions
   "Is likely to scold another child who violated a house rule"
7. Internalized Conduct
   "Can stop her/himself in the middle of doing something forbidden without any intervention from an adult"
8. Empathic, Prosocial Response to Another's Distress
   "Will try to comfort/reassure another in distress"
9. Symbolic Reproduction of/dealing with Wrongdoing
   "During play, will introduce themes of wrongdoing or rule violations"
10. Sensitivity to Flawed Objects, Themes of Wrongdoing
    "Shows concern when toy is broken"

Further information available from: Grazyna Kochanska, Department of Psychology, 11 Seashore Hall East, University of Iowa, Iowa City, Iowa 52242-1407.

Instrument: My Child-Shame and My Child-Guilt
Authors: Ferguson, T. J., Stegge, H., & Barrett, K. C.
Designed for: 5- to 12-years

Brief Description

The My Child-Shame and the My Child-Guilt are modifications of Kochanska's (1992) parental report of internalized conscience (the My Child). The My Child-Shame is designed to measure parental reports of their children's shame-related affects, cognitions, behaviors, and styles of coping or defense, and the second to measure their reports of components related to guilt. Both forms of the My Child have 51 questions. The My Child-Guilt consists of six scales and the My Child-Shame of seven (the seventh subscale, Denial of Feeling, showed poor internal consistency reliability).

Sample Items from the My Child-Guilt

1. General Guilt Behaviors
   "Likely to look remorseful or guilty when caught in the middle of a forbidden activity"
2. Confession
   "May confess to doing something naughty even if unlikely to be caught"
3. Apology and/or Promise Not to Do It Anymore
   "Will spontaneously say 'sorry' after having done something wrong"
4. Reparation/Amends
   "Eager to make amends for doing something naughty"
5. Internalized Standards of Conduct
   "Is enough to prohibit something once and s/he probably will not do it even when alone"
6. Empathic, Prosocial Response to Another's Distress
   "Likely to ask 'what's wrong?' when seeing someone in distress"

Sample Items from the My Child-Shame

1. General Shame Behaviors
   "Tries to disappear, avoids contact after falling short of expectations"

2. Concern over Good Feelings with Parents After Failure or Falling Short
   "After having fallen short, asks for another chance to do well"
3. Excusing/Rationalizing
   "Child blames own failure on others or difficulty of the task"
4. Avoidance Behavior specifically
   "Can't seem to look you in the eye after falling short or being naughty"
5. Standards of Internalized Conduct
   "Even tasks hard for his/her age can be presented to the child and s/he will try them"
6. Self-focus
   "Worries about what other people think of him/her"

Further information available from: Tamara J. Ferguson, Department of Psychology, Utah State University, Logan, UT 84322-2810, e-mail address: UF734@cc.usu.edu.

Instrument: Clown Doll Paradigm
Authors: Barrett, K. C., & Zahn-Waxler, C., and Cole, P. M.
Designed for: 17–36 month olds

Brief Description

Children are invited to play with an experimenter's favorite doll (a clown) while the experimenter attends to some tasks in the other room. Unbeknownst to the children, one of the doll's legs is broken, so that as soon as the child picks up the doll, the leg falls off. The coding procedure focuses on real-time measures of children's behaviors before and after the mishap, and before and after the experimenter returns to display "mild concern" about the broken doll. Behaviors coded as guilt-relevant reflect an amending style that includes discrete behaviors, such as latency to trying to repair the leg or latency to letting the experimenter know that the leg is broken (either through body language or verbalizations directed at the experimenter). Shame-relevant behaviors connote an avoiding style that includes the discrete behaviors of latency to gaze aversion relative to the experimenter, rate of bodily avoidance of the experimenter (movements away from the experimenter, but not toward any other person or object present in the room), and the presence or absence of an embarrassed smile followed, within 5 sec, by gaze aversion from the experimenter.

Further information available from: Karen C. Barrett, Department of HDFS, Colorado State University, Fort Collins, CO 80523.

REFERENCES

Achenbach, T. M., McConaughy, S. H., & Howell, C. T. (1987). Child/adolescent behavioral and emotional problems: Implications of cross-informant correlations for situational specificity. *Psychological Bulletin, 101,* 213–232.

American Psychiatric Association. (1994). *Diagnostic and statistical manual of mental disorders* (4th ed.). Washington, D.C.

Aronfreed, J. (1968). *Conduct and conscience: The socialization of internalized control over behavior.* New York: Academic Press.

Ausubel, D. P. (1955). Relationships between shame and guilt in the socializing process. *Psychological Review, 62,* 378–390.

Averill, J. R. (1994). Emotions becoming and unbecoming. In P. Ekman, & R. J. Davidson (Eds.), *The nature of emotion* (pp. 265–269). New York: Oxford University Press.

Barrett, K. C. (1995). A functionalist approach to shame and guilt. In J. P. Tangney and K. W. Fischer (Eds.), *Self-conscious emotions: The psychology of shame, guilt, embarrassment, and pride* (pp. 25–63). New York: Guilford Press.

Barrett, K. C., Zahn-Waxler, C., & Cole, P. M. (1993). Avoiders versus amenders—Implications for the investigation of guilt and shame during toddlerhood? *Cognition and Emotion, 7,* 481–505.

Baumeister, R. F., Stillwell, A. M., & Heatherton, T. F. (1994). Guilt: An interpersonal approach. *Psychological Bulletin, 115,* 243–267.

Beall, L. (1972). *Shame-Guilt Test.* Berkeley, CA: Wright Institute.

Blatt, S. J., Quinlan, D. M., Chevron, E. S., McDonald, C., & Zuroff, D. (1982). Dependency and self-criticism: Psychological dimensions of depression. *Journal of Consulting and Clinical Psychology, 50,* 113–124.

Brody, L. R. (1996). Gender, emotional expression, and parent–child boundaries. In R. D. Kavanaugh, B. Zimmerberg, & S. Fein (Eds.), *Emotion: Interdisciplinary perspectives* (pp. 139–170). Mahwah, NJ: Erlbaum.

Brody, L. R., & Carter, A. S. (1982). Children's emotional attributions of self versus other: An exploration off an assumption underlying projective techniques. *Journal of Consulting and Clinical Psychology, 50,* 665–671.

Brown, J., & Weiner, B. (1984). Affective consequences of ability versus effort ascriptions: Controversies, resolutions, and quandries. *Journal of Educational Psychology, 76,* 146–158.

Buchsbaum, H. K., & Emde, R. N. (1990). Play narratives in thirty-six month-old children: Early moral development and family relationships. *Psychoanalytic Study of the Child, 45,* 129–155.

Burggraf, S. A., & Tangney, J. P. (1989). *The Self-Conscious Affect and Attributions Inventory for Children (SCAAI-C).* Bryn Mawr, PA: Bryn Mawr College.

Burton, R. V. (1971). Correspondence between behavioral and doll-play measures on conscience. *Developmental Psychology, 5,* 320–332.

Bybee, J., & Williams, C. (1995). *When is guilt adaptive? Relationships to prosocial behavior, academic and social strivings, and mental health.* Manuscript submitted for publication.

Bybee, J., Williams, C., & Merisca, R. (1994, August). *Greater guilt is related to prosocial, academic and socioemotional competence.* Poster presented at the annual convention of the American Psychological Association, Los Angeles, CA.

Bybee, J., Williams, C., & Merisca, R. (1996). *Why might guilt decline during adolescence?* Manuscript submitted for publication.

Bybee, J. A., & Zigler, E. (1991). Self-image and guilt: A further test of the cognitive-developmental formulation. *Journal of Personality, 59,* 733–744.

Cameron, N., & Rychlak, J. F. (1985). *Personality development and psychopathology: A dynamic approach* (2nd ed.). Boston: Houghton Mifflin.

Campos, J. J., Mumme, D. L., Kermoian, R., & Campos, R. G. (1994). A functionalist perspective on the nature of emotion. In N. A. Fox (Ed.), The Development of emotion regulation: Biological and behavioral considerations. *Monographs of the Society for Research in Child Development, 59* (2-3, Serial No. 240).

Chapman, M., Zahn-Waxler, C., Cooperman, G., & Iannotti, R. (1987). Empathy and responsibility in the motivation of children's helping. *Developmental Psychology, 23,* 140–145.

Clark, D., & Watson, L. A. (1994). The vicissitudes of mood: A schematic model. In P. Ekman, & R. J. Davidson (Eds.), *The nature of emotion* (pp. 400–405). New York: Oxford University Press.

Cole, P. M., Michel, M. K., & Teti, L. O. (1994). The development of emotion regulation and dysregulation: A clinical perspective. In N. A. Fox (Ed.), The development of emotion regulation: Biological and behavioral considerations. *Monographs of the Society for Research in Child Development, 59.* (2–3, Serial No. 240)

Compas, B. E., Ey, S., & Grant, K. E. (1993). Taxonomy, assessment, and diagnosis of depression during adolescence. *Psychological Bulletin, 114,* 323–344.

Cook, D. R. (1996). Empirical studies of shame and guilt: The Internalized Shame Scale. In D. Nathanson (Ed.), *Knowing feeling: Affect, script, and psychotherapy* (pp. 132–165). New York: London.

Crandall, V., Crandall, V. J., & Katkovsky, W. (1965). A children's social desirability questionnaire. *Journal of Consulting Psychology, 29,* 27–36.

Crowley, S. L., & Ferguson, T. J. (1994, April). *Guilt revisited: Ruminative guilt and its relationship to shame.* Poster presented at the annual meeting of the Western Psychological Association, Kona, HI.

Crowley, S. L., & Ferguson, T. J. (1995, April). *Guilt and shame: A confirmatory analysis invoking two measurement strategies.* Paper presented at the annual meeting of the American Educational Research Association, San Francisco.

Crowley, S. L., & Ferguson, T. J. (1996, April). *Actual and fantasized behavior: Sex-related differences in the use of defense mechanisms.* Paper presented at the annual meeting of the Rocky Mountain Psychological Association, Park City, UT.

de Rivera, J. (1984). The structure of emotional relationships. In P. Shaver (Ed.), *Review of Personality and Social Psychology: Vol. 5. Emotions, Relationships, and Health* (pp. 116–145). Beverly Hills, CA: Sage.

Derogatis, (1983). *SCL-90-R manual.* St. Petersburg, FL: Clinical Psychometrics.

Edelman, R. J. (1985). Social embarrassment: An analysis of the process. *Journal of Social and Personal Relationships, 2,* 195–213.

Emde, R. N., Johnson, W. F., & Easterbrooks, M. A. (1987). The do's and don'ts of early moral development: Psychoanalytic tradition and current research. In J. Kagan & S. Lamb (Eds.), *The emergence of morality in young children* (pp. 245–277). Chicago: University of Chicago Press.

Epstein, S. (1990). Comment on the effects of aggregation across and within occasions on consistency, specificity, and reliability. *Methodika, 4,* 95–100.

Evans, D. R., Jessup, B. A., & Hearn, M. T. (1975). Development of a reaction inventory to measure guilt. *Journal of Personality Assessment, 39,* 421–423.

Eyre, H. L., & Ferguson, T. J. (1996, April). *Emotional stereotyping of men and women.* Poster presented at the annual meeting of the Rocky Mountain Psychological Association, Park City, UT.

Ferguson, T. J. (1993, August). *Socialization of guilt- and shame-proneness in male and female college students.* Paper presented at the annual meeting of the American Psychological Association. Toronto, Canada.

Ferguson, T. J., & Crowley, S. L. (1993, June). *Gender differences in self-evaluative emotion as mediated by self-consciousness.* Poster presented as the annual meeting of the American Psychological Society, Chicago.

Ferguson, T. J., & Crowley, S. L. (in press). Measure for measure: Guilt is not a unitary construct. *Journal of Personality Assessment.*

Ferguson, T. J., & Denissen, K. (1982). De samenhang tussen de reacties van moeders en hun kindern op overtredingen: Disciplinair gedrag en morele internalisatie [The relationship between mothers' and children's reactions to transgression: Disciplinary behavior and moral internalization]. In M. Boekaerts & C. F. M. van Lieshout (Eds.), *Sociale en motivationele aspecten van hat leren [Social and motivational aspects of learning]* (pp. 137–149). Lisse, The Netherlands: Swets & Zeitlinger.

Ferguson, T. J., & Eyre, H. L. (1996, March). *Multifaceted functions of transient and persistent guilt in adults and children.* Poster presented at the biennial meeting of the Southwestern Society for Research on Human Development, Park City, UT.

Ferguson, T. J., Sorenson, C., Bodrero, R., & Stegge, H. (1996, August). *(Dys)functional guilt and shame in developmental perspective.* Poster presented at the biennial International Society for the Study of Behavioral Development conference, Quebec City, Canada.

Ferguson, T. J., & Stegge, H. (1995). Emotional states and traits in children: The case of guilt and shame. In J. P. Tangney and K. W. Fischer (Eds.), *Self-conscious emotions: The psychology of shame, guilt, embarrassment, and pride* (pp. 174–197). New York: Guilford Press.

Ferguson, T. J., Stegge, H., & Barrett, K. C. (1996). *My Child—Shame and My Child—Guilt.* Unpublished instrument, Utah State University.

Ferguson, T. J., Stegge, H., & Damhuis, I. (1991). Children's understanding of guilt and shame. *Child Development, 62,* 827–839.

Ferguson, T. J., Stegge, H., Miller, E. R. & Olsen, M. E. (1996). *Is guilt "adaptive" or not? A comparison of two measures.* Manuscript submitted for publication.

Ferguson, T. J., & Wells, G. L. (1980). Priming mediators in causal attribution. *Journal of Personality and Social Psychology, 38,* 461–470.

Feshbach, N., & Roe, L. (1968). Empathy in six- and seven-year olds. *Child Development, 39,* 133–145.

Friedman, M. (1985). Toward a reconceptualization of guilt. *Contemporary Psychoanalysis, 21,* 501–547.

Freud, S. (1961). Civilization and its discontents. In J. Strachey (Ed. and Trans.), *The standard edition of the complete psychological works of Sigmund Freud: Vol. 21.* London: Hogarth Press. (Originally published 1930)

Frijda, N. H. (1986). *The emotions.* Cambridge: Cambridge University Press.

Garber, J., Braafladt, N., & Zeman, J. (1991). The regulation of sad affect: An information-processing perspective. In J. Garber & K. A. Dodge (Eds.), *The development of emotion regulation and dysregulation* (pp. 208–240). Cambridge: Cambridge University Press.

Graham, S., Doubleday, C., & Guarino, P. A. (1984). The development of relations between perceived controllability and the emotions of pity, anger, and guilt. *Child Development, 55,* 561–565.

Haimowitz, B. R. (1996). *The assessment of shame and guilt in elementary school children.* Unpublished dissertation, Tufts University.

Harder, D. W. (1990). Additional construct validity evidence for the Harder Personal Feelings Questionnaire measure of shame and guilt proneness. *Psychological Reports, 67,* 288–290.

Harder, D. W. (1995). Shame and guilt assessment, and relationships of shame- and guilt-proneness to psychopathology. In J. P. Tangney and K. W. Fischer (Eds.), *Self-conscious emotions: The psychology of shame, guilt, embarrassment, and pride* (pp. 368–392). New York: Guilford Press.

Harder, D. W., Cutler, L., & Rockart, L. (1992). Assessment of shame and guilt and their relationships to psychopathology. *Journal of Personality Assessment, 59,* 584–604.

Harder, D. W., & Lewis, S. J. (1987). The assessment of shame and guilt. In J. N. Butcher & C. D. Spielberger (Eds.), *Advances in personality assessment: Vol. 6.* (pp. 89–114). Hillsdale, NJ: Erlbaum.

Harder, D. W., & Zalma, A. (1990). Two promising shame and guilt scales: A construct validity comparison. *Journal of Personality Assessment, 55,* 729–745.

Harter, S. (1982). The perceived competence scale for children. *Child Development, 53.* 87–97.

Harter, S. (1983). Children's understanding of multiple emotions: A cognitive-developmental approach. In W. F. Overton (Ed.), *The relationship between social and cognitive development* (pp. 147–194). Hillsdale, NJ: Erlbaum.

Harter, S., & Whitesell, N. (1989). Developmental changes in children's emotion concepts. In C. Saarni & P. L. Harris (Eds.), *Children's understanding of emotions* (pp. 81–116). New York: Cambridge University Press.

Hermans, H. J. M., & Hermans-Jansen E. (1995). *Self-narratives: The construction of meaning in psychotherapy.* New York: Guilford.

Higgins, E. T. (1987). Self-discepancy: A theory relating self and affect. *Psychological Review, 94,* 319–340.

Hoblitzelle, W. (1987). Differentiating and measuring shame and guilt: The relation between shame and depression. In H. B. Lewis (Ed.), *The role of shame in symptom formation* (pp. 207–235). Hillsdale, NJ: Erlbaum.

Hodges, K., McKnew, D., Cytryn, L. & McKnew, D. (1982). The Child Assessment Schedule (CAS) diagnostic interview: A report on reliability and validity. *Journal of the American Academy of Child Psychiatry, 10,* 173–189.

Hoffman, M. L. (1975). Sex differences in moral internalization and values. *Journal of Personality and Social Psychology, 32,* 720–729.

Hoffman, M. L. (1976). Empathy, role taking, guilt, and development of altruistic motives. In T. Likona (Ed.), *Moral development and behavior* (pp. 124–143). New York: Holt, Rinehart, & Winston.

Hoffman, M. L. (1977). Moral internalization: Current theory and research. In L. Berkowitz (Ed.), *Advances in experimental social psychology: Vol. 10* (pp. 85–133). New York: Academic Press.

Hoffman, M. L. (1983a). Affective and cognitive processes in moral internalization. In E. T. Higgins, D. N. Ruble, & W. W. Hartup (Eds.), *Social cognition and social development* (pp. 236–274). New York: Cambridge University Press.

Hoffman, M. L. (1983b). Empathy, guilt, and social cognition. In W. F. Overton (Ed.), *The relationship between social and cognitive development* (pp. 1–51). Hillsdale, NJ: Erlbaum.

Hoffman, M. L., & Salzstein, H. D. (1967). Parent discipline and the child's moral development. *Journal of Personality and Social Psychology, 5,* 45–57.

Izard, C. E. (1977). *Human emotions.* New York: Plenum Press.

Izard, C. E., Blumberg, S. H., & Oyster, C. K. (1985). Age and sex differences in the pattern of emotions in childhood anxiety and depression. In J. T. Spence & C. E. Izard (Eds.), *Motivation, emotion, and personality* (pp. 317–324). North-Holland: Elsevier Science Publishers.

Johnson, R. C., Kim, R. J., & Danko, G. P. (1989). Guilt, shame, and adjustment: A family study. *Personality and Individual Differences, 10,* 71–74.

Jones, E. E., & Davis, K. E. (1965). From acts to dispositions: The attribution process in person perception. In L. Berkowitz (Ed.), *Advances in experimental social psychology: Vol. 2* (pp. 219–266). New York: Academic Press.

Jones, W. H., & Kugler, K. (1993). Interpersonal correlates of The Guilt Inventory. *Journal of Personality Assessment, 61,* 246–258.

Jones, W. H., Kugler, K., & Adams, P. (1995). You always hurt the one you love: Guilt and transgressions against relationship partners. In K. Fischer, & J. P. Tangney (Eds.), *Self-conscious emotions: The psychology of shame, guilt, embarrassment, and pride* (pp. 301–321). New York: Guilford Press.

Josephs, L. (1992). *Character structure and the organization of the self.* New York: Columbia University Press.

Katz, P., & Zigler, E. (1967). Self-image disparity: A developmental approach. *Journal of Personality and Social Psychology, 5,* 186–195.

Kaufman, G. (1992). *Shame: The power of caring* (3rd ed.). Cambridge, MA: Schenkman.

Kelley, H. H. (1967). Attribution theory in social psychology. In D. Levine (Ed.), *Nebraska symposium on motivation Vol. 51* (pp. 192–241). Lincoln: University of Nebraska Press.

Kippax, S., Crawford, J., Benton, P., & Gault, U. (1988). Constructing emotions: Weaving meaning from memories. *British Journal of Social Psychology, 27,* 19–33.

Klass, E. T. (1987). Situational approach to assessment of guilt: Development and validation of a self-report measure. *Journal of Psychopathology and Behavioral Assessment, 9,* 35–48.

Kochanska, G. (1991). Socialization and temperament in the development of guilt and conscience. *Child Development, 62,* 1379–1392.

Kochanska, G. (1992). *My Child Version 2: A preliminary manual.* Unpublished instrument, University of Iowa, Iowa City, IO.

Kochanska, G. (1993a, March). Early conscience: Organization and developmental transitions. In S. Lamb (Chair), *The beginnings of morality.* Symposium conducted at the biennial meeting of the Society for Research in Child Development, New Orleans, LA.

Kochanska, G. (1993b, March). The origins of guilt. In G. Kochanska (Chair) *Towards an integration of socialization and temperament in early development of conscience.* Symposium conducted at the biennial meeting of the Society for Research in Child Development, New Orleans, LA.

Kochanska, G., Aksan, N., & Koenig, A. L. (1995). A longitudinal study of the roots of pre-schooler's conscience: Committed compliance and emerging internalization. *Child Development, 66,* 1752–1769.

Kochanska, G., DeVet, K., Goldman, M., Murray, K., & Putnam, S. (1994). Maternal reports of conscience development and temperament in young children. *Child Development, 65,* 852–868.

Kovacs, M. (1992). *Children's Depression Inventory.* North Tonawanda, NY: Multi-health Systems.

Kubany, E. S., Abueg, F. R., Owens, J. A., Brennan, J. M., Kaplan, A. S., & Watson, S. B. (1995). Initial examination of a multidimensional model of trauma-related guilt: Applications to combat veterans and battered women. *Journal of Psychopathology and Behavioral Assessment, 17,* 353–376.

Kubany, E. S., & Manke, F. P. (1995). Cognitive therapy for trauma-related guilt: Conceptual basis and treatment outlines. *Cognitive and Behavioral Practice, 2,* 27–61.

Kugler, K., & Jones, W. H. (1992). On conceptualizing and assessing guilt. *Journal of Personality and Social Psychology, 62,* 318–327.

Leckman, J. F., Caruso, K. A., Prusoff, B. A., Weissman, M. M., Merikangas, K. R., & Pauls, D. L. (1984). Appetite disturbance and excessive guilt in major depression. *Archives of General Psychiatry, 41,* 839–844.

Lewis, H. B. (1971). *Shame and guilt in neurosis.* New York: International Universities Press.

Lewis, M. (1992a). The self in self-conscious emotions. In D. Stipek, S. Recchia, & S. McClintic (Eds.), Self-evaluation in young children. *Monographs of the Society for Research in Child Development, 57.* (1, Serial No. 226).

Lewis, M. (1992b). *Shame, the exposed self.* New York: Free Press.

Lewis, M. (1993a). The emergence of human emotions. In M. Lewis & J. Haviland (Eds.), *Handbook of emotions.* New York: Guilford.

Lewis, M. (1993b). Self-conscious emotions: Embarrassment, pride, shame, and guilt. In M. Lewis & J. Haviland (Eds.), *Handbook of emotions.* New York: Guilford.

Lewis, M. (1995). Embarrassment: The emotion of self-exposure and evaluation. In J. P. Tangney & K. W. Fischer (Eds.), *Self-conscious emotions: The psychology of shame, guilt, embarrassment, and pride* (pp. 198–218). New York: Guilford.

Lewis, M., Alessandri, S. M., & Sullivan, M. W. (1992). Differences in shame and pride as a function of children's gender and task difficulty. *Child Development, 63,* 630–638.

Lindsay-Hartz, J., de Rivera, J., & Mascolo, M. F. (1995). Differentiating guilt and shame and their effects on motivation. In J. P. Tangney & K. W. Fischer (Eds.), *Self-conscious emotions: The psychology of shame, guilt, embarrassment, and pride* (pp. 274–300). New York: Guilford Press.

Lutz, C. A. (1988). *Unnatural emotions: Everyday sentiments on a Micronesian atoll and their challenges to Western theory.* Chicago, IL: University of Chicago Press.

Magai, C., & McFadden, S. H. (1995). *The role of emotions in social and personality development: History, theory, and research.* New York: Plenum.

Malatesta, C. Z., & Wilson, A. (1988). Emotion cognition interaction in personality development: A discrete emotions, functionalist analysis. *British Journal of Social Psychology, 27,* 91–112.

McGraw, K. M. (1987). Guilt following transgression: An attribution of responsibility approach. *Journal of Personality and Social Psychology, 53,* 247–256.

Merisca, R., & Bybee, J. (1994, April). *Guilt, not moral reasoning, relates to volunteerism, prosocial behavior, lowered aggressiveness, and eschewal of racism.* Poster presented at the annual meeting of the Eastern Psychological Association, Providence, RI.

Merisca, R., & Bybee, J. (1996). *Guilt, not moral reasoning, relates to measures of prosocial attitudes and behaviors.* Manuscript submitted for publication.

Miceli, M. (1992). How to make someone feel guilty: Strategies of guilt inducement and their goals. *Journal for the Theory of Social Behavior, 22,* 81–104.

Modell, A. H. (1971). The origin of certain forms of pre-Oedipal guilt and the implications for a psychoanalytic theory of affects. *International Journal of Psychoanalysis, 52,* 337–346.

Mood, D. W., Johnson, J. E., & Shantz, C. (1978). Social comprehension and affect matching in young children. *Merrill Palmer Quarterly, 24,* 63–66.

Moretti, M. M., & Higgins, E. T. (1990). The development of self-system vulnerabilities: Social and cognitive factors in developmental psychology. In R. J. Sternberg & J. Kolligian, Jr. (Eds.), *Competence considered* (pp. 286–314). New Haven, CT: Yale University Press.

Mosher, D. L. (1966). The development and multi-trait-multi-method matrix analysis of three measures and three aspects of guilt. *Journal of Consulting Psychology, 30,* 25–29.

Mosher, D. L. (1979). The meaning and measurement of guilt. In C. E. Izard (Ed.), *Emotions in personality and psychopathology* (pp. 105–129). New York: Plenum Press.

Moulton, R. W., Burnstein, E., Liberty, P. G., & Altucher, N. (1966). Patterning of parental affection and disciplinary dominance as a determinant of guilt and sex typing. *Journal of Personality and Social Psychology, 4,* 356–363.

Nathanson, D. L. (1987). *The many faces of shame.* New York: Guilford.

Nisbett, R. E., & Wilson, T. D. (1977). Telling more than we can know: Verbal reports on mental processes. *Psychological Review, 84,* 231–259.

Nunner-Winkler, G., & Sodian, B. (1988). Children's understanding of moral emotions. *Child Development, 59,* 1323–1338.

Olsen, M. E., Ferguson, T. J., & Knight, E. (1994, March). *Children's justifications for feeling guilty and ashamed.* Poster presented at the annual meeting of the Rocky Mountain Psychological Association, Las Vegas.

Olver, R. R., Aries, E., & Batgos, J. (1989). Self-other differentiation and the mother–child relationship: The effects of sex and birth order. *Journal of Genetic Psychology, 150,* 311–321.

Orvis, B. R., Cunningham, J. D., & Kelley, H. H. (1975). A closer examination of causal inference: The roles of consensus, distinctiveness, and consistency information. *Journal of Personality and Social Psychology, 32,* 605–616.

Parkinson, B. (1995). *Ideas and realities of emotion.* London: Routledge.

Pedhazur, E. J. (1982). *Multiple regression in behavioral research.* New York: Holt, Rinehart, and Winston.

Piers, G., & Singer, M. (1953). *Shame and guilt.* New York: Norton.

Potter-Efron, R. T. (1989). *Shame, guilt, and alcoholism: Treatment issues in clinical practice.* New York: Haworth Press.

Quiles & Bybee, J. (in press). Chronic and predispositional guilt: Relations to mental health, prosocial behavior, and religiosity. *Journal of Personality Assessment.*

Ridgeway, D., Waters, E., & Kuczaj, S. A. (1985). Acquisition of emotion-descriptive language: Receptive and productive vocabulary norms for ages 18 months to 6 years. *Developmental Psychology, 21,* 901–908.

Robinson, J., Mantz-Simmons, L., MacFie, J., & The MacArthur Narrative Working Group (1995). *Narrative Coding Manual.* Unpublished Instrument.

Rutter, M. (1991). Age changes in depressive disorders: Some developmental considerations. In K. A. Dodge & J. Garber & Eds.), *The development of emotion regulation and dysregulation* (pp. 273–300). Cambridge: Cambridge University Press.

Scheff, T. J. (1988). Shame and conformity: The deference-emotion system. *American Sociological Review, 53,* 395–406.

Shavelson, R. J., Webb, N. M., & Rowley, G. L. (1989). Generalizability theory. *American Psychologist, 44,* 922–932.

Spitzer, R. L., & Endicott, J. (1978). *Schedule for Affective Disorders and Schizophrenia, Life-time version (SADS-L).* New York: Biometrics Research Division, New York State Psychiatric Institute.

Stegge, H., & Ferguson, T. J. (1990). *Child–Child Attribution and Reaction Survey (C-CARS).* Unpublished instrument, Utah State University.

Stegge, H. & Ferguson, T. J. (1994). *Self-Conscious Emotion: Maladaptive and Adaptive Scales (SCEMAS).* Unpublished instrument, Vrije Universiteit Amsterdam and Utah State University.

Stipek, D., & DeCotis, K. M. (1988). Children's understanding of the implications of causal attributions for emotional experiences. *Child Development, 59,* 1601–1610.

Susman, E. J., Trickett, P. K., Iannotti, R. J., Hollenbeck, B. E., & Zahn-Waxler, C. (1985). Child-rearing patterns in depressed, abusive, and normal mothers. *American Journal of Orthopsychiatry, 55,* 237–251.

Tangney, J. P. (1989, April). *Shame-proneness, guilt-proneness, and interpersonal processes.* Paper presented at the annual meeting of the Society for Research in Child Development, Kansas City.

Tangney, J. P. (1990). Assessing individual differences in proneness to shame and guilt: Development of the Self-Conscious Affect and Attribution Inventory. *Journal of Personality and Social Psychology, 59,* 102–111.

Tangney, J. P. (1991). Moral affect: The good, the bad, and the ugly. *Journal of Personality and Social Psychology, 61,* 598–607.

Tangney, J. P. (1992). Situational determinants of shame and guilt in young children. *Personality and Social Psychology Bulletin, 18,* 199–206.

Tangney, J. P. (1993). Shame and guilt. In C. G. Costello (Ed.), *Symptoms of depression* (pp. 161–180). New York: Wiley.

Tangney, J. P. (1995a). Recent advances in the empirical study of shame and guilt. *American Behavioral Scientist, 38,* 1132–1145.

Tangney, J. P. (1995b). Shame and guilt in interpersonal relationships. In J. P. Tangney and K. W. Fischer (Eds.), *Self-conscious emotions: The psychology of shame, guilt, embarrassment, and pride* (pp. 114–142). New York: Guilford Press.

Tangney, J. P. (1996). Conceptual and methodological issues in the assessment of shame and guilt. *Behavior Research and Therapy, 34,* 741–754.

Tangney, J. P., Burggraf, S. A., Hamme, H., & Domingos, B. (1988a). *The Self-Conscious Affect and Attribution Inventory (SCAAI).* Bryn Mawr, PA: Bryn Mawr College.

Tangney, J. P., Burggraf, S. A., Hamme, H., & Domingos, B. (1988b, March). *Assessing individual differences in proneness to shame and guilt: The Self-Conscious Affect and Attribution Inventory.* Poster presented at the meetings of the Eastern Psychological Association, Buffalo, NY.

Tangney, J. P., Burggraf, S. A., & Wagner, P. E. (1995). Shame-proneness, guilt-proneness, and psychological symptoms. In J. P. Tangney and K. W. Fischer (Eds.), *Self-conscious emotions: The psychology of shame, guilt, and pride* (pp. 343–367). New York: Guilford Press.

Tangney, J. P., Ferguson, T. J., Wagner, P. E., Crowley, S. L., & Gramzow, R. (1996). *Test of Self-Conscious Affect, version 2 (TOSCA-2).* Unpublished instrument, George Mason University and Utah State University.

Tangney, J. P., Marschall, D., Rosenberg, K., Barlow, D. H., & Wagner, P. (1993). *Children's and adults' autobiographical accounts of shame, guilt, and pride experiences: A qualitative analysis of situational determinants and interpersonal concerns.* Manuscript submitted for publication.

Tangney, J. P., Wagner, P. E., Burggraf, S. A., Gramzow, R., & Fletcher, C. (1991, June). *Children's shame-proneness, but not guilt proneness, is related to emotional and behavioral maladjustment.* Poster presented at the meeting of the American Psychological Society, Washington, DC.

Tangney, J. P., Wagner, P., Fletcher, C., & Gramzow, R. (1991, April). *Integrational continuities and discontinuities in proneness to shame and proneness to guilt.* Presented at the meetings of the Society for Research in Child Development, Seattle, WA.

Tangney, J. P., Wagner, P. E., Gavlas, J., & Gramzow, R. (1991). *The Test of Self-Conscious Affect for Adolescents (TOSCA-A).* Fairfax, VA: George Mason University.

Tangney, J. P., Wagner, P. E., Gavlas, J., Hill-Barlow, D. E., & Gramzow, R. (1992, August). *Shame, guilt, and constructive vs. destructive anger.* Poster presented at the annual meeting of the American Psychological Association, Washington, DC.

Tangney, J. P., Wagner, P. E., & Gramzow, R. (1989). *The Test of Self-Conscious Affect.* Fairfax, VA: George Mason University.

Tangney, J. P., Wagner, P. E., & Gramzow, R. (1990, June). *Shame-proneness, but not guilt-proneness, is linked to psychological maladjustment.* Poster presented at the meetings of the American Psychological Society, Dallas, TX.

Tangney, J. P., Wagner, P. E., & Gramzow, R. (1992). Proneness to shame, proneness to guilt, and psychopathology. *Journal of Abnormal Psychology, 101,* 1–10.

Tangney, J. P., Wagner, P. E., Hill-Barlow, D., Marschall, D. E., & Gramzow, R. (1996). Relation of shame and guilt to constructive versus destructive anger across the lifespan. *Journal of Personality and Social Psychology, 70,* 797–809.

Thoits, P. A. (1989). The sociology of emotions. *Annual Review of Sociology, 15,* 317–342.

Thompson, B. (1984). *Canonical correlation analysis: Uses and interpretation.* Newbury Park, CA: Sage.

Thompson, R. A., & Hoffman, M. (1980). Empathy and the development of guilt in children. *Developmental Psychology, 16,* 155–156.

Thrane, G. (1979). Shame. *Journal for the Theory of Social Behaviour, 9,* 139–166.

Tomkins, S. S. (1963). *Affect, imagery, consciousness: Vol. II The negative affects.* New York: Springer.

Wallbott, H. G., & Scherer, K. R. (1989). Assessing emotion by questionnaire. In R. Plutchik & H. Kellerman (Eds.), *Emotion: Theory, research, and experience: Vol. 4* (pp. 55–82). New York: Academic Press.

Walsh, J. A., Tomlinson-Keasy, C., & Klieger, D. (1974). Acquisition of the social desirability response. *Genetic Psychology Monographs, 89,* 241–272.

Watson, D., & Clark, L. A. (1992). Affects separable and inseparable: On the hierarchical arrangement of the negative affects. *Journal of Personality and Social Psychology, 62,* 489–505.

Weiner, B. (1986). *An attributional theory of motivation and emotion.* New York: Springer-Verlag.

Wiggers, M., & van Lieshout, C. F. M. (1985). Development of recognition of emotions: Children's reliance on situational and facial expressive cues. *Developmental Psychology, 21,* 338–349.

Williams, C., & Bybee, J. (1994). What do children feel guilty about? Developmental and gender differences. *Developmental Psychology, 30,* 617–623.

Wolfe, V. V., Finch, A. J., Jr., Saylor, C. F., Blount, R. L., Pallmeyer, T. P., & Carek, D. J. (1987). Negative affectivity in children: A multitrait-multimethod investigation. *Journal of Consulting and Clinical Psychology, 55,* 245–250.

Wurmser, L. (1981). Das problem der scham [The problem of shame]. *Jahrbuch der Psychoanalyse, 13,* 11–36.

Zahn-Waxler, C. (1993). Warriers and worriers: Gender and psychopathology. *Development and Psychopathology, 5,* 79–89.

Zahn-Waxler, C., & Chapman, M. (1982). Immediate antecedents of caretakers' methods of discipline. *Child Psychiatry and Human Development, 12,* 179–192.

Zahn-Waxler, C., Cole, P. M., & Barrett, K. C. (1991). Guilt and empathy: Sex differences and implications for the development of depression. In K. A. Dodge & J. Garber (Eds.), *The development of emotion regulation and dysregulation* (pp. 243–272). Cambridge: Cambridge University Press.

Zahn-Waxler, C., Iannotti, R. J., Cummings, E. M., & Denham, S. (1990). Antecedents of problem behaviors in children of depressed mothers. *Development and Psychopathology, 2,* 271–291.

Zahn-Waxler, C., & Kochanska, G. (1990). The origins of guilt. In R. Thompson (Ed.), *Nebraska symposium on motivation: Vol. 6. Socioemotional development* (pp. 183–258). Lincoln: University of Nebraska Press.

Zahn-Waxler, C., Kochanska, G., Krupnick, J., & Mayfield, A. (1988). *Coding manual for Children's Interpretations of Interpersonal Distress and Conflict.* Laboratory of Developmental Psychology, National Institute of Mental Health.

Zahn-Waxler, C., Kochanska, G., Krupnick, J., & McKnew, D. (1990). Patterns of guilt in children of depressed and well mothers. *Developmental Psychology, 26,* 51–59.

Zahn-Waxler, C., Radke-Yarrow, M., & King, R. (1979). Child rearing and children's prosocial initiations towards victims of distress. *Child Development, 50,* 319–330.

Zahn-Waxler, C., Ridgeway, J., Denham, S., Usher, B., & Cole, P. (1993). Pictures of infants' emotions: A task for assessing mothers' and young children's verbal communication about affect. In R. Emde, J. Osofsky, & P. Butterfield (Eds.), *The IFEEL Pictures: A new instrument for interpreting emotions* (pp. 217–236). Madison, CT: International Universities Press.

Zahn-Waxler, C., & Robinson, J. (1995). Empathy and guilt: Early origins of feelings of responsibility. In J. P. Tangney and K. W. Fisher (Eds.), *Self-conscious emotions: The psychology of shame, guilt, embarrassment, and pride* (pp. 143–173). New York: Guilford Press.

Zajonc, R. B. (1980). Feeling and thinking: Preferences need to inferences. *American Psychologist, 35,* 151–175.

PART II

How Does Guilt Develop?

CHAPTER 3

The Origins of Guilt in Early Childhood

Karen Caplovitz Barrett

Colorado State University, Fort Collins, Colorado

INTRODUCTION

This chapter concerns the origins of guilt in very young children—toddlers in the first 3 years of life (For a review encompassing older ages as well, see Zahn-Waxler & Kochanska, 1990). The topic is one that is rife with controversy. Whether or not one views the young child as capable of guilt depends to a large extent on one's theory of guilt. Moreover, even among those who are convinced that guilt is possible at this young age, definitional differences abound. Given these controversies, this chapter will first address selected theories and definitions of guilt. Following the discussion of theories of guilt will be a review of the existing empirical literature on behaviors displayed during toddlerhood that are, at very least, relevant to or precursors to guilt.

THEORIES OF GUILT

Freudian Theory

One reason why the concept of guilt during toddlerhood is controversial is that many theories postulate developmental prerequisites for guilt that are viewed as

Guilt and Children
Copyright © 1998 by Academic Press. All rights of reproduction in any form reserved.

impossible during the toddler years. The classic theory proposing such prerequisites is that of Freud (1930/1961). Freud held that guilt resulted when id impulses (and the ego's attempts to act upon these drives) conflicted with superego dictates and prohibitions. True guilt involved *intrapsychic* conflict, usually over aggressive aims, when superego demands conflicted with actualizing such motives. Apparent guilt from actual aggression was different, and should be labeled as remorse. Thus, guilt was not possible until the Oedipus complex was resolved and the superego established; until that time children behaved morally only if they felt threatened with loss of love:

> At the beginning, therefore, what is bad is whatever causes one to be threatened with loss of love. For fear of that loss, one must avoid it. . . . This state of mind is called a "bad conscience"; but actually it does not deserve this name. . . . A great change takes place only when the authority is internalized through the establishment of a super-ego. . . . Actually, it is not until now that we should speak of conscience or a sense of guilt. (Freud, 1930/1961, pp. 71–72).

Not all psychoanalytic theories require the establishment of the superego for guilt, however. Klein (1975), for example, who emphasizes the drive to make reparation, connects guilt to need for love and believes that guilt is possible much earlier in development.

Cognitive Prerequisite Theories

Freudian theory is not the only theory in which developmental prerequisites for guilt are proposed. A number of theorists suggest that broad cognitive abilities are required for guilt to be experienced; however, exactly when, in development, guilt becomes possible varies by theory.

Kagan's Theory

Jerome Kagan (1984) proposed, for example, that guilt is not possible until children can recognize that they can choose how to behave; until such time (about age 4) they do not see that they could have behaved in a more desirable way. Thus, he sees guilt as emerging at about 4 years of age—later in development than children become capable of reacting to task failure with a shame-like anxiety state.

Lewis's Theory

In contrast, Michael Lewis (1991) sees shame and guilt as emerging at about the same point in development as one another, as a function of the same cognitive prerequisites. Lewis has focused his empirical attention on embarrassment and shame; however, he has discussed guilt theoretically as well. According to his theory (M. Lewis, 1991), both shame and guilt are "self-conscious emotions" that involve self-evaluation relative to standards, rules, and goals. As such, several cognitive developments are necessary before guilt and shame can be experienced. First, children must be capable of "objective self-awareness," which he operationalizes as self-recognition (possible by about 15 to 24 months of age). Next, children must develop a knowledge base of standards, rules, and goals, as well as the ability to evaluate themselves vis-à-vis those standards. Finally, they must be able to make the attribution that they were responsible for the standard violation. M. Lewis (1991) holds that shame is experienced if the person attributes the standard violation to global characteristics of the self and that guilt is experienced if the person attributes the violation to specific characteristics of the self, such as undesired behaviors s/he performed. He proposes that the full set of prerequisites for guilt will not be present until about 3 years of age; thus, guilt is hypothesized to emerge at about that time.

Hoffman's Theory

Martin Hoffman's (1984) theory of guilt development suggests a gradual progression in levels or types of guilt with cognitive development. He proposes that as the self–other distinction becomes increasingly well developed, so does a sense of empathy. As empathy develops, moreover, so does guilt because guilt occurs when one feels empathy for another's distress and also feels responsible for that distress. He also indicates that the development of causal understanding affects the development of guilt, but that a rudimentary sense of causality exists quite early in development.

Even before babies can distinguish clearly between self and other, Hoffman suggests that they may respond to others' displays of pain with a rudimentary guilt feeling, even though they lack a clear-cut view of being the cause of the distress. However, once they clearly distinguish self from other, they can experience true empathic distress when others are hurt, and they may feel guilty if they were responsible for the distress. Next, children become able to experience guilt even when the victim's feelings must be inferred. Then, children become able to experience guilt in response to others' general plight (rather than a specific incident) if they feel responsible for that plight. Eventually, children become able to experience guilt when they *fail* to help another in need (guilt over inaction), and even when contemplating harming someone. Thus, although Hoffman sees cognitive abilities as prerequisites for guilt, he indicates that the requisite cognitions need not be fully developed for some, primitive sense of guilt to be possible. Rather, the level of guilt, and types of situations in which guilt can be aroused, change as the child becomes more cognitively advanced. This view is consistent in many ways with my own view of the role of cognition and cognitive development in the development of emotion (e.g., Barrett, 1995).

A Functionalist Approach

Cognitive Prerequisites?

According to my own functionalist approach, emotion processes, including guilt, are influenced but not defined by cognitive processes. Rather, they are *defined* by a set of functions that the emotion serves for the individual in relation to the relevant environment (e.g., Barrett, 1995; Barrett, in press; Barrett & Campos, 1987). If none of these functions is served, the emotion is not present. In most cases in which emotions are elicited, cognition is involved—a special form of cognitive process (the appreciation) that relates organism to environment, and determines the significance of that organism–environment relationship for the individual's functioning in that context. This cognitive process need not be sophisticated, conscious, nor contemplative, however, and some level of it may be "built in" to the organism by biology. Thus, the lowest level possible for any appreciation may be sufficient to elicit some variant of the relevant emotion, and that lowest level may even be present at birth or soon after birth.

These concepts are very important if one wishes to determine when, in development, guilt is first possible. Although many cognitive abilities seem logical as prerequisites to guilt, one can almost always find less advanced levels of the same class of abilities at younger ages. For example, self-recognition in a mirror does seem to become possible some time between 15 and 24 months in most children. However, children have some sense of themselves and their accomplishments much earlier. In fact, even newborns can learn to suck in particular patterns so as to produce a desired stimulus such as their mother's voice (DeCasper & Fifer, 1980), suggesting at least some, highly rudimentary awareness of what they are doing. Thus, the two requirements Hoffman (1984) specifies as prerequisites for guilt seem to be present at birth in primitive form—in that infants both respond to other infants' crying with like emotion ("empathic crying") and have some rudimentary sense of their responsibility for events.

One still may question whether these two abilities are sufficient for the display of guilt and whether, as an empirical observation, newborns do display guilt. Consistent with many other theorists, I hold that it is highly improbable that newborns can manifest guilt (although this is an empirical question), because guilt seems to involve more than simple apprehension that one's behavior is connected with another's distress; one also needs to have some appreciation that hurting someone is a problem. Typically, guilt results only if one's harm of another has resulted from deviation from a rule or standard. One does not always become involved in a guilt-family process when one hurts someone, even if one feels responsible (e.g., Jones, Kugler, & Adams, 1995). For example, a physician is unlikely to experience guilt after giving a person a shot. An elementary school-aged child is similarly unlikely to show guilt after accidentally dropping a book on her foot. Guilt seems to result when one has some sense of a "should" or "shouldn't" that was violated, producing the harm, and there is no evidence that newborns compare their behavior to even the most primitive "shoulds" and "shouldn'ts" (standards and rules). Moreover, it is extremely implausible that newborns have any sense of "shoulds" and "shouldn'ts," given that these would typically be culturally defined, and conveyed via socialization. Thus, it would seem that the need for sufficient socialization experience is as large or a larger constraint on when, in development, guilt becomes possible than broad cognitive abilities.

The point of this discussion is not to arrive at a new *a priori* age before which guilt cannot occur. As research on Piagetian abilities has demonstrated, the age of onset of most cognitive abilities seems as much determined by what the researcher considers a relevant task and ability as by children's capabilities (e.g., see Lempers, Flavell, & Flavell, 1977; Wellman, Cross, & Bartsch, 1986). Moreover, socialization begins at birth and continues throughout the life. When has "enough" socialization taken place? It is hard to know exactly what level of any given ability or what amount of socialization experience is essential for any emotion.

According to my approach, however, it really is not necessary to determine this; it is more useful to study the emotional process itself, unfolding in context—to see if the expected functions are being served. If the relevant process does not occur in any children of a given age under a particular set of circumstances in which that emotion is predicted, then that emotion is not possible *in that context at that age* (this demonstration still does not indicate that the *emotion* is not ever possible at that age). For example, it seems improbable that any 2 year old would experience a guilt-family emotion as a function of plagiarizing ideas for fantasy play from a television program. However, many 2 year olds might experience a guilt-family process after breaking a parent's possession while playing with it after being told time after time not to play with it. The context has to be one with which children of that age are familiar, and one in which they can appreciate, at some level, that they harmed someone. According to my approach, children become likely to experience most emotions in a wider array of contexts as they grow older. Thus, one form of emotional development is the development of emotional responsiveness to a larger set of situations (see Barrett, 1995; Barrett, in press, for more information). With respect to guilt, the findings of Zahn-Waxler, Robinson, and Emde (1992) that parents report more guilt as toddlers grow older (from 14 to 24 months of age) is consistent with the possibility that they are displaying guilt-like responses to more and more situations.

Emotions as Families

An emotion label, such as "guilt," refers not to a unitary state or feeling, but to a family of related emotion processes that are defined by the functions they serve for the experiencing individual. Although functions often are adaptive in Darwinian terms—to promote survival in the environment of evolutionary adaptiveness—this is not necessary. More typically, the functions promote adaptation in the current, ongoing interaction between the experiencing organism and the external or internal environment. Each emotion serves three functions—social communication, behavior regulation, and internal regulation.

Guilty responses communicate to others that one does not wish to harm people, and that one does wish to repair the wrong one has perpetrated and the relationship with the person who was wronged. Behavior-regulatory functions involve inclination to acknowledge and correct the wrongdoing and to repair the relationship with the victim. Internal-regulatory functions include highlighting the standard that was violated and the harm it caused as well as the capacities of oneself as agent. As is true for any emotion, a feeling state may or may not be present. Given the need to have some sense of the social standard of not harming people, as well as some appreciation that one has harmed someone, it is unlikely that young infants will display guilt in any context. However, it seems quite possible that toddlers can show guilt. I believe that evidence gathered by Carolyn Zahn-Waxler, Marian Radke-Yarrow, and colleagues at the National Institute of Mental Health, by Grazyna Kochanska and her colleagues, and by myself and my colleagues (presented later) all suggest that guilt is possible in toddlers (e.g., Barrett, Zahn-Waxler, & Cole, 1993; Kochanska, Casey, & Fukumoto, 1995; Zahn-Waxler, Radke-Yarrow, & King, 1979).

Guilt versus Shame

Before I discuss this research on guilt-relevant behavior in young children, one more important theoretical issue needs to be discussed. One of the difficulties that arises in the literature on the origins of guilt is inclarity in research as to just what is considered "guilt," and how or whether "guilt" is distinguished from "shame." Some of the researchers who have made some of the most important empirical contributions to the study of guilt-relevant responses in young children include in their conceptual and/or operational definitions of guilt behaviors and/or feelings that others would consider shame-relevant responses. In the past decade, a growing literature, primarily regarding adults, has highlighted the importance of distinguishing clearly between guilt and shame. According to this literature, in our culture shame is more strongly associated with adverse concomitants (including some or all forms of psychopathology, angry outbursts, and "interminable family conflict") than is guilt (e.g., Harder, 1995; Harder, Cutler, & Rockart, 1992; Scheff, 1995; Tangney, 1995; Tangney, Wagner, & Gramzow, 1992). Moreover, there is some interesting evidence using parental report that suggests differential genetic and environmental contributions to the development of guilt versus shame (Zahn-Waxler & Robinson, 1995). Parents reported on their twins' tendencies to display guilt and shame (as well as other emotions) at 14, 20, and 24 months of age. Results indicated that although both guilt and shame had significant heritability at 14 months of age, shared environment also made a significant contribution to guilt (but not to shame).

This shared environmental component in guilt increased with age, such that it was the only significant contributor to guilt at 20 and 24 months. In contrast, heritability made the only significant contribution to shame at 20 and 24 months of age (after the models were corrected for deviations in findings from classic twin-methodological assumptions [negative shared environmental contribution]). These results, too, suggest that it is important to distinguish shame from guilt.

Most of the literature that distinguishes shame clearly from guilt bases this distinction on the work of Helen Block Lewis (1971). Her phenomenological analysis of guilt and shame in individuals who were in therapy suggested several important distinctions between these emotions. Persons experiencing guilt focus on the *misdeed* that they perpetrated, and on repairing that wrong. In contrast, those experiencing shame focus on how bad they are as people. According to H. Lewis (1971), in shame, one both becomes acutely conscious of oneself and of others' evaluation of oneself; and one wishes to disappear, hide, or die rather than feeling activated to confess and make reparation (as in guilt). H. Lewis (1971) also highlighted the disruption of thought processes caused by shame.

In most current views of the distinction between shame and guilt, these concepts of Lewis are preserved. In particular, most theories emphasize the focus on the badness of one's actions (guilt) versus the whole self (shame); and on the contrast between inclinations to make reparation and confess (guilt) versus propensities to make oneself small, to withdraw from others, and to avoid looking at others (shame). However, in some research and theorizing, some of the characteristics of shame are included as characteristics of guilt. For example, in Zahn-Waxler and Kochanska's (1990) recent review of the literature on guilt, they note that a submissive posture (which they associate with guilt) may reduce the likelihood of attack by others. Submissive posture is more typically associated with shame when shame is clearly distinguished from guilt. Similarly, results of a study by Seligman, Peterson, Kaslow, Tanenbaum, Alloy, and Abramson (1984) are discussed by Zahn-Waxler and Kochanska as indicating a connection between guilt and depression in school-aged children because these researchers found that children who attributed bad events to internal, stable, and global causes were more likely to report depression. Again, internal, global attributions are considered shame-relevant by most researchers who make clear distinctions between shame and guilt (e.g., Lewis, 1991; Tangney, 1995). In some of their research, Zahn-Waxler and colleagues have coded guilt in narratives children provide in response to ambiguous pictures (e.g., a mother leaving home, with her child watching her departure). One set of responses coded as indicators of guilt involved bizarre, violent, unrealistic, or extreme elements in the stories. Again, many would assume that disruption of thought, especially in response to "loss of love" associated with the caregiver's departure, is more likely to be a response to shame than to guilt. Thus, unfortunately, some findings that are relevant to the development of guilt in young children may also be relevant to shame (by other researchers and theorists' definitions of these emotions), because the two are intermingled.

RESEARCH ON GUILT-RELEVANT BEHAVIOR IN YOUNG CHILDREN

Measurement Difficulties

The theoretical differences, alluded to above, in views of the distinction (or lack of distinction) between guilt and shame create measurement difficulties, in that the referent for "guilt" may differ across studies. However, when it comes to empirical investigation of guilt in toddlers, another very basic measurement issue arises—just what responses by preverbal or barely verbal individuals clearly indicate guilt?

The systematic study of infant emotion burgeoned beginning in the 1970s when cross-cultural studies seemed to indicate clear-cut, universal facial patterns that were associated with discrete emotions such as joy, anger, fear, and sadness (e.g., Ekman, 1972; Izard, 1971). Although recent research suggests that these facial patterns do not invariably indicate the presence of the emotions with which they are associated, even in relatively unsocialized infants (e.g., see Camras, 1991), they are considered by many to be a strong index of those emotions in babies. However, no such strong facial index has been found for guilt. Moreover, to the extent that one requires a feeling state in one's definition of guilt, guilt cannot be studied in young children, who cannot verbalize fine distinctions among negative emotional states. The primary indices of guilt, reparation, and confession/pointing out the mishap, are ambiguous for those who emphasize feeling, in that one may engage in these behaviors without *feeling* guilty. Perhaps for this reason, much of the empirical work on the origins of guilt in toddlerhood never uses the word guilt in describing or even discussing findings.

From a functionalist perspective, to the extent that a pattern of behavior is manifested that serves an emotion's functions in a context in which those functions are sensible (and the relevant appreciations are sensible), a member of the relevant emotion family may be viewed as ongoing. Thus, if a toddler displays a guilt-relevant *pattern* (behaviors promoting reparation and acknowledgment of/confession for one's harmful acts), in a relevant context (e.g., just after the child breaks another's possession), then there is evidence that a guilt-family response has been manifested. This by no means implies that the toddler experiences guilt in the same way that adults experience it; nor even that the toddler feels guilty. Some researchers might consider the responses to be a precursor to guilt, depending on their definition of guilt. However, if a child who has hurt another child goes over and touches and then kisses the injured location, s/he is demonstrating that s/he knows, at some level, that hurting others is a problem, and is letting the victim know that s/he wants to right the wrong. This set of responses certainly functions like guilt.

Thus, in this review, I will discuss findings that are relevant to guilt-family responses, whether the authors of the study described them as such, or used terminology with wider acceptance, such as helping, reparation, internalization, or conscience. This is necessary, in that only three empirical studies involving toddlers

(Barrett et al., 1993; Kochanska, 1991; Zahn-Waxler et al., 1983) used the term *guilt* in the title. Moreover, of those, one assessed guilt only at the follow-up visit at age 8–10 years; one comprised a summary and interpretation of previously reported and ongoing research, and used "guilt-like" when describing empirical findings; and in the other one, a question mark in the title indicated that some might not view the responses as indicating guilt.

Studies of Guilt-Relevant Behavior in Toddlers

In the late 1970s and early 1980s, exciting research uncovered evidence that even toddlers seem to care about others' feelings. Such research negated the then-prevalent belief that toddlers and even preschoolers were incapable of seeing any view other than their own. A ground-breaking study by Zahn-Waxler et al. (1979) enlisted mothers' assistance in chronicling their children's behavior when they encountered a person in distress. Results revealed that toddlers could be quite sensitive to the plight of others, even displaying altruistic behaviors when they were bystanders to distress and reparative behaviors when they caused others' distress. This study also indicated that differences in parental discipline were associated with differences in children's tendencies to make reparation. The results of this and ensuing studies were supportive of theories such as that of Hoffman (1984), suggesting that young children are capable of having empathy and even guilt; and stood in stark contrast to theories such as that of Piaget (e.g., Piaget & Inhelder, 1948/1969), which had been interpreted as meaning that children could only see their own perspective until they were about 7 years of age.

Zahn-Waxler, Radke-Yarrow, and their colleagues framed this early work in terms of children's ability to help others who were victims of distress—labeling help for distresses to which the child was a bystander as altruism and help for distresses the child had caused as reparation (in keeping with the extant literature). They found that some 90% of the time, children as young as 10 months of age showed some form of response to others' distress, whether they caused the distress (a guilt-relevant situation) or whether they simply observed another's distress. At the youngest ages (10–12 months), children's responses were likely to involve personal distress, rather than prosocial acts, particularly when they caused the distress. Reparative responses occurred on approximately a third of the occasions in which children 15 months old or older harmed another person. Moreover, even some 10–12 month olds performed reparative acts when they hurt someone. Furthermore, as toddlers became older (they were studied until about 2½ years of age), they were increasingly likely to perform altruistic and reparative responses in response to others' distress (Zahn-Waxler et al., 1979, 1983).

Children's likelihood of trying to make reparation after harming someone was systematically associated with the form of discipline technique their parents used (Zahn-Waxler et al., 1979, 1983). Children whose mothers showed empathic caregiving were more likely to be highly altruistic and reparative. Moreover, children who were highly reparative were more likely to have mothers who frequently used affective explanations in disciplining their children, including moralistic statements (e.g., "It's not nice to bite"), prohibitions with explanations (e.g., "Can't you see Al's hurt? Don't push him"), absolute principles (e.g., "We never never hit people"), and love withdrawal (e.g., "When you hurt me, I don't want to be near you."). Mothers who frequently stated absolute principles had children who were most likely to make reparation 4.5 or more months later. Thus, one of the key behaviors associated with guilt, reparation, was evident in young toddlers and was systematically related to maternal child-rearing practices. These findings were startling and exciting for those who thought of toddlers as dependent, egocentric, relatively unsocialized creatures who were incapable of guilt.

A replication-and-extension study of normative and depressed mothers and their toddlers also used the maternal–observer methodology, but involved assessment of self-recognition abilities and observation of the children, with peers, in some simulated distress incidents in the laboratory as well (Zahn-Waxler, Radke-Yarrow, Wagner, & Chapman, 1992). Surprisingly, parental depression was unrelated to children's responses, so groups were collapsed. Again, even very young toddlers sometimes made reparation for harms that they caused. By 13–15 months of age, over half of the children had made some prosocial response to others' distress; by 23–25 months, all but one child had done so. Again, children's prosocial interventions increased with age, both when children were bystanders and causes of others' distress. Interestingly, children were less likely to show empathic concern when they caused distress than when they simply observed it, and this was more true at 18–20 months than at 13–15 or 23–25 months. Moreover, children showed more overt distress and more aggression when they caused (versus observing) another's distress, with boys being especially likely to show more aggression when they cause another's distress. Interestingly, overt distress in response to distresses that children caused at 18–20 months was associated with greater prosocial behavior and empathic concern, suggesting very much a guilt-like *pattern* of response.

Although self-recognition increased with age, it was only significantly associated with prosocial behavior and self-referential behavior (imitation of others' distress) at 23–25 months of age, providing only weak support for a self-recognition as a prerequisite to such behavior. The authors did not separate witnessed from caused distress events in these correlations with self-recognition; however, self-recognition has been proposed as a prerequisite for empathy as well. Thus, this second study primarily replicated the results of the first study, suggesting that children's altruistic and reparative responses to others' distress are rather robust findings.

The only study that systematically investigated patterns of guilt-relevant behavior, as distinguished from patterns of shame-relevant behavior, in toddlers was that of Barrett et al. (1993). In this study, 2 year olds were studied in a laboratory situation in which they were playing with the Experimenter's (E's) rag doll (with E out of the room) when the doll's leg fell off. Children's responses to this mishap typically fit one of two patterns. Avoiders displayed a shame-relevant pattern, avoiding E and avoiding looking E in the face repeatedly after the leg fell off and telling E and repairing the doll only after a long delay (often after E specifically asked about the leg), if at all. In contrast, Amenders displayed a guilt-relevant pattern, repairing the doll quickly after the leg fell off, typically before E even returned; telling E about the mishap soon after E returned following the mishap; and rarely avoiding E via gaze aversion or active avoidance following the mishap (never more than once). Moreover, parents of the Amenders reported that they showed more guilt relative to shame at home than did Avoiders, and that they more frequently had broken others' possessions in the past, suggesting that children with greater experience in similar contexts are more prone to display the guilt-relevant pattern when the situation occurs again.

The differences between Avoiders and Amenders were pronounced. All of the 20 Amenders attempted to repair the leg before E said that it was broken; only 11 of 24 Avoiders did so. Only 1 of 24 Avoiders both attempted to repair the leg and "confessed" (pointed out the broken leg to E) before E pointed out the mishap. In contrast, 15 of the 20 Amenders did so. Moreover, preliminary results in the same paradigm with 17 month olds indicate that the guilt-relevant responses of latency to repair the leg and latency to point out the mishap to E form a separate component (based on Principal Components Analysis) from shame/embarrassment-relevant behaviors of smiling and avoiding E via overt behavior and/or gaze aversion, and that both of these components are distinct from a third component involving nervous touching and body manipulations and latency to touch a forbidden toy. These results provide further support for the belief that even toddlers can show guilt, and that guilt-relevant patterns can be distinguished from other patterns of response to children's infractions of standards.

The finding that guilt-relevant behaviors are distinct from shame-relevant behaviors in toddlers contrasts with results based on self-report methods with adults, which have suggested that guilt and shame are fairly highly correlated. It is difficult to reconcile the child and adult findings, in that they differ on both methodology and age group. Perhaps shame and guilt are distinct patterns in early development, only to become interrelated as the person grows older. Alternatively, adults might confuse the two emotions, thus confounding them when making self-reports. A third possibility is that adults experience *both* of these emotion processes on many occasions in many situations. Perhaps adults' ability to relate to more aspects of the situation enables them to react with both shame and guilt. Further research, with multiple age groups and methodologies, is needed to unconfound age and method.

Kochanska and her colleagues (Kochanska, 1991, 1995; Kochanska & Aksan, 1995; Kochanska, Casey, & Fukumoto, 1995; Kochanska, DeVet, Goldman, Murray, & Putnam, 1994) typically use the terms "internalization," "conscience," and "sensitivity to standards," rather than "guilt" in describing the reactions of toddlers, but many of their findings seem quite relevant to the study of guilt. In an early study in this line of research, Kochanska (1991) examined parent–child disciplinary control interactions, observed child "anxiety" or inhibited temperament, and parentally reported rearing strategies when children were 1½ to 3½ years old. She related these measures to children's verbalizations to six scenarios (depicted in pictures) in which guilt was a potential response, obtained during a follow-up visit when children were 8–10 years old. For three of these scenarios, guilt was an expectable and seemingly appropriate response; children in the pictures were depicted as transgressing. In the other three scenarios, guilt was a potential but not necessarily appropriate response. These were ambiguous scenarios in which blame was not clearly indicated. Kochanska (1991) found no differences between children of depressed and normative mothers, but did find that results depended to some extent on the temperament of the children.

Children were divided into two groups based on the degree to which they displayed anxiety/inhibition at 1½ to 3½ years of age. Then, two measures of parents' degree of punitiveness/power assertion—one observed by the researchers and one self-reported by the parents—were correlated, *separately for the two temperament (low and high anxiety/inhibition) groups,* with the degree to which, at age 8 to 10, children depicted the protagonists in the scenarios as displaying (a) "internalization" and empathy for their victim, (b) reparation for the wrongdoing, and (c) discomfort at transgressing.

Results indicated that, for *"low anxious"* or "uninhibited" children, the degree to which parents reported that they used power assertion when children were toddlers was *uncorrelated* with the degree to which children reported at ages 8 to 10 that the protagonists in the scenarios displayed reparation, distress at transgression, or internalization and empathy. Moreover, lower *observed* parental power assertion directed toward these low anxious children was associated only with greater likelihood that children would report that the protagonists in the stories made reparation. In contrast, for *high inhibited* or anxious children, lower *observed* parental power assertion was associated with children's reports that the protagonists displayed more intense discomfort at transgressing, more empathy/internalization, and more reparation; and parents' lower *self-reported* power assertion was associated with internalization/empathy for their victim's distress and more reparation (moreover, discomfort at transgression approached significance). Thus, parental power assertiveness had more of an impact on "high anxious" children's tendencies to represent transgressors as showing more guilt-like behavior than it did on "low anxious" children's tendencies to do so.

Finally, Kochanska (1991) examined toddlers' compliance to their parents' control demands in relation to their responses (at age 8–10) to the scenarios. She did not divide children according to their temperament for these correlations. Results indicated that compliance during toddlerhood was associated with children's depicting the protagonists as displaying more empathy, reparation, and discomfort at transgressing. Thus, compliance and less power-assertive rearing at 1½–3½ years of age predicted guilt-like responses to semiprojective scenarios at

8–10 years of age, the latter being primarily true for relatively inhibited or anxious children.

A later study of 26- to 41-month-old children (Kochanska, 1995) revealed that warm, reciprocal parent–child interaction patterns were associated with children's increased tendency to obey rules in the absence of surveillance ("internalization"). The particular indicator or feature of warm, reciprocal relationships that was related to "internalization," however, differed depending on whether children had been classified as "fearless" (uninhibited) versus "fearful" (inhibited). For "fearless" or un- inhibited children, attachment security (as measured using the attachment Q-sort) was predictive of such internalization; maternal discipline was not. In contrast, for "fearful" or inhibited children, nonpower assertive discipline style ("gentle disci- pline") and not attachment security was related to "internalization." Moreover, observed discipline was related to observed internalization and reported discipline was related to reported internalization.

Other recent reports from the same study revealed additional relevant informa- tion. One of these reports (Kochanska et al., 1995) described findings regarding children's reactions to flawed and unflawed objects in relation to their responses to two laboratory mishaps—the doll paradigm described earlier, with some modifica- tions, and a paradigm based on one reported in Cole, Barrett, and Zahn-Waxler (1992), in which the child damaged E's T-shirt. Researchers correlated the various measures from the flawed object situation with those from the two laboratory situ- ations separately for each gender, after partialling out children's ages and Peabody Vocabulary scores. Results for girls indicated that (a) greater verbal concern about flawed objects was associated with greater self-blame and attempts to repair labora- tory mishaps, as well as with greater tendency to apologize and/or suggest repara- tion, and to display distress in response to the same mishaps; (b) more positive comments about unflawed objects was associated with more apologetic and repara- tive comments regarding the mishaps; and (c) more physical concern about flawed objects was associated with more self-blame and reparation attempts and with more distress regarding the mishaps. Thus, girls' apparent concern about flawed objects and preference for unflawed objects was related to their tendency to show guilt- relevant behavior following the two mishaps. Results for boys were weaker; only one mishap variable was related to each of two flawed object variables: (a) boys' increased number of positive comments about unflawed objects was associated with more distress to the mishaps; and (b) verbal concern about flawed objects was associated with more apologizing/suggesting reparation for the mishaps (Ko- chanska et al., 1995). All of these findings suggest that toddlers display guilt- relevant behavior in response to mishaps that they believe they caused and that these responses, especially for girls, are associated with their sensitivity to viola- tions of standards.

Moreover, additional analyses of data from the same children revealed that parents' mutually positive parent–child affect predicted parentally reported internalization (a measure that included some guilt-relevant responses), and mutually positive parent–child affect, along with age and gender (although the beta for gender was only marginally significant) predicted observed internalization (committed compliance), again highlighting the importance of a good parent–child interaction pattern or relationship in the development of internalization and guilt-relevant behavior (Kochanska & Aksan, 1995).

Finally, in another study from the same laboratory, it was found that parents of children under 2 years of age reported that their children showed guilt-relevant behavior: (a) 71% reported children's reparation following wrongdoing; (b) 67% reported children's confession following wrongdoing; (c) 29% reported children's apologies; 67% reported children's guilt [although guilt was not clearly distinguished from other emotional responses to similar situations (e.g., shame)]; and (d) 62% reported that their children corrected their own behaviors (Kochanska et al., 1994). These findings further support the idea that guilt and related responses are apparent during the second year of life.

In conclusion, although findings from all of these studies are open to interpretation, they do paint a picture of the toddler as a caring individual who is learning and attending to society's rules, even in the absence of surveillance, is ready to try to repair wrongdoings he or she causes, and shows a pattern of behavior that is highly suggestive of guilt. These behavioral responses and parental reports of guilt are the closest one can get to scientific evidence of guilt in this age group, and they all seem to point to the toddler's capabilities. Now, what is needed is to study additional predictors and sequelae of these guilt-relevant responses. To the extent that findings are consistent with what one would predict for guilt, this should provide even more compelling evidence that the reparative, confessional, and other guilt-relevant responses of toddlers when they violate standards are guilt-related.

Guilt, like all emotions, is adaptive under certain circumstances. Research has indicated that it is associated with positive characteristics, such as empathy and reparation (e.g., Barrett et al., 1993; Tangney, 1995; Zahn-Waxler & Robinson, 1995). Moreover, it is an unusual emotion, in that even though it is considered a "negative" emotion, it is generally considered socially *desirable* to display under certain circumstances. However, most theorists and researchers agree that it is possible for guilt to be maladaptive as well, when it is too pervasive, intense, or stable, when it occurs under inappropriate circumstances, or when it occurs too infrequently under desirable circumstances (e.g., see Barrett, 1995; Bybee & Quiles, chapter 13, this volume; Ferguson, Sorenson, Bodrero, & Stegge, 1996; Quiles & Bybee, in press). It is important for us to study guilt during its origins, before it might become deflected into a maladaptive pattern in some children and entrenched as a permanent feature of personality. Research on guilt in very young children may have important implications for the future development of those children.

REFERENCES

Barrett, K. (1995). A functionalist approach to shame and guilt. In J. P. Tangney & K. W. Fischer (Eds.), *Self-conscious emotions (pp. 25–63).* New York: Guilford Publications.

Barrett, K. C. (in press). A functionalist approach to the development of emotion. In M. F. Mascolo & S. Griffin (Eds.), *What develops in emotional development?* New York: Plenum.

Barrett, K. C., & Campos, J. J. (1987). Perspectives on emotional development: II. A functionalist approach to emotions. In J. Osofsky (Ed.), *Handbook of infant development* (2nd ed., pp. 555–578). New York: Wiley.

Barrett, K. C., Zahn-Waxler, C., & Cole, P. M. (1993). Avoiders versus Amenders—implications for the investigation of guilt and shame during toddlerhood? *Cognition and Emotion, 7,* 481–505.

Camras, L. (1991). Conceptualizing early infant affect; emotions as fact, fiction or artifact? View II: A dynamical systems perspective on expressive development. In K. T. Strongman (Ed.), *International review of studies on emotion* (Vol. 1, pp. 16–28). New York: Wiley.

Cole, P. M., Barrett, K. C., & Zahn-Waxler, C. (1992). Emotion displays in two-year-olds during mishaps. *Child Development, 63,* 314–324.

DeCasper, A. J., & Fifer, W. (1980). Of human bonding: Newborns prefer their mothers' voices. *Science, 208,* 1174–1176.

Ekman, P. (1972). Universals and cultural differences in facial expressions of emotion. In J. Cole (Ed.), *Nebraska Symposium on Motivation, 1971* (Vol. 19, pp. 207–282). Lincoln: University of Nebraska Press.

Ferguson, T. J., Sorenson, C. B., Bodrero, R. & Stegge, H. (1996, August). *(Dys)functional guilt and shame in developmental perspective.* Poster presented at ISSBD, Quebec City, 1996.

Freud, S. (1961). Civilization and its discontents. In J. Strachey (Ed. and Trans.), *The standard edition of the complete psychological works of Sigmund Freud* London: Hogarth Press (Original work published 1930).

Harder, D. W. (1995). Shame and guilt assessment, and relationships of shame- and guilt-proneness to psychopathology. In J. P. Tangney & K. W. Fischer (Eds.), *Self-conscious emotions* (pp. 368–392). New York: Guilford.

Harder, D. W., Cutler, L., & Rockart, L. (1992). Assessment of shame and guilt and their relationships to psychopathology. *Journal of Personality Assessment, 59,* 584–604.

Hoffman, M. (1984). Parent discipline, moral internalization, and development of prosocial motivation. In E. Staub, D. Bar-Tal, J. Karylowski, & J. Reykowski (Eds.), *Development and maintenance of prosocial behavior* (pp. 117–137). New York: Plenum.

Izard, C. (1971). *The face of emotion.* New York: Appleton-Century-Crofts.

Jones, W. H., Kugler, K., & Adams, P. (1995). You always hurt the one you love: Guilt and transgressions against relationship partners. In J. Tangney & K. Fischer (Eds.), *Self-conscious emotions* (pp. 301–321). New York: Guilford Publications.

Kagan, J. (1984). *The nature of the child.* New York: Basic Books.

Klein, M. (1975). *Love, guilt, and reparation and other works, 1921–1945.* New York: Dell.

Kochanska, G. (1991). Socialization and temperament in the development of guilt and conscience. *Child Development, 62,* 1379–1392.

Kochanska, G. (1995). Children's temperament, mothers' discipline, and security of attachment: Multiple pathways to emerging internalization. *Child Development, 66,* 597–615.

Kochanska, G., & Aksan, N. (1995). Mother–child mutually positive affect, the quality of child compliance to requests and prohibitions, and maternal control as correlates of early internalization. *Child Development, 66,* 236–254.

Kochanska, G., Casey, R. J., & Fukumoto, A. (1995). Toddlers' sensitivity to standard violations. *Child Development, 66,* 643–656.

Kochanska, G., DeVet, K., Goldman, M., Murray, K., & Putnam, S. (1994). Maternal reports of conscience development and temperament in young children. *Child Development, 65,* 852–868.

Lempers, J. D., Flavell, E. R., & Flavell, J. H. (1977). The development in very young children of tacit knowledge concerning visual perception. *Genetic Psychology Monographs, 95,* 3–53.

Lewis, H. B. (1971). *Shame and guilt in neurosis.* New York: International Universities Press.

Lewis, M. (1991). Self-conscious emotions and the development of self. In T. Shapiro & R. N. Emde (Eds.), New perspectives on affect and emotion in psychoanalysis. *Journal of the American Psychoanalytic Association (Suppl.), 39,* 45–73.

Piaget, J. & Inhelder, B. (1969). *The child's conception of space* (F. J. Langdon & J. L. Lunzer, Trans.). New York: W. W. Norton. (Original work published 1948).

Quiles, Z., & Bybee, J. (in press). Chronic and predispositional guilt: Rrelations to mental health, prosocial behavior, and religiosity. *Journal of Personality Assessment.*

Scheff, T. J. (1995). Conflict in family systems: The role of shame. In J. P. Tangney & K. W. Fischer (Eds.), *Self-conscious emotions* (pp. 393–412). New York: Guilford.

Seligman, M. E. P., Peterson, C., Kaslow, N., Tanenbaum, R., Alloy, L., & Abramson, L. (1984). Attributional style and depressive symptoms among children. *Journal of Abnormal Psychology, 93,* 235–238.

Tangney, J. P. (1995). Shame and guilt in interpersonal relationships. In J. P. Tangney & K. W. Fischer (Eds.), *Self-conscious emotions* (pp. 114–139). New York: Guilford.

Tangney, J. P., Wagner, P., & Gramzow, R. (1992). Proneness to shame, proneness to guilt, and psychopathology. *Journal of Abnormal Psychology, 101,* 469–478.

Wellman, H. M., Cross, D., & Bartsch, K. (1986). Infant search and object permanence: A meta-analysis of the A-not-B error. *Monographs of the Society for Research in Child Development, 51 (Serial No. 214).*

Zahn-Waxler, C., & Kochanska, G. (1990). The origins of guilt. In R. A. Thompson (Ed.), *Nebraska Symposium on Motivation 1988* (pp. 183–258). Lincoln, NE: University of Nebraska Press.

Zahn-Waxler, C., Radke-Yarrow, M., & King, R. (1979). Child rearing and children's prosocial initiations toward victims of distress. *Child Development, 50,* 319–330.

Zahn-Waxler, C., Radke-Yarrow, M., & King, R. (1983). Early altruism and guilt. *Academic Psychology Bulletin, 5,* 247–259.

Zahn-Waxler, C., Radke-Yarrow, M., Wagner, E., & Chapman, M. (1992). Development of concern for others. *Developmental Psychology, 28,* 126–136.

Zahn-Waxler, C., & Robinson, J. (1995). Empathy and guilt: Early origins of feelings of responsibility. In J. P. Tangney & K. W. Fischer (Eds.), *Self-conscious emotions* (pp. 143–173). New York: Guilford.

Zahn-Waxler, C., Robinson, J., & Ende, R. N. (1992). The development of empathy in twins. *Developmental Psychology, 28,* 1038–1047.

Varieties of Empathy-Based Guilt

Martin L. Hoffman
New York University, New York, New York

INTRODUCTION

The first developmental account of guilt came from Freud. Strangely, Freud's concept of guilt was not the result of harming someone, but a largely unconscious throwback to early childhood, based on anxiety over punishment or abandonment by parents. When the anxiety is activated by hostile feelings, it is transformed into guilt even if the hostility is not expressed. In Freud's words, "A threatening external unhappiness, loss of love and punishment by external authority, has been exchanged for a lasting inner unhappiness, the tension of a sense of guilt," (Freud, 1930, p. 73). Freud recognized the pathological quality of this guilt and suggested humans also feel a more reality-based guilt, but he did not come up with an alternative conception of guilt and its development, nor did his followers. This pathological quality may explain guilt's bad reputation and long neglect by academic psychologists.

In the late 1960s, I advanced an empathy-based theory of interpersonal guilt, defined as an *intensely unpleasant feeling of disesteem for oneself that results from empathic feeling for someone in distress combined with awareness of being the cause of that distress* (Hoffman, 1982; Hoffman & Saltzstein, 1967). Since then, decades of research has provided support both for the existence of empathy-based guilt, and the hypothesis that it serves as a motive for prosocial acts like making reparation to one's victims, helping people who are not one's victims, examining one's values and reordering one's priorities, and resolving to be less selfish and more considerate of others in the future (see review by Baumeister, Stillwell, & Heatherton, 1994).

I am now clarifying and extending the theory by examining the varieties of empathy-based guilt associated with different types of prosocial moral encounters. This is my topic here, but first I summarize the evidence for empathy-based guilt and the five types of moral encounters that may comprise the prosocial moral domain.

EVIDENCE FOR EMPATHY-BASED GUILT

There are several lines of evidence—narrative, correlational, experimental. Narrative evidence is provided by Tangney, Marschall, Rosenberg, Barlow, and Wagner (1996), who found that children and adults often express empathic feelings in the course of describing personal guilt experiences. I found the same thing in my story-completion guilt research years ago, as I will discuss later. Tangney et al. also report significant positive correlations between paper-and-pencil measures of empathy and guilt in college students, in fifth-grade children, and in the fifth-grade children's mothers, fathers, grandmothers, and grandfathers (Tangney, 1991; Tangney, Wagner, Burggraf, Gramzow, & Fletcher, 1991). Indirect correlational support for empathy-based guilt is evident in the 1970s and 1980s parent-discipline research, which showed consistently positive relationships between induction discipline and both empathic distress and guilt. Krevans and Gibbs (1996) also found a positive correlation between empathy and guilt in children whose parents frequently use inductions. Finally, Thompson and Hoffman (1980) did an experiment in which first-, third-, and fifth-grade children were shown stories on slides (also narrated by the experimenter) in which a boy harms someone. The subjects in whom empathy was aroused by asking them how the victim felt obtained higher scores on projective guilt measures than controls who were not asked about the victim, suggesting that empathic arousal may intensify guilt feeling. Putting it all together, it seems reasonable to conclude that empathy-based guilt is a real phenomenon.

TYPES OF MORAL ENCOUNTERS

I recently proposed that a comprehensive prosocial, empathy-based moral theory would encompass at least five types of moral encounters (Hoffman, in press): (a) Innocent bystander: one witnesses someone in pain, danger, or distress. The moral issue is whether one is motivated to help. (b) Transgressor: one has harmed someone, or is about to act in a way that may harm someone. The moral issue is whether one is motivated to avoid the harmful act or at least feels guilty and acts prosocially afterwards. (c) Virtual transgressor: one is innocent but feels oneself a transgressor. (d) Multiple-claimant: an extended bystander model in which one witnesses two or more victims or potential victims but cannot help them all and must make a choice. (e) Caring versus justice: one must choose between acting in accord with a caring principle (we should help people in need) or a justice principle (we should reward people who are productive) when the two are in conflict.

First, I discuss the bystander model, which is a cornerstone of my comprehensive moral scheme. It is also the prototypic moral encounter for empathic distress, and because I deal with guilt based on empathic distress I begin by summarizing my developmental scheme for empathic distress and speculating about guilt in bystanders.

INNOCENT BYSTANDERS

People are bystanders when they witness someone in pain, danger, or distress (physical, emotional, financial). As I noted, the moral question is, are they motivated to help? The bystander model is the prototype for empathic distress and related empathic affects and the context for a stage theory of their development (see Hoffman, 1978, 1984a for details). A summary follows.

Definition of Empathy

Empathy is a feeling more appropriate for someone else's condition than one's own; one's feeling may match the other's but not necessarily. This definition is more complex than a "match" definition but the complexities, and I hope the advantages will be apparent as we go along. As prosocial action involves helping someone in distress, I focus on empathic *distress* and highlight its motivational properties.

Arousal of Empathic Distress

There are at least five arousal modes. Three are primitive, automatic, and most important, involuntary: (a) reflexive newborn's crying at the sound of another's cry. This response by alert, content infants is not simply imitation or a reaction to a noxious stimulus but vigorous, intense, and indistinguishable from the spontaneous cry of an infant in actual discomfort. It must therefore be considered a rudimentary precursor of empathic distress, although the infant probably cannot tell it from actual distress. It may also contribute to empathy development, as the co-occurence of another's cry and self-distress may create the expectation of self-distress whenever one is exposed to another's distress; (b) mimicry, which has two steps: the observer spontaneously imitates the victim's facial, vocal, and postural expression of feeling; the resulting changes in the observer's facial and postural musculature then trigger afferent feedback which produces feelings that match the feelings of the victim; (c) classical conditioning, and direct association of cues in the victim's situation that remind observers of similar experiences in their own past and evoke feelings in them that fit the victim's situation.

Two empathy-arousing modes involve higher-order cognitive processes: (d) mediated association, in which language communicates the victim's emotional state and makes the connection between his situation and the observer's past experience; and (e) role taking, in which observers feel something of the victim's distress by imagining themselves in his place (self-focus); by imagining how he feels, based on knowledge of his experiences or his or her group's behavior in similar situations (other-focus); or by a combination of self- and other-focus. Because role taking is cognitively demanding, it may often be deliberate, but it does occur spontaneously in 9-year-olds (Wilson & Cantor, 1985), as well as in anyone who identifies with characters in novels or films.

The importance of so many modes is they enable observers to respond empathically to whatever distress cues are available. Cues from the victim's face, voice, or posture can be picked up through mimicry; situational cues, through conditioning or association. If the victim expresses his distress verbally or in writing, or someone else describes his situation, observers can be empathically aroused through mediated association or role taking.[1] Empathic distress is thus a multidetermined, hence reliable human response. This fits well with the argument (Hoffman, 1981) that it became a basic part of human nature through natural selection and the finding (Zahn-Waxler, Robinson, & Emde, 1992) that it has a hereditary component.

Empathy Development

Mature empathic distress includes a metacognitive awareness of responding empathically: one knows the stimulus event is impinging on someone else, not on oneself. One may also sense what the victim feels and make causal attributions. Mature empathizers have thus passed the developmental milestones of acquiring a cognitive sense of themselves and others as physically separate and having independent internal states, and being able to distinguish what happens to others from what happens to themselves.

It appears that 7-year-olds and a few 5-year-olds have this metacognitive awareness: they attribute their own feeling to a film character's feeling or situation (Strayer, 1993). This means that children younger than that are empathically aroused without this awareness, and suggests that empathic distress develops along with acquiring a cognitive sense of oneself and others. I identified four broad stages of

---

[1]The involuntary modes can prevent "egoistic drift" and the loss of other-focus that can occur when observers ruminate about past experiences associated with victims' situations.

self and other development, which may interact with children's empathic affect to produce four developmental levels of empathic distress.

Global Empathic Distress

As noted, alert and contented newborns become agitated and distressed at the sound of another's cry. Infants progress after that, but their response to another's distress remains primitive. A 1-year-old saw a friend fall and start to cry. She stared at her friend, began to cry, then put her thumb in her mouth and buried her head in her mother's lap, just as she does when she herself is hurt. We do not know exactly what her behavior means but a parsimonious explanation is that since she behaves the same way whether she or the other is distressed she must equate the two, which suggests she cannot tell the difference between things happening to another and things happening to herself. This fits the well-known mirror-research finding that children lack a clear self-image until 18 months. The child's behavior also shows empathic distress functioning as a motive—to reduce her own distress.

Quasi-Egocentric Empathic Distress

Early in year 2, toddlers can differentiate what happens to others and themselves. They know the other is in distress, but they remain egocentric enough to assume that what helps them will help others. A 14-month-old boy responded to a crying friend with a sad look, then gently took the friend's hand and brought him to his own mother, although the friend's mother was present. His act shows both empathic distress as a prosocial motive (he clearly tries to help the friend) and confusion between his and his friend's needs.

A More Veridical Empathy for Another's Feeling

Later in year 2, toddlers become aware that others have internal states (thoughts, feelings, wants) independent of their own. They can now empathize more accurately with others' feelings and needs in different situations and help them more effectively. The transition is illustrated by a 2-year-old who brought his own teddy bear to comfort a crying friend. It didn't work. He then paused, ran to the next room and returned with the friend's teddy bear; the friend hugged it and stopped crying. The transition to veridical empathy may thus occur when children are cognitively ready to learn from corrective feedback following their "egocentric" mistakes.

This is only the beginning of course. Learning to fully empathize with others is a life-long task: by age 8, for example, children learn that conflicting emotions can coexist in a person (Gnepp, 1989); by 16, they sometimes refrain from helping because they know it may put victims at a social disadvantage (Midlarsky, 1985). Adults know their empathic distress is sometimes more intense than the victim's (the problem means less to him; he has adjusted to it). Therapists learn to hold back on expressing empathic grief because it might keep patients from expressing negative feeling about the relative or friend who died.

Empathic Distress beyond the Situation

Gender and ethnic identity research suggests that children's sense of themselves as coherent and continuous over time is hazy until about 6–9 years. We might infer that this is when they know that others also have identities and lives beyond the immediate situation. We might also expect it to be some time before they can use this knowledge to infer another's current feelings, because of interference from salient situational and expressive cues. Gnepp and Gould's (1985) research seems to suggest otherwise. They told subjects about a child's prior experience (bitten by gerbil; rewarded for excellent dive) and then asked them what the child's emotional reaction would be in a related subsequent event (his turn to feed class gerbil; his turn to dive). Half the second graders and two-thirds of the fifth graders correctly used the prior information. It thus appears that about 10 years is when children's knowledge of others' lives begins to affect their empathic response. But future research may alter this estimate drastically.

Whenever it happens, children should be able to empathize with someone who is chronically ill, emotionally deprived, or hopelessly poor—regardless of his immediate behavior. If he appears sad, knowing his life is sad should intensify their empathic distress. If he appears happy, the contradiction should make them stop and think; and rather than respond to his happy expression with empathic joy they may realize that his sad life is a more compelling index of his well-being and respond with empathic sadness, or a mixture of empathic joy and sadness. Mature empathy is thus a response to a network of cues: from the other person's behavior and expression, his situation, and everything one knows about him.

Sympathetic Distress

In moving from "global" to "quasi-egocentric" empathy, children's empathic distress appears to be qualitatively transformed, owing to advances in self–other differentiation, into a more reciprocal concern for victims. They continue to feel empathic distress but also sympathetic distress, or compassion. From then on developmentally (and from here on in this chapter), empathic distress includes a sympathetic component; and children want to help because they feel sorry for the victim, not just to relieve their own empathic distress.[2] Sympathetic distress may therefore be the child's first truly prosocial motive.

---

[2]Children may not help just to relieve their own empathic distress (except in "empathic overarousal" discussed later), as there are easier ways to do this (turning away or leaving).

Evidence for the shift comes from anecdotes like those I cited showing children progressing developmentally from responding to another's distress by seeking comfort for themselves, to seeking comfort for the victim. Similar developmental advances by 10–14-months-olds were observed by Zahn-Waxler, Radke-Yarrow, and King (1979) and Zahn-Waxler, Robinson, and Emde (1992), who also describe an in-between stage (a 12-month-old whose first prosocial act alternated between gently touching the victim and gently touching himself). And, these researchers found, as did Bischoff-Kohler (1991), that mirror-self-image-recognition at 18 months predicted sympathetic distress and prosocial behavior at 24 months, even with age controlled, in keeping with the hypothesis that advances in self–other differentiation foster development of sympathetic distress.

Cognitively Expanded Bystander Model

Cognitive processes enable humans to form images, represent events, and imagine themselves in another's place. And because represented events can evoke affect (Fiske, 1982; Hoffman, 1985), empathy can be aroused by imagining victims, as in reading about their misfortunes, arguing about economic or political issues, or making Kohlbergian judgments about hypothetical dilemmas. A 13-year-old male subject responded to the question, "Why is it wrong to steal from a store?" as follows: "Because the people who own the store work hard for their money and they deserve to be able to spend it for their family. It's not fair, they sacrifice a lot, and they make plans and then they lost it all because somebody who didn't work for it goes in and takes it." The subject turned an abstract moral question into an empathy-relevant one by imagining a victim's inner states (work motivation, expectation and future plans, disappointment).

In sum, cognitive development expands the bystander model to encompass moral motivation in a variety of situations.

Causal Attribution and Empathic Affects

Most people make spontaneous attributions about the cause of events (Weiner, 1985) and probably do this when observing someone in distress. Depending on the attribution, empathic distress may be reduced or transformed into other empathic affects. It may be reduced if the victim is blamed. Blaming victims may have a factual base (jogging in dangerous places, staying with abusive husbands, having promiscuous sex) in which case empathic distress may be neutralized and observers may feel indifference or even contempt for victims. Even without a factual base, blaming victims may serve to distance bystanders and reduce their guilt or feeling of responsibility. Staub (1996) suggests distancing may occur because it is extremely difficult to see others suffer when one can do nothing about it.

Empathic distress may be transformed into *sympathetic distress* if the cause is natural (accident, illness) or beyond the victim's control (Weiner, 1985); or, if the cause is unclear as in the early developmental transformation of empathic into sympathetic distress. If someone else is the cause, empathic distress may be transformed into *empathic anger*, which is a dual feeling of empathic distress for the victim's pain, and anger at the culprit. Empathic anger is hard to distinguish from direct anger because the behavioral outcomes are similar. A 17-month-old in a doctor's office, who watched his brother get a shot, tried to hit the doctor. A highly aggressive toddler learned to channel his aggression so well that by 6 years he expressed more empathic anger than any of his peers (Chapman et al., 1986). These examples and Levine's (1995) finding that 6-year-olds express empathic anger but cannot tell anger-evoking from sadness-evoking situations, suggest the need to study how empathy, empathic anger, and direct anger interrelate.[3]

People also make attributions about victims' character, often based on reputation or stereotype. Character attributions may decrease empathy when victims are viewed as bad, immoral, lazy, or blamed for their distress, and who therefore deserve their fate. But if victims are viewed as basically good, observers may not only empathize with their personal distress but also view them as victims of injustice ("nonreciprocity" of deeds and outcomes), which may transform empathic distress into an *empathic feeling of injustice* (Gibbs, 1991; Hoffman, 1991).

Most important for present purposes, if observers view themselves as the cause of the victim's distress, the self-blame attribution may transform their empathic distress into a feeling of guilt. As I said earlier, there is evidence that empathy-based guilt can be an effective prosocial motive. It may also play a role in all five types of moral encounters but especially in transgressions and virtual transgressions, as we shall see.

Guilt in Innocent Bystanders

The research has long made clear that empathic distress is reliably aroused in bystanders and functions as a prosocial motive to do something to alleviate the victim's distress (Eisenberg & Miller, 1987). As with other motives, there is no assurance that observers will actually help; more powerful egoistic motives such as fear, not wanting to get involved, or being in a hurry to get where one is going, may intervene. Observers who do not help, however, may often feel guilty about their inaction. In this case, the self-blame attribution that turns empathic distress into guilt is due to the awareness not of causing the victim's distress but of allowing it to happen or continue.

---

[3]Part of empathic anger is empathy with a victim's pain—with his anger, too, if he is angry. Some people who have trouble with direct anger can feel empathic anger with victims who are distressed but not angry. Would these people empathize with victims who are angry?

There is scattered anecdotal evidence that guilt over inaction motivates prosocial behavior. White 1960s civil-rights activists said they would feel guilty if they did nothing because that would allow the Southern black people's victimization to continue (Keniston, 1968). A German who saved Jews from Nazis said, "Unless we helped, they would be killed. I could not stand that thought. I never would have forgiven myself." (Oliner, 1988, p. 168). A college student, "The woman kept hitting her kid. I felt I'd feel bad if I did nothing. So I got my keys and entertained the kid. He responded. The mother then acted better. I felt real good."

In my early guilt research (Hoffman, 1970), I used a story-completion item in which a well-meaning "hero" (same age and sex as subject), is rushing to a movie with a friend and sees a child who seems lost. He suggests they help but the friend talks him out of it. The next day he hears that the child, left alone by his baby-sitter, ran into the street and was killed. The adult version has an elderly person looking for something lost in the snow. In their completions, most subjects (fifth and seventh graders, and parents) had the hero feeling intense guilt over allowing the tragedy to happen. The guilt often included empathic distress for the child or his parents and led to prosocial acts like helping the parents (mow their lawn, run errands), going out of one's way to help children, and free baby-sitting. Older children and adults also had the hero criticize himself ("How could I be so selfish?") and make a vow to reorder his priorities and think of others in the future.

Even when bystanders help, they may feel guilt over hesitating because the victim suffered in the interim. If so, this would mean bystanders always feel guilt except in emergencies requiring immediate action, and the "guilt over hesitating" may add to their motivation to help. This would of course add to guilt's importance as a motive in bystander situations.

TRANSGRESSIONS

Transgressions are situations in which one harms someone or is about to act in a way that might harm someone. They may be provoked, intentional, accidental, by-products of conflict, or violations of another's expectations. The moral issue is whether one is motivated to avoid the harmful act or at least feels guilty and acts prosocially afterwards. The transgression model is the prototypic moral encounter for empathy-based guilt.

The empathy-arousing processes described earlier may work as prosocial moral motives more or less naturally in bystanders. They may not work when children harm or are about to act in a way that might harm someone, because their emotions may blind them to the harm done and override any empathic tendencies. External agents may be needed. This adds the sociocultural dimension and the concept of moral internalization (Hoffman, 1983, 1988) to our account.

Accidents

In accidents where children are aware of the harm done, feel empathic distress and guilt, and engage in a reparative act, intervention is not needed. It is needed when children are unaware of the harm or ignore or laugh at the victim's distress.

Intentional Harm

Most people do not harm others intentionally except in self-defense, retaliation for a past hurt, because they misperceive others' intentions, or in the service of ideology or principle. Children harm others for all but the last reason, and also engage in pranks like throwing stones at school windows that might hurt others. And they hurt others for no apparent reason: a 5-year-old sulked over a scolding; her younger sister approached and offered her a toy; she said "go away, I don't like you," whereupon her sister ran to the living room, buried her head in the couch, and sobbed. Such situations require adult intervention.

Conflicts

A major challenge for moral development and socialization, because of their emotionality and high fequency (Hay, 1984) are conflicts between peers, mainly over possessions (toys, candy, swing, slide, jump rope, climbing apparatus). Child A says it is his turn, grabs a toy from B, who grabs it back. They fight until A pushes B away, grabs the toy and runs, leaving B crying. If A is empathically distressed and comforts B, intervening is unnecessary. It is necessary if A ignores B's cries or B chases and hits A, because powerful egoistic and angry emotions may keep each child from attending both to his own behavior and the other's distress ("decentering"), which is necessary for empathic distress and accepting blame. Blame is something to be avoided anyway, as it is self-deprecatory, painful, and associated with past punishment. Intervention is thus needed to put empathy and especially guilt arousal processes in motion. Besides, someone may get hurt.

Guilt and Moral Socialization in Discipline Encounters

I have long argued that the foundation for guilt and moral internalization necessary for combatting egoistic needs in conflict situations occurs in discipline encounters at home when children harm someone. Whether the harm is accidental, intentional, or conflict-related, and whether the victim is a parent or peer, it is only in discipline encounters that adults make connections between children's motives and actions and their harmful consequences for others, and communicate disapproval of these actions. After three decades of research (from Hoffman, 1963, to Krevans & Gibbs, 1996) it appears that the most effective parental discipline methods for producing guilt and moral internalization are *inductions,* which point up the harmful consequences of children's acts for others.

How Inductions Work

To explain the underlying processes, I made an information-processing analysis of discipline encounters and the cognitive and emotional changes in children between discipline encounters (Hoffman, 1983). I present here a revised analysis, using generalized event representations or "scripts". Scripts are useful because (a) even young children form them to organize social-behavioral experiences and guide actions (Nelson, 1981); (b) like other representations, they become more complex with age through successive assimilation; and (c), most important, they can be charged with affect and thus acquire motive properties. Scripts of behavioral interaction sequences, charged with prosocial moral affects (empathic distress, sympathetic distress, guilt) may thus provide the affective-cognitive-behavioral units of people's prosocial moral motivational structure. My analysis follows:

1. Inductions, like other discipline methods, communicate disapproval of children's harmful acts but they also call attention to both the victims' distress and children's blame for causing it. Making victims salient should activate the empathy-arousal modes described earlier—mimicry if children look at the victim, role taking if they are encouraged to imagine how they would feel in his place, mediated association if relevant past experiences are mentioned—and children may feel empathic distress for victims' pain, hurt feelings, and (eventually) suffering beyond the immediate situation. When they process information about their causal role, the resulting self-blame attribution may transform their empathic distress into guilt feeling (Hoffman, 1970, 1982)—*transgression guilt,* in contrast to guilt over inaction. The parental disapproval reinforces transgression guilt and adds a sense of having done something wrong.

2. After several repetitions of transgression followed by induction, empathic distress, and empathy-based guilt, children form a Transgression $\rightarrow$ Induction $\rightarrow$ Guilt script, which is emotionaly charged (empathic distress, guilt) and therefore has motive properties. The full script may include reparative acts by children, their parent's and victim's positive responses, and their own empathic relief and guilt reduction, which help reinforce the reparative acts' connection to guilt. These are important for the development of prosocial moral behavior, but I exclude them because my focus is moral motivation rather than behavior.

3. Over the years children successively assimilate into their Transgression $\rightarrow$ Induction $\rightarrow$ Guilt scripts the information contained in thousands of inductions[4]— enough to transform them into increasingly complex, generalized structures of

---

[4]"Thousands" is based on Wright's (1967) finding that 2–10-year-olds experienced parental influence attempts every 6 to 9 min (about 50 a day or 15 thousand a year!) and evidence that middle-class parents use "reasoning" half the time (Chapman & Zahn-Waxler, 1982; Ross, Tessla, Kenyon, & Lollis, 1990; Smetana, 1989).

emotionally charged knowledge about effects of their actions on others. Early scripts may consist mainly of kinesthetic representations of one's harmful acts, images of victims' pain and parents' discipline behavior, and associated empathy and guilt. With age, they become less imagistic and more semantic, "propositional," and principle-like (one must not hurt others), while retaining the empathy and guilt.

4. These generalized scripts result from children's active semantic integration of induction content and relating it to their own action and the victim's condition. The children's internal processes are therefore salient, and the scripts should be experienced as their own constructions and part of their internal motive system, despite having originated externally. The internalization process may also be enhanced by the tendency of "episodic" details like the parent's presence to fade from memory, while semantically integrated information endures (Tulving, 1972).

5. The above can be viewed as an explanation of how early encounters between children's egoistic motives and parental demands (discipline encounters) are transformed into encounters between children's egoistic motives and their own internalized prosocial motives (moral encounters). From early on, inductions give discipline encounters an increasingly moral-encounter component that eventually takes over, as parental intervention becomes unnecessary and children "internalize" the motive to consider others even in conflict situations. The scripts, now Transgression → Guilt, are activated directly by children's awareness of doing harm and the associated guilt feels like it comes from within.

Anticipatory Guilt

Guilt's value as a prosocial motive would be limited if it only operated after the fact. But Transgression → Guilt scripts, like other representations, can probably be activated in advance by relevant stimuli, in this case children's anticipatory thoughts and images about harmful effects of their planned action on others. The script's associated guilt is then experienced as "anticipatory guilt," which serves as a motive against committing the act. To feel and act on anticipatory guilt has cognitive and behavior-control requisites: the ability, under fire, to connect intentions, acts, and consequences that have not occurred, to consider other perspectives, and to control impulses.

The term "anticipatory guilt" may be a misnomer: one is not motivated to avoid guilt in the traditional sense of avoiding pain to the self, but simply to avoid harming the other. Instead of feeling guilty after harming someone, one feels guilty at the thought of harming someone. Instead of thinking about ways to undo a harmful act, one may "undo" it in advance—by not doing it.

The Context of Discipline

Discipline occurs in an ongoing relationship, and since inductions' effectiveness requires secure, motivated children, it makes sense that high-induction parents are affectionate and that securely attached toddlers are receptive to parental influence attempts (Hoffman, 1988; Londerville & Main, 1981). A good relationship is not enough, however, and the emotionality of situations in which children harm others at times calls for power assertion (physical force, threats, commands). Although power assertion works against guilt—it arouses emotions (fear, anger) and acts (gaze aversion, withdrawal) that disrupt cognitive processing and undermine inductions (Hoffman, 1963, 1970; Rothbart, 1989)—some power assertion may be necessary to get children to stop, pay attention, and process the information. How much is needed varies: a mild directive if the child is simply unaware ("Don't you see you hurt Mary? Don't pull her hair"). But highly charged conflict situations may require physically removing and calming children before verbalizing inductions, or holding them firmly and insisting they listen. Temperament may also be a factor: less power assertion is required to get fearful children to resist temptation (Kochanska, 1995), and less power assertion is probably required to get empathic children to attend to inductions.

Induction, Guilt, and Prosocial Behavior

Empathy-based transgression guilt was found in Baumeister et al.'s (1994) review to motivate prosocial acts like apologizing, making reparation, and generalized helping. In a recent study by Krevans and Gibbs (1996), the hypothesis that empathic distress and guilt mediate induction's contribution to prosocial behavior was supported: previous findings that induction relates to empathy and prosocial behavior were replicated, but induction's relation to prosocial behavior disappeared when empathy's effect was controlled, in keeping with the empathy-as-mediator hypothesis. Guilt-as-mediator received post hoc support: guilt related to prosocial behavior only in high-empathy children, and to empathy only in children of high-induction parents.

VIRTUAL TRANSGRESSIONS

In virtual transgressions one has not caused another's distress but blames oneself for it anyway. The developmentally earliest instances were reported by Zahn-Waxler et al. (1979). Children 15–20 months old who encountered their mother looking sad or sobbing for no apparent reason, would look sad themselves (empathic distress), approach, and try to comfort the mother. About a third of them seemed to accept responsibility for the mother's distress, saying something like "I sorry, Mommy, did I do anything wrong?" or spanking themselves.

Zahn-Waxler et al. viewed these actions as expressing empathy-based guilt. I was surprised that infants could feel guilty, and ended up explaining it as due to the combined effects of incomplete self–other differentiation, primitive causal schemas based on temporal and geographical contiguity, and a sense of omnipotence—all of which made them confused about the cause—and since they were near the mother at the time, they simply blamed themselves (Hoffman, 1982). But I remained skeptical and suggested they might just be parroting the behavior of others.

However, these same children produced more guilt themes than others in laboratory assessments 5 years later (Cummings, Hollenbeck, Iannotti, Radke-Yarrow, & Zahn-Waxler, 1986). This makes me less skeptical, although I would like to see stronger evidence of guilt. Assuming it is guilt, I view it as a forerunner of a type of guilt that may be inherent in close human relationships: "relationship guilt."

Relationship Guilt

Close relationships may be necessary for a full emotional life but they have a price. Baumeister, Stillwell, and Heatherton (1995) asked adults to describe the most recent instance in which they felt guilty; the largest category was neglecting a relationship-partner and another was failure to live up to an interpersonal obligation. The reason may be that close relationships provide endless opportunities for hurting one's partner and experiencing transgression guilt: "from mundane unintended slights, thoughtless remarks, or forgotten appointments to more serious betrayals of confidence, bald-faced lies, and crushing infidelities" (Tangney & Fischer, 1995, p. 134).

But they also provide endless opportunities for blaming oneself even when innocent, because relationship partners may become so dependent on each other that their feelings and moods depend heavily on the other's feelings, moods, and actions. More important, each one knows the other is similarly dependent on him. Indeed, owing to countless interactions over time, each may become acutely aware of new and unpredictable ways of unintentionally distressing the other. In short, each develops a keen sensitivity to the potential impact of his words and deeds on the other.

It may therefore seem reasonable when one's partner is sad or unhappy and the cause is unclear, not only to feel empathic distress but also to blame oneself. One might not feel guilty if certain of one's innocence but one can never be certain without keeping accurate mental records of previous interactions—which people do not do. Adding to uncertainty are ways of harming others that are unique to close relationships and may involve changing, unpredictable expectations (neglecting obligations, breaking promises, not being attentive enough). Feeling guilty over one's partner's distress may therefore be endemic to close relationships. I call it "relationship guilt" because it is generated more by the relationship than by a particular act, and I count it as a type of virtual transgression because it is not based on an actual transgression but a presumed one.

Relationship guilt may be involved in the infant guilt. Infants cry and mothers run to take care of them. Infants get injured or ill, or hurt the mother (get a hand tangled in her hair and pull), and she responds with vocal, facial, or bodily expressions of pain or sorrow. Infants crawl, walk, or talk for the first time, and mothers express delight. These maternal responses and explicit statements of how important children are may create omnipotence feelings towards mothers. As a result, long before developing a "theory of mind" that enables them to infer the impact of their actions, infants may connect their actions to changes in mothers' moods through simple association. In this context, it is reasonable to expect the mother's sad expression or sobbing without a clear cause to be an ambiguous stimulus to infants, which, together with their undeveloped sense of agency (fuzzy awareness of causing/not causing things to happen), and their physical proximity to mothers may explain the emergence of infants' guilt over harming mothers: "Mother is sad; it must have been something I did".

What accounts for its phasing out, which happens around the end of the second year according to Zahn-Waxler et al.? I suggest it may be due to a confluence of two things: increasingly clear feedback from mothers, and children's cognitive development, especially their improved sense of agency. The increase in feedback clarity may be due to the shift in the primary emphasis of the parental role at the end of the second year from caretaker/nurturer to socializer/discipliner. Whereas few mother–infant interactions before 2 involve discipline attempts, by 2 years well over half of them do (Hoffman, 1975). After that, when children hurt their mothers a discipline encounter ensues in which mothers make it clear that the child hurt them. This contrasts sharply with those occasions in which mothers answer children's "Did I hurt you?" by assuring them they did not. The contrast should add to feedback clarity, and children's cognitive advancement and increasingly accurate sense of agency should help them grasp the difference.

If relationship guilt in infants ends by 2, then why should it show up in adults? My answer is that adult relationships involve peers and are multifaceted, unlike the single nurturer–nurturee-dimensioned mother–infant relationship. Consequently, the simple reassuring feedback that ends infant guilt may not work for adults. Adult relationship guilt is not due to an undeveloped sense of agency but, as dscussed, to adults' learning from experience about the subtle ways of hurting others that may not be apparent until long afterwards, the ways that words and deeds are misinterpreted, and the limitations of one's memory for past encounters that might explain their partner's distress. In sum, adult relationship guilt comes out of a complex web of interactions in which relationship partners are certain of their importance to the other but not of the cause of the other's emotional state at a given time. They are therefore as vulnerable to guilt when the other is distressed without a clear cause, as infants. Here are some examples.

A college student reported feeling "really down one day. My boyfriend was near crying and asked 'What did I do?' I said it's not your fault. He asked again. I said no, it's not your fault. He said, 'Then why are you so down?' I said I don't know but it's not your fault. He said 'I must have done something.' Another student: "My boyfriend seemed worried and I knew right away I must have done something. I asked what was the matter. He didn't know. Then I knew it must have been because he spent too much money on my birthday present." When people commit suicide, partners often feel guilty ("I should have known he was depressed"; "if only I had [or had not] . . .").

Developmental Guilt

If close relationships are the context for virtual transgressions featuring relationship guilt, societies like ours can make growing up and pursuing normal personal goals the context for virtual transgressions involving "developmental guilt": guilt over leaving home, achieving more than one's peers, or benefitting from privileges others lack.

Separation Guilt

Clinicians describe adolescents who are excited about leaving home but feel empathic distress and guilt when they think about it because it will pain their parents (Modell, 1963). Parents may contribute by telling children how important they are. A friend of mine's separation guilt drove him to turn down a top university for a local college (which he still regrets). His mother's saying she would not stand in his way though she would be unhappy if he left, did not help. Children may of course sense parents' anxiety even when they are less explicit.

Guilt over Achievement

A talented child draws a picture that attracts adult attention and wins praise and hugs. His peers look on dejectedly. When teachers start grading children on their performance relative to others, high performers soon realize their achievements make others feel inadequate. Adolescents may feel guilty if they are the first in their family or group to go to college, because they think it lowers the other's self-esteem (it could of course give them vicarious pride: "One of us made it."). The issue is "social comparison," which helps assess performance in the absence of objective standards. But it also tells children their success may lower their peers' self-esteem, and if they empathize they may feel guilty. There is no research on achievement guilt but one reason for "fear of success" found in the 1970s research on the topic was that it makes others feel like failures.

Guilt over Affluence

Older children and adolescents are sensitive to lifestyle differences based on affluence, and being more affluent than others is a potential source of guilt (Hoffman, 1989).

Some 1960s activists seem to have transformed empathic distress for society's disadvantaged into "guilt over affluence" when they became aware of the vast discrepancy between their good life and others' meagre existence; and "guilt by association" when they saw their social class as culpable (Keniston, 1968). A congressional intern expressed this clearly when asked why many middle-class youth were "turned off by the very system that gave them so many advantages and opportunities:

> They feel guilty because while they are enjoying this highest standard of living, American Indians are starving and black ghettoes are overrun by rats . . . This goes on while they eat steak every day. Their sense of moral indignation can't stand this; and they realize that the blame rests on the shoulders of their class. (*New Republic,* November 28, 1970).

Guilt over affluence relates to survivor and "existential" guilt (Hoffman, 1989). It may occur in adults but I class it with developmental guilt because it is more likely in adolescents and may be a significant part of their prosocial moral development.

MULTIPLE CLAIMANTS

In these dilemmas bystanders must choose which victims to help. Obvious examples are people drowning or caught in burning buildings. A less obvious but more familiar example is writing letters of recommendation for a favorite student. The moral claimants are the student who expects one's support, the colleagues who expect candid replies, and the unknown candidates who need the job. These dilemmas involve "caring," and one's motive to act on one or more claimants' behalf is based on empathy or the principle of caring, which is a generalized expression of the value of considering others (we are our brother's keeper; we must alleviate suffering). The moral issue is who one should help.

The scientific issue is who one does help. Evolutionary biology's answer is simple: those with whom one shares the most genes (Hamilton, 1971). Psychology's answer is complex: with single claimants one empathizes with most anyone in distress. With multiple claimants, one may empathize with them all but to a greater degree with those he knows and cares about (Costin & Jones, 1992), those who share his race, gender, or personality profile (Feshbach & Roe, 1968; Klein, 1971; Krebs, 1970), and those whose plight fits his own enduring concerns (Gruen & Mendelsohn, 1986; Houston, 1990).[5] These biases can be transcended when highly principled people are compelled to make life-and-death choices:

> "When asked how many of the Jewish people they helped were strangers, over 90% of the rescuers said at least one. Their universalist view of their ethical obligations sometimes put them in a tragic situation. When they could only choose one person to save, they struggled to find a guiding criterion. Should it be the doctor, the judge, or the poor

[5]By "empathize to a greater degree," I mean one's threshold for empathic distress is lower for these victims than for others.

uneducated person whose life promised little more than survival? The child, the aged, or the frail? This "playing God" with people's lives left its mark: choice itself violated the principle of universal responsibility, and guilt feelings continue to plague some of them as they reflect on the choices they made." (edited quotation from Oliner, 1988, p. 170).

These remarks show the agony of choosing among moral claimants in extreme situations, the fact that principled people who make sacrifices may feel guilt over victims they could not possibly help, and the importance of a transcending principle.

CARING VERSUS JUSTICE

The multiple claimant dilemmas so far lie within the empathy and caring domain: which person should one help? In caring-versus-justice dilemmas one must choose to act in accord with caring or justice. I will touch lightly on these dilemmas because of space limitations and the limited role of empathy-based guilt in them. For more detailed treatment see Hoffman (1990, in press).

Different caring-versus-justice dilemmas are possible, but the prototypic one and the one that interests me the most is the conflict between "caring" (we should help the needy; we are our brothers' keeper) and merit-based distributive justice (people should be rewarded for their output or competence). To illustrate, in the letter of recommendation example I described the writer's conflict about whether to mention his student's weaknesses, and his guilt towards the student if he mentions them, and towards his colleagues if he does not. Both of these outcomes exemplify empathy-based guilt, and the dilemma fits within the caring domain. He could try to resolve the conflict by empathizing with each moral claimant, imagining their distress if he writes a favorable or a candid letter, and feeling appropriate anticipatory guilt. He might then decide what to do on the basis of which claimant's distress would be greater, or what would cause him less guilt, or whether empathy for his student should override any concerns about his colleagues and the other job candidates.

But the writer's dilemma also has a justice component. The academic system places high value on merit (scholarly output and competence) and its integrity rests on recommenders' candid assessments of job applicants, which his colleagues expect. In other words, merit should determine who gets the job. This conflicts head-on with the writer's empathic concern for his student, especially if he believes the student may not be the most competent applicant. If he candidly reveals the student's weaknesses, in keeping with "justice," he violates "caring" and may feel empathy-based guilt over betraying the student. If empathy for the student prevails and he emphasizes the student's strengths and downplays weaknesses, he may not only feel empathy-based guilt over misleading his colleagues, but he may also feel guilt over violating "justice." The latter type of guilt may have little or no empathic base (Hoffman, 1990).

Similar issues are involved in promotion, tenure, and related decisions. An esteemed faculty member died and his wife, a part-time adjunct instructor with below-average teacher ratings, wanted to keep her job. "Caring" and "need" seemed to dictate allowing her to keep it, and some faculty took this position. But others argued that this would be unkind to students ("caring"), or immoral because we should only hire the best people available ("justice").

SUMMARY

Cutting across the varieties of empathy-based guilt are four guilt-arousing processes—processes by which empathic distress and self-blame combine to produce guilt feeling.

1. Arousal and integration of empathic distress and self-blame, driven by external intervention. This is the main guilt-arousal process in development of transgression guilt in children. The key intervention is inductive discipline, which both arouses empathic distress and makes the child aware of the harmful consequences of his action or contemplated action for others. This awareness transforms the empathic distress into guilt feeling.

2. Spontaneous arousal and integration of empathic distress and self-blame when one has harmed someone. This spontaneous empathy-based transgression guilt is the result of inductions continuing to do their job and becoming less necessary over time. Also contributing are advances in cognitive development that enable children spontaneously to feel guilt over the harmful consequences of inaction, and anticipatory guilt over the harmful consequences of actions they may be contemplating.

3. Spontaneous arousal and integration of empathic distress and self-blame, resulting from previous interaction with significant others and ambiguities in their current situation. This is the main process in relationship guilt, although there is an enormous difference in complexity between infants' guilt over distressing their mothers and guilt in relationships among adults.

4. Once the empathy-based transgression guilt becomes independent of the discipline encounters that gave rise to it and part of the child's own repertoire, it may add a feeling of being a transgressor component to the guilt he experiences over inaction in bystander encounters. This is because any guilt feeling, including guilt over inaction, may activate the Transgression → Guilt script. The same thing may happen when one feels relationship guilt, guilt over separation, guilt over achievement, guilt over affluence, or guilt over violating caring or justice principles that are in conflict.

In other words, some empathy-based transgression-guilt may always be experienced, in addition to the guilt feeling characteristic of each type of moral encounter, including those in which one has not committed a transgression.

REFERENCES

Baumeister, R. F., Stillwell, A. M., & Heatherton, T. F., (1994). Guilt: An interpersonal approach. *Psychological Bulletin, 115,* 243–267.
Baumeister, R. F., Stillwell, A. M., & Heatherton, T. F. (1995). Interpersonal aspects of guilt. In J. P. Tangney & K. W. Fischer (Eds.), *Self-conscious emotions: Shame, guilt, embarrassment, and pride* (pp. 255–273). New York: Guilford Press.
Bischoff-Kohler, D. (1991). The development of empathy in infants. In M. Lamb & M. Keller (Eds.), *Infant development: Perspectives from German-speaking countries* (pp. 245–273). Hillsdale, NJ: Erlbaum.
Chapman, M., & Zahn-Waxler, C. (1982). Young children's compliance and noncompliance to parental discipline in a natural setting. *International Journal of Behavior Development, 5,* 81–94.
Costin, S. E., & Jones, C. J. (1992). Friendship as a facilitator of emotional responsiveness and prosocial interventions among young children. *Developmental Psychology, 28,* 941–947.
Cummings, E. M., Hollenbeck, B., Iannotti, R., Radke-Yarrow, M., & Zahn-Waxler, C. (1986). Early organization of altruism and aggression: Developmental patterns and individual differences. In C. Zahn-Waxler, E. M. Cummings, & R. Iannotti (Eds.), *Altruism and aggression: Biological and social origins* (pp. 165–188). New York: Cambridge University Press.
Damon, W. (1977). *The social world of the child,* San Francisco: Jossey-Bass.
Eisenberg, N., & Miller, P. (1987). Relation of empathy to prosocial behavior. *Psychological Bulletin, 101,* 91–119.
Feshbach, N. D., & Roe, K. (1968). Empathy in six- and seven-year olds. *Child Development, 39,* 133–145.
Fiske, S. F. (1982). Schema-triggered affect: Applications to social perception. In M. S. Clark & S. T. Fiske (Eds.), *Affect and cognition: The 17th annual Carnegie symposium on cognition* (pp. 55–78). Hillsdale, NJ: Erlbaum.
Freud, S. (1961). Civilization and its discontents. In J. Strachey (Ed. and Trans.), *The standard edition of the complete psychological works of Sigmund Freud, Vol. 24* (pp. 59–145). London: Hogarth Press. (Originally published in 1930)
Gibbs, J. C. (1993). Moral-cognitive interventions. In A. P. Goldstein & C. R. Huff (Eds.), *The gang intervention handbook,* (pp. 159–185). Champaign, IL: Research Press.
Gnepp, J. C. (1989). Children's use of personal information to understand other people's feelings. In C. Saarni & P. L. Harris (Eds.), *Children's understanding of emotion* (pp. 151–177). New York: Cambridge.
Gnepp, J., & Gould, M. E. (1985). The development of personalized inferences: Understanding other people's emotional reactions in light of their prior experiences. *Child Development, 56,* 1455–1464.
Gruen, R., & Mendelsohn, G. (1986). *Journal of Personality and Social Psychology, 51,* 609–614.
Hamilton, W. D. (1971). Selection of selfish and altruistic behavior in some extreme models. In J. F. Eisenberg & W. F. Sillon (Eds.), *Man and beast: Comparative social behavior.* Washington, DC: Smithsonian Institution Press.
Hay, D. (1984). Social conflict in early childhood. *Annals of Child Development, 1,* 1–44.
Hoffman, M. L. (in press). *Empathy and moral development.* New York: Cambridge University Press.
Hoffman, M. L. (1963). Parent discipline and the child's consideration for others. *Child Development, 34,* 573–588.

Hoffman, M. L. (1970). Conscience, personality, and socialization techniques. *Human Development, 13,* 90–126.

Hoffman, M. L. (1975). Moral internalization, parental power, and the nature of parent–child interaction. *Developmental Psychology, 11,* 228–239.

Hoffman, M. L. (1978). Empathy, its development and prosocial implications. In C. B. Keasey (Ed.), *Nebraska Symposium on Motivation, 25,* 169–218.

Hoffman, M. L. (1981). Is altruism part of human nature? *Journal of Personality and Social Psychology, 40,* 121–137.

Hoffman, M. L. (1982). Development of prosocial motivation: Empathy and guilt. In N. Eisenberg-Berg (Ed.), *Development of Prosocial Behavior* (pp. 281–313). New York: Academic Press.

Hoffman, M. L. (1983). Affective and cognitive processes in moral internalization: An information processing approach. In E. T. Higgins, D. Ruble, & W. Hartup (Eds.), *Social cognition and social development: A socio-cultural perspective* (pp. 236–274). New York: Cambridge University Press.

Hoffman, M. L. (1984). Interaction of affect and cognition in empathy. In C. Izard, J. Kagan, & R. Zajonc (Eds.), *Emotions, cognition, and behavior* (pp. 103–131). New York: Cambridge University Press.

Hoffman, M. L. (1985). Affect, motivation, and cognition. In E. T. Higgins & R. M. Sorrentino (Eds.), *Handbook of motivation and cognition: Foundations of social behavior* (pp. 244–280). New York: Guilford.

Hoffman, M. L. (1988). Moral development. In M. Lamb & M. Bornstein (Eds.), *Developmental psychology: An advanced textbook.* (2nd ed.) (pp. 497–548). Hillsdale, NJ: Erlbaum.

Hoffman, M. L. (1989). Empathy and prosocial activism. In N. Eisenberg, J. Reykowski, & E. Staub (Eds.), *Social and moral values: Individual and societal perspectives* (pp. 65–86). Hillsdale, NJ: Erlbaum.

Hoffman, M. L. (1990). Empathy and justice motivation. *Motivation and Emotion, 4,* 151–172.

Hoffman, M. L. (1991). Toward an integration: Commentary. *Human Development, 34,* 105–110.

Hoffman, M. L., & Saltzstein, H. D. (1967). Parent discipline and the child's moral development. *Journal of Personality and Social Psychology, 5,* 45–57.

Houston, D. A. (1990). Empathy and the Self: Cognitive and Emotional Influences on the Evaluation of Negative Affect in Others. *Journal of Personality and Social Psychology, 59,* 859.

Keniston, K. (1968). *Young radicals.* New York: Harcourt.

Klein, R. (1971). Some factors influencing empathy in six- and seven-year-old children varying in ethnic background (Doctoral dissertation, University of California, Los Angeles, 1970). *Dissertation Abstracts International, 31,* 3960A. (University Microfilms No. 71-3862)

Kochanska, G. (1995). Children's temperament, mother's discipline, and security of attachment: Multiple pathways to emerging internalization. *Child Development, 66,* 597–615.

Krebs, D. L. (1970). Empathy and altruism. *Journal of Personality and Social Psychology, 32,* 1124–1146.

Krevans, J., & Gibbs, J. C. (1996). Parents' use of inductive discipline: Relations to children's empathy and prosocial behavior. *Child Development. 67,* 3263–3277.

Levine, L. J. (1995). Young children's understanding of the causes of anger and sadness. *Child Development, 66,* 697–709.

Londerville, S., & Main, M. (1981). Security of attachment, compliance, and maternal training methods in the second year of life. *Developmental Psychology, 17,* 289–199.

Midlarsky, E., & Hannah, M. E. (1985). Competence, reticence, and helping by children and adolescents. *Developmental Psychology, 21,* 534–541.

Modell, A. H. (1963). On having the right to a life: An aspect of the superego's development. *International Journal of Psychoanalysis, 46,* 323–331.

Nelson, K. (1981). Social cognition in a script framework. In J. H. Flavell & L. Ross (Eds.), *Social cognitive development* (pp. 92–118). Cambridge: Cambridge University Press.

Oliner, S. P., & Oliner, P. M. (1988). *The altruistic personality.* New York: The Free Press.

UNAVAILABLE. *New Republic,* November 28, 1970.

Ross, H., Tesla, C., Kenyon, B., & Lollis, S. (1990). Maternal intervention in toddler peer conflict. The socialization of principles of justice. *Developmental Psychology, 26,* 994–1003.

Smetana, J. G. (1989). Toddler's social interactions in the context of moral and conventional transgression in the home. *Developmental Psychology, 25,* 499–508.

Staub, E. (1996). Responsibility, helping, aggression, and evil. *Psychological Inquiry, 7,* 252.

Strayer, J. (1993). Children's concordant emotions and cognitions in response to observed emotions. *Child Development, 64,* 188–201.

Tangney, J. (1991). Moral affect: The good, the bad, and the ugly. *Journal of Personality and Social Psychology, 61,* 598–607.

Tangney, J., & Fischer, K. (1995). *Self-conscious emotions: Shame, guilt, embarrassment, and pride.* New York: Guilford.

Tangney, J. P., Marschall, D., Rosenberg, K., Barlow, D. H., & Wagner, P. (1996). *Children's and adult's autobiographical accounts of shame, guilt, and pride experiences.* Unpublished manuscript, George Mason University, Fairfax, VA.

Tangney, J. P., Wagner, P. E., Burggraf, S. A., & Fletcher, C. (1991, June). *Children's shame-proneness, but not guilt-proneness, is related to emotional and behavioral maladjustment.* Poster presented at the meeting of the American Psychological Society, Washington, D.C.

Thompson, R. & Hoffman, M. L. (1980). Empathy and the development of guilt in children. *Developmental Psychology, 16,* 155–156.

Tulving, E. (1972). Episodic and semantic memory. In E. Tulving & W. Donaldson (Eds.), *Organization of memory* (pp. 301–403). New York: Academic Press.

Weiner, B. (1985). "Spontaneous" causal thinking. *Psychological Bulletin, 97,* 74–84.

Wilson, B. J., & Cantor, J. (1985). *Journal of Experimental Child Psychology, 39,* 284–299.

Wright, H. F. (1967). *Recording and analyzing child behavior.* New York Harper & Row.

Zahn-Waxler, C., Radke-Yarrow, M., & King, R. (1979). Childrearing and children's prosocial initiations toward victims of distress. *Child Development, 50,* 319–330.

Zahn-Waxler, C., Robinson, J. L., & Emde, N. E. (1992). The development of empathy in twins. *Developmental Psychology, 28,* 1038–1047.

CHAPTER 5

The Emergence of Gender Differences in Guilt during Adolescence

Jane Bybee

Northeastern University, Boston, Massachusetts

Eleanor Maccoby, speaking 15 years later of her now classic book, *The psychology of sex differences* (Maccoby & Jacklin, 1974), notes:

> [T]here were very few attributes on which the average values for the two sexes differed consistently. Furthermore, even when consistent differences were found, the amount of variance accounted for by sex was small. . . . In my judgment, the conclusions are still quite similar to those Jacklin and I arrived at in 1974: There are still some replicable sex differences, of moderate magnitude, in performance on tests of mathematical and spatial abilities. . . . When it comes to attributes in the personality-social domain, results are particularly sparse and inconsistent (Maccoby, 1990).

One individual difference variable that does vary substantially and consistently across sex is the proclivity for guilt. From adolescence onward, studies repeatedly indicate that females compared to males are more strongly predisposed to various forms of guilt (e.g., Evans, 1984; Harder & Zalma, 1990; Merisca & Bybee, 1994; Quiles & Bybee, 1997; Tangney, 1990). What makes these findings all the more intriguing is that many of the strongest correlates of guilt—internalizing disorders, aggression, criminality, empathy and nurturing behavior, and academic achievement—also differ strongly across sex. Disorders linked with more guilt (such as depression and eating disturbances) are more prevalent among women compared to

Guilt and Children
Copyright © 1998 by Academic Press. All rights of reproduction in any form reserved.

men (Bybee, Zigler, Berliner, & Merisca, 1996; Zahn-Waxler, Cole, & Barrett, 1991). Competencies (such as scholastic achievement and caregiving) associated with a greater proclivity for guilt are likewise more evident among females than males (Merisca & Bybee, 1994). Conversely, aggression and criminality are associated with a relative absence of guilt and are less prevalent among women compared to men (Merisca & Bybee, 1994; Persons, 1970; Ruma & Mosher, 1967; Tangney, Wagner, Fletcher, & Gramzow, 1992a; Wilson & Herrnstein, 1984). Researchers have suggested that gender differences in guilt may explain, in part, disparities across sex in the prevalence of certain mental illnesses and important social behaviors (Zahn-Waxler et al., 1991).

Yet gender differences in guilt have often been ignored. With a few notable exceptions (e.g., Zahn-Waxler et al., 1991; Zahn-Waxler & Robinson, 1995; Zahn-Waxler & Kochanska, 1990), there has been little recent theoretical work on gender differences in guilt and a number of empirical studies neither discuss or assess effects of gender (e.g., Tangney, Wagner, & Gramzow, 1992b; Baumeister, Stillwell, & Heatherton, 1995). One factor that may have stymied research efforts is that previous conceptualizations of gender differences in guilt such as those contained in the psychoanalytic literature and particularly the influential works of Helen Block Lewis (e.g., 1979a, 1979b) have proved to be wrong. According to the psychoanalytic view, females compared to males do not develop as strong or exacting a superego and are less prone to guilt (Freud, 1925/1961; Lewis, 1979a, 1979b). Research findings typically fall in a direction opposite of these suppositions.

OVERVIEW

Why do women compared to men have a higher proclivity for guilt? As discussed later, gender differences in guilt intensity and frequency are not consistent among young children. Clear differences across sex apparently emerge around puberty. From adolescence onward, females are consistently more prone to guilt than are males.

During adolescence, guilt becomes less intense, and drops more precipitously for males than females (Williams & Bybee, 1994b). Traditional wisdom holds that the processes of socialization, the pressures of civilization, and the move toward internalization of mores and standards result in more moral, responsible thoughts and actions with development. Yet according to Zahn-Waxler and Robinson (1995, p. 163), "The notion of increased morality with age may reflect as much developmental myth as fact." During adolescence, for example, crime rates increase dramatically (Wilson & Herrnstein, 1984). Indicators of irresponsible, self-injurious behaviors such as alcohol and drug abuse and noncompliance to medical regimes skyrocket (Achenbach & Edelbrock, 1981; Bybee, Leckman, Lavietes, & Tamborlane, 1991). Against this backdrop, findings that guilt does not increase in intensity during adolescence, but rather declines markedly (Williams & Bybee, 1994b) appear less counterintuitive. Age-related decreases in guilt intensity are found for both sexes, but seem to be more pronounced among males (Williams &

Bybee, 1994b). In order to interpret these findings, we must consider the possibility that forces, both internal and external to the individual, may act to alleviate, offset, or desensitize adolescents to experiences of guilt.

What precipitates the decrease in guilt around puberty and why is the decline apparently steeper for males than for females? Gender differences do not appear solely in the intensity of guilt, but are evident also in what children feel guilty about, who makes them feel guilty, and how they react to guilt-producing situations. These gender differences receive attention first in our review. Males are more likely than females to mention feeling guilt over aggression. Guilt over aggression declines with development for both sexes. Peers and parents alike tolerate aggressive behavior among boys and do little to induce feelings of guilt among males. Peers are less likely to judge males (compared to females) as blameworthy. Moreover, males' reactions to guilt-producing events are generally effective in alleviating feelings of guilt. In sum, these influences may result in an age-related decline in guilt among males.

In contrast, females are more likely than males to mention feeling guilty about inconsiderate and dishonest behavior. Males and females both report more guilt over inconsiderate and dishonest behavior with development. Peers and parents alike are condemning of transgressions among females, hold girls to higher standards than boys, and actively attempt to make young females feel guilty over lapses. Furthermore, prototypical female reactions (such as rumination and admission of blameworthiness) prolong and intensity feelings of guilt. These factors may, in combination, dull or offset age-related declines in guilt. Sex differences are now reviewed in more detail.

Gender Differences in What Males Versus Females Feel Guilty About

According to Williams and Bybee (1994a), a greater percentage of female compared to male adolescents mention guilt over lying and inconsiderate behavior. Similarly, among undergraduates, Tangney (1992) finds that women compared to men are more likely to mention guilt over lying.

In contrast, males are more likely to feel guilty over aggressive, boisterous activities. A greater proportion of males, compared to females, mention guilt over property damage, fighting, and victimizing animals (Williams & Bybee, 1994a). Among adults, men are more likely than women to mention guilt over not helping others (Tangney, 1992).

Gender Differences in Who Makes Males Versus Females Feel Guilty

Compared to males, females more frequently mention guilt arising in the context of close interpersonal relationships. A greater percentage of females compared to males mention family members when describing guilt-producing incidents. Females are more likely than males to mention parents as a source of guilt (Williams & Bybee, 1994a). Moreover, extended family members are mentioned three times as frequently by females as compared to males (Williams & Bybee, 1994a).

Males, in contrast, are more likely to mention guilt involving people with whom they are superficially involved. Males are twice as likely as females to mention casual acquaintances and adults who are not relatives when describing guilt-producing incidents (Williams & Bybee, 1994a).

Gender Differences in How Individuals React to Guilt-Producing Incidents

Females are more likely to admit culpability. Females compared to males offer more numerous and complex concessions for wrongdoing (Gonzales, Manning, & Haugen, 1992, Studies 1 & 2). Females also ruminate more over wrongdoing (Lyubomirsky & Nolen-Hoeksema, 1993). Such responses may prolong and intensify feelings of guilt.

When asked to account for misbehavior, males compared to females are more likely to fabricate lies (Gonzales et al., 1992). Denial may serve to minimize feelings of guilt.

Gender Differences in How Guilty Peers Believe Males Versus Females Should Feel

Peers hold females more accountable for their actions. Among 5th, 8th, and 11th graders, females compared to males believe same-sex peers should feel more guilt over lapses (Williams & Bybee, 1994b).

DEVELOPMENTAL CHANGES IN THE INTENSITY AND FREQUENCY OF GUILT

Researchers who have assessed developmental changes in the intensity and frequency of guilt feelings have uncovered a complex developmental path. Developmentalists generally acknowledge that guilt feelings first emerge around age 2 when the child becomes aware of another's distress and cognizant that they themselves are the source of that distress (e.g., Hoffman, 1978). From this time onward through grade school, guilt feelings apparently become more frequent and intense. During adolescence, however, guilt feelings become less intense. Finally, as individuals approach and pass through adulthood, guilt feelings may again increase in intensity.

Guilt Increases during Childhood

In one longitudinal study of children tested at 14, 20, and 24 months, mothers were asked to rate the prevalence of guilt feelings among their children over the past week (Zahn-Waxler, Robinson, & Emde, 1992). Guilt became significantly more prevalent with age. From the second to third year of life, Stipek, Gralinski, and Kopp (1990) likewise report an increase in children's behaviors indicative of remorse as rated by the mother.

In a sample of first, third, and fifth graders, Thompson and Hoffman (1980) gave children stories describing experiences a child might commonly encounter such as neglecting to help after an accident, taking another child's toys, or cheating at checkers. Children were asked to assume the role of the harm doer and to describe how much guilt they would feel to provide a measure of guilt intensity. Children's explanations of why they felt the way they did and whether or not they would feel differently if the act remained undetected were used to derive a measure of concern for the victim and to assess the justice principles used. Thompson and Hoffman found more intense guilt, greater concern for the victim's welfare, and more frequent use of internal principles of right and wrong among older children.

Finally, Zahn-Waxler and her colleagues (Chapman, Zahn-Waxler, Iannotti, & Cooperman, 1987; Zahn-Waxler, Kochanska, Krupnick & McKnew, 1990) presented children, ranging in age from 4 to 10, with hypothetical situations of interpersonal distress and conflict and assessed children's spontaneous comments and responses to probe questions. Results consistently indicated age-related increases in the mean number of guilt themes expressed by children of nondepressed mothers.

Guilt Declines during Adolescence

In pointed contrast to studies among children, studies consistently indicate that guilt feelings become less intense during adolescence. In two samples of inner-city youth, older compared to younger adolescents were less likely to indicate that they themselves would feel guilty in reaction to guilt-evoking incidents described in a series of vignettes (Bybee, Merisca, & Zigler, 1995). Students were also less likely at older age levels to indicate that same-sex others should feel guilty. Similarly, among both urban and suburban 5th, 8th, and 11th graders, there were significant declines with grade in personality proclivity for guilt, though effects varied across gender and apparently leveled off and even increased from the 8th to the 11th grade for certain subgroups (Bybee & Williams, 1997).

Guilt May Increase from Young to Middle Adulthood

Guilt increased in intensity from the 8th to the 11th grades among urban females (Bybee & Williams, 1997). Similarly, a recently completed study by Bybee, Zielonka, and Mayne (1997) points to a positive correlation between age and guilt among both heterosexual and homosexual men in their twenties and thirties.

THE EMERGENCE OF GENDER DIFFERENCES IN THE INTENSITY OF GUILT

Before adolescence, males and females do not consistently differ in the intensity of feelings of guilt. Indeed, several studies point to higher levels of guilt among males than among females among young children. Among 2-year-olds, for example, more boys than girls are classified as amenders, a group showing guilt-type reactions (Barrett, Zahn-Waxler, & Cole, 1993). Thompson and Hoffman (1980) find more intense guilt among boys than girls in their sample of 1st, 3rd, and 5th graders.

In a slightly older sample of students from grades 4 through 7, however, Perry, Perry, and Weiss (1989) find girls compared to boys expect more guilt from behaving aggressively, findings that replicated earlier results from Perry, Perry, and Rasmussen (1986). It is unclear whether findings from the Perry et al. (1986, 1989) studies should be interpreted as reflective of a developmental shift in gender differences in guilt from the early to late elementary school years or whether they are indicative of inconsistencies in gender differences prior to adolescence.

From adolescence onward, it is clear that females compared to males consistently report more guilt. Two studies indicate more state guilt among females. Buss and Brock (1963) find that, among college students, women compared to men report more guilt in reaction to administering electric shocks. Females also report more state guilt than males on a pen-and-pencil inventory (Kugler & Jones, 1992). These studies indicate that the phenomenological or affective experience of guilt is apparently more pronounced among females.

Females are more prone to predispositional guilt than are males. In other words, females compared to males more often report feeling guilt in response to eliciting events. Gender differences are found among college students (Evans, 1984; Merisca & Bybee, 1994; Quiles & Bybee, 1997), adolescents with Type I diabetes (Bybee et al., 1991), and urban and suburban 5th through 11th graders (Bybee & Williams, 1997) on the Mosher scales and derivatives. Similarly, females score higher than males on predispositional guilt assessed by other measures in both adolescent and adult samples (Harder, Cutler, & Rockart, 1992; Tangney, 1990).

Females score higher than males on indices of chronic guilt in college samples (Harder & Zalma, 1990; Quiles & Bybee, 1997). Differences in chronic, ongoing, unalleviated forms of guilt, however, appear to be less robust than gender differences in other forms of guilt. No gender differences in chronic guilt are reported by Harder et al. (1992) or by Kugler and Jones (1992).

Using vignettes containing guilt-evoking situations, females compared to males also indicate they would feel more intense guilt (Williams & Bybee, 1994b). Gender differences were apparent when the precipitating situation involved an incident and were less apparent when failure to attain an ideal or inequity was involved.

WHY MIGHT GENDER DIFFERENCES IN THE INTENSITY OF GUILT EMERGE WITH DEVELOPMENT?

Nine possible explanations for gender differences in guilt intensity are as follows:

1. *Males, because they commit a greater number of aggressive acts, may become more inured to resultant experiences of guilt.* As reviewed earlier, males compared to females are more likely to mention aggressive events as guilt-producing. Males' greater proclivity for physical aggression and criminal behavior has been well established (e.g., Eagly & Steffen, 1986; Maccoby & Jacklin, 1974). The question, then, becomes do males feel *more* guilt than females because of their greater proclivity for aggressiveness or do they feel *less* guilt because they become used to aggressing against others and develop defenses that neutralize feelings of guilt?

The presumption of psychoanalytic theorists is that male's greater proclivity for aggressive or immoral behavior will result in greater guilt. According to Helen Block Lewis (1979a, 1979b), two major factors conjoin to predispose men to greater guilt. First, young boys' anaclitic identification with and emulation of their mother are, with resolution of the Oedipal complex, superceded by defensive identification with the father (Lewis, 1979b). Renunciation of anaclitic identifications, according to the psychoanalytic perspective, leads males to become more aggressive and to experience more early guilt (Horney, 1932). Secondly, according to Lewis (1979a), males are forced into aggressive behavior in order to successfully earn a livelihood in competitive economic systems. According to Lewis, men have more opportunities for moral transgression because of their more direct participation in the workplace and are more likely to commit transgressions because they are under greater pressure to make money. Implicit in both of these conceptualizations is the assumption that males' greater aggression will result in more guilt. It is possible that the greater early aggressiveness of males compared to females provides a partial explanation for findings such as those of Thompson and Hoffman (1980) that young males compared to females are more prone to guilt. Young boys who, compared to young girls, transgress more often may experience guilt more frequently and perhaps more intensely.

Among adults, however, guilt is not proportionate to wrongdoing. Consider the following passage from Brown's (1957) classic text, *Social Psychology*.

> If everyone had the same sort of conscience, same in content and in severity, then each man should feel guilt proportionate to his wickedness. We know they do not do so. People who are as harmless as anyone can be may, nevertheless, sink into a guilty depression. On the other hand, psychopaths can murder and torture without suffering guilt.

Guilt is not directly proportionate to wickedness and so consciences must vary in content and in severity. Freud has even proposed, in *Civilization and its Discontents* (1930), that guilt is inversely related to wickedness: "The more righteous a man is, the stricter and more suspicious will his conscience be, so that ultimately it is precisely those people who have carried holiness farthest who reproach themselves with the deepest sinfulness" (p. 114). Why should this be so? Reverse the order of Freud's statements and you take away all their surprise— "The stricter and more suspicious a man's conscience is, the more righteous will he be." Of course.

Individuals who commit more aggressive acts (compared to individuals who rarely commit such transgressions) may become more inured to resultant feelings of discomfort and guilt. With advancements in cognitive reasoning, adolescents may be better able to justify and excuse immoral or substandard actions, thereby minimizing feelings of guilt (see Bybee, Merisca, & Velasco, chapter 9, this volume). Males, who compared to females more often commit aggressive acts, may develop an arsenal of rationalizations over time for misbehavior.

2. *Males may be less likely than females to punish themselves with guilt feelings for aggression because they are more likely to see aggressive behavior as normative for their gender.* Aggression is more common among males and more likely to be seen as part of the males' sex-role stereotype (Perry et al., 1989). Children are more likely to punish themselves for antisocial acts when they believe few of their peers would behave the same (Perry, Perry, Bussey, English, & Arnold, 1980).

3. *From infancy onward, males compared to females are viewed less negatively for commiting acts of aggression.* Research findings indicate that parents and peers alike treat male aggressors less harshly than female aggressors. One observational study of 3- and 6-month-old infants indicates that mothers react to anger expressions by girls in a negative manner (by frowning, for instance), whereas mothers react to anger expressions by boys in an empathetic manner (Malatesta & Haviland, 1982). Aggression is likewise more readily tolerated by parents of boys compared to parents of girls (Condrey & Ross, 1985). Observational data examining toddlers also indicate that mothers of girls compared to boys are more likely to require their child to relinquish toys to their peers (Ross, Tesla, Kenyon, & Lollis, 1990). Among 2-year-olds, observational data indicate that mothers of girls compared to boys are more likely to use other-oriented reasoning, pointing out the harmful consequences of aggressive behavior (Smetana, 1989). Among elementary school-aged children, boys expect less parental disapproval than do girls for aggression, at least for aggression provoked by other males (Perry et al., 1989).

Similarly, boys expect less peer disapproval and rejection than do girls for aggression aimed at same-sex peers (Boldizar, Perry, & Perry, 1989; Perry et al., 1986). Further, when 5th-, 8th-, and 11th graders are asked to judge the blameworthiness of same-sex peers in a series of vignettes involving transgressions, inactions, and other lapses, females are judged more severely than are males (Williams & Bybee, 1994b).

4. In addition, among adolescents, *boys expect more tangible rewards than do girls for aggression aimed at same-sex peers* (Perry et al., 1986). Males are also more likely than girls to believe that aggression will serve to increase the self-esteem of the

perpetrator (Slaby & Guerra, 1988). Boys are also less likely to expect negative self-evaluation, upset, and guilt after committing an aggressive act (Boldizar et al., 1989; Perry et al., 1989).

5. *With development during childhood and adolescence, externalizing behaviors and aggression become less prevalent* (Achenbach & Edelbrock, 1981; Zahn-Waxler et al., 1991). Males are more likely than females to mention aggressive, boisterous acts as precipitators of guilt (Williams & Bybee, 1994a). Thus, the very events—acts of aggression—that males compared to females more frequently mention as precipitators of guilt decline with age. Moreover, with development, adolescents of both sexes express less guilt over aggressive, boisterous acts (Williams & Bybee, 1994a).

6. Conversely, several developmental changes may converge that offset tendencies toward decline in levels of guilt among females. *Around adolescence, internalizing symptoms and disorders increase and this rise is much more pronounced for females than for males* (Achenbach & Edelbrock, 1981). Increased feelings of self-blame and self-hatred, characteristic internalizing symptoms, may be manifested in greater feelings of guilt among females.

7. *Parental discipline techniques vary across gender.* Parents act to encourage girls to feel guilty. Parents are more likely to use induction with girls than with boys (Hoffman, 1975) and to point out the consequences of the child's actions for others (Smetana, 1989), discipline techniques that elicit empathy, a response closely linked with guilt.

8. *Although the prevalence of lying and inconsiderate behaviors declines with development (Achenbach & Edelbrock, 1981; Berndt, 1981), both males and females are more likely to feel guilt over these behaviors at higher age levels (Williams & Bybee, 1994a).* Females are more likely than are males to mention feeling guilty over lying and inconsiderate behavior as mentioned earlier. Thus, the events that females compared to males more often mention as guilt-evoking become more common sources of guilt for both sexes with development.

9. *Females may be more likely than males to punish themselves with guilt feelings for inconsiderate behavior because they are less likely to see insensitivity as normative for their gender.* Nurturing, caregiving behavior is part of the female sex-role stereotype (Zahn-Waxler et al., 1991). Inconsiderate, disingenuous behavior is not, then, normative behavior for females, but instead runs counter to the sex-role stereotype. As mentioned earlier, individuals are particularly likely to punish themselves for behaviors they believe to be nonnormative (Perry et al., 1980).

CONCLUSIONS

In sum, then, males and females differ not only in the intensity of guilt feelings from adolescence onward, but in what and who causes them to feel guilty. Males are more likely to feel guilt about aggressive behaviors and in the presence of strangers. Aggressiveness is seen as normative for males and parents and peers alike may tolerate this type of behavior. Males are more likely than females to deny culpability for their actions and are less likely to experience ongoing, unalleviated feelings of guilt. Males feel less intense guilt with development during adolescence.

In contrast, females are more likely to feel guilt about inconsiderate behavior and around family members. Inconsiderateness is seen as nonnormative for females, and females may be especially harsh in punishing themselves for misbehavior that runs counter to sex-role stereotypes. Guilt over inconsiderate behavior becomes more prevalent with development for females (as well as for males). Peers hold females compared to males more accountable for their actions. Parents likewise are less tolerant of misbehavior among females than males and are more likely to use discipline techniques with daughters that lead to guilt. Females compared to males are more willing to concede responsibility for misdeeds and apparently have more difficulty expelling feelings of guilt as evidenced by their higher scores on chronic guilt.

Females' greater proclivity for guilt may be both a blessing and a curse. Chronic feelings of guilt, unchannelled and unresolved, may provide an ongoing source of self-degradation, serve as an endless reminder of the failing that evoked the emotion, and may be a precipitating factor in the development of depression and eating disorders (Bybee et al., 1996; Harder et al., 1992; Quiles & Bybee, 1997). In turn, perceived inadequacies inherent in depression and eating-related disturbances (such as purging and starvation) and attendant attributional patterns may fuel feelings of guilt. Yet the high levels of guilt found among females may also be of benefit. Guilt may provide a powerful deterrent and punishment for past wrongdoings and may interrupt ongoing action sequences midstream and redirect them (Baumeister, Stillwell, & Heatherton, 1994; Bybee & Zigler, 1991; Merisca & Bybee, 1994). A greater predisposition for guilt may play a role in enabling women to inhibit aggressive behavior, engage in more nurturing behavior and caregiving, and exhibit more conscientious behavior in the classroom. Statements about causal relationships remain speculative. Nonetheless, the pronounced gender differences in various forms of guilt stand in contrast to the meager yield of gender differences in most social-personality variables. The strong relationships of guilt to mental illnesses and social behaviors that show pronounced differences across sex are intriguing.

REFERENCES

Achenbach, T. M., & Edelbrock, C. S. (1981). Behavioral problems and competencies reported by parents of normal and disturbed children aged four through sixteen. *Monographs of the Society for Research in Child Development, 46* (1, Serial No. 188).

Barrett, K. C., Zahn-Waxler, C., & Cole, P. M. (1993). Avoiders vs. amenders: Implications for the investigation of shame during toddlerhood? *Cognition and Emotion, 7,* 481–505.

Baumeister, R. F., Stillwell, A. M., & Heatherton, T. F. (1994). Guilt: An interpersonal approach. *Psychological Bulletin, 115,* 243–267.

Baumeister, R. F., Stillwell, A. M., & Heatherton, T. F. (1995). Personal narratives about guilt: Role in action control and interpersonal relationships. *Basic and Applied Social Psychology, 17,* 173–198.

Berndt, T. J. (1981). Age changes and changes over time in prosocial intentions and behavior between friends. *Developmental Psychology, 17,* 408–416.

Boldizar, J. P., Perry, D. G., & Perry, L. C. (1989). Outcome values and aggression. *Child Development, 60,* 571–579.

Brown, R. (1957). *Social psychology.* New York: Free Press.

Buss, A. H., & Brock, T. C. (1963). Repression and guilt in relation to aggression. *Journal of Abnormal and Social Psychology, 66,* 345–350.

Bybee, J. A., Leckman, J. F., Lavietes, S., & Tamborlane, W. (1991, April). *Guilt, depressive symptoms, and the quality of diabetic adherence among adolescents with Insulin-Dependent Diabetes Mellitus.* Paper presented at the Annual Meeting of the Eastern Psychological Association. New York, NY.

Bybee, J., Merisca, R., & Zigler, E. (1995, August). *Developmental, situational, and gender differences in the intensity of guilt reactions.* Poster presented at the Annual Meeting of the American Psychological Society. New York, NY.

Bybee, J. A., & Williams, C. (1997). *When is guilt adaptive? Relationships to prosocial behavior, academic and social strivings, and mental health.* Manuscript submitted for publication, Northeastern University, Boston, MA.

Bybee, J., Zielonka, E., & Mayne, T. (1997). *Guilt and shame among heterosexual and homosexual men: Relationships to sexual behavior and mental health.* Unpublished manuscript, Northeastern University, Boston, MA.

Bybee, J. A., & Zigler, E. (1991). The self-image and guilt: A further test of the cognitive-developmental formulation. *Journal of Personality, 59,* 733–745.

Bybee, J. A., Zigler, E., Berliner, D., & Merisca, R. (1996). Guilt, guilt-evoking events, depression and eating disorders. *Current Psychology: Developmental, Learning, Personality, Social, 15,* 113–127.

Chapman, M., Zahn-Waxler, C., Iannotti, R., & Cooperman, G. (1987). Empathy and responsibility in the motivation of children's helping. *Developmental Psychology, 23,* 140–145.

Condrey, J. C., & Ross, D. F. (1985). Sex and aggression: The influence of gender label on the perception of aggression in children. *Child Development, 51,* 943–967.

Eagly, A. H., & Steffen, V. J. (1986). Gender and aggressive behavior: A meta-analytic review of the social-psychological literature. *Psychological Bulletin, 100,* 309–330.

Evans, R. G. (1984). Hostility and sex guilt: Perceptions of self and others as a function of gender and sex-role orientation. *Sex Roles, 10,* 207–215.

Freud, S. (1958). *Civilization and its discontents.* New York: Doubleday Anchor. (Original work published 1930).

Freud, S. (1961). Some psychical consequences of the anatomical distinction between the sexes. In J. Strachy (Ed. and Trans.), *The standard edition of the complete psychological works of Sigmund Freud* (Vol. 19). London: Hogarth Press. (Original work published 1925).

Gonzales, M. H., Manning, D. J., & Haugen, J. A. (1992). Explaining our sins: Factors influencing offender accounts and anticipated victim responses. *Journal of Personality and Social Psychology, 62,* 958–971.

Harder, D. W., Cutler, L., & Rockart, L. (1992). Assessment of shame and guilt and their relationships to psychopathology. *Journal of Personality Assessment, 59,* 584–604.

Harder, D. W., & Zalma, A. (1990). Two promising shame and guilt scales: A construct validity comparison. *Journal of Personality Assessment, 55,* 729–745.

Hoffman, M. L. (1975). Sex differences in moral internalization and values. *Journal of Personality and Social Psychology, 32,* 720–729.

Hoffman, M. L. (1978). Toward a theory of empathic arousal and development. In M. Lewis & L. Rosenblum (Eds.), *The development of affect, Genesis of Behavior, Vol. 1* (pp. 205–226). New York: Plenum.

Horney, K. (1932). The dread of women. *International Journal of Psychoanalysis, 13,* 348–361.

Kugler, K., & Jones, W. H. (1992). On conceptualizing and assessing guilt. *Journal of Personality and Social Psychology, 62,* 318–327.

Lewis, H. B. (1979a). Shame in depression and hysteria. In C. E. Izard (Ed.), *Emotions in personality and psychopathology* (pp. 371–396). New York: Plenum.

Lewis, H. B. (1979b). Guilt in obsession and paranoia. In C. E. Izard (Ed.), *Emotions in personality and psychopathology* (pp. 399–414). New York: Plenum.

Lyubomirsky, S., & Nolen-Hoeksema, S. (1993). Self-perpetuating properties of dysphoric rumination. *Journal of Personality and Social Psychology, 65,* 339–349.

Maccoby, E. E. (1990). Gender and relationships: A developmental account. *American Psychologist, 45,* 513–520.

Maccoby, E. E., & Jacklin, C. N. (1974). *The psychology of sex differences.* Stanford, CA: Stanford University Press.

Malatesta, C. Z., & Haviland, J. (1982). Learning display rules: The socialization of emotion expression in infancy. *Child Development, 53,* 991–1003.

Merisca, R., & Bybee, J. A. (1994, April). *Guilt, not moral reasoning, relates to volunteerism, prosocial behavior, lowered aggressiveness, and eschewal of racism.* Poster presented at the Annual Meeting of the Eastern Psychological Association, Providence, Rhode Island.

Perry, D. G., Perry, L. C., Bussey, K., English, D., & Arnold, G. (1980). Processes of attribution and children's self-punishment following misbehavior. *Child Development, 51,* 545–551.

Perry, D. G., Perry, L. C., & Rasmussen, P. (1986). Cognitive social learning mediators of aggression. *Child Development, 57,* 700–711.

Perry, D. G., Perry, L. C., & Weiss, R. J. (1989). Sex differences in the consequences that children anticipate for aggression. *Developmental Psychology, 25,* 312–319.

Persons, R. W. (1970). Intermittent reinforcement, guilt, and crime. *Psychological Reports, 26,* 421–422.

Quiles, Z., & Bybee, J. (1997). Chronic and predispositional guilt: Relations to mental health, prosocial behavior, and religiosity. *Journal of Personality Assessment, 69,* 104–126.

Ross, H., Tesla, C., Kenyon, B., & Lollis, S. (1990). Maternal intervention in toddler peer conflict: The socialization of principles of justice. *Developmental Psychology, 26,* 994–1003.

Ruma, E. H., & Mosher, D. L. (1967). Relationship between moral judgment and guilt in delinquent boys. *Journal of Abnormal Psychology, 72,* 122–127.

Slaby, R. G., & Guerra, N. G. (1988). Cognitive mediators of aggression in adolescent offenders: 1. Assessment. *Developmental Psychology, 24,* 580–588.

Smetana, J. G. (1989). Toddlers' social interactions in the context of moral and conventional transgressions in the home. *Developmental Psychology, 25,* 499–509.

Stipek, D. J., Gralinski, J. H., & Kopp, C. B. (1990). Self-concept development in the toddler years. *Developmental Psychology, 26,* 972–977.

Tangney, J. P. (1990). Assessing individual differences in proneness to shame and guilt: Development of the Self-Conscious Affect and Attribution Inventory. *Journal of Personality and Social Psychology, 59,* 102–111.

Tangney, J. P. (1992). Situational determinants of shame and guilt in young adulthood. *Personality and Social Psychology Bulletin, 18,* 199–206.

Tangney, J. P., Wagner, P., Fletcher, C., & Gramzow, R. (1992a). Shamed into anger? The relation of shame and guilt to anger and self-reported aggression. *Journal of Personality and Social Psychology, 62,* 669–675.

Tangney, J. P., Wagner, P., & Gramzow, R. (1992b). Proneness to shame, proneness to guilt, and psychopathology. *Journal of Abnormal Psychology, 101,* 469–478.

Thompson, R. A., & Hoffman, M. L. (1980). Empathy and the development of guilt in children. *Developmental Psychology, 16,* 155–156.

Williams, C., & Bybee, J. (1994a). What do children feel guilty about? Developmental and gender differences. *Developmental Psychology, 30,* 617–623.

Williams, C., & Bybee, J. (1994b). *Do grade level, peer delinquency, emotionality, and gender affect ratings of own and other's guilt?* Paper presented at the Annual Meeting of the Eastern Psychological Association, Providence, Rhode Island.

Wilson, J. Q., & Herrnstein, R. J. (1984). *Crime and human nature.* New York: Simon & Schuster.

Zahn-Waxler, C., Cole, P. M., & Barrett, K. C. (1991). Guilt and empathy: Sex differences and implications for the development of depression. In J. Garber & K. Dodge (Ed.), *The development of emotion regulation and dysregulation* (pp. 243–272). Cambridge: Cambridge University Press.

Zahn-Waxler, C., & Kochanska, G. (1990). The origins of guilt. In R. A. Thompson (Ed.), *The 36th Annual Nebraska Symposium on Motivation: Socioemotional Development* (pp. 183–258). Lincoln: University of Nebraska Press.

Zahn-Waxler, C., Kochanska, G., Krupnick, J., & McKnew, D. (1990). Patterns of guilt in children of depressed and well mothers. *Developmental Psychology, 26,* 51–59.

Zahn-Waxler, C., & Robinson, J. (1995). Empathy and guilt: Early origins of feelings of responsibility. In J. P. Tangney & K. W. Fischer (Eds.), *Self-conscious emotions: The psychology of shame, guilt, embarrassment, and pride* (pp. 143–173). New York: Guilford.

Zahn-Waxler, C., Robinson, J., & Emde, R. (1992). The development of empathy in twins. *Developmental Psychology, 28,* 1038–1047.

PART III

Inducing, Instilling, and Alleviating Guilt

CHAPTER 6

Inducing Guilt

Roy F. Baumeister
Case Western Reserve University, Cleveland, Ohio

INDUCING GUILT

Should parents make their children feel guilty? I suspect that the quick answer would be a resounding "No!" On the other hand, if one were to ask whether parents actually do make their children feel guilty, the answer—at least from the children—would almost certainly be "Yes." At first glance, then, inducing guilt is one problematic pattern in filial relationships. The gap between ideals and reality suggests that parents, at least, succumb to temptation and do things that they and the broader culture find objectionable.

My own work on guilt has suggested a very different view. The thrust of my approach has been to understand guilt as a largely interpersonal emotion that functions primarily and powerfully to improve interpersonal relationships (Baumeister, Stillwell, & Heatherton, 1994). Despite its terrible reputation, guilt may actually be a good, positive phenomenon. From that perspective, parents should perhaps stop feeling so, well, guilty about inducing guilt in their children.

Lest this cautiously positive view of guilt be mistaken for a blanket endorsement, I hasten to point out that guilt is capable of being harmful and destructive. I certainly do not wish to suggest that we should all always strive for more guilt in ourselves

Guilt and Children
Copyright © 1998 by Academic Press. All rights of reproduction in any form reserved.

127

and our families. Perhaps the best way to think about guilt is as a tool, similar to a knife or hammer. Such tools can cause considerable harm, especially when used in malicious or careless ways. Still, the occasional harm should not blind us to the fact that guilt is frequently used in a proper and constructive fashion, with beneficial results.

The view of guilt as an interpersonal emotion runs contrary to an established tradition that considers guilt as a solitary, private phenomenon. In this traditional view, people compare their actions against abstract standards of proper behavior, and when they fall short of these standards they feel guilty. No one else need be involved: Guilt is something between a person and his or her conscience. In contrast, our view treats guilt as arising out of interpersonal bonds and interactions. Guilt is thus primarily an emotion that signals an interpersonal problem or disturbance, and it functions to motivate people to maintain better relationships.

In this brief chapter, I will attempt to summarize my own research findings and then explain the implications for parent–child interactions. Even though such interactions have not been the direct focus of my research efforts, they have surfaced repeatedly in our work, and the extension of implications to them is straightforward, at least once several basic assumptions can be established.

First it is necessary to take a view of the family that differs somewhat from the standard images and stereotypes of loving, nurturant parents and grateful children. On the contrary: the interests of parents and children are often in conflict. The desires of one may run opposite to the preferences of the other. The issue may be large or small, but the potential for conflict is often there, ranging from decisions about whether the child may take a job after school or not, to the small but familiar debate over whether the child may stay up a little longer than usual.

Resolving such conflicts depends on influence tactics. Power, usually in the form of parental control over the child's outcomes, is often a factor. A parent can remove a child's resources or privileges and even physically coerce the child. Children are not without power, of course. A child can make a public spectacle that will embarrass the parent and, more generally, children can make their parents' life unpleasant in a variety of ways.

The operation of guilt, especially manipulations of guilt, can then be understood in the context of conflict and power dynamics. Inducing guilt is an alternative to exerting power. Inducing guilt is a form of influence that does not rely on direct coercion or on controlling the other's outcomes. Guilt is thus one of the quintessential weapons of the weak.

This analysis suggests that children would be more likely than parents to use guilt, because they lack direct power and hence would be the first to resort to the alternative. But this is not correct. Parents have more need of influence than children, because part of the parent's job is socializing the children to behave properly. That is, the child's self-interest may require influencing the parent, but this is a limited matter, whereas the parent sees a much bigger project in shaping the behavior of the child even when direct and immediate self-interests (of the parent) are not involved.

Cultural relativity and variation undoubtedly play a role in determining the frequency (and perhaps efficacy) of filial guilt manipulations. Donenberg and Weisz's finding (chapter 12, this volume) that parents rely more on guilt induction as the child grows older and physical coercion becomes less viable is consistent with this analysis. In some cultures, the exertion of direct physical force as a form of coercion is permissible and corporal punishment is considered acceptable and tolerable. Parents may also exert considerable control throughout their children's lives when the parents own and control the family's assets, land, and means of livelihood, and when the parents hold the power of arranging marriages and determining their child's occupation. In contrast, in other societies (such as our own), corporal punishment is widely disapproved of and, in certain cases, outlawed. Intergenerational transmission of wealth is but one avenue for achieving financial security, and indeed social status and position are more fluid and merit-based. When parents cannot assert physical and financial control, they may be more likely to induce guilt to gain control over their offspring. Guilt is just one of the parents' arsenal of weapons for controlling the child's behavior, and relative availability of other weapons in the arsenal (as shaped by sociocultural constraints) helps determine how often a parent may resort to inducing guilt.

THEORY

In this section I shall briefly summarize the theoretical understanding of guilt that has guided (and emeged from) my research. Guilt originates as an emotional response to hurting or harming someone with whom one has a positive social bond. Harm or hurt is understood broadly, so as to include neglecting or disappointing that person or causing emotional distress. The positive social bond is important: The prototypical cause of guilt would be hurting someone that the person loves. The ready applicability of this to the family is obvious, because of the strength and love that often characterize family bonds.

There are two main emotional roots of guilt. One is empathy: when someone else suffers, the empathic observer suffers too (Hoffman, 1982). This emphatic distress turns into full-fledged guilt when the onlooker judges himself or herself to be the cause of the other's suffering. Moreover, empathy is strongly linked to similarity (see Batson, Duncan, Ackerman, Buckley, & Birch, 1981). People feel most empathy toward a similar other person. Empathy is also increased when the individual knows the other person well, because such familiarity increases insight into the other's inner feeling states. On both counts, of course, guilt should be especially strong in families.

The second emotional root of guilt is exclusion or separation anxiety. Guilt can be understood as one derivative form of anxiety. Anxiety is most commonly associated with social exclusion, in the sense that anxiety results from being rejected by desired groups or relationship partners (e.g., Baumeister & Tice, 1990; Leary & Kowalski, 1995). Hence hurting a relationship partner may cause the perpetrator to feel guilt because hurting the partner increases the probability that the partner may abandon or reject the perpetrator at some point. Again, this means that family relationships should be particularly likely to breed guilt. To be rejected by a parent or child can be quite devastating, and in the historical/evolutionary past, social exclusion could even be life-threatening.

Guilt is also anticipatory, and indeed it functions best in that way. That is, guilt may arise with the recognition that one's current actions (or inactions) could potentially result in social exclusion, rejection, or ostracism. Guilt can thus prevent the person from doing wrong things or hurting relationship partners.

Inducing guilt capitalizes on this basic structure of guilt. The message that lies at the core of guilt induction is "Look how you are hurting me." The other person changes his or her behavior to avoid the guilt that would follow from hurting you. As already noted, guilt is thus a widely available influence strategy because it does not require formal power or control over material outcomes. It is available even to the relatively weak and powerless, as a means to allow them to get their way.

Guilt does however depend on the emotional bond, in two ways. First, the person will feel guilty only to the extent that he or she empathizes with other's suffering. Emotional bonds increase empathy and mutual concern. The greater difficulty that people may have in empathizing with a total stranger makes it relatively difficult for a stranger to induce guilt. Second, the person has to want to preserve the relationship. "Look how you are hurting me" will not elicit much guilt if the response is "So what?" Thus, again, strangers and casual acquaintances are at a substantial relative disadvantage in terms of their ability to induce guilt. Hence the capacity to induce guilt will be directly proportional to the other person's positive caring about you. The stronger the social and emotional bond between two people, the greater the capacity for manipulating guilt feelings.

Inducing guilt is not without its costs. Two types of costs have been identified. First, manipulating guilt can breed resentment, and so even if the guilt inducer gets his or her way, he or she may have to be content with a residue of ill will and resistance to future attempts at guilt induction. At the extreme, accumulated resentment over guilt manipulations could even damage or break up the relationship, although I have not found any systematic studies showing this.

The second potential cost of using guilt as an influence strategy is *metaguilt*— that is, guilt over inducing guilt. Metaguilt may arise from the following sequence of events. The inductor leads the relationship partner to feel or become guilty. Guilt is itself a form of distress and mental suffering. The recognition that one has caused a relationship partner to feel anguished may, in turn, generate guilt in the inducer.

One last theoretical point concerns the nature of the social relationships that give rise to guilt. Although I have emphasized close relationships, perhaps the more precise construct would be *communal* relationships (e.g., Clark, 1984; Clark & Mills, 1979). Such relationships are defined by norms that people should care about each other's welfare, independent of material self-interest. In contrast to communal relationships, *exchange* relationships are based on fair transactions in which each partner seeks his or her own self-interested benefits. There is little need for guilt in exchange relationships, because the other person is only participating as long as and to the extent that he or she derives sufficient benefits. Communal relationships, however, are vulnerable to exploitation and abuse, if one person continually claims benefits based on the other's concern but does not reciprocate. Hence guilt can help keep such relationships mutually advantageous.

RELATIONSHIPS AND GUILT INDUCTION

The relationship context of guilt has been established in several studies. Guilt emerged in our research as a heavily interpersonal phenomenon, contrary to the traditional view that treated guilt as a solitary phenomenon. In several studies, people's account of feeling guilty generally involved interpersonal harm, and indeed we found only a handful of exceptions to the principle that guilt arises from inter- personal transgressions (Baumeister, Reis, & Delespaul, 1995; Baumeister, Stillwell, & Heatherton, 1995). Other studies have pointed to similar conclusions (Jones, Kugler, & Adams, 1995). We found that people do sometimes feel guilty when they are alone—but even that guilt is usually associated with thinking about an interper- sonal transgression. Apart from the occasional failure to fulfill one's personal reso- lutions or vows, such as in dieting or exercising, guilt is linked to hurting other people.

Moreover, guilt is mainly linked to hurting people with whom one has a close relationship. In one study (Baumeister, Reis, & Delespaul, 1995) we asked partici- pants to describe one incident for each of six unpleasant emotions: guilt, fear, anxiety, anger or irritation, frustration, and sadness. We then coded these on a six- point scale as to who else was involved: solitary events were coded as zero, strangers with no prospect of future interaction were coded 1, strangers with whom there was a likelihood of future interaction were coded 2, role-based relationships were coded 3, acquaintances or roommates as 4, and intimate partners (including roman- tic partners, family members, and best friends) as 5. These codings thus served as an index of the interpersonal closeness of the emotion.

Guilt received the highest score of the six emotions. Comparing the emotions in pairs revealed that guilt was significantly more interpersonal than any of the other emotions except sadness, and it was significantly higher than each of the others except sadness. Moreover, guilt stories were more likely than any other emotion to receive the highest coding (5). These results confirmed that guilt is more likely than other emotions to arise in the context of close relationships.

Although guilt-evoking situations are mostly interpersonal, the specific induc- tion of guilt is even more closely linked with a relationship context. We conducted one study that asked people either to describe an incident in which someone made them feel guilty or to describe an incident in which they made someone feel guilty, and we conducted a similar coding for relationship closeness on those accounts

(Baumeister, Stillwell, & Heatherton, 1995; see also Vangelisti, Daly, & Rudnick, 1991). Nearly all of the descriptions (95%) involved a partner in a close relationship. When we coded for communal rather than close relationships, the same pattern emerged. (Communal relationships are defined by certain norms and expectations, especially mutual caring.) Guilt is almost exclusively induced in the context of communal relationships.

Why should inducing guilt be so strongly linked to close, communal relationships? As already proposed, one has to invoke the other's concern in order to induce guilt. If the other does not mind hurting you, then claiming to be hurt is not likely to alter the other's behavior. But people who care about you do not want to hurt you, and so claiming to be hurt may generate guilt and alter their behavior. Mutual concern is the defining feature of communal relationships and is essential to the strategy of inducing guilt.

Parent–child relationships are thus well suited for inducing guilt. Parents and children normally care very much about each other and are motivated to avoid hurting each other. They have strong empathic links. And, of course, they have plenty of reasons for wanting to alter each other's behavior.

To illustrate these points, I present the following account of filial guilt induction. This was furnished by a participant in one of our studies (Baumeister, Stillwell, & Heatherton, 1995). She was asked to describe an incident in which someone made her feel guilty, and she chose to write about how her parents induced guilt over her dating behavior when they disapproved:

> Generally my parents are very old-fashioned, and when it comes to the people I date they definitely have an opinion. Now, I generally do not agree with their point of view, but since they are my parents they have an uncanny ability to make me feel guilty. They would say things like, "Can't you see what you're doing to yourself," "Can't you see what you're doing to us?" "This really hurts us," "All we've ever wanted was the best for you," and so on. As you can imagine this leads to quite a bit of distress. On one side I feel that my opinions are correct and "right," but I don't like to "hurt" my parents either.

This example illustrates several theoretical themes. First, the relationship bond is an important basis for guilt, and indeed the author seems quite aware that the emotional connection is a condition that makes the guilt induction possible: She says "since they are my parents" they are able to induce guilt. The implication is that similar ploys by other people, particularly others with whom she had less of a bond, would not succeed.

Second, the story shows that guilt is used to influence behavior in a conflict situation. In this case, the writer has certain preferences as to her own dating activities and partners, and the parents have different ones ("I generally do not agree with their point of view"). They use guilt to sway her behavior toward their standards and expectations.

Third, the author of this account clearly resents the parental use of guilt to alter her behavior. The parents may indeed get their way in terms of altering their daughter's behavior, but their victory is not without cost, and indeed the risk of long-term damage to the relationship is apparent. Parents have sought throughout history to influence the mating choices of their offspring, and although we do not know how this particular case has been resolved, it is no secret that one common outcome involves the young person defying the parental pressure and eventually making the choice of which they disapprove—leaving a lasting dose of bitterness and alienation in the family.

Fourth, the guilt induction is explicitly presented as a matter of telling the daughter that her actions inflict pain and distress on the parents. Her summary of their comments indicates that they say things such as, "This really hurts us," to alter her behavior. She obviously does not think that her own motive in choosing dating partners is to inflict maximal pain and distress on her parents, but as long as they can convince her that her actions do end up hurting them, she feels guilty.

Last, is there any evidence of the positive or constructive side of guilt in this story? If there is anything good about guilt, it does not seem apparent to this particular participant in this incident. Nonetheless, if the guilt is successful in swaying the daughter to make an eventual mate choice who will be at least somewhat acceptable to the parents, her relationship to them may end up stronger than if she chooses someone whom they can not stand. Such an outcome would not be fully satisfactory according to the romanticized views of love and mating that prevail in modern Western culture, and it may even be one that the woman herself would regard as nonoptimal. But it might just be better for her relationship to her parents.

NEGLECT

Another question that has guided our research is what do people actually feel guilty for doing? Like other researchers, we have sought to categorize the types of incidents that people describe as causing guilt. In every study, we found the same category to be the largest (Baumeister, Reis, & Delespaul, 1995; Baumeister, Stillwell, & Heatherton, 1995). This category consisted of interpersonal neglect: failing to pay attention to or spend time with someone. Our results suggest that interpersonal neglect is the number one sin of omission in today's United States.

Interpersonal neglect also stood out in Baumeister, Reis, and Delespaul's (1995) study on inducing guilt. The perception that someone has failed to pay attention to you or spend sufficient time with you is the most common reason that people report for inducing guilt in another person. (It is also the most common reason given in people's account of being made to feel guilty by someone else.)

The dominance of the interpersonal neglect category underscored for us the importance of guilt as a mechanism for preserving relationships. After all, interpersonal neglect is probably the simplest and most passive reason that relationships may fail. If you ignore someone long enough, that person will eventually form an attachment with someone else. If guilt can indeed reduce interpersonal neglect, it will keep relationships strong and prevent deterioration.

Neglect can occur on either side of a filial relationship. Most adult offspring are probably familiar with the guilty feeling that they have not spent enough time with their parents. Many parents are lonely or find their lives dull, and they look to their offspring to provide stimulation. The pressure to call, write, and visit is often suffered and not infrequently resented, especially when the offsrping are busy with their own lives. Even merely staying at the parental home may not be enough, because guilt can arise over a lack of attention or interaction. In one study, for example, we had several accounts by college students who went back to their parents' home over the holidays but then felt guilty (or were made to feel guilty) because they had spent most of the vacation with their old friends rather than interacting with their parents.

Thus, offspring feel guilty when they neglect their parents. The reverse is also common, however, particularly earlier in the child's life when the child has a greater appetite for parental attention. Many young parents find themselves coping with job demands and other pressures, as a result of which they cannot spend as much time with their children as they feel they ought. Working mothers in particular are often subject to mixed messages that tell them to pursue their own careers but also to be certain to give the child all it needs—including time and attention.

Hence many parents are prepared to feel guilty spontaneously. Under such circumstances, it would not take much for the child to learn to play on those feelings and possibly to manipulate them for the child's own advantage. Privileges, money, and toys or other possessions can be extracted from the parent in a steady stream simply by making the parent feel guilty for not being available when the child wanted some contact. For example, if the child can show distress over a parent's impending business trip, the parent may feel guilty enough to spend most of the free hours during the trip shopping for a special gift that will make it up to the child. And it does not take much skill for such a child to extract a bedtime extension on the day the parent returns.

RESENTMENT AND METAGUILT

In our research, we found that guilt is not without its costs. Inducing guilt may be an effective strategy to allow people to get their way in close relationships without using power or coercion, but it cannot be considered an ideal mode of influence. As suggested earlier, resentment and metaguilt may result, and these outcomes carry considerable costs.

Resentment is a negative response on the part of the target of guilt induction. In our studies many people indicated that they complied with the other's wishes when the other person made them feel guilty—but they resented this. In such cases, the influencer's victory is slightly hollow. The person does get his or her way, but the bad feeling held by the other may reduce the other's willingness to continue to provide benefits or affection.

In theory, the accumulation of such resentment could eventually damage the relationship. Anecdotally, some people do claim that their resentment over being made to feel guilty frequently has caused them to break off relationships. If this is correct, it may help explain why mothers are sometimes regarded as the ultimate guilt inducers. No matter how much one resents having guilt feelings manipulated, one cannot break up with or divorce one's mother. (Of course, mothers are suited in others ways to the role of guilt inducer: They have often lacked the formal or material power that many fathers have, and they cultivate the strong emotional attachments that form the basis for inducing guilt.)

The filial bond may, however, end up in a close relationship that is highly ambivalent, if frequent guilt induction builds up a residue of resentment. Again, whether guilt actually contributes to ambivalence in parent–child relations remains a question for further investigation.

Metaguilt is guilt that one feels over inducing guilt. We noted that guilt arises from hurting another person, and guilt is itself sufficiently unpleasant so as to qualify as a form of hurt (loosely defined), and so inflicting guilt can be understood as one kind of harm infliction. People may therefore feel guilty about causing their children to feel guilty. This may be particularly true in societies like today's United States, because guilt has a very unsavory reputation and is reputed to be harmful to well-being and detrimental to mental and physical health. Parents may therefore think that making their children feel guilty is a form of emotional abuse.

Metaguilt thus penalizes the inducer of guilt, even while that person may be penalizing the target of guilt induction. Or, more specifically, parents may feel guilty at the same time that they induce guilt in their children. Metaguilt would not necessarily diminish the effectiveness of the parent's attempt to influence the child, as long as it is merely a matter of the parent's feelings. If the parent is deterred by metaguilt from using guilt to shape the child's behavior, however, metaguilt may end up discouraging parents from using one of their effective tools of socialization.

GUILT AND SELF-ESTEEM

The preceding comments about metaguilt raise the broader question of whether it is a good idea for parents to induce guilt in their children. As I have already suggested, guilt suffers from a terrible reputation in modern American culture, partly from an overgeneralized, bastardized Freudian doctrine that depicts guilt as an unhealthy mechanism that stifles personal growth and thwarts the natural, spontaneous expressiveness of the human psyche. Parents see their role as facilitating their child's growth, not hampering it, and so they may fear that inducing guilt will make them bad parents.

Yet such fears are misguided and largely groundless. Much metaguilt may be based on a mistaken sense of the harmful nature of guilt. It may be possible to make one's child neurotic by instilling large amounts of guilt, or by failing to teach (or honor) constructive means of guilt alleviation such as apologies and restitution that prevent feelings from becoming chronic (see Bybee & Quiles, Chapter 13, this volume). Still, such cases are probably rare. Guilt is typically a prosocial and benefi- cial emotion, however, and instilling too little guilt may be more harmful to the child in the long run than instilling too much. At the extreme, the absence of the sense of guilt is one defining feature of the psychopath, who preys on other people and often ends up in various forms of trouble, ranging from unsatisfying intimate relationships to prison.

More important, guilt serves valuable prosocial functions, and a failure to instill an adequate sense of guilt does the child a serious disservice. The view of guilt promoted in this chapter and in my other recent works (Baumeister, Stillwell, & Heatherton, 1994; see also Tangney, 1995) emphasizes the positive, desirable nature of guilt as a vital means of maintaining good interpersonal relationships. Someone raised without guilt is poorly equipped to have good, durable close relationships or to be a useful, valued member of a small group. In simpler terms, only a fool would marry or hire someone who lacked an adequate sense of guilt.

It is useful to contrast parental attitudes about guilt with those about self-esteem. During the past two decades, the United States has witnessed a self-esteem move- ment that has gradually convinced many parents (along with schoolteachers, therapists, policymakers, and many others) that instilling self-esteem should be a top priority in raising children (e.g., California Task Force, 1990). I have criticized this policy in other places (Baumeister, 1993; see also Adelson, 1996; Dowes, 1994), partly on the basis that the negative, problematic side of high self-esteem such as its link to violence is too readily ignored (Baumeister, Smart, & Boden, 1996).

For present purposes, though, the key contrast involves the distribution of costs and benefits of self-esteem as opposed to guilt. Self-esteem fosters a comfortable, potentially arrogant sense of superiority that feels very good to the individual but is potentially a problem for the people who live and work with him or her. Anyone who has ever worked with a person who has a huge, inflated ego can probably attest to the constant difficulty of adjusting one's behavior to accommodate that person's egotism. Thus, the benefits of self-esteem come mainly to the individual self, while the costs are borne by others.

The opposite is true for guilt. Guilt is an important mechanism that induces people to relinquish their own gratifications when they come at the expense of others, particularly the suffering of others. Guilt deters people from stealing from their friends, cheating on their spouses, or betraying their employers. More gener- ally, then, the costs of guilt are borne by the individual, while the direct or imme- diate benefits accrue primarily to those associated with him or her.

It is therefore not surprising that a highly individualistic culture such as today's United States has developed an exalted view of the wonderfulness of self-esteem and an exaggerated negative view of guilt. If one considers only the perspective of the individual self, particularly in terms of material and emotional benefits, self- esteem is a plus and guilt is a minus.

This individualistic view is however one-sided and ultimately unrealistic, because people do not exist as individual units but rather must live their lives in ongoing relationships with other people (Baumeister & Leary, 1995). In principle, a person might find happiness by cultivating an extremely high self-esteem while living in social isolation, but in practice social isolation is incompatible with happiness (see Baumeister, 1991; Myers, 1992, for reviews). To be happy, it is necessary to get along well with at least a small circle of friends and intimates. And guilt is helpful and possibly essential for making that possible.

Moreover, our society might be better off if parents recognized that the obligations of parenthood are not exclusively focused on the child: that is, parents should perhaps acknowledge that they have some duty to society at large to raise a child who will be a useful, productive, law-abiding citizen. Guilt is clearly central in achieving that goal. It is plausible that the high rates of crime and other antisocial behaviors that currently plague the United States would be much lower if many individuals had been brought up with a stronger sense of guilt and a weaker sense of personal superiority and entitlement (i.e., self-esteem).

Thus, although the modern American *Zeitgeist* exhorts parents to instill self-esteem and avoid instilling guilt, this approach may be short-sighted and self-destructive. I am not advocating a complete reversal, but a more balanced and equitable mixture of self-esteem and guilt might in the long run be best for the individual child (and eventual adult), for the people who will live and work with that individual, and for society as a whole.

CONCLUSION AND SUMMARY

Guilt is a widely misunderstood emotion, and our culture has emphasized its negative, destructive, and unpleasant side while largely overlooking its benefits. Guilt can serve valuable functions in strengthening close, communal relationships and motivating people to behave in prosocial, desirable ways.

Parents and children do induce guilt in each other in a variety of ways. In general, guilt is induced in relationships marked by norms of mutual concern and by strong emotional bonds, and so the parent–child relationship is in some ways an ideal context for inducing guilt. Children may make parents feel guilty in order to help them (the children) get their way. Parents induce guilt in children not only to get their way but also to help socialize the children by shaping their behavior to conform to the parents' standards and expectations, and presumably those of the broader culture as well. Guilt is often an important tool that parents can use to help mold their children into decent, successful, productive citizens.

Guilt trades on emotional bonds and on mutual concern that parents and children have for each other. The strategy of inducing guilt is most commonly based on conveying to the other person that the other's behavior is causing oneself pain or distress. Guilt is thus a mechanism for influencing the other's behavior without using coercion or other forms of power. Inducing guilt is not inherently bad nor does it broadly or generally lead to destructive consequences. It can have costs and drawbacks, such as resentment, but then so do more aggressive and coercive forms of influence.

Given its power and value and its suitability to filial relationships, guilt provides a potent and effective tool that parents may employ in the socialization of their child and in the maintenance of close interpersonal ties. Some may deplore the fact that parents make their children feel guilty, but apart from the abuses and excesses of this influence strategy it has much to recommend it.

REFERENCES

Adelson, J. (1996: February). Down with self-esteem. *Commentary, 34*–38.

Batson, C. D., Duncan, B. D., Ackerman, P., Buckley, T., & Birch, K. (1981). Is empathic emotion a source of altruistic motivation? *Journal of Personality and Social Psychology, 40,* 290–302.

Baumeister, R. F. (1991). *Meanings of life.* New York: Guilford Press.

Baumeister, R. F. (1993). Understanding the inner nature of low self-esteem: Uncertain, fragile, protective, and conflicted. In R. Baumeister (Ed.), *Self-esteem: The puzzle of low self-regard* (pp. 201–218). New York: Plenum.

Baumeister, R. F., & Leary, M. R. (1995). The need to belong: Desire for interpersonal attachments as a fundamental human motivation. *Psychological Bulletin, 117,* 497–529.

Baumeister, R. F., Reis, H. T., & Delespaul, P. A. E. G. (1995). Subjective and experiential correlates of guilt in everyday life. *Personality and Social Psychology Bulletin, 21,* 1256–1268.

Baumeister, R. F., Smart, L., & Boden, J. M. (1996). Relation of threatened egotism to violence and aggression: The dark side of high self-esteem. *Psychological Review, 103,* 5–33.

Baumeister, R. F., Stillwell, A. M., & Heatherton, T. F. (1994). Guilt: An interpersonal approach. *Psychological Bulletin, 115,* 243–267.

Baumeister, R. F., Stillwell, A. M., & Heatherton, T. F. (1995). Personal narratives about guilt: Role in action control and interpersonal relationships. *Basic and Applied Social Psychology, 17,* 173–198.

Baumeister, R. F., & Tice, D. M. (1990). Anxiety and social exclusion. *Journal of Social and Clinical Psychology, 9,* 165–195.

California Task Force to Promote Self-Esteem and Personal and Social Responsibility (1990). *Toward a state of self-esteem.* Sacramento, CA: California State Department of Education.

Clark, M. S. (1984). Record keeping in two types of relationships. *Journal of Personality and Social Psychology, 47,* 549–557.

Clark, M. S., & Mills, J. (1979). Interpersonal attraction in exchange and communal relationships. *Journal of Personality and Social Psychology, 37,* 12–24.

Dawes, R. M. (1994). *House of cards: Psychology and psychotherapy built on myth.* New York: Free Press.

Hoffman, M. L. (1982). Development of prosocial motivation: Empathy and guilt. In N. Eisenberg (Ed.), *The development of prosocial behavior* (pp. 281–313). New York: Academic Press.

Jones, W. H., Kugler, K., & Adams, P. (1995). You always hurt the one you love: Guilt and transgressions against relationship partners. In J. Tangney & K. Fischer (Eds.), *The self-conscious emotions* (pp. 301–321). New York: Guilford.

Leary, M. R., & Kowalski, R. (1995). *Social anxiety.* New York: Guilford.

Myers, D. (1992). *The pursuit of happiness.* New York: Morrow.

Tangney, J. P. (1995). Shame and guilt in interpersonal relationships. In J. Tangney & K. Fischer (Eds.), *The self-conscious emotions* (pp. 114–139). New York: Guilford.

Vangelisti, A. L., Daly, J. A., & Rudnick, J. R. (1991). Making people feel guilty in conversations: Techniques and correlates. *Human Communication Research, 18,* 3–39.

CHAPTER 7

Religion and Guilt in Childhood

Lane Fischer and P. Scott Richards

Brigham Young University, Provo, Utah

INTRODUCTION

Historically, psychology has neglected or discounted religion. Lehr and Spilka (1989), in a review of psychology textbooks, conclude that, "essentially nothing was offered on religious development, experience, or beliefs or on their relationships to a broad range of expressions in personality and social behavior" (p. 370). Wells (1998) likewise finds that little research has been conducted in the developmental or child clinical literature on children's experience with religion. Indeed, the negative regard in which religion has traditionally been held by psychologists is acknowledged in the cover story of the *APA Monitor* in August, 1996 (Clay, 1996).

In the present chapter, we explore reasons for the neglect of religion in theoretical and empirical work in psychology. We point out that, contrary to prevailing theoretical tenets, religiosity is not necessarily related to poor mental health and worse socioemotional well-being. We argue for more refined definitions and measurement of both religion and guilt. Empirical evidence indicates that intrinsic religiosity is associated with a healthy guilt response to actual wrongdoing and to good physical health and lowered rates of substance abuse, delinquency, and suicidality. Extrinsic religiosity, in contrast, is associated with more unhealthy, neurotic forms

Guilt and Children
Copyright © 1998 by Academic Press. All rights of reproduction in any form reserved.

of worry and guilt and poor adjustment on self-report indices of mental well-being. In order to informally explore how different religions and religious leaders differ in their conceptualizations of guilt and means of alleviating guilt, we present a synopsis of interviews with individuals following Sikhism, Judaism, Catholicism, Episcopalianism, Presbyterianism, and Mormonism. We close with thoughts on the development of guilt and religion.

WHY HAVE PSYCHOLOGISTS IGNORED THE INTERRELATIONSHIP OF GUILT AND RELIGION AMONG CHILDREN?

Why is there a lack of literature connecting two ubiquitous phenomena in children's lives: guilt and religion? Early leaders in the behavioral sciences portrayed religious beliefs and behaviors in negative ways, perhaps because of their personal beliefs regarding religion, perhaps because of their borrowed philosophy, and perhaps because science in the late 19th and early 20th centuries was vigorously challenging religious authority and tradition. In "The Future of an Illusion," Freud states that religious ideas "are illusions, fulfillments of the oldest, strongest and most urgent wishes of mankind" (Freud, 1927/1961, p. 30). He also says that religion is "the universal obsessional neurosis of humanity" (Freud, 1927/1961, p. 43). Freud compares religious beliefs to a "sleeping draught" and says that "the effect of religious consolations may be likened to that of a narcotic" (Freud, 1927/1961, p. 29).

Freud (1913/1950) clearly ties guilt and religion together in *Totem and Taboo*, and leaves the reader with the distinct impression that to experience religion is to be naive or neurotic. In fact, the subtitle of, *Totem and Taboo*, is *Some Points of Agreement Between the Mental Lives of Savages and Neurotics*. Freud maintains that Oedipal strivings and conflicts lead to murderous intents as the child seeks to do away with the father to have unlimited access to, and the full attention of, the mother. Resultant remorse and deferred obedience to the father figure are embodied by the totem. Totemism is described as the first attempt by religion to incorporate the two cardinal taboos: incest and murder. Totemism and all subsequent religious behavior are interpreted as a neurotic solution to the Oedipal problem. Religion and guilt are seen as interrelated: To be religious is pathological. To experience guilt is pathological. To be free of religion is to be enlightened. Indeed, Freud's (1910/1964) analysis of Leonardo da Vinci portrays him as one of the most luminescent figures of the Renaissance because he freed himself of his religious and familial fetters.

In *Civilization and Its Discontents* Freud (1930/1961) traces the origins of guilt to the child's fear of retaliation by authority figures for aggressive instincts and acts. Guilt and accompanying fear of retribution is said to lead to the renunciation of aggression. Freud posits that psychological development involves the introjection of aggressive impulses. Hostility, previously aimed outward and against others, is hypothesized to turn inward and against the self as the superego regulatory functions sharpen and strengthen. Conscience or fear of an internalized authority figure then leads to a renunciation of instinctual drives.

Consider another powerful influence in psychotherapy, Albert Ellis. Ellis (1980) states that, "Religiosity is in many respects equivalent to irrational thinking and emotional disturbance." Ellis allows that people can be healthy and religious when they are not dogmatic about religion and when the religion they choose undogmatically ascribes to "the freedom of the individual, the desirability of unconditional self-acceptance, the tolerance and forgiveness of others who act poorly and other forms of liberal religion." Ellis (1980) states that "such individuals would benefit more without the belief in the intervening variable of religion or God" (p. 637–638). Only recently has Ellis (1996) softened his stance on religion.

John B. Watson, one of the founders of behaviorism, basically ignored spiritual behavior, but on those occasions when he did mention it, his writings revealed his bias against religion. In his book, *Psychology from the Standpoint of a Behaviorist,* for example, Watson said, "Psychology, up to very recent times, has been held so rigidly under the dominance both of traditional religion and of philosophy—the two great bulwarks of medievalism—that it has never been able to free itself and become a natural science" (Watson, 1983/1924, p. 1). In arguing why psychology should not concern itself with studying consciousness, Watson said, 'States of consciousness,' like the so-called phenomena of spiritualism, are not objectively verifiable and for that reason can never become data for science" (Watson, 1983/1924, p. 1). Watson viewed religious behavior as an irrelevant conditioned response that was unworthy of scientific study.

RELIGION AND MENTAL HEALTH

Although over 70 years have passed since religious beliefs were first widely regarded in mainstream psychiatry and psychology as unhealthy and unproductive, this viewpoint has persisted until recent years (Bergin, 1980, 1983, 1991; Ellis, 1980; Jensen & Bergin, 1988). This negative bias has remained despite the fact that research investigating the relationship between religion and mental health has been surprisingly sparse, and perhaps because early reviews of what research there was were unfavorable and reflective of the older antireligious zeitgeist (Dittes, 1971; Sanua, 1969).

In response to renewed allegations that religiosity is "equivalent to irrational thinking and emotional disturbance" (Ellis, 1980, p. 637), Bergin (1983) examined the limited research literature that up to the time that had investigated the relationship between religiosity and mental health, reviewing correlations of religiosity with traditional paper–pencil measures of mental health (e.g., MMPI, manifest anxiety, neuroticism, self-esteem, irrational beliefs, ego strength, and psychic adequacy). Of the 30 reported correlations, "only 7, or 23%, manifested the negative relationship

TABLE I   Relationship in the Literature between Religious Commitment and Mental Health Factors[a]

Religion associated with mental health		
Physical health	Mortality	Suicide
Drug use	Alcohol use	Delinquency
Well-being	Outcome	Depression
Divorce and marital satisfaction		
Ambiguous or complex associations between religion and mental health		
Anxiety	Psychosis	Self-esteem
Sexual disorders	Prejudice	Intelligence/Education
Religion associated with psychopathology		
Authoritarianism	Dogmatism/Tolerance	
Suggestibility/Dependence	of ambiguity/Rigidity	
Temporal lobe epilepsy	Self-Actualization	

[a]Adapted from Gartner, Larson, & Allen (1991). Reprinted by permission of Rosemead School of Psychology, Biola University.

between religion and mental health assumed by Ellis and others. Forty-seven percent indicated a positive relationship and 30% a zero relationship. Thus 77% of the obtained results are contrary to the negative effect of religion theory . . ." (p. 176). Bergin also pointed out, however, that most of the results (23 out of 30) were not statistically significant and that the overall (average) mean correlation across all studies was almost zero (.09).

Bergin (1983) discussed reasons why the overall mean was so small and attributes it in part to problems in measurement and methodology in this domain. He encouraged future researchers to use greater specificity in definitions and measures of both religiousness and mental health rather than relying on global indicators. Since Bergin's review, many additional studies have examined the relationship of religiousness to emotional or social functioning. Overall, the findings have not supported the "religiosity–emotional disturbance" hypothesis but, to the contrary, have provided evidence that religious beliefs and behaviors are correlated with positive indicators of physical and mental health (Batson, Schoenrode, & Ventis, 1993; Gartner, Larson, & Allen, 1991; Matthews et al., in press; Payne, Bergin, Bielema, & Jenkins, 1991).

Gartner et al. (1991) reviewed over 200 studies on religion and mental health. Religious commitment showed strong correlations with indicators of mental health and social functioning, such as good physical health and lowered rates of mortality, suicide, drug and alcohol use, delinquency, and divorce (see Table I).

The relation of religion to better functioning was most evident when the aforementioned "real life" behaviors were considered. Gartner et al. (1991) also con-

cluded that "measures of actual religious behavior, that is, measures of religious participation such as church attendance, were more powerfully related to mental health than
were attitude scales measuring religiosity" (p. 16). On paper-and-pencil measures of
psychological functioning, the relationship of religion to adjustment was often ambiguous or negative. Gartner et al. (1991) argued that some of these negative relationships
can be attributed to use of personality and mental health measures that are biased against
religiously committed people. Some mental health measures, for example, define religious beliefs and behaviors, ipso facto, as indicators of poor mental health (Bergin, 1983).
In research with paper-and-pencil measures of religiosity, Gartner et al. (1991) also
noted that distinguishing between different types of religiousness reveals that some
types of religiousness (e.g., intrinsic, devout) are related to good emotional functioning
whereas others (e.g., extrinsic) are unrelated or negatively related to adaptive behaviors.
Studies by Bergin, Masters, and Richards (1987) and Richards (1991) as well as reviews
by Payne et al. (1991) and Batson et al. (1993) show similar findings.

Batson et al.'s (1993) review clearly illustrates how the relationship between
religiousness and mental health differs depending on the definitions of religiousness
and mental health that are used. It is also especially pertinent to this chapter because
it presents data regarding the relationship between religion and guilt. An intrinsic
religious orientation (i.e., being involved in religion and internally committed to it
because one truly believes in one's faith) is associated with appropriate social
behavior, personal competence and control, unification and organization, an absence of illness, and *freedom from worry and guilt*. It is typically not correlated with
self-acceptance/self-actualization and open-mindedness and flexibility (see Table II).
In contrast, an extrinsic religious orientation (i.e., involved in religion for the social
and personal benefits it offers) is seemingly unhealthy and is *inversely* associated with
appropriate social behavior, personal competence and control, open-mindedness and
flexibility, absence of illness, and *freedom from worry and guilt*.

Batson et al.'s (1993) review clearly illustrates that there are healthy ways of being
religious and less healthy ways. In regard to guilt, their review suggests that extrinsically religious persons may be more susceptible to the emotion than are more
devout, intrinsic persons. At first Batson et al.'s findings would appear to conflict
with Richards's (1991) finding that intrinsically religious college students were more
guilt prone than were extrinsically religious ones. Richards, however, used a measure, the Shame Guilt Test—Richard Williams (SGT-RW) (Bupp, 1983; Richards
& Williams, 1989; Smith, 1972) that is thought to reflect a *healthy* guilt response to
actual wrongdoing, whereas the studies in Batson et al.'s review appears to focus on
more *unhealthy, neurotic forms of worry and guilt*. These findings suggest, therefore,
that intrinsically religious persons may be more likely to experience healthy guilt
responses to actual transgressions and wrongdoing, but less likely to experience
irrational or neurotic guilt (or shame) over imagined wrongdoing, minor mistakes,
and perceived personal inadequacies.

Meek, Albright, and McMinn (1995) confirm Richards's (1991) finding that
intrinsically religious people are more likely than extrinsically religious people to

TABLE II   Line Score on Research Examining the Relationship between Mental Health and Three Different Dimensions of Individual Religion[a]

| Conception of mental health | Dimension of individual religion[b] | | | | | |
| | Extrinsic, means | | | Intrinsic, end | | |
	+	?	−	+	?	−
Absence of illness	1	7	11	11	7	1
Appropriate social behavior	0	1	4	5	0	1
Freedom from worry and guilt	0	7	15	15	5	4
Personal competence and control	0	4	9	11	4	3
Self-acceptance, self-actualization	0	5	3	1	8	3
Unification and organization	0	3	0	5	0	0
Open-mindedness and flexibility	0	4	6	1	6	2
Total	1	31	48	49	30	14

[a]Adapted from Batson, Schoenrode, & Ventis (1993). Copyright © 1993 by C. D. Batson, P. Schoentrade, W. C. Wentis. Used by permission of Oxford University Press, Inc.

[b]The three columns under each dimension of individual religion indicate first the number of reports of a positive relationship with each conception of mental health (+); second, the number of reports of no clear relationship (?); and third, the number of reports of a negative relationship (−).

experience guilt over wrongdoing. They also are more likely to confess their errors and to forgive themselves. Meek et al. interpret guilt as a mediating factor between religious orientation and outcomes, such as propensity to reoffend. Intrinsically religious people, while enduring guilt, are more likely to repair the error, avoid future errors, forgive themselves, and get on with life.

This work is in its nascency and much more research on the relationship between the various types of religiousness and guilt is needed before we will adequately understand the religion and guilt relationship. The following principles will enhance the quality and clarity of findings in this domain.

Guilt Is Not a Unitary Construct

Much of the literature in the past has oversimplified the term *guilt*. Tangney, Wagner, Burggraf, Gramzow, and Fletcher (1990) distinguish guilt from shame, finding that the two emotions have distinct psychological and behavioral correlates (see also Tangney, Chapter 1, this volume). Quiles and Bybee (1997) distinguish two forms of guilt: chronic and predispositional guilt. The authors define chronic guilt as an ongoing condition, unattached to immediate events. They define predispositional guilt as a personal proclivity for experiencing guilt in reaction to circumscribed precipitating events. By differentiating a previously unitary construct, guilt, into two separate constructs, the authors are able to demonstrate that chronic guilt shows stronger relationships with symptoms of depression and psychopathology than predispositional guilt. Predispositional guilt is more strongly associated with lowered hostility, increased volunteerism, and participation in religious activity.

The Richards (1991) and Meek et al. (1995) studies illustrate that it is crucial for researchers to carefully define what type of guilt they are studying. Perhaps even greater clarity would have been possible in the Batson et al. (1993) study if they would have distinguished between the various types of guilt that were measured in the studies they reviewed.

Religion Is Not a Unitary Construct

Religion has historically been oversimplified. Bergin (1983) concludes that one of the reasons that there was such a diversity of findings in his meta-analysis was that the term *religion* can refer to as many as 21 different factors, yet all are called by the same name. Ellis (1980) states that "devout orthodox, or dogmatic religion (or what might be called religiosity) is significantly correlated with emotional disturbance" (p. 637). Morgan (1995) empirically tested whether or not variables such as devoutness, orthodoxy, and dogmatism are synonymous with religiousness. Devoutness is an aspect of religious behavior that may be characterized in terms of the earnestness of its expression. Devoutness is often measured using the Religious Orientation Scale (Allport & Ross, 1967), which identifies the intrinsic/extrinsic nature of a person's religious behavior. Orthodoxy is a feature of religiousness that is related to the content of a person's belief system. Fundamentalism is a feature of religious experience related to the strategy by which religion is interpreted. Fundamentalism is usually thought of in terms of the literalness of scriptural interpretation or the rigidity or permeability of boundaries around the religion. Morgan assesses intrinsicness, orthodoxy, and fundamentalism as measures of "the why, the what, and the how" of religious practice. Morgan shows that although there is some commonality among these concepts in that they are all related to the superordinate construct of religion, the correlations are not strong enough to conclude that they are interchangeable.

Even after clearly defining and measuring any factor of religious experience, it is important to assess the level of the ecology in which that factor is operating. Factors may operate at a cultural, subcultural, family, or individual level. A factor such as devoutness, for example, may be shared by families within a culture and yet be experienced very differently by individuals within the same family. More refined models of the environment take into account the influence of shared and nonshared factors as well as the level (e.g., global, familial) at which they occur (Fischer, 1991).

QUALITATIVE INQUIRY

We sought to explore what representatives from various religions would say about how their particular religion conceptualizes guilt and what processes or rituals were used to alleviate guilt in their followers. The underlying assumptions behind these interviews was that religion is not a unitary construct and that it would not have a consistent effect on conceptions of, or reactions to, guilt. Different religious environments differentially influence the texture and tambour of a child's experience of guilt. It is more precise to consider what specific postulates a child's religion presented about guilt rather than simply whether the child was raised in a "religious" environment.

Each of the six interviews, conducted by the first author, had its own character. The interviews ranged from .05 to 4 hours in length and generally covered the issues of each religion's belief and practices related to (a) the nature of humans and purpose of life, (b) the origin of guilt, (c) the function of guilt, and (d) practices or ordinances designed to alleviate guilt. Some interviews focused more directly on children's experience than others.

An individual pastor, rabbi, or bishop may not represent the religion accurately and may be affected by their own experiences and viewpoints. Variation naturally occurs across parishes, across families, and across individuals within a family in how they experience, interpret, and integrate their religious experience. These interviews are not meant to be representative of each faith as a whole, but are presented rather as an exploration of how individual religious leaders portray guilt, its socialization, and channels of alleviation.

The authors are indebted to the following religious leaders for their time and the care with which they approached this task: Karandeep Singh, Brandeis University, Waltham, MA; Rabbi Fred Wenger, Congregation Kohl Ami, Salt Lake City, Utah; Sister Janet Stankowski, St. Francis Catholic Church, Provo, Utah; Reverend Allen Tull, Theologian to the Episcopal Bishop of Utah, Orem, Utah; Pastor Leslie Davies, Community Presbyterian Church of Springville, Utah; and Bishop Steve Merrell, The Church of Jesus Christ of Latter Day Saints, Minneapolis, Minnesota.

Sikhism

Karandeep Singh is a Sikh who formerly taught comparative religion at Brigham Young University. "Sikh" means disciple. According to Karandeep, the purpose of existence is for humans to become "one with God." Sikhism does not recognize original guilt or any sense of the fall. Sikhs believe that perfection and union with God is attainable. In fact, humans are to become fully integrated with God. One is not fully human until one is fully divine. The quest is to transcend the dualistic world that is created by human ego and to integrate with the one. Ego becomes the Satanic equivalent. It is the boundary that humans establish that keeps them from becoming one with God. Karandeep quoted a classic Sikh teaching that one becomes what one loves: dust or God. Guilt is an awareness of loving dust over God.

Sikh children are taught that they are a child of Babaji. Babaji is a familial and beloved term for God. Parents strive to create a close relationship between Babaji and the child. Babaji is characterized as the loving, forgiving, giving parent who is omnipresent for the child. Children are taught that there is a close, one-on-one relationship between the child and God. Children's early conception is of God as a external being who has a constant companionship with the child. As children mature, their construction of God is that Babaji is within, that God is constantly accompanying them from within. Maturity brings an awareness that everything in the cosmos is within one's self, including God.

With this sense, sins represent any disruption of the relationship between God and the child. For Sikh children, the loss of constant companionship of God is a powerful experience. Such a loss or disruption is experienced as guilt. Sikhs are taught that, because it is his nature to be unconditionally forgiving, a simple apology to God is sufficient to restore the relationship. God cannot help but be forgiving.

There are no rituals to assist Sikhs in reconnecting with God within. Baptism is the only ordinance in Sikhism. Any five baptized Sikhs can baptize a new disciple. At baptism, the disciple accepts vows that include proscriptions against extramarital sex and the use of alcohol, and a ban on cutting one's hair. If individuals should break any of those vows, they present themselves before a quorum of five baptized Sikhs, who give penance and prescribe some active community service as a way to atone for the violation of the vows and to restore them to the path of becoming one with God.

Judaism

Rabbi Wenger began the interview with a classic joke: "A mother took her child to the psychiatrist, who after interviewing the child reported, 'The good news is that your child doesn't have a guilt complex; however, he is guilty.'" For Jews, guilt is real and related to the nature of being human and the existence of God. In Judaism, according to Rabbi Wenger, humans are conceived of as partners with God in the act of creation. The more they align themselves with God, the more human they are. The less they align themselves with God, the less human they are. There are 613 commandments that have evolved from the original 10 commandments. The existence of these commandments implies the existence of a commander who is God. The commandments are expectations that God sets for humans. Life is centered around those commandments. As Rabbi Wenger portrays it, the experience of Judaism is the attempt to live up to the demand of the commandments in response to a covenant between God and Jews.

There is no concept of "original sin" in Judaism. Guilt is a universal human condition related to being imperfect people guided by God. However, as Jews identify themselves as the chosen people, they feel a keen responsibility to be moral agents. Although such is required of all people, according to Rabbi Wenger, Jews feel it more so. Violation of the commandments results in guilt.

Judiasm involves experiences that help to articulate and alleviate sin and guilt. Devout Jews pray three times daily. In each prayer, there is a section of confession in which the worshiper acknowledges his or her imperfection and inability to completely comply with all the commandments. There are also prayers of atonement after specific violations.

Children are trained in these daily observances and progress to a point where they take full individual responsibility before God for their actions. Bar Mitzvah and Bat Mitzvah is a celebration of that transition. Just how seriously Judaism approaches the idea of ethical responsibility can be seen in one of the parental statements in the Bar Mitzvah ceremony. The parent states, "Praised art thou, oh Lord our God, Ruler of the Universe, who has freed me from the ethical responsibility of this child." Up until age 13, a parent is morally responsible for the behavior of a child. At age 13, the young person is morally responsible for their own behavior in relation to the commandments. Until the age of 13, children are taught how to be a Jew. After the age of 13, they are taught why they are a Jew.

One of the observances in Judaism related to guilt and forgiveness is Yom Kippur. "Yom Kippur" is translated as "Day of Atonement." The observance involves fasting and prayers in recognition of all of one's unresolved errors and weaknesses. These are symbolically forgiven and the worshiper is cleansed. It is a period during which worshipers approach one another in seeking and giving forgiveness as well as approaching God in asking forgiveness.

Catholicism

Sister Janet spoke directly to the questions and referred the interviewer to the Catechism of the Catholic Church (1995). She believes that humans' purpose on earth is to know, love, and serve God and others. The light at the end of the path is God. Guilt is innate. It has existed since the fall of Adam and Eve. Humans share in the sin and guilt that accompanies life in an imperfect world and that is part of being imperfect beings. According to Sister Janet, guilt is a universal experience that serves as a checkpoint. The function of guilt is to assist people in evaluting themselves and changing their actions. Guilt leads sinners back to the path that leads to God.

Several sacraments in Catholicism help people along this path. According to Sister Janet, when Jesus left the earth, the Church created the sacraments so that people would experience forgiveness. Jesus is a visible reminder of God's forgiveness. The sacraments of Baptism, Confirmation, and Eucharist are sacraments of Christian initiation that children and adolescents experience. Baptism is the first ordinance administered to infants, which cleanses them of original guilt. For Catholics, baptism is the means by which one is born into God's family. Baptism represents a choice to have God at the end of the path of life. Confirmation perfects baptism and includes a renewal of baptismal promises. Eucharist is the administration of consecrated bread and wine that represents Christ's body and blood. The Eucharist is designed to nourish the soul, wipe away sins, and preserve the participant from future sins. The Sacrament of the Eucharist is usually administered in association with Mass. Sister Janet characterized Mass as a perfect prayer which articulates the need and request for mercy. Mass involves a prayer of praise, adoration, thanksgiving, sorrow, petition, acceptance of forgiveness, and statement of beliefs. These three sacraments help alleviate original and personal guilt.

The Sacrament of Penance and Reconciliation involves acknowledgment of sins of commission and omission through confession and sorrow, which leads to being reunited with God. Although God forgives a person at the moment one is sorry, the sacrament helps people let go of guilt. Another ordinance is The Sacrament of Anointing of the Sick, formerly called Extreme Unction. This sacrament is performed when a person is in danger of death because of old age or illness. The priest anoints the person with consecrated oil and sometimes offers the Eucharist. One function of this sacrament is to provide forgiveness of sins if a sick or dying person was not able to obtain forgiveness through the Sacrament of Penance. It prepares the person to pass over into eternal life cleansed of guilt.

Episcopalianism

Reverend Tull pointed out the importance of Easter and the Resurrection in guilt and forgiveness. Worshipers continually rediscover the resurrection and newness of life. Christianity is seen as a way to escape the past and to live in a new way. By nature, humans are loving beings in a community of others. Guilt is part of the human experience that emerges when one behaves in an unloving way that is not consistent with who one truly is. According to Reverend Tull, guilt is a signal that reminds humans to be loving in the community and to be who they truly are. Absolution is a setting aside of those behaviors and conditions that are part of violating one's true self in a community. Forgiveness is a gift from a loving God. The community is extremely important according to Reverend Tull because humans discover their worth through their relationships with others.

There are some activities that assist in the process of creating newness. The Eucharist is an observance that includes a summary of faith, a prayer for the world, and a confession of sin with a prayer of thanksgiving for grace and forgiveness. Communion is the administration of bread and wine representing the body and blood of Christ, which is the acting out of restoration to the community. It is an invitation to return to the table of fellowship. Clergy have a special place and authority to declare God's forgiveness to the community. On an individual basis, clergy can engage in the Reconciliation of a Penitent. In this process, the priest is to help an individual objectify their sins, but the sin remains between the person and God.

Excommunication is rare, but represents being cut off from Communion with the community of believers. Excommunication occurs when the behavior is scandalous or notoriously evil. In essence, when one's behavior seriously disrupts the functioning of the community, it would result in expulsion from the community. In general, however, worshipers are welcomed to fellowship and to continually seek a newness of life and to be true to their underlying, basic, loving selves.

Presbyterianism

Pastor Davies was quite succinct in characterizing the experience of guilt and forgiveness in her religion. Although humans live in a sinful world and are by nature sinful, the emphasis for Presbyterians is on the fact that they are children of a loving God who forgives. Forgiveness is not dependent on particular rituals as much as on an individual's acceptance of the grace of Christ to forgive. She emphasized that from this perspective, rituals were not important. Forgiveness emerges directly through Christ. Guilt is not something to weigh people down, but to be lifted from them. Guilt is a signal that reminds one of sinfulness and to accept grace and forgiveness. The weekly service involves a prayer of confession that reminds the congregation that no one is perfect. This is followed by an assurance of forgiveness, which is articulated by the pastor to the congregation. The service is designed to heighten awareness of one's need to accept the grace of a loving God who will forgive.

Mormonism

Bishop Merrell stated that, in the Mormon view, humans are the literal children of a Heavenly Father; children with the potential to become like God. Humans and God are of the same ilk. The purpose of life is to learn to be like God. Perfection is possible through a combination of self-discipline and the grace of God.

People are endowed by God with an innate gift called the "Light of Christ." The Light of Christ leads people towards a healthy life and away from actions and behaviors that will make them less than they really are. Movement toward goodness brings peace and joy, while movement away from goodness brings guilt. The peace and guilt messages of the Light of Christ are signals that help foster spiritual development.

Latter-Day Saints do not believe in original guilt. People are free agents, accountable only for their own behavior. Children are sinless, guiltless, and "alive in Christ." They become accountable for their actions before God at age eight. Parents are responsible for teaching their children about their true nature and about the commandments, which are given through ancient and modern prophets. The commandments are guidelines that map out behaviors that are in keeping with humans' true nature as children of God.

Violation of the commandments leads to guilt, which requires repentance. Repentance requires recognition of the error, sorrow, personal labor to restore all that can be restored, as well as personal prayer to ask for forgiveness and grace. Some grievous sins such as fornication require confession to an ecclesiastical leader who counsels with the person to help them take positive steps to change behavior. After age 12, adolescents meet with their Bishop on an annual basis at least to discuss their development and receive counsel.

Two ordinances support the repentance process: baptism and the sacrament of the Lord's supper. At baptism, people make a covenant with God to take upon themselves the name of Christ, repent of their sins, keep the commandments, and bear one another's burdens. Their sins are symbolically washed away. Children enter the covenant at age 8 when they become personally accountable for their sins according to the Mormon religion. The sacrament of the Lord's supper is administered weekly and represents a renewal of the baptism covenant. Latter-Day Saints engage in a weekly repentance process, remembering Christ's sacrifice and partaking of bread and water to recommit themselves to the covenant and to receive forgiveness.

DIRECTIONS FOR RESEARCH ON INDIVIDUAL RELIGIONS

From the foregoing interviews the reader can imagine that guilt and the alleviation of guilt might be shaped and formulated differently in each religious congregation and by individuals in each unit. Fundamental differences in the definition of humans and God lead to various explanations of, and responses to, guilt. Sikhism and Mormonism teach that perfection is possible and that becoming one with God, or becoming like God, is the goal of existence. Rather than seeking perfection as in Sikhism and Mormonism, Presbyterianism seems to remind parishioners that perfection is not attainable but that forgiveness is. While Sikhs and Mormons state that a moral life leads one to be more divine, Jews state that a moral life leads one to be more human. Differences may make one religious group more vulnerable to chronic guilt or to guilt over failure to attain ideals. Intuitively, for example, Mormons may be more likely to suffer from guilt associated with perfectionism than other groups that emphasize that perfection is not possible.

Such differences lead to different definitions of sin and guilt. A Sikh family may emphasize the disruption of harmony with God as a bad state of affairs, whereas an Episcopal family may be more concerned with the disruption of harmony in the community, whereas a Jewish family might emphasize the violation of clearly articulated commandments as cause for guilt. Whereas a Catholic family might clearly categorize sins as venial or mortal, a Presbyterian family might focus on the general fallability of humans.

Such differences also shape the way a child is taught to alleviate their guilt. Whereas a Presbyterian family might teach a child to ask directly for grace without any ritual, a Catholic family might highlight the need to pursue sacraments to reify one's repentance process. A Mormon family may emphasize personal labor to directly restore any damage done by the error, whereas an Episcopal family may encourage one to discontinue the behavior and renew fellowship. Whereas a Jewish family may have children look forward to annual communal holy days as a time of forgiveness, a Sikh family may eschew all ritual and emphasize an individualized process of repentance.

Additional questions are raised by examination of this qualitative data that may be addressed through quantitative inquiry. Bybee, Merisca, and Velasco (chapter 9, this volume) review findings that confession as part of religious experience served to alleviate guilt. There are many other questions to be addressed including the following:

- Are there differences between children from different religious groups as to why they experience guilt?
- Are there significant differences in the type and intensity of self-conscious affects—guilt, shame, embarrassment, and pride—experienced by children from different religions?
- Are there differences between children in different religious groups in chronic and predispositional guilt?
- What features of religious life such as orthodoxy, fundamentalism, or intrinsicness are related to what features of guilt?

With emerging models of religious experience, refinements in defining and measuring guilt, and an acceptance of the legitimacy of religion in human being's lives as something other than a pathological adaptation, the stage is set to begin to explore the true correlates between guilt and religion as experienced by children.

THE DEVELOPMENT OF CHILDREN'S RELIGIOUS EXPERIENCES

No review of guilt and religion in children would be complete without at least some consideration of the role of development. There is little empirical data on this important topic, although several recent developmental models address children's experience with religion. Elkind (1978) offers three stages of religious understanding in development that closely parallel Piaget's stages of cognitive development. During Stage 1, children are quite undifferentiated in their identification with institutional religion and in their personal experience with prayer. Stage 2 evidences greater cognitive awareness and parallels Piaget's concrete operational stage. Children can identify themselves and others as being of different religions because of concrete outward manifestations of such. Prayer is identified by the actual behaviors associated with praying, whatever those cultural forms might be. Stage 3 parallels the emergence of Piaget's formal operational stage. At this stage children disavow religious identity by outward forms, but define themselves and others according to abstractions of inner belief. Prayer becomes an inner mental function that is private and intimate and not so dependent on outward form.

Fowler (1991) presents a stage model of religious/faith development that builds upon both Piaget's cognitive and Kohlberg's moral development models. The first four of seven stages occur prior to adulthood. The first stage is "Primal Faith" which predates birth and language. It is centered on the caring behaviors and rituals that parents provide to meet the child's needs. The pattern of responsiveness by the parent establishes the foundation for later stages of faith. The second stage, "Intuitive-Projective Faith," is characterized by constructions of transcendent ideals that are analogs of those of the children's parents. The third stage is "Mythic-Literal Faith" and is characterized by a shift from fantasy to more concrete reasoning about life and the core values. The fourth stage is "Synthetic-Conventional Faith" which emerges with formal operational thinking and adolescence. The adolescent's ability to abstract, reflect, and relate unseen forms emerges at a time when identity formation is paramount. Capturing an internalized sense of self that incorporates a set of personal religious beliefs and values, a relationship with God or the transcendent principle, and a community of like-minded fellows is crucial at this stage.

Oser (1991) describes a model of religious development that requires integration of seven sets of constructs that appear to be polar opposites. As children develop, they may focus on one pole more than another, but mature religious judgment involves a recognition that each pole depends on the other for its existence. The shifts and crises inherent in struggling toward such integration are identified in five stages, four of which occur during childhood and adolescence. The seven polar dimensions are freedom versus dependence, transcendence versus immanence, hope versus absurdity, transparency versus opacity, faith versus fear, holy versus profane, and eternity versus ephemerity. Considering only the dimension of freedom versus dependence, Stage 1 is characterized by total dependence on an all-powerful God who exercises unidirectional power and control. Stage 2 evidences some bidirectional influence and weakening dependency. Children at this stage believe that their obedience and good deeds influence God's behavior towards them. Stage 3 shows a decided shift toward the freedom side of the dimension. Children see themselves as autonomous and the Ultimate Being as having its own autonomous responsibilities. Children in stage 4 acknowledge the limits of autonomy and begin to capture their freedom in terms of community and God's sustaining influence on their freedom. Stage 5 is a rare paradoxical state in which the poles are truly integrated. People in stage 5 are described as "finding freedom in utter commitment and obedience, which to others appears as a loss of freedom" (p. 13).

Will studies indicate that guilt increases in intensity as individuals progress to higher stages of religious development or will their greater capacity for abstraction enable them to construe more ambiguity into situations and invent more effective guilt-reducing rationalizations with maturity as suggested by Bybee, Merisca, and Velasco (chapter 9, this volume)? Will progression through these stages be paralleled by a differentiation of guilt into discrete variants? As children become capable of envisioning guilt over transcendent ideals, for instance, might guilt over failure to attain these ideals emerge in a parallel fashion? These and other questions await empirical study.

REFERENCES

Allport, G. W., & Ross, J. M. (1967). Personal religious orientation and prejudice. *Journal of Personality and Social Psychology, 5,* 432–443.

Batson, C. D., Schoenrade, P., & Ventis, W. C. (1993). *Religion and the individual: A social-psychological perspective.* New York: Oxford University Press.

Bergin, A. E. (1980). Psychotherapy and religious values. *Journal of Consulting and Clinical Psychology, 48,* 75–105.

Bergin, A. E. (1983). Religiosity and mental health: A critical reevaluation and meta-analysis. *Professional Psychology, 14,* 170–184.

Bergin, A. E. (1991). Values and religious issues in psychotherapy and mental health. *American Psychologist, 46,* 394–403.

Bergin, A. E., Masters, K. S., & Richards, P. S. (1987). Religiousness and mental health reconsidered: A study of an intrinsically religious sample. *Journal of Counseling Psychology, 34,* 197–204.

Bupp, C. S. (1983). *An examination of shame and guilt among veterans of the Vietnam conflict.* Unpublished doctoral dissertation, University of Minnesota, Minneapolis.

Catechism of the Catholic Church (1995). New York, NY. First Image/Doubleday.

Clay, R. A. (1996, August). Psychologists' faith in religion begins to grow. *The APA Monitor, 27,* 8, 1.

Dittes, J. E. (1971). Religion, prejudice, and personality. In M. Strommen (Ed.), *Research on religious development: A comprehensive handbook* (pp. 355–390). New York: Hawthorn.

Elkind, D. (1978). *The child's reality: Three developmental themes.* Hillsdale, NJ: Erlbaum.

Ellis, A. (1980). Psychotherapy and atheistic values: A response to A. E. Bergin's "Psychotherapy and religious values." *Journal of Consulting and Clinical Psychology, 48,* 635–639.

Ellis, A. E. (1996, August). *Can rational emotive behavior therapy (REBT) be effectively used with people who have devout beliefs in god and religion?* Symposium conducted at the 104th Annual Convention of the American Psychological Association, Toronto, Canada.

Fischer, L. (1991). *The relationships among family functioning, IQ, and mental health outcomes in transracially adoptive families.* Unpublished doctoral dissertation, University of Minnesota, Minneapolis.

Fowler, J. W. (1991). Stages in faith consciousness. In F. K. Oser & W. G. Scarlett (Eds.), *Religious development in childhood and adolescence* (pp. 27–45). San Francisco: Jossey-Bass.

Freud, S. (1950). *Totem and taboo: Some points of agreement between the mental lives of savages and neurotics.* (J. Strachey, Trans.). New York: W. W. Norton. (Original work published 1913)

Freud, S. (1961). *Civilization and its discontents.* (J. Strachey, Trans.). New York: W. W. Norton. (Original work published 1930)

Freud, S. (1961). *The future of an illusion.* (J. Strachey, Trans. & Ed.). Norton & Company: New York. (Original work published in 1927)

Freud, S. (1964). *Leonardo da Vinci and a memory of his childhood.* (A. Tyson, Trans.). New York: W. W. Norton. (Original work published 1910)

Gartner, J., Larson, D. B., & Allen, G. D. (1991). Religious commitment and mental health: A review of the empirical literature. *Journal of Psychology and Theology, 19,* 6–25.

Jensen, J. P., & Bergin, A. E. (1988). Mental health values of professional therapists: A national interdisciplinary study. *Professional Psychology, 19,* 290–297.

Lehr, E., & Spilka, B. (1989). Religion in the introductory psychology textbook: A comparison of three decades. *Journal for the Scientific Study of Religion, 28,* 366–371.

Matthews, D. A., McCullough, M., Larson, D. B., Koenig, H. G., Swyers, J. P., & Milano, M. G. (in press). Religious commitment and health: A review of the research and implications for family medicine. *Archives of Family Medicine.*

Meek, K. R., Albright, J. S., & McMinn, M. R. (1995). Religious orientation, guilt, confession, and forgiveness. *Journal of Psychology and Theology, 23,* 190–197.

Morgan, D. T. (1995). *Intrinsic religiousness, religious orthodoxy, and religious fundamentalism as predictors of social and emotional functioning.* Unpublished master's thesis, Brigham Young University, Provo, Utah.

Oser, F. K. (1991). The development of religious judgment. In F. K. Oser & W. G. Scarlett (Eds.), *Religious development in childhood and adolescence* (pp. 5–25). San Francisco: Jossey-Bass.

Payne, I. R., Bergin, A. E., Bielma, K., & Jenkins, P. (1991). Review of religion and mental health: Prevention and the enhancement of psychosocial functioning. *Prevention in Human Services, 9,* No. 2, 11–40.

Quiles, Z. N., & Bybee, J. (1997). Chronic and predispositional guilt: Relations to mental health, prosocial behavior and religiosity. *Journal of Personal Assessment, 69,* 104–126.

Richards, P. S. (1991). Religious devoutness in college students: Relations with emotional adjustment and psychological separation from parents. *Journal of Counseling Psychology, 2,* 189–196.

Richards, P. S., & Williams, R. C. (1989, August). *The assessment of shame and guilt proneness in counseling.* Paper presented at the 97th Annual Convention of the American Psychological Association, New Orleans, LA.

Rowe, D. C., & Plomin, R. (1981). The importance of non-shared (E_1) environmental influences in behavioral development. *Developmental Psychology, 17,* 517–531.

Sanua, V. D. (1969). Religion, mental health, and personality: A review of empirical studies. *American Journal of Psychiatry, 125,* 1203–1213.

Smith, R. L. (1972). *The relative proneness to shame or guilt as an indicator of defensive style.* (Doctoral dissertation, Northwestern University, 1972). Dissertation Abstracts International, 33, 2823B–2824B.

Tangney, J. P., Wagner, P. E., Burggraf, S. A., Gramzow, R., & Fletcher, C. (1990). *The test of self-conscious affect for children (TOSCA-C).* Fairfax, VA: George Mason University.

Watson, J. B. (1983). *Psychology from the standpoint of a behaviorist.* Dover, NH: Frances Pinter. (Original work published in 1924)

Wells, M. G. (1998). The context of religion in clinical child psychology. In W. K. Silverman & T. H. Ollendick (Eds.), *Developmental issues in the clinical treatment of children.* Boston: Allyn & Bacon.

CHAPTER 8

Guilt and Sexuality in Adolescents

Donald L. Mosher

University of Connecticut, Storrs, Connecticut

What is new in the minds of adolescents? According to Kohlberg and Gilligan (1971, p. 1060), "If there is anything that can be safely said about what is new in the minds of adolescents, it is that they, like their elders, have sex on their minds." Moreover, according to Gagnon and Simon (1973, p. 42), "Despite our present capacity as a society to generate high levels of public discourse about sexual matters, it is probably not unreasonable to assert that learning about sex in our society is learning about guilt; conversely, learning how to manage sexuality constitutes learning how to manage guilt."

Three decades ago, Mosher (1966) published a classic paper that introduced three measures of three aspects of guilt. These measures of guilt as a personality disposition generated a few hundred research investigations, selectively reviewed by Mosher (1994a,b) and Byrne and Schulte (1990). Recently, Mosher conceptualized guilt (1994a) and involvement during sexual intercourse (1996) within Silvan Tomkins's script theory. In this chapter, sex guilt is discussed as an affect-control script, script theory is applied to adolescent sexuality, and guidelines for the sex education of adolescents from the perspective of a critical morality are offered.

Guilt and Children
Copyright © 1998 by Academic Press. All rights of reproduction in any form reserved.

SEX GUILT AS AN AFFECT-CONTROL SCRIPT

This section introduces many concepts from Silvan Tomkins's (1991) script theory. Learning to use a complex theory requires that the reader understand the meanings assigned to theoretical terms. By introducing theoretical distinctions, a theorist helps us perceive what he or she has conceived. A good theory keeps us from being blind and dumb by helping us to perceive and conceive the new. With a genius like Tomkins, this is a challenge to be faced by interested scholars; if this summary proves too dense for your purposes, skip ahead to the section on *The Role of Parents*.

From the perspective of Tomkins's script theory, affects are sets of muscular and glandular responses located in the skin of the face and also widely distributed throughout the body that generate sensory feedback that is either inherently acceptable and rewarding or inherently unacceptable and punishing. Affects are *discrete,* with specific neural programs that are variously experienced: two with the positive qualia of interest-excitement or enjoyment-joy, one with the neutral quale of surprise-startle, and six with distinctive negative qualia of fear-terror, distress-anguish, anger-rage, shame, disgust, and dissmell (dissmell is to olfaction as disgust is to gustation).

The most important concepts in script theory for understanding persons are *scenes* and *scripts*. A scene is defined as a happening with a beginning and an end that forms an organized whole. At a theoretical minimum, all scenes must contain at least one *affect* that is *invested* in its *object* (any psychological entity), which is usually the *source* or *target* of affect. For example, imagine that Tim is hot (affect of sexual excitement) for Tina (object), that his fantasies of being sexual with her are the source of his sexual excitement, that she is the target of his sexual excitement, and that Tim invests his sexual affect in Tina by valuing her as sexually desirable.

Sexual scenes, particularly interpersonal ones, usually contain more elements than a single affect and its object. Sexual scenes often include a cast of sexual actors interacting at a particular time and place, with all of the sexual props, events, actions, affects, and other psychological functions that make up a culturally defined sexual episode as a set of transactions between two actors.

Sexual guilt is an *auxiliary* affect that functions as a barrier to sexual excitement and enjoyment within certain sexual scenes; an auxiliary affect because it is innately activated by the temporary interruption and attenuation of already activated positive affects. Such conflicted scenes contain erotic events (things that happen), actions (actors' purposive behavior), or psychological functions (perception, memory, imagination, and like) that are invested with sexual meanings that conflict with the individual's moral code. That is, as an affect, sexual guilt is an interruptive or inhibitory auxiliary affective response (see also Barmeister, Stillwell, & Heatherton, 1994) to already activated affective excitement or enjoyment that is invested in morally taboo sexual objects. The function of the negative affect of guilt is *affect control,* attenuating or inhibiting excitement or enjoyment of sexual objects. Because affect is the principal motivator in the human being, action is consequently deliberately suppressed or indirectly inhibited. When joined with a *report* (a conscious message) of a moral rule, affective guilt provides a moral reason for restraining affect and action in this sexual scene.

However, the affect of guilt is not always conscious, reasoned, or reasonable. Not only that, reasons are not causes. According to Tomkins (1962), the activation of affects as biological entities is based upon specific innate profiles of neural stimulation. Although fantasizing and remembering often induce sexual affect, the activation of affect does not require cognition (see Barrett, chapter 3, this volume). How would a baby have learned the cry of distress as it leaves the birth canal? Does it appraise the world as a vale of tears? Instead, any learned activator operates by mimicking the profile of the innate activator; activation in any learned affect script is built upon the innate affect script.

Because discrete affects have the properties of abstractness and generality in Tomkins's (1991) theory, there are no affects that are specific to sexuality until they are concretized and specified by the sexual nature of their source or target within the context of an unfolding scene. The expressions, *sexual affect* and *sexual guilt,* are short-hand terms for a discrete positive affect invested in sexual objects and guilt over sexual excitement, enjoyment, sensation, perception, cognition, or action.

Following the socialization of affects in the infant or child, sexual guilt controls illicit affects, actions, and sexual responses in sexual scenes by operating as a *script.* A script is defined by Tomkins (1991) as a set of affect-invested rules for ordering information in a connected set of scenes that share a family resemblance. Information in the family of scenes is *ordered* in the sense that events and actions become predictable, producible, interpretable, manageable, or defensible through the use of the rules. The *rule* is an instruction that orders information to govern how the person functions psychologically: how to see, hear, feel, imagine, analyze, and do. When not innate, the rule is a product of learning, becoming a skilled process that at first compresses and then later expands information; because it is skilled, the compression–expansion transformation is no longer in consciousness. The person responds to new and familiar information in the scene with compressed information in the form of rules that expand as a function of contingencies in the unfolding scene.

Learned rules in a personality script are a product of a process of *psychological magnification.* During psychological magnification, the person coassembles a set of affect-invested scenes, usually in consciousness, in order to devise tactics and strategies to make the outcomes of those scenes closer to the heart's desire. As a product of affect-invested learning, the rule possesses both *information advantage* and *magnification advantage.* Information advantage is a function of the ratio of the number of scenes ordered (its power) in the numerator when divided by the simplicity of the ordering rule in the denominator. A scientific law, like the laws of thermodynamics or Tomkins's principle of the density of neural firing in the innate activation of affects (1962, p. 250), has information advantage, accounting for a multitude of observations of events with a simpler principle. Magnification advantage results when the power of ordered information in the numerator is multiplied by *affect density* (the intensity, duration, and repetition of affect invested in the information-advantaged rules). The affect invested in rules occurs not only in the scenes that have led to the search for rules but also during the process of psychological magnification itself when fresh affect is invested in the rules. The affect experienced in the scene and during psychological magnification may be the same or different. For example, a person may feel sexually excited and free from guilt during a sexual scene with a friend's partner. But, later on, after coassembling the scene with other sexual scenes that contain moral violations, the person decides that having sex with the partner of a friend is wrong. So, the person now invests fresh guilty affect in a rule that adds a condition, the partner of friends, to an older rule of when to avoid sexual contact.

Affects *amplify* by analogy all ongoing and recruited psychological processes in a scene, making them *more so*. In a sexual scene, through affect amplification by guilt, the taboo sexual source and target become more guilt-filled and the attenuated sexual response more guilt-tinged, altogether more analogous to the qualia of guilty affect. Affect amplification thereby correlates both source and response as guiltily alike, through their sharing of an experienced qualia and temporal profile of guilt-interrupted and guilt-attenuated sexual excitement and enjoyment.

In contrast, psychological magnification *reamplifies* the already once amplified scenes with fresh affect, making thematic issues *more so through time*. In a family of similar or analogous guilty sexual scenes, the issue of sexual sin becomes a recurrent theme of sexual temptation leading to excitement and enjoyment that becomes an occasion of sin and subsequent guilty regret. Whether the scenes were amplified by guilt initially or not, the fresh guilt experienced when reviewing the set of scenes may generate rules of remorse, confession, penance, or undoing. If the set of scenes were already invested with guilt, the fresh guilt reamplifies the guilt invested in the original scenes, making the already guilt-filled scenes, more so through time as a rule-governed script. Psychological magnification validates the sinfulness of sexuality, making it more sinfully so through time by constellating new but analogous scenes to its sex-guilt family. In the script, cognition as analysis, imagination, and memory—transformed into and conserved as rules—has bound time through its ability to represent and rerepresent affectively urgent information. The rules in the sex-guilt script contain answers in the form of instructions about how to respond to the problematics in the family of sexual scenes. If sexual temptation becomes newly problematic in the script, rules for the avoidance of temptation and for the inhibition of sexual desire, which is exciting, imagined temptation, will join the earlier rules for controlling excitement and enjoyment from past sexual scenes.

Thus, affects are a change-amplifying and correlating mechanism within a scene; whereas magnified rules conserve earlier possible solutions to families of scenes. These automatic strategies often prove to be more self-validating than self-fulfilling. For example, a sex-guilt script validates the person as a sinner more often than it sexually fulfills or creates a valued moral life. For the adolescent, sexual awakening evokes sexual temptation and guilt more than it brings untrammeled pleasure. In a culture that condemns sexual experimentation, youthful experiences with mastur-bation, petting, and coitus validate the sex-guilt script more readily than they con-tribute to an affluent script of sexual pleasure. Yet, responding with conserved guilt to socially permissible sexual scenes in adulthood based upon childhood's rules dulls sexual excitement, degrades enjoyment, and transforms the meanings of adult sexual scenes from self-fulfilling pleasure to validated moral disgrace.

A rule is both a *product* and *process* of the *minding system* (the integrated cognitive and motivational subsystems of the human being; Tomkins, 1992). The minding system duplicates itself by a feedback system that uses information to reduce the difference between a predetermined image (purpose) and the current state to zero. Rules are the product of learning patterned skills, tactics, and strategies. Following compression into memory, the rule is stored as a product. When activated as a process during an unfolding scene, the rule is retrieved as stored content. During an unfolding scene, as compressed information, rules interact with newly gathered auxiliary information from sensory, perceptual, and affective sources. Then, rules expand as scripted instructions about what and how to think, act, and speak.

Rules are open-ended instructions that have certain features. These features define the nature of the rules. Rules are *selective* in their application to specific scenes, *incomplete* in that they require supplementation by auxiliary information gathered in the ongoing scene to fulfill their conditions, variously *accurate* or *inaccu-rate* in their ordering of information (predictions, strategies, defenses, and the like), and continually *changing* and reordering based upon outcomes and evaluations of new scenes.

The rules in a *sexual-script* order information about how to interpret and respond when in a set of scenes sharing a family resemblance among their sexual elements. A *family resemblance* is an incompletely overlapping set that is connected, in the case of positive affect, through sharing similarities as *variants* around an unchanging core that distinguishes the family, or, in the case of negative affect, through *analogs* that make what might otherwise be familial differences somehow the same by analogy. When compared to positive affects, the mind's facile capacity for forming analogies means that negative affect more rapidly constellates new scenes to its growing family. Negative affect can snowball in a positive feedback loop.

All scripts are *modular*. Thus, along with trial-and-error responding to novel scenes, an individual has available a multiplicity of scripts that can decompose and recombine to govern psychological responses to any scene that somehow resembles a scripted family of scenes. The modular element of the script is the rule.

Classifying Sexual Scripts

The most important modular rules are used to help classify scripts. Tomkins's taxonomy includes four major classes: (a) Script of Orientation and Evaluation, (b) Affect Scripts, (c) Ratio Scripts, and (d) Change-Review Scripts. For present purposes, the most important exemplars are Ideological Scripts as a subclass of Evaluative Scripts and Affect Control Scripts as a subclass of Affect Scripts.

Sexual scripts are modularly complex. They combine rules from attachment scripts from infancy with rules from gender and interpersonal scripts from early childhood (Orientation Scripts), with rules from discrete affect scripts about excitement, enjoyment, and sensory pleasure in nonsexual scenes from childhood, with rules from affect ratio scripts that are learned in adolescent sexual scenes of masturbation, kissing and petting, and the like, with rules from change-review scripts of love and jealousy drawn from childhood and adolescence, along with prior interpersonal scenes involving the specific actors that provide a plot and map for any ongoing sexual scene. Of course, sexual scripts also contain rules derived from scenes in which guilt and other negative affects such as distress, fear, anger, disgust, dissmell, and shame were psychologically magnified.

Shame as a Theoretical Construct That Includes Guilt

For Tomkins, shame is a theoretical construct that includes guilt among other aspects of shame. The essential condition for the activation of shame is, "I want, but . . ." The essential condition for the instigation of sexual guilt is, "I want you sexually, but I feel guilty." The more general conditionality of shame includes guilt's specific essential condition. Shame and guilt are innately activated when already instigated positive affect is confronted with a temporary barrier, like social inferiority or morality, that interrupts and attenuates excitement or enjoyment.

When observing persons who were experiencing shame or guilt, Tomkins noted that their affective response was characterized by the same facial behavior: eyes and head down, face averted and blushing. What was different was their psychological experience as manifested in different reports of perceived causes and consequences. Tomkins noted that the origin of this facial behavior was the shyness response of infants after they were able to conserve familiar faces; their excited looking and smiling was interrupted and attenuated by a stranger. After the eyes and head were lowered, the blushing and averted face might just display renewed eye-gaze interest in the stranger and another smile of enjoyment.

Tomkins (1987) recognized that shame is used today to refer more to feelings of inferiority than to feeling of guilt and to proving oneself good as superior rather than good as moral. Nonetheless, he regarded shame as a *theoretical construct* that was not necessarily best defined for scientific purposes by contemporary usage. Shame is considered to be the same affect in spite of feeling quite different when it is coassembled as complex reports of an identical affect, along with different sources and responses, and with different perceived causes and consequences.

Affects are evolutionary, biological adaptations that are general and abstract rather than specific to different psychological sources and responses. Thus, anxiety and phobia can be psychologically differentiated as either having no identifiable source and as having a focused source, although both remain exemplars of the discrete affect of fear-terror. Also, responses to the identical affect of fear can vary from starving from fear of eating in anorexia to eating from fear of starving (or emptiness) in bulimia. Psychological distinctions can generate a list of "affects" as long as its abundant affective vocabulary. Not all of these are theoretically or empirically trivial, but not all of them are discrete affects that carve nature at its joints. In describing discrete affects, one must be parsimonious.

The different sources and responses associated with affective shame can lead to shame, now regarding it as a theoretical construct, to be experienced variously as embarrassment, shyness, discouragement, inferiority, guilt, alienation, and more. Nonetheless, regardless of how the affect of shame is differentially experienced in consciousness, it remains identical as a subcortical, stored, innate neural program or script. Thus, guilt is considered to be a form of moral shame rather than a separate discrete affect (Tomkins, 1987). From Tomkins's perspective, shame and guilt share a single discrete neural affect program, yet remain experientially distinct because they usually are coassembled with different psychological reports reflecting different interpretations of the scene. Examples are: "I am too hot and may embarrass myself"; "I am too hot and my partner may embarrass me"; "I am so excited that I must be brazen, which is shameful"; "I am so excited, that my partner may think I am brazen, which is shameful"; "I am so excited that this act must be sinful"; "I am so excited that I feel guilty for my lust but not for this sexual act"; "I am so excited that this sexual linkage or partner must be shameful to me, my partner, or my society"; "I am so excited that this sexual linkage or partner must be sinful because anything that feels this good must be evil"; "I am ashamed that I don't feel guilty over my excitement"; "I am ashamed that I do feel guilty over my excitement"; "I am ashamed that I feel ashamed of my excitement"; "I feel guilty that I am not more ashamed of my excitement"; "I feel guilty that I am so ashamed of my excitement"; "I feel both ashamed and guilty over my excitement"; "I am so excited that I no longer feel either ashamed or guilty"; and many more.

In all of these instances, already instigated sexual excitement is interrupted and attenuated or inhibited by shame or guilt as a controlling affect. Although many conceptual and empirical distinctions can be made between shame and guilt, their paramount similarity is their shared innate neurological program and status as an auxiliary interruptive affect of already instigated positive affect.

As discussed later, what is even more important for Tomkins than the distinctions between shame and guilt are the distinctions, not usually made by psychologists, between shame or guilt and the affects of disgust and dissmell, which are the more toxic affects. As always, Tomkins stressed the role of affect in the face, believing that the experience of facial affect was the most important component of the experience of affect. As noted, he found differences between shame and guilt only in reports of sources and responses but not in facial affect. However, disgust and dissmell—two innate auxiliary responses to the oxygen, thirst, and hunger drives—revealed distinctive facial changes. In disgust, the head is forward and down while the lower lip is lowered and protruded. Whereas, in dissmell, the head is pulled back while the upper lip is raised and the nose, elevated.

The Role of the Parent

Parents introduce negative affect into scenes with sexual meaning during the socialization of children's affect because human sexuality itself is invested with affective value and meaning. As an important example of scripts of Orientation and Evaluation, Ideological Scripts contain a view of human nature that includes what is valued in the socialization of children and their sexuality. Containing the central values of a culture and the sanctions for their violation, ideology begins in cosmology and religion and ends in social criticism. The socialization of affect prepares the individual for a life of ideological partisanship. This is because the affects that are psychologically magnified as personal scripts during affect socialization and certain ideological postures, which are systems of belief that are enculturated by learning during socialization, *resonate*.

In the psychological process of resonance, a person with both guilty affect *and* an idealized and internalized cognitive system of moral beliefs experiences the onset of either affect or cognition as instigating and amplifying the other. The three rules are: "If you know sin, then feel guilty; if you feel guilty, then you know sin; continue this alternation and intensify it. Resonating affect and ideology itensify and prolong one another as reciprocating sources and targets. Thus, a guilty personality and an ideology of sin mutually resonate as one form of psychological magnification of sex-guilt scripts.

For Tomkins (1965), Western history revealed a polarity of left versus right in ideological stance, from the humanist, who values positive affect and the child as an end it itself, to the normative, who values normative standards to be met by the child before positive affect is deserved. The humanist identifies with the oppressed and social change; the normative, with the oppressor and the status quo. The ideology of the humanist parent encourages a rewarding socialization of the child's affect, including affect invested in sexuality; just as the ideology of the normative parent requires the opposite, a punitive socialization of affect-invested sexuality.

The critical ideological question is whether the child and the child's sexuality is to be regarded as a valued end, or must the child's will be broken so as not to jeopardize the parent's comfort and society's mores. For the humanist parent, empathy with the child's sexual interest and enjoyment follows from the acceptance of sexuality as a human good. For the normative parent, sexuality is an alien entity to be controlled in self and child, lest its urgency be magnified until all control is lost and perversion triumphs. For the humanist, human nature and natural sexuality are good; whereas for the normative, the nature of the human being and sexuality are evil.

The sexual interest and response of children elicits negative affect in normative parents who deliberately and self-righteously trigger negative affect in their child in order to inhibit any sexual response, whether affect or action, that they view as morally unacceptable. When the interruption of sexual affect by parents is joined with a verbalized moral belief that is drawn from a normative ideology of sexual morality, it conjoins affect control with moral cognitions, producing resonance. When such parental control elicits a guilty response in the child, it is socialization and socialized response that inscribe the sex-guilt-script. For example, in conventional Roman Catholic morality, having sexual intercourse is acceptable only within a monogamous marriage for purposes of procreation without experiencing too much sensory pleasure. Initially externalized admonitions to avoid sex before marriage for moral reasons that also trigger affective guilt (perhaps because the interruptive pattern occurred during a scene of exciting sexual longing) can become an internalized barrier to interest, excitement, and activity in sexual scenes. The magnification advantage of the sex-guilt script is enhanced by the resonance between affect and ideology. Psychologically magnified childhood scenes in which sexual excitement and enjoyment were transformed into sexual guilt by parental induction of guilty affect resonate with the ideological belief that sexuality is morally problematic. Thus, affective sex-guilt and a sex-negative ideology mutually extend and augment one another by joining a guilty affective *caring* with an ideological *knowing* that defines reality.

In America, because of extensive normative ideological beliefs about the dangerous and disgusting nature of sexuality, the socialization of affect invested in sexual objects is characteristically vigilant, insistent, strident, and pious. Tomkins specified four types of dynamic operators: (a) affect amplification, (b) psychological magnification, (c) idealization, and (d) sacralization. Through the dynamic operator of amplification, the affect of guilt makes all sexual responses more guiltily, sexually so. Through the dynamic operator of psychologically magnification, the sex-guilt script makes all selected sexual scenes more guiltily familiar through time. Through the dynamic operator of idealization, guilt over profaning or polluting an ideal sexual image becomes most guiltily so. For example, idealization of the mother can produce a Madonna-whore complex. But, the dynamic operator of *sacralization* makes all moral rules divine and absolute; thus, the sanction of eternal damnation in hell's fire awaits the sinfully, sexually guilty.

Socialization of Affects in Development

Tomkins's vision of the socialization of affects introduced a radically different theory of development to psychology than those offered by behavioral, psychodynamic, or stage theorists. First, for Tomkins, what is socialized is affect itself, rather than behavior, the id, or cognition. The theoretical units of analysis are scene and script. Affect and its object are the crucial theoretical elements within the scene. Coassembled families of remembered and imagined scenes that share similarities or analogies in aspects of their origin, source, target, response, and consequences of affect investment are analyzed when psychologically seeking to understand the rules of scripts.

Second, during affect socialization, the observed unit of analysis must be enlarged to a *sequence of scenes* because thematically meaningful scenes unfold through time as related episodes. The sequence of scenes includes (a) the scenes leading up to the socialization scene, (b) the child's immediate and delayed, observable and internal, responses to the parent's punishing transaction in the specific socialization scene, and (c) the subsequent scenes of parent's and child's responses and transactions to the earlier scenes.

Moreover, the socialization of excitement and enjoyment invested in sexuality is not independent but is conjoined with the socialization of negative affects used to control sexuality. Furthermore, a punitive socialization of sexual affect may be relatively isolated (specific) or quite typical (general) of a larger reign of terror, rage, and dissmell, and when it is general and toxic, this creates a more stable negative equilibrium, making change harder. The conceptual complexity introduced by making the child an autonomous actor who responds variously to socialization transactions, to his or her own affective inertia, and to changeable or stable scripts does full justice to the intricacy of both the human beings' intellectual *and* affective freedom. These theoretical complexities bear a cost of requiring hard thinking and much learning from psychologists who wish to understand and appreciate Tomkins, but his fruitful theory promises the benefits of continually expanding advantaged information.

Because the minding system both represents these affective and transactional responses in scenes and rerepresents these coassembled interactions through time, quite different consequences are produced by what might appear to observers to be a similar socializing scene as a function of different existing ratios of preexisting affects (For example, is guilt relatively more shameful or disgusting?) and different forms of Affect Ratio Scripts (For example, given a favorable or unfavorable overall ratio of positive to negative affect across life's scenes, is the person relatively optimistic or pessimistic about sexuality and morality?). As a simplified example, consider the child who has been warned about the evils and dangers of masturbation, yet does so anyway and is caught (versus a child who, without warning, is unexpectedly caught in his or her initial exploration of his or her genitals). The parent can respond variously by expressing concerns for the health of the child that is either distressing ("I don't want you to hurt yourself") or fear-inducing ("If you don't stop playing with that thing, I'll cut it off"); by instilling moral shame directly by pointing out the moral weakness of the child ("You know that you shouldn't touch yourself there. It's bad."), or indirectly by blushing and hanging their own head; by angrily slapping the child's hands while saying, "Don't ever do that again!" or by slapping without verbal comment; by displaying a disgust face with or without also uttering, "filthy child," and so on. Then, the child can feel either angry, guilty, ashamed, disgusted, or the like and can cease masturbation for now or forever, or vow to fight back against such moral hypocrisy, or to become sexually brazen, or to better conceal his or her sexual interest, or to continue secretly while feeling distressed or ashamed or guilty or disgusted or afraid, and so on. Such responses vary as a function of the affects experienced by the child in the scene, scripts developed in prior scenes that select this scene as relevant to their thematic concern, and the inertia of generated affect that can continue to amplify further responses. The excited child may begin masturbating again when the parent leaves the room, whereas, the disgusted child may become reluctant ever to touch his or another's genitals ever again. The child's affect and recruited responses may or may not be overt and correctly interpreted by the parents. When the child responds overtly, then, the parent will make more socializing responses to whatever affective or behavioral response is detected in the child, and the child will respond again, and so on.

What's more, the socialization of affects continues throughout life, deepening or attenuating the earlier patterns, introducing or reducing conflict or ambiguity, reversing directions of affect (from negative to positive or the other way around), or changing dominant affective responses (from control by shame to control by disgust), or recasting the sexual scene as scenes of revenge ("I'll do to my kids what my parents did to me."), undoing ("I'll never do to my kids what my parents did to me."), or of celebration ("I live for sex and feeling guilty" [in perpetual alternation]).

Because affects are personally experienced as urgent, are socially contagious (See Campos, 1994), and are prone to social escalation, society rarely permits the free expression of unmodulated affect. If my sexual excitement is urgent, you may find it contagious, and we may escalate each other's excitement. But what if we are strangers, both men or women, in church rather than in bed, afflicted by sexual dysfunction or a sexually transmitted disease, an adolescent? Given the social problematics of sexuality, societies and families script children for affect control.

The Affect-Control Script

The *affect-control script* contains affect-invested rules for controlling the consciousness, density, display, expression, communication, action, consequences, conditionality, and specificity of unacceptable affective responses. The control of affect is principally maintained through a specific process called an *affect bind*. An affect bind is defined as a learned reduction of an activated affect by a controlling affect that is automatically activated by the initial affect as a learned sequence.

The principal dynamic in the formation of sex-guilt scripts is consequential dense affect change, most often experienced as a good-scene-turned-bad because a dense positive affect has been transformed into a dense negative affect. When parents characteristically use a specific affect to control the child's excitement and enjoyment in scenes given sexual meaning, the child may learn to use the same affect to control his or her own excitement or enjoyment in sexual scenes. Parental induction of guilt in socializing sexual scenes can lead to a skilled learning of an excitement-guilt or an enjoyment-guilt affective bind by the child who now has learned how to attenuate or inhibit his or her positive affects in future sexual scenes by a skilled and automatic activation of affective guilt. Because the affect bind has become skilled and automatic, it does not require a conscious moral cognition, but the person may search for the source of the affect and correctly (or incorrectly) conclude a moral rule has been or might be transgressed. But also, the person might just experience the uncomfortable qualia of the negative affect without being able to identify its source as a "moral" barrier or even to label the affect as "guilt" when it is experienced only as a cognitively vague but urgent discomfort that requires reducing.

Whether the discrete affect will be labeled guilt or shame by the individual, we have argued, is largely a function of contextual cues and learned cue assignment. One person's guilt is another person's shame. If a professor has sex with a student, he or she may feel guilty ("I feel guilty for breaking an important moral rule.") or ashamed (I feel ashamed for breaking an important social rule.") or both, "I feel guilty and ashamed for having sex with that student."), or neither ("Morality and society be damned; I found that sexual experience to be exciting and enjoyable."). The protagonist's interpretations select subsequent responses as the scripted expressions of shame or guilt, whether they are concealment or confession, continuation or cessation. These interpretations-as-rules have been psychologically magnified in past sexual scenes, becoming rules in this family.

At its simplest, intensifying sexual excitement can be inhibited by an affect bind that controls noisy and passionate sexual expression within the sexual scene. The affect bind is an automatic learned sequence in which the affect of excitement (or enjoyment) amplifying passionate sexual response reaches a level that elicits a controlling affect, like guilt. When the controlling affect is elicited as a learned affect control sequence, the rule is, "If too much excitement (or enjoyment), then turndown (attenuate) or turn-off (inhibit) excitement when guilt begins." At its most complex, the scripts of shame and guilt over sexuality can lead to ritual suicide and self-mutilation. Such run-away magnification of ashamed and guilty scripts over sexuality intensify by conjoining multiple affects from multiple sources.

For example, a samurai is charged with securing secrets from a geisha before strangling her, but he finds himself impotent in the scene. His multiple sources of shame in the scene include shameful feelings of sexual inferiority for not having an erection; a deep shame over discovering that he is not who he thought he was in multiple senses; discouragement over failing to fulfill his mission as well as his manhood; shameful defeat at his triple failure of penis, self, and Shogun; alienation from the world of pleasure and of duty; alienation from the self beset with guilty self-recriminations because he believes that he must somehow have wanted to fail if he did not succeed; that he failed in three ways, sexually, not finding out the secret, and not strangling the geisha after eliciting her secret; that he failed because he was morally reluctant to kill the woman; that he had failed not only the master to whom he had pledged his loyalty by writing his pledge in blood, but also his ancestors and deities that were written on the scroll that was burned, and whose ashes he swallowed. Not only does he experience multiple sources of shame and guilt, but he also experiences multiple affects that amplify the shame and guilt. He is distressed as he remembers, ruminates, and imagines; afraid of his master; disgusted by his multiple weakness; feeling dissmell toward the geisha and himself for the sexual failure; surprised because he had never failed before; angry at himself, the geisha, and the master; guilty for feeling angry at his master, and he magnifies these multiple sources of guilt, shame, inferiority, discouragement, defeat, and alienation with a fresh affect of deep shame. These multiple affects and multiple sources of affects magnify the painful guilty shame until he realizes that his affective regret, humiliation, terror, anguish, repulsion, and alienation can be ended and atoned for only by ritual suicide as *hara-kiri* or *seppuku*.

For a more guilt-loaded scenario, imagine the Victorian boy warned that masturbation, the solitary or secret vice, is the precursor of the social vice in any boy who cannot control his lust. Not only is he lacking in self-discipline, he also is sinful and has the disease of concupiscence. His parents vow to break his evil will by torturing his penis. Before sleeping, a metal device to prevent masturbation is placed upon his penis, a torture in which pins will prick his penis if it becomes erect, which, of course, it must during every REM period. Next, his foreskin is sewn shut so it cannot sensuously slide over the glans; later, it is circumcised without anesthesia as per the next doctor's advice. He learns that masturbation produces not only degeneracy but also a myriad of diseases, from syphilis to sterility, from epilepsy to madness, from nosebleeds to heart murmurs, from homosexuality to the penis drying up and falling off. Yet he continues to masturbate, vows never to do it again, but masturbates still. Guilt from multiple sources as well as terror over the inevitable consequences on earth and in heaven, disgust at his self-pollution, and dissmell for that offending organ are ended by self-multilation. If thy eye offend thee, pluck it out.

When Does Guilt Inhibit Sexual Enjoyment and Control Sexual Behavior?

Will she or won't she? Will the affect bind of guilt controlling sexual excitement and enjoyment win the day, or will the sexual scene continue in spite of guilt-attenuated excitement and enjoyment? The fate of an affect-bind rule in a particular scene is a joint function of auxiliary information arising from what happens in the unfolding scene and the innate relationships between affects that Tomkins described as interaffect dynamics. Using his theory of innate activators of affect and as few additional assumptions as necessary, Tomkins (1962) hypothesized 19 innate affect dynamics. Central to understanding guilt is the dynamic specifying that the innate activator of shame or guilt is the interruption and attenuation of excitement or joy by an inner or outer barrier. In contrast to the attenuation (partial reduction) of excitement in shame, a complete reduction of activated excitement produces joy. For example, intense and prolonged sexual excitement that is reduced by orgasm elicits the smile of joy; whereas, guilt-attenuated and partially reduced excitement might trigger shame at sexual failure or guilty withdrawal from the sexual scene or guilty postscene evaluations.

Successful control by an affect bind is dependent on the relative intensities of the instigated affect and the controlling affect. According to Tomkins (1962, p. 294). "The instigation of maximum-intensity positive affect is antagonistic to the maintenance of maximum intensity negative affect and the instigation of negative affect is similarly antagonistic to the maintenance of positive affect with respect to maximum intensity." Suppose an adolescent woman's sexual script permits her to give and receive sexual pleasure so long as she does not have coitus, which is proscribed as morally wrong, and that any transaction to initiate sexual intercourse by her partner characteristically onsets an affective guilt bind. If her guilt is maximally strong, it may control her sexual excitement because of its antagonistic effect, but if her sexual excitement on this occasion is of maximal intensity then it may override her less intense guilt, in spite of the affect-bind rule in her sex-guilt script. Not only that, but also the affect dynamic of induction (p. 295) hypothesizes, "if weak or moderate instigated negative affect does not reduce the intensity of ongoing positive affect, the intensity of the positive affect will be increased to an intensity which will reduce the antagonistic response." Thus, the induction dynamic asserts that weak or moderate sexual guilt that does not reduce the intensity of ongoing sexual excitement and enjoyment will, instead, paradoxically increase those positive affects to an intensity that will reduce the antagonistic affect bind of guilt. This dynamic also explains the appeal of socially and morally taboo sex for those in whom affect binds are characteristically only weak or moderate, whereas guilt successfully proscribes illicit sex in those whose affect binds onset at maximal intensity. If you are not too guilty, you may discover the excitement and enjoyment of tabooed sexual linkages or partners. But, if you are really guilt prone, you cannot even imagine it.

These two rules, that guilt attenuates positive affect and the innate affect-dynamic rule that maximally instigated negative affect is antagonistic to positive affect, are general and innate. A psychologically magnified affect-control script functions through rules whose instructions are also more specific. Specifically, the affect-control script contains learned affect-invested rules for controlling these specific *parameters* of affect: (a) consciousness, (b) density, (c) display, (d) expression, (e) communication, (f) action, (g) consequences, (h) conditionality, and (i) specificity. Although the affect-control script may focus on controlling both excitement and enjoyment or, through partitioning, perhaps one but not the other, or one more than the other, its rules also address various parameters of these two positive discrete affects. Considering *consciousness* of affect, Betty may be aware that she enjoys kissing but not that it excites her sexually. If others act as if you are not sexual, not capable of sexual excitement, ignoring it when you are, you may not learn to be aware or to label such feeling as being sexually turned on.

There are a myriad of rules about just how *dense* sexual excitement and enjoyment can be without eliciting a controlling affect to reduce sexual affects' density. These rules of density control the intensity, duration, or frequency of permissible positive affects in sexual scenes. People may be able to have sex so long as they do not become too intensely excited, or they may be capable of intense excitement if sexual activity is not too frequent, or they may enjoy brief sex—a quickie—but not the prolonged enjoyment or intense ecstasy of deep involvement in a sensuous or dramatic sexual scene. Affect binds targeting the density of affect keep individuals from being too sexy, horny, sensual, excited, or ecstatic.

The *display* of sexual affect in the face and voice is disciplined by admonitions not to make too much noise or someone will hear, not to leer, not to look at me like that, to take that sluttish look off your face. Because most boys masturbate in cultures that deride their masturbation, they learn to cum quietly and to mask their face when sexually interested. They may manifest these scripted rules by playing it cool in future scenes even when in the throes of coital climax.

Both the face and the voice can be masked to reduce intensity and consciousness and display of affect. To cry out in excitement or to shed tears of joy or relief during orgasm may violate multiple parameters of affect control. The vocal *expression* of excited and joyous sexuality can be diminished by teaching that it is unladylike or unmanly or immoral to moan in naked pleasure, to breathe too fast and too hard, to groan and strain to reach orgasm, to scream in excited joy. Facial but not vocal display may be inhibited, or the other way around. For example, excitement might be displayed in the face so long as it is not vocally expressed above certain decibel levels.

The parameter of verbal *communication* of sexual excitement and enjoyment is widely controlled in America. When people agree to have sex, they rarely specify verbally just who will do what to whom, when, how, and for how long. Much less do they transmit their sexual history in the midst of a seduction. Not talking about sex at all precludes the exploration of what is exciting and what not, what is enjoyable and how to make it more so.

Few adolescents can imagine their parents having sex; fewer still can imagine them having passionate, excited, ecstatic sex complete with sexy faces, voices, words, and action. The adult and adolescent generations mutually make consciousness of the other generation's sexuality magically disappear by instilling conditionality, display, and communication blackouts on one another by socializing rules to see no sex, hear no sex, and speak no sex across parent–child generations.

Rules for the control of sexual *action* are a ubiquitous subject of socialization, often by spelling out the *consequences* of sexual action as potential perils. "No one will respect you; you'll get AIDS and die," and the like. No one is supposed to be doing it. Everyone is to just say no. Yet the pull of tabooed sexuality is increased by the struggle over controlling sexuality and the freeing loss of control over sexuality. One of the master motives of the human being, according to Tomkins, is that affect inhibition should be minimized. Tomkins states, (1962, p. 330) "The inhibition of the overt expression of any affect will ordinarily produce a residual form of the affect which is at once heightened, distorted, and chronic and which is severely punitive." Small wonder that adolescents feel caught in a bind between "the wages of sin is death" and "the wages of sexual repression is inhibition and neurosis."

The *conditionality* of sexuality includes times, places, partners, relationships, and activities, conditions which also impact on rules for consciousness, density, display, vocalization, and verbalization of affect. Such rules limit who can do what with whom sexually. Finally, the rules for affect in sexual scenes may be *general or specific:* all excitement is to be controlled as too crude, or only sexual excitement is restricted. The same modular rules may be general across all scenes of sexual excitement or enjoyment. Or, sexual scenes may be partitioned into different families, each requiring their own specific rules, as when a husband may have one set of rules for sex with his wife and another for sex with his mistress.

The present state of an individual's affect-control script for sexual excitement/ enjoyment is a function of the socialization of affects that is begun by the parent but continues throughout life. The affect binds employed by the parent to control sexuality will be replicated initially in the controlling affect and in the rules for the parameters of control, to be reexperienced whenever an affect-bind rule is retrieved and expanded in a sexual scene until further validated or disconfirmed. Disconfirmation can lead to alterations in specific rules. For example, a woman's pleasure at a man's passionate sexual expression may disconfirm his rule that density or expression of excitement or enjoyment should be limited as guilt-worthy. If disconfirmation is massive and intense, it can lead to a process of magnification that onsets a change-review script, a review that is undertaken whenever significantly changing events are taken to mean that life will never be the same again. Suddenly, all of the rules of the script are open to reinterpretation.

For example, a characteristically guilty married man has a rule against adultery, but finds his sexual desire, excitement, and enjoyment are at such a maximal intensity that his guilt is reduced, leading to adulterous intercourse with a single woman. His guilt script is disconfirmed by his rule-breaking action and the density of his positive affect without guilt. This may lead to a change-review script in which his disenchantment with his wife is confirmed, and he falls in love with his new and idealized partner. The partner, now idealized as loved, by being who she is and how she is, has made all of their sexuality free of guilt.

The Toxicity of Controlling Affects

I am arguing that the toxicity of the controlling affect in an affect-control script is important. The toxicity of affects in psychology is an analogy to the toxicity of chemicals in pharmacology. In distinguishing between distress-anguish and fear-terror, Tomkins believed that two negative affects were evolutionarily necessary at two different levels of toxicity. On the one hand, fear is highly urgent and toxic but lasts only a brief time. On the other hand, distress is bearable if it lasts a lifetime. Although it may not prepare the person for problem solving, fear-terror demands immediate attention by its biological urgency as an emergency motivator, whereas, distress-anguish is biologically useful because it can be borne while a problem is solved and it also can be put aside when frightened or excited or angry, only to return when these more urgent affects have had their say.

The toxicity of an affect is directly proportional to the intensity its punishing qualia and inversely proportional to its duration of activation and the usual duration of its activator. If the negative affect is too toxic, it replaces the focus on the threatening situation with the conscious experience of its own activation. Overcome with terror, we freeze rather than flee. Tomkins reasoned (1963, p. 9), "The evolutionary solution to such a problem was to coordinate the toxicity of the self-punishing response to its duration and to the probable duration of its activator."

For the psychologist, the crucial but often overlooked question is: how toxic is the discrete affect that is controlling sexuality? People who are conflicted over sexuality have affect control scripts in which the controlling affect is usually either guilt or disgust. In guilt, the frame is, "I want sex, but I feel guilty." In disgust, the frame is, "I want sex, but also I don't want sex because it is disgusting."

Among the negative affects, an affect bind with shame or guilt as the controlling affect is less toxic, being a temporary interruption and attenuation of positive affect. As an auxiliary to the hunger and thirst drives, disgust is used extensively to control sexual appetite and affects. Disgust is the affect of ambivalence, of purity and impurity, of contamination and decontamination, of initially taking in and then spitting or vomiting out. It is more toxic because its activator is longer lasting and the experience of disgust is more self-punishing in its qualia. It lasts longer because when you are sexually polluted you are dirty both inside and outside. Recall how commonplace disgust over semen and menstruation is in human cultures; when taken in as disgusting, bodily fluids must be spit out or vomited. Following sex, which is more self punishing: to hang your head in guilt or to vomit in disgust? For all of us who have experienced both guilt and self-disgust over our sexual contacts, the phenomenologically more toxic affect is easily identified.

Like shame or guilt, disgust operates only after excitement or enjoyment have been activated. According to Tomkins (1991, p. 334), "When it is the control of sex and aggression which is the focus of socialization, the affects of shame and self-disgust are experienced as 'guilt." Having written about guilt for many years, I now urge psychologists to distinguish between guilt and disgust. In my own revised measure of guilt (Mosher, 1988), I failed to make a clear distinction between guilt and shame, which in retrospect I view as a positive, but I also failed to make a distinction between guilt originating in shame and guilt originating in self-disgust, which was a mistake. Six examples of potential forced-choice items that make such a distinction follow: "The practice of homosexuality is . . . morally wrong; (or, repugnant)." "If I (did) masturbate, I('d) feel . . . guilty for sinning; (or, disgusted with myself for being so weak.)" "I feel . . . guilty over my premarital sexual activity; (or, disgusted with my self or my partner for our premarital sexual activity)." "The worst part of sex for me is that I feel so . . . guilty afterward, that I have sinned; (or, impure, that I have dirtied myself)." "My guilt (or disgust) keeps me from really enjoying premarital sex." "My guilt (or disgust) keeps me from becoming really sexually excited."

I argue that this difference is psychologically important because of the greater toxicity of disgust. Antisexual ideologues make significant use of disgust, dissmell, and contempt. For example, pornography is argued by opponents to be not only dangerous, invoking fear, but polluting, invoking disgust. Homosexuals and transsexuals are treated with contempt. When, under the guise of sex education, human sexuality is equated with danger and pollution in antisexual ideology, fear and disgust is evoked in adolescents. Dissmell is the affect of prejudice, it instills contempt for sexual sinners and "deviants."

The ideological polarity predicts differential parental use of shame and disgust during socialization. The child socialized by humanist parents will experience guilt as a variant of shame; whereas the child socialized by normative parents will experience guilt as self-disgust. When the culture defines sex as immoral and impure, the complex in consciousness of reports of source, affect, and target can vary considerably and still be labeled as "guilt." Nonetheless, the greater toxicity of disgust compared to shame within the complex of guilt makes this distinction crucial for a theory of guilt. Whereas guilt as shame calls for repair in temporarily interrupted empathic relationships, guilt as self-disgust often produces nuclear scripts of contamination that must be continually decontaminated with little chance of success.

The most toxic affects used to control sexuality are fear-terror, anger-rage, and dissmell (an affect that is auxiliary to the thirst, food, and oxygen drives). The most pathological instances of "guilt" as a personality script involve these toxic–antitoxic scripts. For instance, an affect-control script in which terror binds sexual excitement, when joined with rage at the socializing parent or an analog of the parent and with dissmell for the victimized sexual object, appears to characterize the FBI's (1985) disorganized lust murderer.

Shame, disgust, and dissmell are all affects of rejection, whether of self or others. They differ among themselves in the dimensions of time and distance. Shame is a *temporary* barrier to continuing social intimacy and sexual excitement and enjoyment. Shame bespeaks of empathy for others, as when the parent is shamed but empathic with a child who displays his or her genitals or fondles them in public. Disgust interrupts a positive sexual response by contaminating it, requiring decontamination. A currently popular image of contamination is the warning, "When you have sexual intercourse with one person, you are really having sexual intercourse with all of that person's partners." Such an image is intended to invoke simultaneously disgust through contamination, dissmell at promiscuity, and fear of sexually transmitted diseases. Preaching abstinence as the only safe sex insures moral purity and brands all other sex as dangerously and disgustingly contaminating.

Disgust is intermediate in distance and longer lasting than shame because pleasure is not only temporarily interrupted but is also lastingly contaminated. Shame can be lessened by repairing the temporarily interrupted relationship; but, disgust requires a thorough decontamination in a context of interpersonal ambivalence that requires making the impure more pure, when the sexual impurity is affectively multivalent and conceptually confusing. In this sex-negative culture, the prescription for purity is virginal abstinence; another is required for regaining purity: the bad woman is made pure through marriage; the bad man, by monogamy. The new abstinence involves pretending that you are a virgin because to be sexually impure is disgusting. However, monogamous marriage does not necessarily end the affect bind of disgust controlling sexual affect.

Still worse, dissmell involves rejection at a *distance* that must remain *permanent*. In folklore the Other is accused of being bad-smelling; they must permanently be kept at a distance, in their inferior place. Contempt, as displayed in the face as a learned, unilateral sneer, combines dissmell and anger. For Tomkins the general distinction between shame or guilt on the one hand and contempt, disgust, dissmell on the other hand is clear: guilt and shame are linked with love and identification with the oppressed, just as contempt-disgust-dissmell are linked with rejection and hatred for the oppressed. Contempt is the mark of the oppressor, and it imprints that mark on children who are punitively socialized by parents who must permanently maintain their hierarchical distance and moral superiority.

To terrorize a child is more pernicious than to be disgusted by a child, but guilt based upon a shame bind is less toxic to the child and preferable to both as a socializing strategy. Some control of sexuality is necessary because the adolescent needs to learn how to differentiate, grade, and modulate sexual excitement and enjoyment. The adolescent must learn a flexible control that includes knowing how to restore the positive affects of excitement and enjoyment following any affect bind. Also, it is desirable that there be a minimal reduction of affect consciousness, density, display, vocalization, and verbalization of affect in sexual scenes. The conditionality of sexual activity needs to include those conditions that respect the rights and privacy of others as well as the right of sexual autonomy for the adolescent. If you love your child, you identify and empathize with him or her, so you use shame or guilt in socialization to teach them what is right and good, but you always help them find their way back to interpersonal reconciliation. But a critical morality does not require a complete restriction of all sexual activity by adolescents, nor should fear of danger and disgust at contamination be the affects chosen to induce "moral" control. If a parent feels disgusted by his child's impure, evil, or dangerous sexuality, he must permanently contaminate it by disgust or stamp it out through dissmell. As with angry disgust and dissmell, contempt is the principal weapon of the self-righteous parent, who must break the sexual will of the child before they pollute themselves. If the adolescent becomes toxically polluted by their sexuality (or drug use or partner choice or what have you), then that youth must be rejected and kept at a permanent distance. When faced by such contempt, the adolescent will feel alienated, a stranger in a strange land, or become, countercontemptuous, a rebel with a cause—adult hypocrisy. Thus, the most important information in this chapter is this: because affects differ in their toxicity, psychologists must make crucial distinctions, and help parents and educators to distinguish among the specific affects that are used control sexual affect and action.

CHANGE-REVIEW SCRIPTS IN
ADOLESCENT SEXUALITY

Theorists offering definitions of adolescence agree that it is a transitional developmental period between childhood and adulthood with a poorly marked onset and endpoint that includes the biological changes of puberty that announce socially that the individual can sexually participate and reproduce. This change in social status from childhood to adulthood is a central cultural concern because it indicates the individual is prepared to assume responsibility in roles as worker, parent, and citizen.

Van Gennep (1960) proposed that rites of passage consisted of three stages: (a) separation, (b) limen (threshold), and (c) aggregation. In the separation phase, the individual leaves childhood behind, usually by creating a spatial distance from the family of origin. In the liminal phase, the adolescent is marginal, a teenager who is betwixt and between. Turner (1969) posited that this phase emphasized stepping out of space and time for a while to experience youth's common bonds with each other, their *communitas,* an equal fellowship with others. In the phase of aggregation, after having successfully undergone an ordeal, the initiates are welcomed into the larger community. In American culture, the adolescent lacks clear-cut rituals that are introduced by adults to mark their rite of passage from childhood to adulthood. They must find their own way betwixt and between.

From a psychological perspective, the transition from childhood to adulthood entails changes in the psychosocial issues of identity, attachment, autonomy, achievement, intimacy, gender, and sexuality. The issue of identity is concerned with "Who am I in this scene?" and "Who am I in this life?" The issue of attachment must address, "How am I to be related to my family of origin and to my peers as I prepare to enter my family of procreation?" The issue of autonomy poses choices, "What do I choose and how do I decide responsibility?" The issue of achievement asks, "What must I learn in order to do what is productive and meaningful?" The issue of intimacy requires that the adolescent learn "How close can I be to another and still be myself?" The issue of gender asks, "How can I be a real man or a real woman?" The issue of sexuality demands, "Who am I sexually? And, "How do I express my sexuality?" The issue of identity can be chosen as a central unifying theme for the adolescent who seeks to put away childish things and to become an attached, autonomous, achieving, intimate, and sexual man or woman.

From the perspective of script theory, the transition from childhood to adulthood requires that certain scenes elicit a *change-review script.* A change-review script addresses radical changes in the self, requiring confrontation and review of the consequences of the perceived radical change. Because the origin of a change-review script is a scene in which change is both radical and real, the person responds by realizing that life will never be the same again. When a consequential scene means that "I will never be the same again," such a momentous scene requires a substantial modification in all of the adolescent's scripts.

Four scenes are prime candidates for suddenly instantiating an adolescent change-review script: (a) the physical changes of puberty, and more specifically, menarche or first ejaculation, (b) falling in love, (3) first coitus, and (4) coming out. No one can predict just which of these events will prove most crucial in Western societies because they depend upon the individual adolescent's responses, including the affect invested in these scenes. Not only that, each may contribute, along with other scenes, to a more slowly dawning realization that "I will never be a child again; now, I am an adult."

Menarche and First Ejaculation

Menarche and first ejaculation are gender dimorphic biological, cultural, and psychological experiences that, because they are not socially celebrated by ritual, become relatively unique experiences for each adolescent in America. Frayser (1985) reported that first menstruation was regarded as important by 39 of 42 technologically simple societies. The meanings assigned to first menstruation included the physical—a sign that the girl is mature enough to engage in sexual intercourse or to reproduce—and, more common, the social—a sign that the girl is eligible for marriage and adulthood. In America, first menstruation is a warning signal of potential or emergent sexuality rather than the achievement of a transitional status that is ritually celebrated. First ejaculation is less visible in its residues and less likely to elicit educational information, not even about personal hygiene. Americans unrealistically fear that sexuality discussed is sexuality unleashed.

The sex-segregated worlds of pre- and early adolescents ensures that scripts of sexuality will build upon the foundations of learned gender scripts. Moreover, the youth culture resembles a secret society that keeps secret the guilty knowledge of the adolescent's sexual exploration from the world of parents and authority, while providing its own prestige system for gender-linked success. Furthermore, the sex-segregated youth cultures are estranged from each other, prescribing different meanings for what is prestigious for each gender: sexual conquest or love and marriage.

Despite sharing the experience of transition from childhood, the developmental pathways of male and female adolescents estrange each from the other's existential experience of their sexuality (Gagnon & Simon, 1973). For adolescent males between boyhood and manhood, the onset of secret sexual activity in the form of masturbation is common. They cited Kinsey's data on masturbation to orgasm for men and women. It revealed rates masturbation to orgasm for men by age 12, of 21%, by age 15, 82%, and by age 20, 92%; whereas, the comparable figures for women, respectively for the same age groups, were only 12, 20, and 33%. The males are variously supported and teased by their male peers for their masturbation, and its meaning is linked to the idea that as real adolescent men they will have coitus instead of masturbating if they are to gain prestige. Thus, as they masturbate, their principal fantasy is of "scoring" with desirable females. Nonetheless, although masturbation is pleasurable, it is accompanied by guilt and anxiety. It is fair to describe this male youth culture as phallocentric because it is centered on penile pleasure and the domination of women. Female masturbation is not only less common, young women's experience is more idiosyncratic, infrequent, and less likely to be linked to collective social meanings.

The adolescent girls becoming women are sharing a homosocial world that values love and marriage, a world of affectively significant relationships. Thus, the adolescent woman is being prepared for heterosociality, not heterosexuality. Gagnon and Simon (1973, p. 56) assert, "The key difference between males and females is that for the latter the organizing experience of puberty is the encouraging and furthering of the reality of marriage rather than, as for the former, the reality of sexual activity." In early adolescence, the homosocial, sex-segregated worlds of both boy and girls are taking normative precedence over heterosexual influence.

Falling In Love

Falling in love is a prototypic change-review script of enchantment. Flirting often includes the excited gaze in alternation with shame's temporary lowering of the eyes and head. But, for love to blossom, just as in the experience of mother and child bonding, the face-to-face, eye-to-eye contact becomes not only unashamed but also joyous in it smiles. As you each fall into the excited eyes of your smiling partner, two fall in love, becoming one. The excitement and joy found in the loved partner's gaze and facial affect can produce an idealization in which the loved partner's presence is the source of much or all of life's excitement and joy and the absence of the partner seems the source of much or all of life's negative affect. This experience of love is both radical and real enough to create the belief that "I will never be the same person again." The physical changes of puberty place the new-found love outside the category of puppy love because the sexual desire and possibility of sharing both sex and reproduction generate a vision of a possible future.

Limerence, the state of being smitten by love (Tennov, 1979), is an example of psychological magnification in which actual, past and, possible future scenes involving the loved partner are coassembled, rerepresented in consciousness, and amplified by fresh affect. With a mutual and deeply shared love, these already loving scenes are reamplified by deep excitement and joy that amplifies the already exciting and joyous scenes. When the love bond is threatened by jealousy, the family of scenes may be reamplified, that is psychologically magnified, by fear, distress, and rage. When the lover is absent, the heart grows fonder by magnifying these already once amplified loving scenes by a distressed lovesickness at the imagined or real possibilities of lost love. An enchantment script remains open to gradual or sudden disenchantment, to the discovery of another real and radical change, that this idealized partner is not who I thought her or him to be. Scripts change as the continuing scenes in a life validate or disconfirm their rules.

First Coitus

Recognizing that first sexual intercourse is a major life transition, Sprecher, Barbee, and Schwartz (1995) examined gender differences in the emotional reactions of pleasure, anxiety, and guilt to first coitus. Using data from 1,659 college students, they found that men reported experiencing more pleasure, more anxiety, and less guilt than women following first intercourse. Men's greater pleasure was explained, in part, by their greater likelihood of experiencing orgasm. Both men and women reported more pleasure and anxiety but less guilt when first sexual intercourse occurred in a close rather than a casual relationship. Women's higher level of guilt was more highly associated than men's with casual rather than serious relationships. According to Sprecher et al. (1995, p. 13), "These results suggest that love and sexual pleasure do go together—that sex is more pleasurable when there is love or commitment."

Coming Out

Although homosexuality has not been classified as a mental illness for over two decades, coming out as a lesbian or gay man is still problematic for a teenager. Our society ensures this is so by making the following assumptions (Herdt, 1989): (a) the presumption of heterosexuality: gay youths are presumed heterosexual, necessarily producing feelings of difference and alienation; (b) the presumption of inversion: gay teenagers face the stigmatizing stereotype that they are gender-role inverted—effeminate men or masculine women—pressing the youths against a normative standard of being "unnatural" and, in the more restrictive cultures, toward either adopting the stereotype or camping in protest of this stigmatization as an invert; (c) the presumption of stigmatization: gay adolescents are marked by stigma and must pass through this societal oppression successfully to develop pride in their gay identity; and (d) the presumption of homogeneity: gay teenagers are stereotyped not only as inverted but also as necessarily as identical kinds of pathological persons, impoverishing their range of choices for a unique identity as expressed through decisions about communication, intimacy, achievement, autonomy, attachment, gender-presentation, and sexuality.

To become an adult the adolescent must make a series of life-directing decisions that determine who she or he is to be as an adult. For Tomkins, duplication and change were a central biological and psychological process; personality was the preserving of an identity in the face of transformative change (Mosher, 1992). Whether considering life or identity, sameness is the special case, change is the general rule. Adolescence holds a mirror to change while the child is duplicatively changed into an adult.

Sexuality is a part of that identity and only a part of it. In order to become that person who we most truly are, we become a unified whole, duplicating an identity as the same person in all of life's varied scenes in spite of the real changes in life and the transformative changes in self. In a deep sense we become what we most value, and we value what we have invested with affect because we are scripted to validate our identities through duplication.

Because sexuality is so invested with affect, whether positive or negative or, as is most common, both positive and negative, our sexuality is a core component of our adult identity. Becoming adult always entails becoming a sexual actor. No other adolescent path to adult maturity is so strewn with land mines by the good intentions of adults.

GUIDELINES FOR THE SEX EDUCATION OF ADOLESCENTS

Being betwixt and between, adolescents are gored on the horns of the conservative religious dilemma of original innocence and original sin (Money, 1980). As children, adolescents are innocent, unaware of sexuality, and not to be sullied and polluted by sexual information; but as sexually mature, they are lustful and must be controlled or punished. The threat to sexual freedom is that an immoral but moralistic intolerance instills a spiral of silence in which most people, feeling unsure of their grounding in a critical morality, fail to speak out against intolerance and oppression of sexual minorities, including teenagers (Mosher, 1989). Hart (1959/1988) distinguished between "positive [conventional or traditional] morality," the morality accepted by a given social group, and "critical morality," the rationally justified set of moral principles used to criticize existing social institutions, including positive morality. At the heart of the conflict over tolerance versus so-called moral disgust and repugnance at sexual expression is whether cruelty is ever justified as moral retribution; although private sexual acts between consenting partners have not produced any harmful and wrongful setbacks of interest to self or other, moralists claim to be offended when they merely imagine their occurrence (Mosher, 1994c). The experience of disgust with other is not a true test within a critical morality. The affective experience of disgust with other may reflect the individual's sex-negative ideology and their own history of a punitive socialization of sexuality. It is asserted that neither cruelty nor intolerance is ever moral, being instead always evil.

Adolescents need a sex education that teaches both tolerance and responsibility. According to Guggenheim and Sussman (1985, p. 249), "Young people [adolescents] have the constitutional right to the freedom of speech, expression, and thought—the core qualities of the First Amendment—which may not be abridged except for 'compelling' reasons." Yet the greatest threat to sex education in the public schools is posed by those conservatives who falsely claim that sex education materials are obscene and that discussing homosexuality as a lifestyle promotes it. Their political strategy seeks to deny funds to programs that might adequately discuss safer sex alternatives like masturbation or condom usage by falsely claiming

TABLE I   Gert's (1988) Ten Moral Rules

1. Don't kill.	6. Don't deceive.
2. Don't cause pain.	7. Keep your promises.
3. Don't disable.	8. Don't cheat.
4. Don't deprive of freedom.	9. Obey the law.
5. Don't deprive of pleasure.	10. Do your duty.

that public funds are being used to promote immorality and deviance at the expense of the traditional (and patriarchal) family.

One implication of the present script theoretic analysis is that an affect-control script serves the individual and society best when the controlling affect is shame-based guilt rather than the more toxic affects of disgust, terror, rage, and dissmell at sex and sexuality. A positive socialization of sexual affect requires graded sexual experiences like (masturbation and petting) that are conjoined with communication, peer discussion, and rational ethical judgment. Education should foster responsible sexual choices for the self and social tolerance for others by developing empathy for others who make legitimate but different sexual choices.

According to Mosher (1994c, p. 381), "Sexual conduct is governed by the same moral rules as human conduct in general, although the intimacy of sexual conduct may evoke moral ideals as well." Moral philosophers explain and justify the rules of a critical morality. According to Gert (1988, p. 6, original italics), *"Morality is a public system applying to all rational persons governing behavior which affects others and which has the minimization of evil as its end, and which includes what are commonly known as moral rules at its core."* Table I presents ten moral rules that Gert argued were impartial, rational, and justified. Given their universality and generality, these rules apply equally to sexual and other interpersonal conduct.

These justified moral rules provide a basis for teaching a critical morality during sex education in schools. Moral rules aim at preventing evils like inducing pain and negative affect, creating disability, and denying freedom and pleasure. These moral rules can be obeyed impartially by all rational persons throughout a day and for a lifetime. These moral rules have the advantages of simplicity, clarity, and intuitiveness. They respect the separation of church and state while offering moral guidelines for preventing evil. They are not specific to sexuality but are equally applicable to all moral dilemmas.

Moral ideals advocate promoting goods and virtues, such as ability [autonomy], freedom, positive affect, pleasure, honesty, and trustworthiness. However, moral ideals cannot always be followed impartially by all rational persons because this duty exceeds the human being's grasp since it is expansive and unending. Gert believed the most that can be morally justified is, "Always be just; be kind when you can." For Gert (1988, p. 69), tolerance is required by the first five moral rules, "an intolerant person is necessarily an immoral person, for he violates a moral rule unjustifiably."

Several moral ideals appear morally valuable in the context of the sex education of adolescents. Sexual freedom is a right derived from the universal principle of respect for persons that has a correlative ideal duty—to be sexually responsible. Mosher (1989, p. 505) offered three questions, which are presented in Table II, to improve the process of making responsible sexual choices.

These three questions focus the person's attention on three aspects of duty to self, others, and society. The first question honors self-respect and relational, long-term thinking about how the individual's sexuality fits into their plan for life. The second question extends the idea of informed consent to sexuality by defining responsible sexuality as informed and voluntary. Not only should the person not deprive the other person of freedom, he or she should not deceive, cheat, or break promises. Furthermore, there is a positive duty derived from the special intimacy of shared sex to be self-disclosing about both your feelings for your partner and any relevant personal, sexual, or medical history. The third question advocates taking a stance of impartiality in weighing your interests with those of your partner and society. It argues that sex is only a private matter when it benefits both partners impartially and has no predictable costs for society.

A responsible sex education of adolescents must eschew the use of fear, disgust, and dissmell to control adolescent sexuality in favor of teaching justified moral rules and promoting moral ideals and virtues. Moralistic intolerance is an evil, never a good. Philosophically justified moral rules and ideals serve as a basis for a moral perspective on the free flow of ideas about sexuality that the First Amendment promises to us as citizens. No ideas about human sexuality should be prohibited on moral or Constitutional grounds. Speech about human sexuality is political speech; separation of church and state requires the disestablishment of traditional religious perspectives that are homophobic and intolerant of ideas and information about adolescent sexuality in the public schools.

TABLE II   Mosher's (1989) Questions for Sexual Responsibility

Duty to self:	Is this sexual choice compatible with my need for personal respect and rationally congruent with my plan for life?
Duty to partner:	Have I fully informed my partner of all known risks and benefits and being sexual with me to ensure my partner's consent is both informed and voluntary?
Duty to society:	Have I considered my sexual interests impartially, allotting them no more but also no less weight than those of my partner and society?

REFERENCES

Baumeister, R. F., Stillwell, A. M., & Heatherton, T. F. (1994). Guilt: An interpersonal approach. *Psychological Bulletin, 115,* 243–267.

Byrne, D., & Schulte, L. (1990). Personality dispositions as mediators of sexual responses. In J. Bancroft (Ed.), *Annual review of sex research, 1,* 93–117.

Campos, J. (1994). The new functionalism in emotion. *SCRD Newsletter, Spring,* 1–14.

FBI Law Enforcement Bulletin (1985). Crime scene and profile characteristics of organized and disorganized murderers, *54,* 18–25.

Frayser, S. G. (1985). *Varieties of sexual experience: An anthropological perspective on human sexuality.* New Haven: HRAF Press.

Gagnon, J. H., & Simon, W. (1973). *Sexual conduct: The sources of human sexuality.* Chicago: Aldine.

Gert, B. (1988). *Morality: A new justification of the moral rules.* New York: Oxford University Press.

Guggenheim, M., & Sussman, A. (1985). *The rights of young people.* New York: Bantam Books.

Hart, H. L. A. (1959/1988). Immorality and treason. In R. M. Baird & S. E. Rosenbaum, (Eds.), *Morality and law* (pp. 47–53). Buffalo, NY: Prometheus Press.

Herdt, G. (1989). Introduction: Gay and lesbian youth, emergent identities, and cultural scenes at home and abroad. In G. Herdt (Ed.), *Gay and lesbian youth* (pp. 1–42). New York: Harrington Park Press.

Kohlberg, L., & Gilligan, C. (1971). The adolescent as philosopher: The discovery of the self in a postconventional world. *Daedalus, 100,* 1051–1086.

Money, J. (1980). *Love and love sickness: The science of sex, gender difference, and pair-bonding.* Baltimore: Johns Hopkins University Press.

Mosher, D. L. (1966). The development and multitrait–multimethod matrix analysis of three measure of three aspects of guilt. *Journal of Consulting Psychology, 30,* 25–29.

Mosher, D. L. (1988). Revised Mosher Guilt Inventory. In C. M. Davis, W. L. Yarber, & S. L. Davis (Eds.), *Sexuality-related measures: A compendium* (pp. 152–155). Lake Mills, IA: Graphic.

Mosher, D. L. (1989). Threat to sexual freedom: Moralistic intolerance instills a spiral of silence. *The Journal of Sex Research, 26,* 492–509.

Mosher, D. L. (1992). Epilogue: A paean to human freedom. In S. S. Tomkins (Ed.), *Affect, imagery, consciousness, cognition: Duplication and transformation of information, Vol. IV* (pp. 355–372). New York: Springer.

Mosher, D. L. (1994a). Guilt. In V. S. Ramachandran (Ed.), *Encyclopedia of human behavior, Vol. 2.* (pp. 467–475). New York: Academic Press.

Mosher, D. L. (1994b). Guilt: Sex guilt. In V. L. Bullough & B. Bullough (Eds.), *Human sexuality: An encyclopedia* (pp. 261–263). New York: Garland Publishing.

Mosher, D. L. (1994c). Public policy and sex offenses: Social toleration versus criminalization. In J. J. Krivacska & J. Money (Eds.), *The handbook of forensic sexology: Biomedical & criminological perspectives* (pp. 369–396). Amherst, NY: Prometheus Books.

Mosher, D. L. (1996). Script theory and human sexual response: A glossary of postulates, corollaries, and definitions. In D. L. Nathanson (Ed.), *Knowing feeling: Affect, script, and psychotherapy* (pp. 105–131). New York: Norton.

Sprecher, S., Barbee, A., & Schwartz, P. (1995). "Was it good for you, too?": Gender differences in first sexual intercourse experiences. *The Journal of Sex Research, 32,* 3–15.

Tennov, D. (1979). *Love and limerence: The experience of being in love.* New York: Stein and Day.

Tomkins, S. S. (1962). *Affect imagery consciousness: The positive affects, Vol. 1.* New York: Springer.

Tomkins, S. S. (1963). *Affect imagery consciousness: The positive affects, Vol. 2.* New York: Springer.

Tomkins, S. S. (1965). Affect and the psychology of knowledge. In S. S. Tomkins & C. E. Izard (Eds.), *Affect, cognition, and personality* (72–97). New York: Springer.

Tomkins, S. S. (1987). Shame. In D. L. Nathanson, (Ed.), *The many face of shame* (pp. 133–161). New York: Guilford.

Tomkins, S. S. (1991). *Affect imagery consciousness: The negative affects: Anger and fear, Vol. 3*. New York: Springer.

Tomkins, S. S. (1992). *Affect imagery consciousness: Cognition: Duplication and transformation of information, Vol. 4*. New York: Springer.

Turner, V. W. (1969). *The ritual process: Structure and anti-structure*. Chicago: Aldine.

van Gennep, A. (1960). *The rites of passage*. Chicago: University of Chicago Press.

CHAPTER 9

The Development of Reactions to Guilt-Producing Events

Jane Bybee, Rolande Merisca, and Rashid Velasco

Northeastern University, Boston, Massachusetts

INTRODUCTION

Serial killer Ted Bundy describes his first physical assault on a woman in the following way, using a third-person narrative (Michaud & Aynesworth, 1983).

> He saw a woman park her car and walk up to her door and fumble for her keys. He walked up behind her and struck her with a piece of wood he was carrying. She fell down and began screaming. He panicked and ran. What he had done terrified him, purely terrified him. Full of remorse and remonstrating with himself for the suicidal nature of that activity, the ugliness of it all, he quickly sobered up. He was horrified by the recognition that he had the capacity to do such a thing. He was fearful, terribly fearful, that for some reason or another he might be apprehended. . . . [H]e sat back and swore to himself that he wouldn't do something like that again, or even anything that would lead to it. . . . For a period of months, the enormity of what he did stuck with him. . . . [B]ut . . . gradually, . . . it would reemerge. This individual would say, "Well, just one trip to the bookstore. Just once around the neighborhood . . ." What happened was this entity inside him was not capable of being controlled any longer at least not for any considerable period of time. It began to try to justify itself, to create rationalizations for what it was doing. (p. 109–111)

Guilt and Children
Copyright © 1998 by Academic Press. All rights of reproduction in any form reserved.

Of his first rape and murder of a young woman abducted from her bedroom, Bundy states:

> A nominally normal individual who has become somewhat subordinate to bizarre desires and abducts a woman and kills her finds himself in a great deal of panic. In the days and weeks following the killing, there would be an undercurrent of anxiety that comes with wondering just what was seen. . . . As far as remorse over the act, that would last for a period of time. But it could all be justified. He would say, "Well, listen. You fucked up this time, but you're never gonna do it again". . . . The approach is, say, "Don't ever do it again." But as time passes, the emphasis is on "Don't get caught." (p. 116)

And from death row, after conviction in the brutal rape, mutilation, and slaying of a 12-year-old girl and the double murder of two sorority women as well as suspected involvement in at least 21 total killings, he reflects:

> [W]hatever I've done in the past—you know, the emotions of omissions or commissions—doesn't bother me. Try to touch the past! Try to deal with the past. It's not *real*. It's just a dream . . . I don't think I need to feel guilty anymore, because I try to do what's right, right *now*. . . . (p. 300)
>
> People disappear every day. It happens all the time. . . . There are so many people. It shouldn't be a problem. What's one less person on the face of the earth, anyway? (p. 310–311)

Fear of punishment, recognition of wrongdoing, remorse, renunciation, justifications, excuses: we see all these reactions to guilt-producing events at play in the mind of a psychopath in these excerpts from interviews of Ted Bundy by Michaud and Aynesworth (1983). The absence of guilt is widely held to be a primary marker of the psychopath (Harper, Hakstian, & Hare, 1988). But how does guilt become absent? Bundy repeatedly acknowledges feelings of remorse, especially when he first began assaulting, abducting, and murdering women. After countless hours of interviews with the killer, Michaud and Aynesworth conclude that one of the keys to understanding his entire mental edifice was that intellectually, he was profoundly dissociative, a compartmentalizer, and a superb rationalizer (p. 10). In short, what set Bundy apart were his *reactions* to guilt-producing events, his ability to neutralize feelings of guilt and remorse through intellectualizations.

What are normal reactions to guilt-producing events, how do reactions develop, and what purpose do they serve? We address these questions in the present chapter. We review, in turn, reconciliation and action tendencies, self-blame and intropunitive responses, rationalizations, avoidance, detection and punishment concerns, and hedonistic responses.

Beyond providing insights into the roots of evil, examination of reactions to guilt-producing events and their development may help us to understand which reactions enable guilt to serve as a source of motivation and goal direction and which reactions prolong and aggravate feelings of guilt. Results may provide insights into how individuals can effectively manage guilt and prevent guilt from becoming chronic and injurious to mental health. We rely on original empirical data as well as a review of the literature to provide descriptions of responses and an account of developmental changes. In the first study,[1] we ask 205 adolescents drawn from the 5th, 8th, and 11th grades to describe guilt-producing incidents and what happened afterward. We examine the prevalence of different reactions to guilt-producing events in the sample overall and changes across grade level in the percentage of students mentioning each event. Illustrative excerpts of these descriptions may be seen in Table I. Descriptive statistics and analyses are presented in Tables II and III. Results are discussed section by section throughout the chapter. In Study 2, we examine the relationship of reliance on justifications and excuses to self-esteem, guilt alleviation, prosocial actions and aggression as reported by peers, self-reported racist attitudes, and depression among 109 college students. Results of this study are reported in Table IV and in the section on rationalizations. We now turn to the first major type of reaction to guilt-producing events: reconciliation and action tendencies.

RECONCILIATION AND ACTION TENDENCIES

Individuals experiencing shame report a concern with inadequacies of the self and a desire to run away, retreat, and shrink from the precipitating event (Ferguson & Stegge, 1995; Ferguson, Stegge, & Damhuis, 1991; Tangney, 1995; Tangney, Wagner, Fletcher, & Gramzow, 1992a). In guilt, the concern is with the act and injury suffered by the victim. The individual experiences a pressing need to approach the situation, to confess, apologize, rectify, make reparation, and set things right (Ferguson & Stegge, 1995; Tangney, 1995). Many of these responses are intrinsically prosocial in nature. Other responses may prompt corrective and remediative behaviors that contain and control damage and prevent recurrences. Reconciliatory responses may help alleviate guilt and prevent feelings from becoming chronic (Bybee, Berliner, Zigler, & Merisca, 1996; Quiles & Bybee, 1997). We consider, in turn, the specific reactions reported by adolescents in the Study 1 sample.

---

[1]We examined 70 fifth graders (33 male, 37 female), 72 eighth graders (38 male, 34 female), and 63 eleventh graders (38 male, 25 female). Students were ethnically diverse and attended urban public schools located in working or lower class neighborhoods in the Northeast. Students were asked to describe in writing three guilt-producing events. After they described each incident, they were asked to write down what they thought or did next. Reactions to the guilt-producing incidents were coded for content using the 26 categories presented in Table 2. Categories mentioned one or more times in the student's descriptions received a score of *1*, whereas categories not mentioned were scored as *0*. Total scores presented for each category, then, represent the percentage of students who mentioned that category in their descriptions. To assess the reliability of the classification system, responses from 25 randomly selected participants were coded again by a second rater who was unaware of subject characteristics and experimental hypotheses. Ninety-eight percent of the content categories scored by the initial rater matched those scored by the second rater. We examined effects of grade level through use of logistic regressions using the CATMOD procedure in Statistical Analysis System (SAS).

TABLE I   Excerpts of the Reactions of Adolescents to Guilt-Producing Events

---

Reconciliation/Action tendency responses

Victim-oriented concern

This girl was fat so I started making fun of her.

I shouldn't have done it cause *I made her feel bad*. I took her aside and apologized. I told her they were just words and *I know those words hurt*.

Me and my three cousins jumped this girl. It was wrong.

I put myself in her place then I said sorry and it won't happen again.

Confession

When I was throwing my He-Man vehicle and it hit the wondow and broke and my sister got in trouble for it.

I told my mother that I did it and said sorry.

I broke an old lady's window when I was playing with a ball on a accident.

Then I went to her house and *told her the truth*.

Apologies

During football practice I gave a guy a cheap shot (tackle).

After practice I apologized to the guy and gave him a handshake.

I threw my sister's Barbie doll head over the fence.

I told her I was sorry, I cried half the day. Then I looked for the head.

Reparation

When I yelled at my niece. I think her feelings were hurt because of the expression on her face.

So I told her I was sorry and try not to make me yell at her then *I brought her some ice cream and let her play with my games and my dolls*.

I broke my aunt's drinking glass and put it in the garbage and said nothing.

I told her the next day and *I saved my money and brought her another set of glasses*. I also apologized.

Reestablish relationship

I got into an argument with one of my friends.

I talked to him and asked for a truce.

I felt guilty about flirting with other boys while I had a boyfriend.

I told my boyfriend what happen and why I flirted and *we worked through it*.

(continues)

Victim-Oriented Concern

We might expect concern for the victim to rise with development as empathy and role-playing skills increase and the adolescent is better able to imagine themselves in the victim's place (Kohlberg, 1969; Zahn-Waxler, Radke-Yarrow, Wagner, & Chapman, 1992). Tangney, Marschall, Rosenberg, Barlow, and Wagner (1996) report that victim-oriented concern is one of the strongest distinguishing features of guilt as compared to shame during childhood. Tangney et al. (1996) also report that concern for the victim is more common among adults compared to children. Expressions of concern for the victim were infrequent in Study 1, however, and showed no changes with development during adolescence.

TABLE I *(continued)*

Renunciation
I felt really bad when I cheated once in school. It was on a test and I said I didn't.
I got punished anyway. I cheated a few times since then, and I always felt terrible, because it was so dishonest. So I just stopped one day. *I refuse to cheat now in any form.* I even make a big deal when my friends do it. They think I'm too strict about cheating. I think eventually it'll catch up with them or their conscience.
I feel guilty when I listen in on my mother's phone conversations and find out about stuff I'm not supposed to know about. And she gives me respect when I am on the phone.
After I got caught and I got grounded *I never EVER listen in on any of her conversations.*

Good intentions
I misplaced my mother's gold ring.
I thought of buying her one back but I couldn't do it without her size.
Once I stole some candy out the store. I didn't want to, but peer pressure got to me.
I thought about taking it back but I didn't, I just dropped those friends who made me do it.

Self-blame and intropunitive responses
Recognition of wrongdoing
Stole a remote control car from a store.
I took the car back because *I realized it was wrong to do it.*
In the second grade we had a metrethon. I came in first and one of my friend came in fourth. I laughed at her.
I knew that was wrong so I tried to apologize but she wouldn't speak to me.

Intensifiers
Myself and all my other friends have always been mean to our so called friend P—. We always make fun of him and make him feel low.
He has been dealt pretty bad cards and we shouldn't do it. I feel sorry for him but I never stop bothering him. I really (feel) bad as I watch this happen, and I think I could stop it and then again I think I can't.
I felt bad when my mother saw my report card which had mostly bad grades.
I feel bad because all my other cousins are graduating from either the 8th or the 12th grade and their mothers are bragging and they are proud when there's nothing for my mother to brag or be proud about. I told her I had a feeling of how she felt and that I was sorry and would try to better next time (which I did).

(continues)

Confession

Confession is an admission of wrongdoing. If the victim is unaware that a transgression has occurred, the transgressor may inform them of the wrongdoing. Children may confess to parents, teachers, and other authorities who were not directly victimized, but whose rules and regulations were broken (see C. Williams & Bybee, 1994a). Individuals may also confess to people such as classmates or political constituents who were not party to the act, but who might make judgments of blameworthiness. Confession may also be performed as a part of religious rituals. Certain religions (e.g., Catholicism) have formally institutionalized confession as a sacrament. In the

TABLE I *(continued)*

Self-hatred and self-punishment
   I had a huge fight with my mother and I slammed my room door and walked out.
   I was mad at myself and at her. I walked around and then I came back and apologized.
   I hated myself when I hit the baseball and the car window and my father had to pay for it.
   When I hit my girlfriend because she said I was cheating on her.
      I let her beat the crap out of me.
   Getting down on myself too much for doing something wrong like after I don't do well in a sport
   and I lose.
      I start hitting my head and kick the ground.
Rumination
   When I was involved in talking about someone. Then tried to ack like I wasn't in it.
      I kept thinking why did I say or do that. It was on my mind for a while.
   I called one of my friends a name and he didn't talk to me for a day.
      I felt bad. *I kept thinking about it.*
Remorse/regret
   I felt guilty about missing a shot in a basketball game because we were down by two points and I
   missed the shot.
   I feel bad when I don't call my mother for a couple of days and then I call her for money.
Rationalization responses
   Justification
      I felt guilty for when I hit my friend
         I thought I was right he kept aggravating me.
      Next store to my friend's house lives an old hag. She stores flower pots behind her garage. We
      threw bricks on them and they break.
         I feel a little sorry for her but she is a hag. We took the remaining flower pots and took turns
         throwing a baseball at the flower pots.
   Excuse
      I forgot my homework paper.
         I forgot my homework paper because my teacher told me to write it down on the back and I forgot to write it
         do and it was almost 8:30 A.M.
      I felt bad about stealing a comic book as a kid.
         I stole it because I thought I had enough money for one for me and one for my sister so I stole the one for me.

(continues)

Study 1 sample, confession was one of the 10 most prevalent reactions to guilt-producing situations among adolescents.

Confession serves to reduce guilt. When secrets are shared, there may be an immediate sense of relief, and if the secret is acceptingly received, the confessor may feel cleansed or refreshed, as if a great weight or burden has been put down (Shepard, 1976). The time, energy, and concentration previously devoted to keeping the secret buried may be free to expend on other pursuits (Shepard, 1976). Roman Catholics who attend sacramental confession report fewer guilt feelings than those who merely converse with the experimenter (Otterbacher & Munz, 1973). Indirect

TABLE I *(continued)*

Avoidance responses
  Distancing
    I always feel sorry when I get into arguments with my grandmother.
      I'd go up to my room and watch T. V.
    I felt guilty when my mother gave me $50.00 and I went out with my friends and boy-
    friend and I spent about $30.00 on him for his birthday. I lied and told my mother I lost
    the money.
      I went in my room closed & locked the door and put the music on full blast for about
      10 minutes.

  Suppression
    I called one of my friends a name, and he didn't talk to me for a day.
      I felt bad, I kept thinking about it. I was going to apologize, but when he started to
      talk to me again, *I tried to forget it.*
    I took part in jumping a few people in my time.
      I kept thinking about the person but then *I tried to do things to get it off my mind.*

Concern with detection/punishment responses
  Preoccupation with punishment
    When I was smoking and my parents didn't know about it.
      But I quit because I thought I would get caught.
    One day I was combing my baby sister's hair and I had made a knot in it. I took the scissors and
    cut it and she (Mom) didn't notice.
      I was so nervous. I thought my mother was going to kill me. But she never found out about what I did to
      my homegirl (sister).

  Cover-up
    I felt guilty for the time I shot a whole bunch of pigeons off my roof with my
    b.b. gun.
      I thought I would get in trouble if they found them, so I thought *I'd collect all of them*
      throw them in a bag and hid them.
    I crashed our car, a minor crash that is.
      I told my parents that I found it that way on the street where I parked it. I was a financial decision
      because I would have had to pay for the damages had I not lied. I felt guilty, but better off.
      I covered it up. That's what the situation called for.

(continues)

evidence that confession lowers guilt is provided by J. W. Regan (1971), who reports that participants who are given an opportunity to talk with a third party after transgression are less likely to use other methods of guilt reduction. When confession is made to a third party, observers judge the confessor to be less blame-worthy or guilty (Weiner, Graham, Peter, & Amuidinas, 1991b). Finally, Stice (1992) provides direct evidence that confession reduces personal feelings of guilt.

According to Todd (1985), the curative power of confession has been known for centuries. Public or group confession is used for its therapeutic value in Alcoholics Anonymous, in live-in programs for drug addicts, and in numerous self-help group

TABLE I *(continued)*

Hedonistic responses
  Pleasure
    One day I was mad at my mother for screaming at me, and then I got her lipstick and wasted it all! Then I went on *still feel good about it.*
    I burst a dog's head open with a brick.
      I laughed.

  Lack of remorse
    I once went beserk because somebody had kept calling me names and I kicked them in the face. *I felt no pity toward the person I kicked. I really hated him.*
    I punched my schoolmate because he got me in trouble with the teacher.
      Not a bit sorry.

Unresponsive action responses
  Did nothing
    I felt real bad on January 26, 1985. Mrs. P—, my teacher, got mad at me and sent me to the office so as to call my mother to bring this schoolbook. I didn't call my mother, instead I ran around the school, came back to class, and said my mother was not home.
      I didn't really do anything. Why should I tell my teacher about that?
    I feel bad for not visiting my boyfriend's family while he's locked up.
      I haven't done anything yet.

  Continuation
    I feel responsible for the teacher's being stressed.
      I kept on doing what I usually do. As I say, don't worry be happy.
    I went skating once and this boy asked me if I had a boyfriend and I told him yes. And he left and later on I was skating with a boy named David (he was 22) and I saw the same boy sitting on the floor watching us skate and my friend brought him to my attention.
      And I felt guilty. *I looked at him and kept on skating.*

settings (Mowrer, 1976). Individuals who disclose traumatic, emotion-laden information show beneficial immediate as well as long-term physiological effects (Petrie, Booth, Pennebaker, & Davidson, 1995). Individuals who write or talk about traumatic experiences show fewer physical illnesses, have better immune system functioning, and require fewer medical visits over the next year than do individuals who are not asked to disclose emotionally charged events (e.g., Berry & Pennebaker, 1993). Confession may be good for mental health as well as physical health. Bybee et al. (1996) report that women who tell others about guilt-producing incidents involving eating and exercise have fewer symptoms of eating disturbances.

Confession may also strengthen interpersonal bonds and mutual liking. Admissions of blame signal recognition that a moral rule has been violated and affirm that the guilty party values that rule (Darby & Schlenker, 1982; Lindsay-Hartz, 1984). Confession is particularly beneficial when it is freely given rather than offered following an accusation and in ambiguous causal situations (Weiner et al., 1991b). Confession results in attributions that are more external, that assign more blame to

TABLE II   Reactions to Guilt-Producing Events

Reaction	Students mentioning category (%)[a]
Remorse/regret	37.5
Apology	15.1
Preoccupation with punishment	13.9
Reparation	13.4
Renunciation	9.1
Confession	7.6
Suppression	6.1
Reestablish relationship	5.8
Justification	4.3
Cover-up	4.1
Rumination	4.1
Continuation	4.0
Distancing	3.5
Did nothing	3.5
Recognition of wrongdoing	3.5
Excuse	3.3
Victim-oriented concern	2.7
Good intentions	1.7
Need to undo	1.3
Pleasure	1.3
Lack of remorse	1.2
Intensifier	0.7
Self-hatred	0.7
Somatization	0.5
Self-punishment	0.3
Miscellaneous	13.4

[a]Numbers represent the percentage of students mentioning each reaction to self-described guilt-producing events.

uncontrollable factors, and that minimize negative dispositional or trait inferences (Weiner et al., 1991b). In a series of studies, Weiner et al. (1991b) demonstrate that individuals who confess are generally perceived more favorably by others and are more likely to be forgiven than individuals who do not confess.

Confession has downsides as well. Even under the most favorable of circumstances, individuals who confess a transgression are perceived less favorably than individuals who are innocent of wrongdoing (Weiner et al., 1991b). Indeed, confession may result in punishment for deeds that might otherwise have gone undetected. Whitesell and Harter (1989) report that young children in their study were afraid to confess because of fear of punishment.

Moreover, individuals who confess may be less likely to engage in reparative and prosocial behaviors. Participants who confess to a third party after transgression are less likely to engage in altruistic behaviors (J. W. Regan, 1971). Men are less likely

TABLE III   Differences across Grade Level in Reactions to Guilt-Producing Events

	Grade level			
Reactions	5th	8th	11th	X^2
Reconciliation/action tendency				
Victim-oriented concern	2.9	1.4	3.8	2.09
Confession	9.2	6.1	7.6	1.40
Apologies	16.5	11.3	17.8	3.71
Reparation	14.1	10.8	15.7	2.07
Need to undo	1.0	1.4	1.6	.33
Reestablish relationship	3.9	2.8	11.4	13.48***
Renunciation	3.4	12.7	11.4	11.04***
Good intentions	1.0	2.4	1.6	1.18
Self-blame/intropunitive responses				
Recognition/intensifier	1.5	3.8	7.0	6.90*
Self-hatred/self-punishment	1.0	0.5	1.6	1.21
Rumination	3.4	5.2	3.8	.92
Remorse/regret	27.2	36.8	49.7	20.75****
Rationalization				
Justifications/excuses	5.8	6.6	10.3	3.07
Avoidance				
Distancing	2.4	4.2	3.8	1.08
Suppression	2.9	7.1	8.6	5.60
Detection and punishment preoccupation				
Punishment preoccupation	19.4	12.7	9.2	8.62**
Cover-up	2.9	5.2	4.3	1.35
Hedonistic responses				
Pleasure/lack of remorse	2.4	2.4	2.7	.05
Unresponsiveness				
Did nothing/continuation	7.8	6.6	7.6	.24
Miscellaneous	15.5	18.9	4.9	15.65***

[a]Numbers represent the percentage of students at each grade level mentioning each reaction to self-described guilt-producing events.

$*p < .05.$ $**p < .01.$ $***p < .001.$ $****p < .0001$

to donate money to a charitable cause after rather than before religious confession (the pattern is reversed for females; Harris, Benson, & Hall, 1975). Because confession alleviates guilt, it may reduce internal pressure for rectification or sublimation. Confession to peers who are overly accepting of wrongdoing, anonymous radio talk shows, or the like may do more harm than good. Confession may assuage the conscience of the guilty party and reduce their compulsion to talk about the incident to the party to the act or authority figures, thereby concealing involvement and reducing the chances for rectification.

Whitesell and Harter (1989) report that older children are more likely to confess than younger children. Older children place less importance on punishment concerns and put more emphasis on the relief that confession provides from agonizing feelings of guilt. In Study 1, we also find that punishment concerns diminish with age, but find no developmental differences in mentions of confession.

Apologies

Apologies are admissions of blameworthiness and regret for transgression. Apologies arise frequently in response to guilt-producing events. Among adolescents in Study 1, apologies are the second most common reaction to guilt-producing events and appear with similar frequency throughout adolescence. Indeed, apologies appear very early in development. Zahn-Waxler and Robinson (1995) report that children as young as 2 have developed a moral sense that is evident in behavior as well as language.

As Walster, Bersheid, and Walster (1973) point out, apologies may serve several functions: they may convince the victim that the harm-doer's justifications for the transgression are plausible; they may convey the harm-doer's remorse and suffering; or they may acknowledge the transgression but point out that it cannot be rectified and ask the victim to "forgive and forget." Apologies place a burden on the recipient to grant forgiveness. Individuals who do not accept apologies from others are not liked as well by observers (Bennett & Dewberry, 1994).

Apologies minimize wrath and retaliatory intentions of the victim (Bramel, Taub, & Blum, 1968; Goffman, 1971; Schlenker, 1980). Children as young as 3 judge actors in stories who apologize less harshly than actors who do not apologize (Irwin & Moore, 1971). Among kindergarteners, elaborate apologies produce less blame, more forgiveness, more liking, more positive evaluations, greater attributions of remorse and (usually) less punishment (Darby & Schlenker, 1982). With development from kindergarten to the fourth and seventh grades, judgments become even more affected by apologies (Darby & Schlenker, 1982).

Apologies may be perfunctory or elaborate. When the event is minor, simply saying, "sorry," or "pardon me," may suffice. As the consequences of events become more severe, apologies become more elaborate, incorporating expressions of remorse and offers of assistance (Schlenker & Darby, 1981). Indeed, when the harm is more severe, more extensive apologies may be needed to assuage the victim's anger and desires for retaliation (Ohbuchi, Kameda, & Agarie, 1989). In addition, with development, apologies become less perfunctory and more elaborate (Sell & Rice, 1988).

As with confession, there may be a downside to apologies. Knoecni (1972) found that participants in a field study who do not help the confederate whose belongings they had knocked onto the sidewalk, instead offer profuse apologies. Confessions or apologies may be provided in the place of tangible assistance when the event has minor consequences. When the ramifications are more severe, however, there is evidence that rather than showing one reaction, the transgressor may show multiple responses, such as apologizing, offering assistance, and expressing concern for the victim (Schlenker & Darby, 1981).

Reparation and Undoing

Reparation was among the five most commonly mentioned responses to guilt-producing events among adolescents in our sample and showed no effects of age level. Reparation may take a number of forms. Individuals may compensate the victim for injuries or harm by providing restitution. Adolescents in Study 1 describe financially reimbursing the victim, replacing a broken object with something comparable, and performing acts of kindness intended to make up for the wrongdoing. An indirect route to reparation involves engaging in compensation. Adolescents may try to make up for letting down their parents in one area by making them proud in another by, for example, getting good grades or following household rules. A rather odd "eye-for-an-eye" restitution appeared in adolescents' descriptions as well. Adolescents who had destroyed their siblings' property (e.g., breaking record albums) let the victim retaliate to make things even. Adolescents also reported letting peers and siblings hit them back or even beat them up to restore equity.

Another person need not be involved or mentioned for reparative acts to occur. Students who feel guilty about performing poorly on a test, for example, may compensate by studying harder for the next one. Dieters may atone for overeating by starvation, purging, or exercising. Athletes may compensate for missing a practice by putting in twice as much time the next day.

Participants in experimental settings often spontaneously attempt to compensate their victims after transgression (Bersheid & Walster, 1967; Brock & Becker, 1966; Konoske, Staple, & Graf, 1979; Walster & Prestholdt, 1966). The robustness of this finding in a number of studies indicates that wrongdoers commonly compensate their victims. Interestingly, studies indicate that participants are most likely to reimburse others to restore exact equity. When the cost is too high or too low, they are more likely to choose to do nothing rather than compensating the other party.

Individuals may also make up for transgressions by behaving in an altruistic manner. Atonement or sublimation may provide a way of giving meaning to a painful event, an opportunity to restore self-esteem or make peace with God, or a way to maintain a view of the world as just and oneself as a moral being. Experimental participants who have committed a transgression are more likely than control individuals to help a third party who was not victimized (Darlington & Macker, 1966; Rawlings, 1968; D. T. Regan, M. Williams, & Sparling, 1972).

A typical study demonstrating that altruism is a common method of reacting to guilt-producing events is that of Carlsmith and Gross (1969). Participants in the guilt condition administered shocks to a confederate as punishment for incorrect responses in a learning task. Those in the control condition observed but did not deliver the shocks. After the experiment was ostensibly over, participants in the experimental condition were three times more willing than those in the control condition to make telephone calls to line up support for a petition supporting an environmental cause and, among volunteers, offered to make twice as many calls. Results suggest that the need to behave altruistically after transgression may be even stronger than the need to compensate the victim. Konoske et al. (1979) report that although participants who were required to lie to the experimenter were more likely to make nondeceptive telephone calls for the experimenter (e.g., the victim) than were members of the control group, they were less likely than the controls to make calls for the experimenter when these calls involve deception. In this case, the need to behave ethically to compensate for wrongdoing outweighed the need to provide direct restitution to the victim.

Reestablish Relationship

In some instances, the guilty party is unwilling to apologize or make reparation. Perhaps the other party is equally or more at fault. Perhaps the act in question is justifiable. Perhaps pride prevents admission of wrongdoing. Individuals may restore a damaged relationship by talking things through and explaining their viewpoint. They may agree to disagree or put events behind them by inviting the other person to join them in a mutually enjoyable activity such as playing tennis or shooting baskets. They may, without accepting blame, underscore the importance of the relationship and their affection for the other person. In Study 1, we find that reestablishing relationships in the absence of apologies or admission of wrongdoing is a relatively common reaction to guilt-producing events. This reaction becomes more prevalent with development during adolescence.

Renunciation

Descriptions of guilt-producing incidents occasionally contain events that happened quite a long time ago. Students will mention, for example, an incident of shoplifting that happened 5 or 10 years before that still torments them or persistently nags at their conscience. Students may write as if thinking aloud that they are not sure why this distant event still bothers them. The description may be offered almost apologetically with disclaimers. Adolescents may preface descriptions, for example, by acknowledging that the event happened long ago, then say they are going to describe it anyway because it keeps coming to mind. When asked to describe what happened after the event, students typically note they never again repeated that action or similar acts. With the zeal of the newly converted, some students mention that not only have they foresworn the act, but they do not tolerate this type of behavior in others either. Although renunciation has received little attention in the literature, we find that it is among the five most frequently mentioned reactions to guilt-producing incidents. Moreover, with development during adolescence, mentions of renunciation rise sharply.

Good Intentions

In the aftermath of guilt-producing incidents, students may think about apologizing or making reparation or foreswearing an act, but fail to carry through. Good intentions were infrequently mentioned and did not show age-related changes.

SELF-BLAME AND INTROPUNITIVE RESPONSES

The reactions covered in the last section involve a pattern of turning outward and toward others (e.g., by confessing, apologizing, and making reparation). The reactions covered in the present section, in contrast, involve a pattern of turning inward and against the self. Individuals faced with wrongdoing may look inside themselves, ruminating, brooding, searching for motives, trying to draw meaning from events. They may chastise themselves, saying that they should have known better, that they were clearly at fault. They may be devoured by self-hatred or consumed with sorrow or remorse. All of these reactions may serve to prolong and intensify feelings of self-hatred. Bybee et al. (1996) have linked intropunitive responses resulting from guilt-evoking events to an increased incidence of symptoms of depression and eating disorders.

Self-blame and intropunitive responses may play an adaptive role as well. Bybee and C. Williams (1996) report that higher guilt-as indexed by both reconciliatory and intropunitive responses—is related to goal-related strivings. In daily living, individuals may not have the time or inclination to scrutinize their every action in order to choose the morally principled path (Merisca & Bybee, 1994). Unpleasant pangs of conscience may play an adaptive role by interrupting an ongoing action sequence midstream and redirecting it (Baumeister, Stillwell, & Heatherton, 1994). Indeed, Merisca and Bybee (1994) find that it is guilt rather than level of moral reasoning that is more closely associated with prosocial actions. Intropunitive responses may also serve to punish the individual for transgressions, ensuring that lessons are remembered. Anticipation of self-punitive responses may serve as a deterrent, preventing the individual from imagining, planning, or committing transgressions. Reflection and introspection may result in a dawning awareness of personal shortcomings or an epiphany that leads the individual to reshape, rededicate, or reconceptualize their self. In and of themselves, righteous suffering and sorrow may add depth and dimension to character. Indeed, as discussed later, highly unfavorable character assessments are given to individuals who do not suffer or feel remorse for wrongdoing.

Recognition of Wrongdoing and Intensifiers

Some students in Study 1 reported that following a guilt-producing incident, they came to realize that what they had done was wrong. Students catalogued the adverse ramifications of their actions, pointed out additional details that made their behavior even worse, and berated themselves by saying that they should have known better or that there was no excuse for their behavior. With development, improved cognitive reasoning abilities may increasingly enable individuals to marshall reasons why their behavior was contemptible. Indeed, the percentage of students who spontaneously disavowed their own behavior doubled from the 5th to the 8th grade, and doubled again from the 8th to the 11th grade.

Self-Hatred and Self-Punishment

Self-hatred is widely held to be a concomitant of guilt. This association is so well accepted that many of the most widely used guilt inventories for adults include self-hatred items (e.g., Kugler & Jones, 1992; Mosher, 1966). In the Study 1 sample, however, we find that adolescents rarely mention self-hatred or a desire for self-punishment after guilt-producing events. A scant 1% of our participants mentioned hating themselves or desiring punishment outside direct retribution to the victim. We found no significant age-related changes in this category.

Wallington (1973) demonstrates that adult harm-doers sometimes punish themselves for wrongdoings. In her study, participants were asked to administer electric shocks to themselves as part of a learning task. Participants who had been forced to lie to the experimenter, compared to controls, exhibited greater self-aggression, administering much more intense shocks to themselves.

Findings that self-hatred is a rare response to guilt-eliciting events among adolescents is not entirely discordant with theory. As Tangney, Burggraf, and Wagner (1995) point out, in shame, attention is turned to the self and relatively stable negative attributions about the self may be made, whereas in guilt, the attention is turned to the wrongfulness of the act and attributions are less stable. Self-approbation in guilt may take the form of recognition of wrongdoing and self-castigation for allowing that act to occur, but this chastisement may not be converted into hatred or punishment of the self as it may in reactions involving shame. Even so, the very low incidence of self-hatred is quite remarkable in that guilt and shame often co-occur. The Study 1 results suggest that, at least prior to early adulthood, self-hatred is not a common reaction to guilt-producing situations.

Rumination

When faced with a guilt-producing event, individuals may replay the event over and over again, thinking about how the event came about and how it could have been avoided. Individuals may engage in introspective thinking, searching deep inside for unconscious motives, for possible character flaws, or other unpleasant truths. They may look for deeper meaning by connecting the event to a pattern of similar events. They may become preoccupied with the pain, disappointment, or even heartbreak they may have caused others to feel. Individuals may not be able to stop thinking about the guilt-evoking event. Thoughts of the event may become intrusive, interrupting everyday functioning by undermining the ability to concentrate and continuing on into the night, leading to fitful sleep and rude or feverish awakenings.

At its best, rumination may help individuals learn a lesson from events and perhaps even reconstruct themselves or a part of their personality to become a more sensitive, caring, or responsible person. At its worst, rumination may give rise to psychopathology. Ruminative responses prolong and exacerbate depressed mood states (Nolen-Hoeksema, Morrow, & Fredrickson, 1993). Females compared to males are more likely to exhibit a ruminative coping style, and this gender difference appears to explain in part females' greater proclivity for depression (Lyubomirsky & Nolen-Hoeksema, 1993).

With development, symptoms of internalizing disorders increase, and thoughts become ever more abstract (Achenbach & Edelbrock, 1981). Yet, in Study 1, grade level had no effect on mentions of rumination. Indeed, only 5% of the sample reported ruminating over the event (note that preoccupation with punishment, which was coded separately, fell with development). It is possible that rumination rises later in development. Just as the incidence of depression increases after puberty (Achenbach & Edelbrock, 1981), rumination might rise only as individuals approach or reach adulthood.

Remorse and Regret

Remorse and regret are often used in guilt inventories as operational indices of the emotion (Harder & Zalma, 1990; Kugler & Jones, 1992; Mosher, 1966; Tangney, Wagner, & Gramzow, 1989). Among adolescents in the Study 1 sample, we find regret and remorse are the most common reactions to guilt-producing events overall and at each age level. Adolescents often experience wishes that they could do things over differently. Students report crying, feeling bad, terrible, or in pain, and wishing that the event had never happened. Reports of regret and remorse become more prevalent with age, more than doubling from the 5th to the 11th grade.

The anguish, remorse, and regret accompanying guilt can be exceedingly painful and emotionally devastating. Indeed, intense remorse and regret may adversely affect mental health and may even be a factor in suicidality. In one large-scale study of female suicide attempters, females who later killed themselves compared to females who did not were more likely to have experienced severe feelings of remorse (Wandrei, 1985).

Remorse and regret, when appropriate to the situation, may be viewed by others as signs of a well-functioning conscience. Remorse may be seen as a step toward righting the injustice caused the victim and a form of punishment in its own right. Perpetrators who express remorse after an aggressive act are perceived more favorably: observers rated them as less aggressive and reduced the degree of intent attributed to them (Schwartz, Kane, Joseph, & Tedeschi, 1978). Wrongdoers who express remorse are seen as less likely to commit a similar act in the future and are given more lenient punishment (Rosen & Adams, 1974; Schwartz et al., 1978). Moreover, actual sentences given to criminal offenders convicted of murder and first-degree assault are less severe when offenders show remorse for their crimes rather than denying guilt (Felson & Ribner, 1981).

RATIONALIZATIONS

How can intelligent people perform unconscionable acts? How can Serb soldiers butcher Bosnian Muslim children in front of their parents, line up scores of men in a field and shoot them to death, and rape women as a matter of state policy? On a domestic level, how can spouses stand complacently by, knowing that their partner is sexually abusing their child? How can family members silently pocket funds illbegotten by siphoning off disabled seniors' pensions or gained when feeble elders are pressured to disinherit other relatives?

Rationalizations allow unconscionable acts to occur. The soldier in the field says he was only following orders. The terrorist points to the greater good served by advancing political causes (or some other idealistic goal). The spouse argues that looking the other way was necessary to keep the family together. Family members maintain they were entitled to the money or were taking the most straightforward course by following (and benefiting from) a recently and suspiciously changed will. Even though in each of the aforementioned cases, individuals may be well aware of societal and ethical mores and standards, and may be capable of rendering judgment against others who commit similar violations of ethical codes, they are able to assuage their own feelings of guilt by utilizing justifications and excuses.

Distinguishing Justifications and Excuses

According to Scott and Lyman (1968), individuals using justifications accept responsibility for the act in question, but deny the pejorative quality associated with it. Justifications represent an attempt to convince others that the offense was more normative, more understandable, and less serious than it seems (Gonzales, Manning, & Haugen, 1992). In contrast, individuals using excuses admit that the act in question is immoral or wrong, but deny full responsibility for the commission of the act. Individuals excuse their actions by highlighting or inventing external, uncontrollable, specific, and unintentional causes and withholding reasons for their behaviors that lead to less favorable attributions (Snyder & Higgins, 1988; Weiner, Amirkhan, Folkes, & Verette, 1987; Weiner, Figueroa-Munoz, & Kakihara, 1991a).

Justifications

There are a number of variants of justifications. An individual may deny that an injury occurred or claim that the effects of the injury were minimal or trifling. Evidence that individuals tend to minimize the suffering of their victims comes from Brock and Buss (1962). Participants who had previously indicated their opposition to electric shock read a communication stating that shock is harmful. Participants who administered electric shocks to others in a verbal learning task recalled significantly less of the communication than did controls. A second form of justification according to Scott and Lyman (1968) involves denial of victim. Transgressors may assert that their victims deserve their fate or search for some fault in the victim that might have contributed to their unfortunate situation and then weight its importance disproportionately. Harm-doers derogate their victims after transgression (Walster & Prestholdt, 1966), especially when they do not expect retaliation (Bersheid, Boye, & Walster, 1968) or when they perceive themselves to be responsible for the other's fate (Lerner & Matthews, 1967).

Another form of justification suggested by Scott and Lyman involves appeal to loyalties. Third parties may benefit from unconscionable acts and may even request that they be performed. Instead of questioning whether the act itself is wrong or right, the event may be construed as one of balancing obligations to the victim against an unbreakable allegiance or inalterable responsibility to follow the will, wishes, or orders of a relative, friend, or superior. Attention is thus drawn away from the morality or fairness of the act. A fourth form is the device of condemnation of the condemners where the transgressor admits performing the act, but asserts that others go unpunished or unnoticed for committing even worse acts (Scott & Lyman, 1968). Who has not observed a family member arguing, often indignantly, that their misdeeds pale in comparison with those of a sister or brother, as if this makes their own misdeed okay and the accuser a villain for daring to broach the issue?

Excuses

Individuals employing excuses deny full responsibility for their actions. Physical ailments, lack of sleep, impaired judgment as a result of alcohol or drug use, traffic jams, and other commitments are all commonly offered excuses that individuals offer for not doing what was expected of them or for declining invitations to, missing, or being late to events (Weiner et al., 1987, 1991a). Individuals may deny intent and claim that they would not have acted in the way they did had they been fully informed or foreseen the results. They may point to accidents, blame their actions on uncontrollable or external factors, and note that the lapse was specific and highly unusual. They may scapegoat someone else for leading them down the wrong path. An individual also might deny responsibility by claiming she was obligated to transgress by the experimental situation. Participants who commit acts involving higher levels of aggression report that they were under more obligation to administer these shocks than subjects in low aggression conditions (Brock & Buss, 1962).

Rationalizations and Adjustment

In justifying an immoral action, individuals show a disregard for the moral code, minimalizing transgressions and denying the wrongfulness of unethical behavior. The individual making an excuse, in contrast, does acknowledge the wrongfulness of the act in question. Indeed, proliferate excuses may be seen as an expression of the individuals' need to convey to the listener that the lapse never would have occurred had it not been for extremely extenuating circumstances. Potentially more unfavorable attributions may be made about individuals offering justifications than individuals offering excuses as the former individuals may be seen as evil or wicked if their account is not believed, whereas the latter may be seen as only having been negligent or irresponsible. Numerous other divergent predictions might be made as well. In our own and others' research, differences between justifications and excuses are sometimes found in relations to mental health (e.g., Bybee et al., 1996).

Common to both devices when used routinely, however, may be an underlying defense mechanism of intellectualization. We found, among a sample of 109 undergraduates in Study 2, that reliance on justifications was highly correlated ($r = .86$) with reliance on excuses and the two measures showed highly similar correlations with criterion measures. We combined the justification and excuse measures to form an index of reliance on rationalizations and examined correlations of this index with indicators of adjustment. Results of Study 2 are presented in Table 4 and discussed in the following sections.[2]

[2]Participants were provided with a series of vignettes describing events that had been determined in pretesting to be guilt-evoking among a high percentage of college undergraduates. The five events included lying to parents about college grades, not calling someone with whom they had made social plans, cheating on a boy- or girlfriend who was living out of town (e.g., over summer vacation), staying out all night with friends while living at parents' house, lying to boss about having a family emergency so they could have time off work to socialize. The vignettes were repeated, appearing each time with a different rationalization (16 excuses, 16 justifications). The vignette describing lying to mother about grades, for example, was followed by the excuse, "I had just come back from a friend's graduation party and had had several glasses of champagne. I was in a great mood and I made things seem better than they were," and elsewhere by the justification, "The way I view it is I am going to have the rest of my life to get serious and worry about my career, mortgages, and other responsibilities. I'm only in college once and I should enjoy it and get my mother off my back." Justifications and excuses were designed to be exemplars of categories from Scott and Lyman (1968). Students were asked to rate the culpability of the main character taking into account the rationale provided. Assessments of higher culpability were said to reflect less honoring of rationalizations.

Self-esteem

Rationalizations preserve feelings of self-worth. Correlations of rationalizations to self-esteem, assessed globally and in specific content domains, are shown in Table 4. Individuals who use rationalizations to reduce their feelings of guilt have higher levels of self-esteem in the social confidence and physical appearance content domains. Perhaps not coincidentally, these are the two domains most closely associated with image and outward appearance. As discussed later, one of the primary functions of rationalizations is to help save face. As Baumeister (chapter 6, this volume) points out, the protection and maintenance of self-esteem is not always a laudable goal. People who commit unconscionable acts often believe themselves to be good, ethical people. Serial murderers and violent offenders, for example, often have inordinately high self-esteem (Baumeister, chapter 6, this volume). Indeed, the father who commits incest, the doctor who has sex with the babysitter, the uncle who pockets his nieces' inheritance may see themselves as pillars of society, churchgoers, influential and well-respected members of their community.

Guilt Alleviation

Rationalizations reduce guilt. Weiner (1985) reports that external attributions for failure minimize personal feelings of guilt. Conversely, individuals who are prone to guilt may recoil at the idea of using justifications and excuses rather than accepting responsibility for their actions. We find that a personality proclivity for guilt is inversely related to use of rationalizations (see Table IV).

Prosocial Actions

With feelings of guilt neutralized, individuals may no longer feel a pressing need to rectify the situation through reparative or prosocial actions. Indeed, as shown in Table 4, rationalizations are correlated with less prosocial behavior. Students who rationalize more are seen by their peers (roommates) as less caring, helpful, and thoughtful individuals.

Aggression

As shown in the table, rationalizations are associated with greater aggressiveness. Among the undergraduates we examined, those who relied more on rationalizations to assuage their feelings of guilt are, according to their peers, more rude, disruptive, and hostile. These findings are consistent with other research reports. Justifications are used by individuals committing a host of immoral, violent, or unpalatable acts. Child molesters and convicted rapists commonly use justifications and excuses (see DeYoung, 1989; Scully & Marolla, 1984). Murderers as well com-

TABLE IV   Relationship of Rationalizations to Self-Esteem, Guilt, Depression, and Social Attitudes and Behaviors[a]

Measures	Rationalizations
Self-esteem	
Social confidence	.33**
School abilities	.18
Physical abilities	.17
Physical appearance	.30**
General self-regard	.16
Guilt	−.49****
Racism	.26*
Peer ratings	
Prosocial behavior	−.28**
Aggressiveness	.25*
Depression	−.13

[a]The Self-Rating Scale (Fleming & Courtney, 1984), Mosher Forced-Choice Guilt Scale (Mosher, 1966, 1979), Beck Depression Inventory (Beck, 1972), Modern Racism Scale (modified from McConahay [1986] by Merisca & Bybee [1994]) and Peer Ratings of Prosocial Behavior and Aggressiveness (Merisca & Bybee, 1994) were used.
*$p < .05$.   **$p < .01$.   ****$p < .0001$

monly proffer justifications and excuses for their violent behavior (Henderson & Hewstone, 1984).

Racist Attitudes

Rationalizations are related to racist attitudes as shown in Table 4. Derogation of the victim, minimization of others' suffering, and appeal to ingroup, family, or ethnic loyalties may all result in racism and ethnic hatred.

Mental Health

Intellectualizations may be helpful in preserving mental health. Benefits may be especially apparent when the rationalization is tailored to a particular distressing event. In the eating and exercise domain, for example, individuals may place unrealistically high expectations upon themselves to exercise vigorously for hour-long stretches daily, to never eat sweets, to avoid fats, to never overeat. Lapses may cause considerable and painful chronic feelings of guilt. Bybee et al. (1996) find that women who are better able to justify or excuse guilt over eating and exercise are less prone to eating disturbances and depression.

As shown in Table 4, however, we found no correlation between rationalizations and depression. Even though individuals who routinely use intellectualizations may feel good about themselves, their bad deeds may return to haunt them. Rationalizers, because they are less likely to engage in prosocial actions and are more prone to aggression, may build ill will and undermine their social support network. Benefits to mental health from a high sense of self-esteem may be offset by the adverse consequences of having poor interpersonal relationships.

Functions of Excuses in Communication

Weiner (et al., 1987, 1991a; Weiner & Handel, 1985) provides a riveting account of the role that excuses play in communication and causal perceptions. By proffering excuses that draw attention to external, unstable, and highly specific reasons for lapses, the communicator may avoid damaging the self-esteem of the rejected party, prevent the other party from becoming or remaining angry, and convince the other party that the act will not be repeated (Weiner et al., 1987, 1991a; Weiner & Handel, 1985). How might we reconcile these findings pointing to positive interpersonal functions of excuses with our own, underscoring negative interpersonal correlates of rationalizations? We suggest that excuses compared to justifications are less damaging to interpersonal relationships because the wrongfulness of the act is acknowledged. In addition, a one-time occurrence of excuse giving, such as that studied by Weiner and his colleagues, may be perceived more favorably than a characterological proclivity for rationalizing such as that assessed in Study 2.

Development of Rationalizations

Rationalizations appear very early in development. Children as young as 36 months commonly use justifications in disputes with their mothers and siblings (Dunn & Munn, 1987). Children aged 5–12, in providing accounts, withhold information in order to avoid attributing their behavior to controllable causes and likewise avoid explanations that would damage the other person's self-esteem (Weiner & Handel, 1985; Yirmiya & Weiner, 1986).

Returning to the first study of the present chapter, we find that reliance on justifications and excuses increases with grade level. Although the effect only approaches significance, the percentage of students who spontaneously mention rationalizations doubles from the fifth to the eighth grade.

Most theories of moral development offer an ontological model of development. According to Kohlberg (e.g., Kohlberg & Candee, 1984), for example, higher stages of moral reasoning necessarily involve more ethical modes of thought. Yet as Zahn-Waxler and Robinson (1995) note, "The notion of increased morality with age may reflect as much developmental myth as fact" (p. 163). Indeed, as Zahn-Waxler and Robinson observe, brutality, indifference, violence, and insensitivity are a part of human nature in both childhood and adulthood. C. Williams and Bybee (1994b) find that guilt declines markedly during adolescence. We maintain that the decrease in guilt goes hand in glove with increases in rationalizations. As individuals become better able to marshall intellectual defenses, they become better able to harden their hearts.

AVOIDANCE

Distancing

As mentioned earlier, shame is typically accompanied by a desire to shrink away, to hide, and to leave the situation, whereas guilt is typically accompanied by a desire to confess, approach, apologize, and set things right (e.g., Ferguson & Stegge, 1995; Tangney, 1995). Faced with feelings of guilt, some students do retreat. They take walks, turn on the stereo or television, or retire to their rooms. This is, however, a relatively infrequent response. Less than 5% of the adolescents in our sample report distancing themselves from guilt-producing situations, and developmental differences did not approach significance.

Suppression

With development, children are better able to regulate and control their emotions (Cole, Michel, & Teti, 1994). We found a grade-related trend: At higher grade levels, adolescents increasingly reported attempts to actively suppress guilt-producing thoughts. Mentions tripled from the 5th to the 11th grades.

DETECTION AND PUNISHMENT CONCERNS

Preoccupation with Punishment

When theorists describe phenomenological experiences of guilt, they sometimes describe a condition called guilty fear (Hoffman, 1985). Perpetrators of an act may worry feverishly that they will be uncovered, exposed, grilled with questions, and subjected to censure and disapproval. They may weigh possible punishments if they confess against even greater retribution if they are found to be covering up the act and against living with a guilty conscience if they are not caught. When detection or confession is certain, the time that lapses between the deed and the arrival of the authority figure may be tense and painful. Individuals may mentally rehearse the moment of truth, imagining their own responses and those of their parent or teacher. The perpetrator may try to think of explanations and ways to lessen or avoid punishment and worry about exactly what form the punishment will take.

We find that preoccupation with punishment is extremely common among adolescents and, indeed, is the third most prevalent response to guilt-evoking situations.

In Study 1, preoccupation with punishment becomes much less prevalent with age, dropping significantly from the younger to the older age groups. This may reflect a developmental progression in moral reasoning away from preconventional concerns with punishment (Kohlberg, 1969). Older adolescents may also be less likely than younger adolescents to be formally punished.

Cover-up

When faced with a guilt-producing event, some participants try to cover their tracks, literally hide the evidence, and lie to protect themselves. Cover-ups were relatively infrequent and showed no age-related changes.

HEDONISTIC RESPONSES

Pleasure and Lack of Remorse

Perhaps the most chilling responses to guilt-evoking situations involve enjoyment over the deed. One adolescent male graphically described beating up another student, noting the satisfaction he drew from pummeling his enemy. Other students almost defiantly noted that they did not feel bad at all over the deed in question. Fortunately, few adolescents in our sample mentioned taking pleasure from hurting others or lack of remorse.

UNRESPONSIVENESS

Some children in Study 1 report doing nothing about the lapse or continuing to perform the same untoward act. All told, just under 10% of our sample highlighted their own unresponsiveness. There were no age-related changes in this category. This may reflect mindless, automated behavior. It may also be that children do not know what to do about their actions, how to rectify or make sense of the situation, so they take the course of least resistance and do nothing.

GENERAL CONCLUSIONS

In this volume, Baumeister (chapter 6) suggests that one of the most important tasks facing parents and caregivers is to induce, instill, and inculcate healthy feelings of guilt and personal responsibility in children. Of equal importance may be the task of teaching children to deal effectively and ethically with feelings of guilt. The challenge is to encourage and reward a healthy predisposition for guilt. Responses that remove the onus of responsibility from the individual such as justifications and excuses hold the potential for extinguishing future as well as past guilt feelings. As mentioned at the beginning of this chapter, the absence of guilt is closely associated with sociopathy. Indeed, in Study 2, we find rationalizations are associated with greater aggression and lowered prosocial behavior as reported by peers and more self-reported racist attitudes. At the other extreme, chronic feelings of guilt are associated with poor mental health (and apparently with antisocial behavior as well—see Bybee & Quiles, chapter 13, this volume). Reconciliatory reactions may help channel guilt into positive behaviors and prevent the feelings from becoming chronic.

Individuals typically do not show a single reaction to guilt-producing incidents. In our Study 1, we found that adolescents often reacted with two, three, or more responses. Perhaps the most healthy individuals tailor their reactions to the precipitating event and are flexible in the responses shown across different incidents. If used after minor incidents or after successful attempts at reparation, rationalizations may play a healthy role in preserving self-esteem. If one reaction is used predominantly and inflexibly, it may backfire. We might imagine that even reconciliatory responses would become harmful if used exclusively or inappropriately, triggering endless and fruitless attempts at appeasement. The well-adjusted person may have an arsenal of responses at their disposal and the wisdom and character to apply them in a flexible and appropriate manner.

The present findings have implications for the assessment of guilt. Certain reactions, such as self-hatred, regret, remorse, concern for the victim, need for reparation, and apologies, are so closely associated with guilt that they are used as operational indicators in the most widely used measures for adults (Harder & Zalma, 1990; Kugler & Jones, 1992; Mosher, 1966; Tangney et al., 1989). Our findings suggest that some of the reactions such as self-hatred do not appear to characterize responses of children. Other common reactions to guilt-producing situations are largely absent from major guilt inventories and have received far less attention in theoretical and empirical work. Children often may react to guilt-producing events by renouncing or foreswearing the act in question, by engaging in rationalizations, or by becoming preoccupied with possible discovery and punishment. These reactions have received little attention in studies of guilt in children, and items have not made their way into guilt inventories.

REFERENCES

Achenbach, T. M., & Edelbrock, C. S. (1981). Behavioral problems and competencies reported by parents of normal and disturbed children aged four through sixteen. *Monographs of the Society for Research in Child Development, 46 (1, Serial No. 188)*.

Baumeister, R. F., Stillwell, A. M., & Heatherton, T. F. (1994). Guilt: An interpersonal approach. *Psychological Bulletin, 115*, 243–267.

Beck, A. T. (1972). Measuring depression: The depression inventory. In T. A. Williams, M. M. Katz, & J. A. Shields (Eds.), *Recent advances in the psychobiology of the depressive illnesses* (pp. 299–302). Washington, DC: US Government Printing Office.

Bennett, M., & Dewberry, C. (1994). "I've said I'm sorry, haven't I?" A study of the identity implications and constraints that apologies create for their recipients. *Current Psychology: Developmental, Learning, Personality, Social, 13*, 10–20.

Berry, D. S., & Pennebaker, J. W. (1993). Nonverbal and verbal emotional expression and health. *Psychotherapy and Psychosomatics, 59*, 11–19.

Bersheid, E., Boye, D., & Walster, E. (1968). Retaliation as a means of restoring equity. *Journal of Personality and Social Psychology, 10*, 370–376.

Bersheid, E., & Walster, E. (1967). When does a harm-doer compensate a victim? *Journal of Personality and Social Psychology, 6*, 435–441.

Bramel, D., Taub, B., & Blum, B. (1968). An observer's reaction to the suffering of his enemy. *Journal of Personality and Social Psychology, 8*, 384–392.

Brock, T. C., & Becker, L. A. (1966). "Debriefing" and susceptibility to subsequent experimental manipulation. *Journal of Experimental Social Psychology, 2*, 314–323.

Brock, T. C., & Buss, A. H. (1962). Dissonance, aggression and the evaluation of pain. *Journal of Abnormal and Social Psychology, 65*, 197–202.

Bybee, J. A., Berliner, D., Zigler, E., & Merisca, R. (1996). Guilt, guilt-evoking events, depression, and eating disorders. *Current Psychology: Developmental, Learning, Personality, Social, 15*, 113–127.

Bybee, J. A., & Williams, C. (1996). *When is guilt adaptive? Relationships to prosocial behavior, academic and social strivings, and mental health.* Manuscript submitted for publication.

Carlsmith, J. M., & Gross, A. (1969). Some effects of guilt on compliance. *Journal of Personality and Social Psychology, 11*, 232–244.

Cole, P. M., Michel, M. K., & Teti, L. O. (1994). The development of emotion regulation and dysregulation: A clinical perspective. In N. A. Fox (Ed.), *The development of emotion regulation: Biological and behavioral considerations. Monographs of the Society for Research in Child Development, 59*, (2–3 Serial No. 240).

Darby, B. W., & Schlenker, B. R. (1982). Children's reactions to guilt. *Journal of Personality and Social Psychology, 43*, 742–753.

Darlington, R. B., & Macker, C. E. (1966). Displacement of guilt-produced altruistic behavior. *Journal of Personality and Social Psychology, 4*, 442–443.

DeYoung, M. (1989). The world according to NAMBLA: Accounting for deviance. *Journal of Sociology and Social Welfare, 16*, 111–126.

Dunn, J., & Munn, P. (1987). Development of justification in disputes with mother and sibling. *Developmental Psychology, 23*, 791–798.

Felson, R. B., & Ribner, S. A. (1981). An attributional approach to accounts and sanctions for criminal violence. *Social Psychology Quarterly, 44*, 137–142.

Ferguson, T. J., & Stegge, H. (1995). Emotional states and traits in children: The case of guilt and shame. In J. P. Tangney & K. W. Fischer (Eds.). *Self-conscious emotions: The psychology of shame, guilt, embarrassment, and pride.* New York: Guilford Press.

Ferguson, T. J., Stegge, H., & Damhuis, I. (1991). Children's understanding of guilt and shame. *Child Development, 62*, 827–839.

Fleming, J. S., & Courtney, B. E. (1984). The dimensionality of self-esteem: II. Hierarchical facet model for revised measurement scales. *Journal of Personality and Social Psychology, 46*, 404–421.

Goffman, B. (1971). *Relations in public.* New York: Harper Colophon.

Gonzales, M. H., Manning, D. J., & Haugen, J. A. (1992). Explaining our sins: Factors influencing offender accounts and anticipated victim responses. *Journal of Personality and Social Psychology, 62*, 958–971.

Harder, D. W., & Zalma, A. (1990). Two promising shame and guilt scales: A construct validity comparison. *Journal of Personality Assessment, 55,* 729–745.

Harpur, T. J., Hakstian, A. R., & Hare, R. D. (1988). Factor structure of the psychopathy checklist. *Journal of Consulting and Clinical Psychology, 56,* 741–747.

Harris, M. B., Benson, S. M., & Hall, C. L. (1975). The effects of confession on altruism. *Journal of Social Psychology, 96,* 187–192.

Henderson, M., & Hewstone, M. R. (1984). Prison inmates' explanations for interpersonal violence: Accounts and attributions. *Journal of Consulting and Clinical Psychology, 52,* 789–794.

Hoffman, M. (1985). Affect, motivation, and cognition. In E. T. Higgins & R. M. Sorrentino (Eds.), *Handbook of motivation and cognition: Foundations of social behavior* (pp. 244–280). New York: Guilford.

Irwin, D. M., & Moore, S. G. (1971). The young child's understanding of social justice. *Developmental Psychology, 5,* 406–410.

Kohlberg, L. (1969). Stage and sequence: The cognitive-developmental approach to socialization. In D. A. Goslin (Ed.), *Handbook of socialization theory and research* (pp. 347–480). Chicago: Rand McNally.

Kohlberg, L., & Candee, D. (1984). The relationship of moral judgment to moral action. In L. Kohlberg (Ed.), *Essays on moral development: Vol. 2. The psychology of moral development* (pp. 498–581). San Francisco: Harper & Row.

Knoecni, V. J. (1972). Some effects of guilt on compliance: A field replication. *Journal of Personality and Social Psychology, 23,* 30–32.

Konoske, P., Staple, S., & Graf, R. G. (1979). Compliant reactions to guilt, self-esteem and self-punishment. *Journal of Social Psychology, 18,* 207–211.

Kugler, K., & Jones, W. H. (1992). On conceptualizing and assessing guilt. *Journal of Personality and Social Psychology, 62,* 318–327.

Lerner, M. J., & Matthews, G. (1967). Reactions to suffering of others under conditions of indirect responsibility. *Journal of Personality and Social Psychology, 5,* 319–325.

Lindsay-Hartz, J. (1984). Contrasting experiences of shame and guilt. *American Behavioral Scientist, 27,* 689–704.

Lyubomirsky, S., & Nolen-Hoeksema, S. (1993). Self-perpetuating properties of dysphoric rumination. *Journal of Personality and Social Psychology, 65,* 339–349.

McConahay, J. (1986). Modern racism, ambivalence, and the modern racism scale. In J. F. Dovidio & S. L. Gaertner (Eds.), *Prejudice, discrimination, and racism.* Orlando: Academic Press.

Merisca, R. & Bybee, J. (1994, April). *Guilt, not moral reasoning, relates to volunteerism, prosocial behavior, lowered aggressiveness, and eschewal of racism.* Poster presented at the Annual Meeting of the Eastern Psychological Association, Providence, Rhode Island.

Michaud, S. G., & Aynesworth, H. (1983). *The only living witness.* New York: Simon & Schuster.

Mosher, D. L. (1966). The development and multi-trait-multi-method matrix analysis of three measures of guilt. *Journal of Consulting Psychology, 30,* 25–29.

Mosher, D. L. (1979). The meaning and measurement of guilt. In C. E. Izard (Ed.), *Emotions in personality and psychopathology* (pp. 105–129). New York: Plenum.

Mowrer, H. O. (1976). Changing conceptions of neurosis and the small-groups movement. *Education, 97,* 24–62.

Nolen-Hoeksema, S., Morrow, J., & Fredrickson, B. L. (1993). Response styles and the duration of episodes of depressed mood. *Journal of Abnormal Psychology, 102,* 20–28.

Ohbuchi, K. I., Kameda, M., & Agarie, N. (1989). Apology as aggression control: Its role in mediating appraisal of and response to harm. *Journal of Personality and Social Psychology, 56,* 219–227.

Otterbacher, J. R., & Munz, D. C. (1973). State–trait measure of experimental guilt. *Journal of Consulting and Clinical Psychology, 40,* 115–121.

Perry, D. G. (1980). Processes of attribution and children's self-punishment following misbehavior. *Child Development, 51,* 545–551.

Petrie, K. J., Booth, R. J., Pennebaker, J. W., & Davidson, K. P. (1995). Disclosure of trauma and immune response to a hepatitis B vaccination program. *Journal of Consulting and Clinical Psychology, 63,* 787–792.

Quiles, Z., & Bybee, J. (1997). Chronic and predispositional guilt: Relations to mental health, prosocial behavior, and religiosity. *Journal of Personality Assessment.*

Rawlings, E. I. (1968). Witnessing harm to others: A reassessment of the role of guilt in altruistic behavior. *Journal of Personality and Social Psychology, 10,* 377–380.

Regan, D. T., Williams, M., & Sparling, S. (1972). Voluntary expiation of guilt: A field experiment. *Journal of Personality and Social Psychology, 24,* 42–45.

Regan, J. W. (1971). Guilt, perceived injustice and altruistic behavior. *Journal of Personality and Social Psychology, 18,* 124–132.

Rosen, B., & Adams, S. J. (1974). Organizational cover-ups: Factors influencing the discipline of information gatekeepers. *Journal of Applied Social Psychology, 4,* 375–384.

Schlenker, B. R. (1980). *Impression management: The self concept, social identity, and interpersonal relations.* Monterey, CA: Brooks/Cole.

Schlenker, B. R., & Darby, B. W. (1981). The use of apologies in social predicaments. *Social Psychology Quarterly, 44,* 271–278.

Schwartz, G. S., Kane, T. R., Joseph, J. M., & Tedeschi, J. T. (1978). The effects of post-transgression remorse on perceived aggression, attributions of intent, and level of punishment. *British Journal of Social and Clinical Psychology, 17,* 293–297.

Scott, M. B., & Lyman, S. M. (1968). Accounts. *American Sociological Review, 23,* 46–62.

Scully, D., & Marolla, J. (1984). Convicted rapists' vocabulary of motive: Excuses and justifications. *Social Problems, 31,* 530–544.

Sell, M., & Rice, M. (1988). Girls' excuses: Listener, severity of violation, and developmental effects. *Discourse Processes, 11,* 35–85.

Shepard, M. (1976). *The Do It Yourself Psychotherapy Guide.* New York: Permanent Press.

Snyder, C. R., & Higgins, R. L. (1988). Excuses: Their effective role in the negotiation of reality. *Psychological Bulletin, 104,* 23–35.

Stice, E. (1992). The similarities between cognitive dissonance and guilt: Confession as a relief of dissonance. *Current Psychology: Research and Reviews, 11,* 69–77.

Tangney, J. P. (1995). Shame and guilt in interpersonal relationships. In J. P. Tangney & K. W. Fischer (Eds.), *Self-conscious emotions: The psychology of shame, guilt, embarrassment, and pride* (pp. 114–139). New York: Guilford Press.

Tangney, J. P., Burggraf, S. A., & Wagner, P. E. (1995). Shame-proneness, guilt-proneness, and psychological symptoms. In J. P. Tangney & K. W. Fischer (Eds.), *Self-conscious emotions: The psychology of shame, guilt, embarrassment, and pride* (pp. 343–367). New York: Guilford Press.

Tangney, J. P., Marschall, D. E., Rosenberg, K., Barlow, D. H., & Wagner, P. E. (1996). *Children's and adult's autobiographical accounts of shame, guilt, and pride experiences: A qualitative analysis of situational determinants and interpersonal concerns.* Manuscript submitted for publication.

Tangney, J. P., Wagner, P., Fletcher, C., & Gramzow, R. (1992a). Shamed into anger? The relation of shame and guilt to anger and self-reported aggression. *Personality and Social Psychology Bulletin, 18,* 199–206.

Tangney, J. P., Wagner, P., & Gramzow, R. (1989). *The Test of Self-Conscious Affect.* Fairfax, VA: George Mason University.

Tangney, J. P., Wagner, P., & Gramzow, R. (1992b). Proneness to shame, proneness to guilt, and psychopathology. *Journal of Abnormal Psychology, 101,* 469–478.

Tedeschi, J. T., & Riordan, C. A. (1981). Impression management and prosocial behavior following transgression. In J. T. Tedeschi (Ed.), *Impression management theory and social psychological research* (pp. 223–243). New York: Academic Press.

Todd, E. (1985). The value of confession and forgiveness according to Jung. *Journal of Religion and Health, 24,* 39–48.

Wallington, S. A. (1973). Consequences of transgression: Self-punishment and depression. *Journal of Personality and Social Psychology, 28,* 1–7.

Walster, E., Bersheid, E., & Walster, G. W. (1973). New directions in equity research. *Journal of Personality and Social Psychology, 25,* 151–176.

Walster, E., & Prestholdt, P. (1966). The effect of misjudging another: Overcompensation or dissonance reduction? *Journal of Personality and Social Psychology, 2,* 85–97.

Wandrei, K. E. (1985). Identifying potential suicides among high-risk women. *Social Work, 30,* 511–517.

Weiner, B. (1985). An attributional analysis of achievement, motivation and emotion. *Psychological Review, 92,* 548–573.

Weiner, B., Amirkham, J., Folkes, V., & Verette, J. A. (1987). An attributional analysis of excuse giving: Studies of a naive theory of emotion. *Journal of Personality and Social Psychology, 52,* 316–324.

Weiner, B., Figueroa-Munoz, A., & Kakihara, C. (1991a). The goals of excuses and communication strategies related to causal perceptions. *Personality and Social Psychology Bulletin, 17,* 4–13.

Weiner, B., Graham, S., Peter, O., & Zmuidinas, M. (1991b). Public confession and forgiveness. *Journal of Personality, 59,* 281–312.

Weiner, B., & Handel, S. (1985). Anticipated emotional consequences of causal communications and reported communication strategy. *Developmental Psychology, 21,* 102–107.

Whitesell, N. R., & Harter, S. (1989). Children's reports of conflict between simultaneous opposite-valence emotions. *Child Development, 60,* 673–682.

Williams, C., & Bybee, J. (1994a). What do children feel guilty about? Developmental and gender differences. *Developmental Psychology, 30,* 617–623.

Williams, C., & Bybee, J. (1994b). *Do grade level, peer delinquency, emotionality, and gender affect ratings of own and others' guilt?* Paper presented at the Annual Meeting of the Eastern Psychological Association, Providence, Rhode Island.

Yirmiya, N., & Weiner, B. (1986). Perceptions of controllability and anticipated anger. *Cognitive Development, 1,* 273–280.

Zahn-Waxler, C., Cole, P. M., & Barrett, K. C. (1991). Guilt and empathy: Sex differences and implications for the development of depression. In J. Garber & K. Dodge (Eds.). *The development of emotion regulation and dysregulation.* Cambridge: Cambridge University Press.

Zahn-Waxler, C., Radke-Yarrow, M., Wagner, E., & Chapman, M. (1992). Development of concern for others. *Developmental Psychology, 28,* 126–136.

Zahn-Waxler, C., & Robinson, J. (1995). Empathy and guilt: Early origins of feelings of responsibility. In J. P. Tangney & K. W. Fischer (Eds.). *Self-conscious emotions: The psychology of shame, guilt, embarrassment, and pride* (pp. 143–173). New York: Guilford Press.

PART IV

Guilt and Adjustment

CHAPTER 10

Avoiding and Alleviating Guilt through Prosocial Behavior

Mica Estrada-Hollenbeck

Harvard University, Cambridge, Massachusetts

Todd F. Heatherton

Dartmouth College, Hanover, New Hampshire

INTRODUCTION

Good deeds are often motivated by feelings of guilt. When we feel guilty over neglecting our mothers, we phone them. When we feel guilty over damaging property, we offer to pay for it. When we intentionally or unintentionally hurt our relationship partners, we apologize. Guilt is a negative emotional state associated with an internal experience of tension, remorse, and agitation (Ferguson, Stegge, & Damhuis, 1991; Tangney, 1992). Guilt is an integral component of conscience. Empirical evidence suggests that feelings of guilt play an important role in motivating behaviors that preserve, strengthen, and sustain social bonds (Baumeister, Stillwell, & Heatherton, 1994, 1995a, 1995b; Tangney, 1995) and prevent individuals from being ostracized (Kochanska, 1993). In this chapter, we briefly define guilt and prosocial behavior and examine their development. We examine how guilt may repair damaged relationships, help people refrain from committing proscribed actions, and spontaneously engage in relationship-enhancing behavior. Finally, we examine how the processes of forgiveness ameliorate feelings of guilt.

Guilt and Children
Copyright © 1998 by Academic Press. All rights of reproduction in any form reserved.

215

GUILT

When Do We Feel Guilty?

Guilt may occur when someone feels responsible for another person's negative affective state or over harming another person. Hoffman (1994a) points out that guilt may arise from actions (such as lying) or from inactions (such as forgetting somebody's birthday). Baumeister et al. (1994) note that guilt arises even when individuals do not feel personally responsible for another's negative situation. Guilt by association, for example, may arise when an individual who did not personally injure someone was part of a group who did (Hoffman, 1994a). Moreover, existential or survivor guilt may result when a person did not commit a transgression but, "feels culpable owing to life circumstances beyond one's control" (p. 170), such as being both wealthy and aware of the suffering of those in extreme poverty. In each of these situations, the guilty party is sensitive to the welfare of others, feels an interpersonal connection—however remote—with them, and/or is aware of a condition of inequity.

The Social Functions of Guilt

The initation, maintenance, and avoidance of guilt serves a number of useful functions inside the context of interpersonal interactions (Baumeister, Stillwell, & Heatherton, 1994, 1995a,b; Tangney, 1995; Vangelisti & Sprague, 1998). Differences between guilt and other negative affective states such as shame (see Tangney, chapter 1, this volume) may help explain why guilt is more typically associated with prosocial behavior. Feelings of guilt promote victim-oriented concern and attempts to increase social contact. Guilt, unlike shame, is associated with action tendencies such as apologies, attempts at reparation, and reconciliatory actions that are inherently prosocial in nature. Feelings of shame prompt avoidance, social withdrawal, and attempts to hide or cover up (Tangney, 1995).

Guilt typically arises in reaction to a specific event, situation, or outcome, whereas shame arises from a negative evaluation of the entire self (Tangney, 1992, 1995; Tangney, Miller, Flicker, & Barlow, 1996). It may be easier to undo or repair a circumscribed event than to remake or recast the self (Tangney, chapter 1, this volume). A person who unintentionally bumps into a table, knocking over and breaking someone's cup of coffee, for example, might react with guilt over the damage that was caused or shame over their own clumsiness. An individual may be readily able and willing to apologize or provide compensation (such as financial restitution for the property damage), but may feel daunted by and paralyzed into inactivity at the prospect of trying to become permanently more graceful or attentive.

Furthermore, among individuals experiencing guilt, the concern is with the transgression or lapse, whereas with shame, the concern is more often with what onlookers or observers will think (Lewis, 1979). Guilt compared to shame may more often give rise to attempts to manage and improve one's social relationships, whereas shame compared to guilt may motivate attempts at impression management.

Guilt serves a number of interpersonal functions, such as prompting people to treat others well and helping people to avoid actions that would harm those around them. Guilt may redistribute power within unbalanced relationships, enabling the person with less power to sometimes get their way by making the other person feel guilty (Baumeister et al., 1994). Indeed, guilt can be used as a tool to manipulate and influence others to behave in ways that benefit the inducer (Baumeister, chapter 5, this volume; Baumeister et al., 1995a). Because guilt motivates prosocial behaviors, individuals inducing guilt may expect to benefit from positive responses (such as apologies and attempts at reparation) that the emotion engenders.

The Emergence of Guilt as a Social Emotion

Social emotions, such as guilt, have attracted increasing attention recently among developmental psychologists. Although the empirical base of data on the emergence of guilt among children is still quite small, theorists point to the importance of empathy in its development (Hoffman, 1982; Kochanska, 1993; Zahn-Waxler & Kochanska, 1990). Guilt is thought to emerge early in development when children empathize with another person's anger, sadness, or distress *and* are aware that they are responsible for the other person's affective state (Hoffman, 1994a, 1994b; Zahn-Waxler & Radke-Yarrow, 1990). Hoffman (1994b) suggests that, "blaming oneself becomes possible once one has acquired the cognitive capacity to recognize the consequences of his action for others and to be aware that he has choice and control over his own behavior" (p. 139).

It is difficult to observe exactly when children begin to feel guilty, since unlike sadness, anger, or surprise, the emotion is accompanied by few objective facial expressions or physical characteristics. Children may also lack the linguistic sophistication necessary to understand the multiple and sometimes ambiguous definitions of guilt. Indeed, adults often have difficulty articulating differences between guilt and closely related emotional states such as shame. In attempts to identify early markers of guilt, some researchers rely on a subjective appraisal of the child's discomfort when viewing a distressed or injured person as evidence of the emotion. Indicators suggest this form of discomfort appears during the second year of life (Kagan, 1981; Zahn-Waxler & Radke-Yarrow, 1990; Zahn-Waxler & Robinson,

1995), and there is general agreement that guilt feelings among children emerge around this time. Evidence suggests, however, that very young children have difficulty distinguishing between harm they cause and harm they observe. Guilt feelings among young children may not be proportionate to their degree of personal responsibility (Zahn-Waxler & Kochanska, 1990). Interestingly, even among adolescents, guilt feelings are common even when the individual is not at fault (Williams & Bybee, 1994). Individuals may, for example, feel guilt by association or guilt over accidents.

Recent evidence indicates that effects of socialization are particularly important in the evolution of guilt. Zahn-Waxler and Robinson (1995) report results from a longitudinal study of the impact of socialization on the development of a variety of negative emotions, including guilt. They compared monozygotic (MZ) and dizygotic (DZ) twins at ages 14, 20, and 24 months. They found that all negative emotions (including guilt) showed considerable genetic influence (as evidenced by higher concordance rates for MZ compared to DZ twins), but guilt was unique in that it was also highly affected by the social environment. With age, the influence of shared environment on guilt became stronger, while the effects of genetic factors decreased.

Parental warmth has been linked with greater guilt in children (Zahn-Waxler & Kochanska, 1990). Indeed, feelings of guilt are common in healthy and happy relationships (see Baumeister et al., 1994). Within warm, communal relationships, feelings of empathy may thrive, and empathy in turn may give rise to guilt. In addition, as Baumeister (chapter 6, this volume) notes, it may be necessary to care about another person in order to experience guilt over hurting them. In family situations where caring and compassionate behaviors abound, the potential for guilt may be maximized.

From adolescence onward, females are more prone to feelings of guilt than are males (Bybee & Miller, chapter 5, this volume; Tangney, 1990; Zahn-Waxler & Kochaska, 1990). There are also gender differences in the situations that evoke guilt. Williams and Bybee (1994), in a content analysis of self-reports given by 5th, 8th, and 11th graders, found that proportionately more males compared to females reported feeling guilty about externally directed aggression (e.g., property damage, fighting, and victimization of animals), whereas females more commonly reported feeling guilty about violating norms of compassion and trust (e.g., inconsiderateness and lying). Females compared to males were more likely to allude to intimate others (e.g., parents and extended family) when mentioning individuals who evoke guilt. Gender differences in guilt-evoking situations and individuals may reflect a greater sense of communality among women (Gilligan, 1982). Findings that females, who compared to males, more often mention guilt as occurring within close interpersonal contexts and also experience higher levels of guilt are consistent with Baumeister et al.'s (1994) assertion that guilt is frequently evoked within the context of important interpersonal relationships.

PROSOCIAL BEHAVIOR

What Is Prosocial Behavior?

Many types of behavior share the common feature of providing benefits for someone else. Doing favors, offering assistance, paying compliments, resisting the temptation to insult, or simply being cooperative all benefit those around us and therefore can be considered prosocial behaviors. Prosocial behavior is generally defined as encompassing actions that are voluntary and that specifically benefit another person (e.g., Franzoi, 1996). In our view, prosocial actions are those performed with the intention of helping others which commonly results in promoting positive interpersonal relationships.

Why do people help others? A variety of explanations have been offered ranging from the selfless to the selfish and from the biological to the philosophical. Cialdini and his colleagues (e.g., Cialdini & Kenrick, 1976; Cialdini et al., 1987) have argued that most instances of prosocial behavior can be explained by selfish motives, such as trying to manage one's public impression or relieve a negative mood state. Similarly, Salovey, Mayer, and Rosenhan (1992) point out that helping behavior can benefit the individuals who provide assistance, not only by repairing current bad moods, but also by regulating long-term mood states. Dispositional factors (such as abilities and knowledge) may also affect rates of prosocial actions (Knight, Johnson, Carlo, & Eisenberg, 1994; Kochanska, 1993).

Alternatively, some researchers have proposed that motives for prosocial behavior are linked to a fundamental need to belong (Baumeister & Leary, 1995; Bowlby, 1969, 1973). From this perspective, prosocial actions not only benefit others, but also strengthen the sense of community. Prosocial actions may reinforce social bonds by satisfying our desire to have others value, need, and appreciate us, and satisfy our need to be esteemed and valued by a social group (see also Fiske, 1992).

Batson and his colleagues (Batson, Turk, Shaw, & Klein, 1995; Batson et al., 1988) argue that the motivation for truly altruistic behavior is *not* to serve egoistic needs such as avoiding guilt, shame, or censure. Nor in this view is truly altruistic behavior motivated by the need to receive praise or boosts to self- or social esteem. Rather, altruistic behaviors are said to occur when the person values the welfare of the other person. For Batson, prosocial behavior is motivated by simple empathy rather than by egocentric rewards or punishment. For Batson, then, behaviors prompted by the avoiding of guilt are not truly altruistic. We take issue with this position, arguing that prosocial behavior is any behavior that benefits others.

The number of behaviors that can be considered "prosocial" is staggering, especially if one includes abstention from antisocial action. For present purposes, we focus on two major categories of prosocial behavior: *relationship-enhancing behaviors* that promote, develop, or sustain relationships, and *relationship-mending behaviors* that repair or restore relationships. In Table I, we provide examples of relationship-mending and relationship-enhancing behaviors.

TABLE I   Examples of Relationship-Mending and Relationship-Enhancing Behaviors

---

Relationship-mending prosocial behaviors

- Gestures of reparation and restitution
- Making amends
- Apologizing
- Confession
- Expressing guilt or remorse to the harmed individual
- Concession and admission of blameworthiness
- Compensation

Relationship-enhancing, developing, and sustaining behaviors

- Politeness; kindness, considerateness; thoughtfulness; being encouraging, caring, friendly and benevolent to others, attempting to maintain common spirit.
- Honesty and trustworthiness
- Helping behaviors, generosity
- Comforting
- Understanding others
- Good classroom conduct
- Volunteerism, contributing to a charity
- Well-developed conscience, sense of right and wrong
- Reliability, carrying out requests responsibly

Development of Prosocial Behaviors

As with guilt, prosocial behaviors emerge during the second year of life (Zahn-Waxler & Radke-Yarrow, 1990). Although children are responsive to the emotional reactions of others almost from birth, they do not display prosocial behaviors, such as helping, sharing, or comforting until their second year. This increase in prosocial behaviors coincides with the child's sense of growing autonomy and the concomitant increase in the ability to take another's perspective and empathize with their emotional distress. One of the most informative studies was conducted by Zahn-Waxler and Radke-Yarrow (1990) who trained mothers to observe and report on their 1- to 2½-year-old's responses to distressed others. Situations were included in which the children were or were not responsible for the other person's distress and situations. In addition, the researchers examined children's reactions to their mothers' simulated distress. Rudimentary prosocial behaviors emerged just after the first birthday when young children provided physical comfort (e.g., pats and hugs) to self or others when observing someone who was emotionally upset. As children matured, their responses became more sophisticated and appropriate to the situation such as asking why someone was crying or trying to remedy the problem. "Children are observed to help, share, provide physical comfort, provide verbal sympathy, protect, and defend victims in distress" (Zahn-Waxler & Radke-Yarrow, 1990, p. 114). Both relationship-mending and relationship-enhancing behaviors are apparently present during the second year of life.

Prosocial behaviors are generally more likely to occur when the other person is someone with whom we are personally involved. Darley (1991) notes, for example, that in the original Latané and Darley study of bystander intervention, any degree of acquaintance among subjects led to increased helping (see also Gottlieb & Carver, 1980). With development, individuals become increasingly likely to help others outside the context of close relationships. Costin and Jones (1992) had children watch a puppet show in which the hurt character was described as either a friend or an acquaintance. They found that the children described strategies to improve the target's mood mainly when the target was a friend. This would indicate that, at least initially, prosocial actions are most likely to occur in the context of close relationships. Zahn-Waxler and Radke-Yarrow (1990) note that comforting interventions (such as trying to cheer up or physically comfort the distressed person) are initially directed only towards caregivers or close family members and only later towards distress in strangers.

THE LINK BETWEEN GUILT AND PROSOCIAL BEHAVIOR

Our limited review of guilt and prosocial behavior indicates several apparent similarities. Guilt and prosocial behaviors are both closely linked with empathy, both occur most commonly within the context of close interpersonal relationships, and both function to strengthen interpersonal bonds and social cohesion. In the next section, we develop two principles: (a) that people engage in relationship-mending behaviors in order to alleviate guilt and (b) that people engage in relationship-enhancing behaviors to avoid guilt.

Relationship-Mending Functions of Guilt

When people transgress against others, studies indicate that they spontaneously engage in a number of reconciliatory actions such as confession, concession, and apology to repair those relationships (Gonzales, Manning, Haugen, 1992; Gonzales, Peterson, Manning, & Wetter, 1990; Ohbuchi, Kameda, & Agarie, 1989; Schlenker & Darby, 1981). As the offense becomes more severe or the transgressor becomes more blameworthy, so does the elaborateness of the response (Gonzales et al., 1992; Schlenker & Darby, 1981). Apologies, for example, become more involved and an array of reconciliatory responses rather than just one may be made. When people engage in reconciliatory behaviors, evidence suggests that these efforts are generally successful in mending or minimizing damage to relationships. An apology from the perpetrator or information attributing the lapse to causes other than harmful intent typically reduces the victim's feelings of anger, aggressiveness, and desire for retaliation (Baron, 1990; Ohbuchi et al., 1989).

Results of these studies complement those of earlier investigations from the late 1960s and 1970s that sought to examine the effects of guilt over transgression on compliance and victim compensation. Individuals who committed a transgression (staged by the experimenter such as "breaking" an expensive piece of equipment or bumping into and knocking over a confederate) were more likely to compensate the victim or agree to a request for assistance from the experimenter or an ostensibly unrelated individual (e.g., Knoecni, 1972; D. T. Regan, Williams, & Sparling, 1972; J. W. Regan, 1971). The lack of manipulation checks confirming that guilt was the mediating variable between the transgression and prosocial behavior, however, led critics to propose alternative interpretations, such as impression management or general negative affect, for the findings (e.g., Cialdini, Darby, & Vincent, 1973). These and other contemporaneous critiques preceded a period of relative dormancy in research on guilt and, indeed, may have triggered this retreat.

More recently, narrative studies have been used to understand guilt-producing incidents (Baumeister et al., 1995b; Tangney, 1992). Researchers find that both transgressors and victims report attempts to make amends when they feel guilty. Indeed, Baumeister et al. (1995b) find that people purposefully induce guilt in order to receive an apology. For instance, sometimes the transgressors are unaware that their actions have caused someone else harm (such as when they had not phoned often enough to satisfy their partner). In these situations, the victim mentions resultant pain and suffering in order to make the transgressor feel guilty and take reparative action. This often works, but not without feelings of resentment and anger occasionally arising among those transgressors who may believe they have done nothing wrong. If overused, guilt induction may lose effectiveness as an influence technique. Making someone feel guilty does, however, make the inducer feel better (Baumeister et al., 1995b), primarily because when the inducer successfully provokes guilty feelings in another person, this provides a social signal that the other person values the relationship. Thus, guilt following transgression may prompt prosocial behavior and send a social signal that serves to repair and strengthen interpersonal relationships.

Studies of young children, preadolescents, adolescents, and young adults confirm that guilt feelings follow transgressions (Barrett, Zahn-Waxler, & Cole, 1993; Ferguson et al., 1991; Harwas-Napierala, 1992; Williams & Bybee, 1994). Narrative accounts by children indicate that guilt is associated with having done something wrong and is accompanied by regret, a need to provide reparation and make amends, and anger with the self (Ferguson et al., 1991). Barrett et al. (1993) identified a group among 2-year-olds who, when they believe they have broken a favorite toy of the experimenter exhibit a constellation of guilt-related behaviors: they attempt to amend the transgression by confession and by trying to fix the broken toy. In contrast to this amenders group, Barrett et al. identify a group they call avoiders who engage in prototypic shame reactions such as withdrawing and attempting to hide the toy. Whether guilt leads to reparative behaviors or whether they are both manifestations of the same underlying construct remains unclear, but links between the indices appear clear at a very early age.

Relationship-Enhancing Functions of Guilt

According to Merisca and Bybee (1994), "Guilt may . . . not only prompt recon-ciliatory actions, but may also initiate prosocial behavior unprompted by a precipi-tating event" (p. 17). Surprisingly, there has been relatively little research linking guilt with relationship-enhancing functions. Although considerable research has examined how guilt may prompt people to redress injuries they have caused and to help others through reconciliatory actions, relatively few studies have examined how guilt may prompt helping behavior in the absence of a precipitating transgres-sion. Yet prosocial behavior that occurs spontaneously rather than in reaction to some previous wrongdoing may be critically important in maintaining good inter-personal relationships. Work by Rusbult and her colleagues (e.g., Rusbult, Verette, Whiteney, Slovik, & Lipkus, 1991), for example, demonstrates that sacrificing for the sake of the relationship (referred to as *accommodating*) is one of the best predictors of marital satisfaction and commitment. Moreover, accommodation is greater among those who value their relationships, acting as an important factor in the strengthening and maintenance of social bonds.

Baumeister et al. (1994) propose that the anticipation of guilt helps prevent behavior that would otherwise threaten a relationship. Feeling guilty also provides a valuable lesson and a reminder not to repeat the offending behavior. Indeed, indi-viduals commonly report learning from past guilt-inducing transgressions (Baumeister et al., 1995b). When a person chooses to forego a hedonistic experience in order to not hurt their relationship partner, their actions (or inactions) communicate to the other party that the relationship is important. Thus, individuals who forego marital infidelity, who control rude, impulsive behaviors, and who work hard to avoid disappointing their loved ones are all engaging in behavior that benefits their rela-tionship partners and prevents feelings of guilt from occurring.

Merisca and Bybee (1994) provide evidence that guilt is related to prosocial behaviors that are not forms of redress, apology, or reparation. These researchers had college students complete questionnaires measuring predispositional guilt and racist attitudes, and then had roommates of these students provide ratings of pro-social behavior. Phone calls to participants from an on-campus volunteer group were used to collect information on their past history of volunteer charity work. Greater guilt was related to more caring, trustworthy, and thoughtful behavior as rated by roommates. Greater guilt was correlated with less self-reported racism. Finally, individuals scoring higher on guilt were more likely to have engaged in volunteer charity work.

The few studies among children that have examined guilt in relation to spontaneous prosocial behavior corroborate findings among college students. Children with a higher predisposition for guilt are more likely to spontaneously help small animals, infants, and adults (Chapman, Zahn-Waxler, Cooperman, & Iannotti, 1987). Bybee and Williams (1994) had 5th, 8th, and 11th graders complete inventories measuring guilt and asked their teachers to rate prosocial behavior. Greater self-reported guilt was associated with less acting-out behavior. In a second study, students high in self-reported guilt were nominated as ranking among the most caring and considerate members of their class by peers. Higher guilt was also correlated with honest and trustworthy behavior as assessed by peer nominations. These findings together indicate that young people who are high on predispositional guilt avoid transgressing against others (e.g., are less prone to acting out) and spontaneously show considerate and ethical behavior.

Zahn-Waxler and Robinson (1995) note that, among young children, an important feature of guilt is its ability to aid in the inhibition and control of behavior. Consistent with this position, studies indicate that children with a greater predisposition for guilt are less likely to play with forbidden toys (Kochanska, DeVet, Goldman, Murray, & Putnam, 1994), are more likely to perform well in school (Bybee & Williams, 1994; Bybee & Zigler, 1991; Merisca & Bybee, 1994), and score higher on frustration tolerance (Bybee & Williams, 1994). Baumeister et al. (1994) argue that guilt may be one of the few emotions capable of interrupting an action sequence midstream and redirecting it. Guilt may prevent antisocial behavior from occurring by interrupting antisocial thoughts and actions and may imbue individuals with the self-control and motivation necessary to engage in prosocial actions.

A cautionary note is in order, however. Individuals who experience chronic guilt show *less* prosocial behavior (Bybee & Williams, 1994; Zahn-Waxler & Kochanska, 1990). Baumeister et al. (1994) point out that although guilt has a number of relationship-enhancing features, it may be maladaptive when it becomes excessive. When guilt feelings are continuous, unresolved, and unalleviated, they may become incapable of fostering prosocial behavior (Bybee & Williams, 1994). Moreover, guilt induction may backfire as a social influence technique.

In summary, currently available evidence suggests that a healthy sense of guilt based on empathetic concern and value of relationships promotes a variety of prosocial behaviors. This healthy sense of guilt is socialized through parental affection and trust, and appears to convey a number of lifelong benefits, both to the people who experience guilt and to those around them.

THE PROCESSES OF FORGIVENESS

Just as guilt prompts confession, apologies, and reparation, reconciliatory responses may, in turn, moderate and alleviate feelings of guilt. The role that reactions to guilt-producing events may play in alleviating guilt feelings is covered elsewhere (see Bybee, Merisca, & Velasco, chapter 9, this volume). The processes of forgiveness, however, have been almost entirely neglected by social psychologists. Common sense suggests that guilt and prosocial behaviors, such as apology, play an important role in the forgiveness process. Perpetrators seek to be forgiven and sometimes victims wish to forgive as a means of dealing with guilt that arises from transgression. Being forgiven may help individuals alleviate feelings of guilt, whereas being denied forgiveness may exacerbate guilt and even lead to other negative emotions (e.g., shame, anger, resentment). In the next section, we describe a narrative study that was conducted to examine the role that feelings of guilt and prosocial behavior play in the forgiveness process and how forgiveness affects interpersonal outcomes.

An Original Study Based on Autobiographical Narratives and Self-Report Data

Micronarratives are personal accounts that focus on specific events, experiences, or memories. They represent one person's beliefs about the factors most important to the situation (such as the various motives and strategies that the person used to affect the situation), as well as precipitating events and consequences. These stories may be biased in multiple ways. People may, for instance, selectively construct, retrieve, and distort personal accounts. A strength of micronarratives is that they contain information that the narrator believes to be most important (Baumeister et al., 1990). Micronarratives are useful for studying topics such as divorce (Harvey, Flanary, & Morgan, 1988; Harvey, Weber, Galvin, Huszit, & Garnick, 1986), life changes (Heatherton & Nichols, 1994), criminal activity (Katz, 1988), anger (Baumeister, Stillwell, & Wotman, 1990), guilt (Baumeister et al., 1995a,b; Ferguson et al., 1991; Tangney, 1992), and forgiveness that are difficult to test using conventional laboratory methods.

In this research, 80 participants (students from Harvard University and local community members) were randomly assigned to one of four conditions that varied according to perspective (victim or perpetrator) and forgiveness outcome (occurred or did not occur). Participants were asked to write a personal account of a meaningful event that involved forgiveness. They were instructed to take as long as they needed to tell the full story, and they were also asked to provide as much detail as possible. The four conditions were as follows:

1. Please describe a meaningful life situation in which you wanted to forgive someone and *did not*.

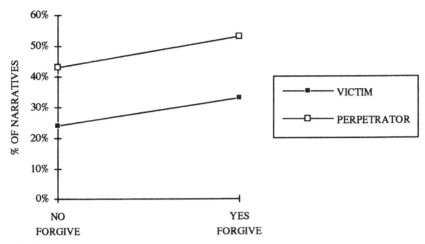

FIGURE 10.1   Percentage of narratives that contained descriptions of the perpetrator apologizing or making amends in situations where forgiveness of the perpetrator occurred versus did not occur and in descriptions provided by the victim versus those provided by the perpetrator.

2. Please describe a meaningful life situation in which you wanted to be forgiven by someone and *were not*.
3. Please describe a meaningful life situation in which you wanted to forgive someone and *did*.
4. Please describe a meaningful life situation in which you wanted to be forgiven by someone and *were*.

The responses were then content-analyzed and coded for themes theoretically relevant to guilt, forgiveness, or prosocial action. Because of the lack of research in this area, this study was exploratory in nature.

We found that perpetrators often performed prosocial actions in an attempt to be forgiven. Consistent with Baumeister et al. (1994), both perpetrators and victims noted that perpetrators apologized and attempted to make amends following a transgression. One perpetrator wrote, "I felt so low I wrote him a letter of apology and called him . . . to explain my story and apologize." A victim wrote, "He sent me flowers. They were beautiful flowers. The card attached was his apology for not having the answer that he knew I deserved." Compared to accounts written from the victim's perspective, accounts written by the perpetrator more often mentioned that the perpetrator apologized, $F(1, 78) = 3.20$; $p < .08$, and attempted to make amends, $F(1,78) = 4.13$; $p < .05$. These finding suggests that there may be a reporting bias depending on perspective. (The percentage of narratives that contained descriptions of the perpetrator apologizing or making amends are shown in Figure 10.1.)

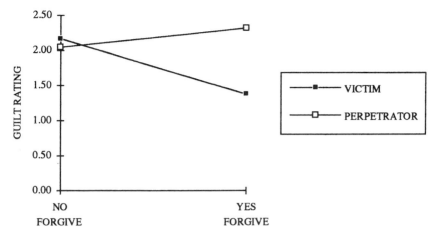

FIGURE 10.2   Self-reported guilt felt by the victim versus guilt felt by the perpetrator in situations where forgiveness of the perpetrator occurred versus did not occur.

Is guilt reduced by forgiveness? Participants completed a guilt inventory after they wrote the micronarrative account. Perpetrators' reported level of guilt after writing the narrative indicates that they still feel guilty for their prior transgression even when they feel forgiven. There were no significant differences in current guilt feelings between those perpetrators who wanted to be forgiven and felt that they were ($M = 2.3$) and those who wanted to be forgiven and felt they were not ($M = 2.0$), $t = n.s.$ It is possible that forgiveness did reduce guilt at the time, but that recalling the incident made perpetrators feel guilty again. It is clear, however, that guilt over transgression continues to be experienced even when the person feels forgiven (see Figure 10.2).

In contrast, victims who forgave the perpetrator felt less guilty ($M = 1.4$) than those who did not forgive the perpetrator ($M = 2.8$), $F(1,81) = 5.54$, $p < .05$. This finding suggests that offering forgiveness to another person for their misdeeds leads to more permanent alleviation of guilt than does being forgiven for one's own transgressions. Interestingly, individuals who did not forgive the transgressor reported levels of guilt commensurate with or higher than individuals who actually committed the transgression. The data, then, clearly suggest that not forgiving a perpetrator you want to forgive leads to increased guilt feelings among victims. This may represent an example of metaguilt (Baumeister et al., 1994) in which the victim feels guilty for making the perpetrator feel guilty. Alternatively, victims who make no attempt to induce guilt, but who intentionally or unintentionally ignore the transgressor, especially when the transgressor is remorseful, may nonetheless feel guilty. In sum, forgiveness may be a more important process for the victim than for the perpetrator in terms of alleviating guilt feelings.

We also examined attitudes towards the interpersonal relationship when forgiveness did or did not occur. In a questionnaire filled out after completion of the narrative, we found that *before* the incident, both victims and perpetrators reported feeling relatively positive about the other person, and there were no differences between those relationships in which forgiveness occurred ($M = 5.6$) or those in which it did not ($M = 5.4$). *After* the incident, however, people rated relationship quality as better when forgiveness occurred ($M = 4.04$) than when it did not occur ($M = 3.2$), $F(1,81) = 4.72$, $p < .05$. This pattern held true for both perpetrators and victims. In addition, perpetrators and victims felt more positively toward one another when forgiveness occurred ($M = 4.8$) than when it did not ($M = 4.0$), $F(1,81) = 3.46$, $p < .06$. In general, transgression led to negative feelings about the other person for both victims and perpetrators. Negative feelings were stronger, however, when forgiveness did not occur.

CONCLUSION

Feelings of guilt motivate individuals to engage in prosocial actions that mend, repair, or remedy damaged relationships once transgressions occur. These guilt feelings also help individuals avoid behaviors that threaten or damage relationships. Prosocial behaviors benefit both the victim and the perpetrator in that the victim benefits from reparative acts (or is spared being the victim of transgression) and both the victim and perpetrator benefit from strengthened social bonds. Expressions of guilt and reparative acts show that the transgressor values the relationship. Such findings have implications for how to facilitate, teach, and promote prosocial behavior in children as well as how to create a social climate that supports prosocial behavior among adults. In conclusion, although guilt has traditionally been viewed as undesirable, recent research demonstrates that feelings of guilt play an important role in the initiation, development, and maintenance of important personal relationships. Although chronic guilt is unhealthy, predispositional guilt may be an indispensible ingredient in a healthy social life.

REFERENCES

Baron, R. A. (1990). Countering the effects of destructive criticism: The relative efficacy of four interventions. *Journal of Applied Psychology, 75,* 235–245.

Barrett, K., Zahn-Waxler, C., & Cole, P. M. (1993). Avoiders vs. amenders: Implications for the investigation of guilt and shame during toddlerhood. *Cognition and Emotion, 7,* 481–505.

Batson, C. D., Turk, C. L., Shaw, L. L., & Klein, T. (1995). Information function of empathic emotion: Learning that we value the other's welfare. *Journal of Personality and Social Psychology, 68,* 300–313.

Batson, C. D., Dyck, J. L., Brandt, J. R., Batson, J. G., Powell, A. L., McMaster, M. R., & Griffitt, C. (1988). Five studies testing two new egoistic alternatives to the empathy-altruism hypothesis. *Journal of Personality and Social Psychology, 55,* 52–77.

Baumeister, R. F., & Leary, M. R. (1995). The need to belong: Desire for interpersonal attachments as a fundamental human motivation. *Psychological Bulletin, 117,* 497–529.

Baumeister, R., Stillwell, A., & Heatherton, T. (1994). Guilt: An interpersonal approach. *Psychological Bulletin, 115,* 243–267.

Baumeister, R., Stillwell, A., & Heatherton, T. (1995a). Personal narratives about guilt: Role in action control and interpersonal relationships. *Basic and Applied Social Psychology, 17,* 173–198.

Baumeister, R. F., Stillwell, A. M., & Heatherton, T. F. (1995b). Interpersonal aspects of guilt: Evidence from narrative studies. In J. P. Tangney & K. W. Fischer (Eds.), *Self-conscious emotions: Shame, guilt, embarrassment, and pride,* (pp. 255–273). New York: Guilford.

Baumeister, R., Stillwell, A., & Wotman, S. R. (1990). Victim and perpetrator accounts of interpersonal conflict: Autobiographical narratives about anger. *Journal of Personality and Social Psychology, 59,* 994–1005.

Bowlby, J. (1969). *Attachment and loss. Vol. 1: Attachment.* New York: Basic Books.

Bowlby, J. (1973). *Attachment and loss. Vol. 2: Separation anxiety and anger.* New York: Basic Books.

Bybee, J., & Williams, C. (1994, April). *When is guilt adaptive? Relationships to prosocial behavior, academic and social strivings, and mental health.* Presented at the 13th Biennial Conference on Human Development, Pittsburgh, PA.

Bybee, J. A., & Zigler, E. (1991). Self-image and guilt: A further test of the cognitive-developmental formulation. *Journal of Personality, 59,* 733–745.

Chapman, M., Zahn-Waxler, C., Cooperman, G., & Iannotti, R. (1987). Empathy and responsibility in the motivation of children's helping. *Developmental Psychology, 23,* 140–145.

Cialdini, R. B., Darby, B. L., & Vincent, J. E. (1973). Transgression and altruism: A case for hedonism. *Journal of Experimental Social Psychology, 9,* 502, 516.

Cialdini, R. B., & Kenrick, D. T. (1976). Altruism as hedonism: A social development perspective on the relationship of negative mood state and helping. *Journal of Personality and Social Psychology, 34,* 907–914.

Cialdini, R. B., Shaller, M., Houlihan, D., Arps, K., Fultz, J., & Beaman, A. L. (1987). Empathy-based helping: Is it selflessly or selfishly motivated? *Journal of Personality and Social Psychology, 52,* 749–758.

Costin, S. E., & Jones, D. C. (1992). Friendship as a facilitator of emotional responsiveness and prosocial interventions among young children. *Developmental Psychology, 28,* 941–947.

Darley, J. M. (1991). Altruism and prosocial behavior research: Reflections and prospects. In M. S. Clark (Ed.), *Prosocial Behavior: Review of Personality and Social Psychology, 12,* 312–327. Newbury Park: Sage.

Ferguson, T. J., Stegge, H., & Damhuis, I. (1991). Children's understanding of guilt and shame. *Child Development, 62,* 827–839.

Fiske, A. P. (1992). The cultural relativity of selfish individualism: Anthropological evidence that humans are inherently sociable. In M. S. Clark (Ed.), *Prosocial Behavior: Review of Personality and Social Psychology, 12,* 176–214. Newbury Park: Sage.

Franzoi, S. L. (1996). *Social psychology.* Madison, WI: Brown & Benchmark.

Gilligan, C. (1982). *In a different voice: Psychological theory and women's development.* Cambridge, MA: Harvard University Press.

Gonzales, M. H., Manning, D., & Haugen, J. (1992). Explaining our sins: Factors influencing offender accounts and anticipated victim responses. *Journal of Personality and Social Psychology, 62,* 958–971.

Gonzales, M., Peterson, J., Manning, D., & Wetter, D. (1990). Pardon my gaffe: Effects of sex, status, and consequence severity on accounts. *Journal of Personality and Social Psychology, 58,* 610–621.

Gottlieb, J., & Carver, C. (1980). Anticipation of future interaction and the bystander effect. *Journal of Experimental Social Psychology, 16,* 253–260.

Harvey, J. H., Flanary, R., & Morgan, M. (1988). Vivid memories of vivid loves gone by. *Journal of Social and Personal Relationships, 3,* 359–373.

Harvey, J. H., Weber, A. L., Galvin, K. S., Huszit, H. C., & Garnick, N. N. (1986). Attribution in the termination of close relationships: A special focus on the account. In R. Gilmour & S. Duck (Eds.), *The emerging field of personal relationships* (pp. 189–201). Hillsdale, NJ: Erlbaum.

Harwas-Napierala, B. (1992). Some psychological aspects of shame and guilt in school children. *Acta Paedopsychiatrica, 55*, 251–254.

Heatherton, T. F. & Nichols, P. A. (1994). Personal accounts of successful versus failed attempts at life change. *Personality and Social Psychology Bulletin, 20*, 664–675.

Hoffman, M. L. (1982). Development of prosocial motivation: Empathy and guilt. In N. Eisenberg (Ed.), *The development of prosocial behavior* (pp. 281–313). NY: Academic Press.

Hoffman, M. L. (1994a). The contribution of empathy to justice and moral judgment. In B. Puka (Ed.), *Reaching out: Caring, altruism, and prosocial behavior. Moral development: A compendium*, Vol. 7 (pp. 161–194). New York: Garland.

Hoffman, M. (1994b). Empathy, role taking, guilt, and development of altruistic motives. In B. Puka (Ed.), *Reaching out: Caring, altruism, and prosocial behavior. Moral development: A compendium*, Vol. 7 (pp. 196–218). New York: Garland.

Kagan, J. (1981). *The second year: The emergence of self-awareness.* Cambridge, MA: Harvard University Press.

Katz, J. (1988). *Seduction of crime: The moral and sensual attractions of doing evil.* New York: Basic.

Knight, G. P., Johnson, L. G., Carlo, G., & Eisenberg, N. (1994). A multiplicative model of the dispositional antecedents of a prosocial behavior: Predicting more of the people more of the time. *Journal of Personality and Social Psychology, 66*, 178–183.

Knoecni, V. J. (1972). Some effects of guilt on compliance: A field replication. *Journal of Personality and Social Psychology, 23*, 30–32.

Kochanska, G. (1993). Toward a synthesis of parental socialization and child temperament in early development of conscience. *Child Development, 64*, 325–347.

Kochanska, G., DeVet, K., Goldman, M., Murray, K., & Putnam, S. (1994). Maternal reports of conscience development and temperament in young children. *Child Development, 65*, 852–868.

Lewis, H. B. (1979). Guilt in obsession and paranoia. In C. E. Izard (Ed.), *Emotions in personality and psychopathology* (pp. 399–414). New York: Plenum.

Merisca, R., & Bybee, J. (1994, April). *Guilt, not moral reasoning, relates to measures of prosocial attitudes and behaviors.* Paper presented at the meeting of the Eastern Psychological Association, Providence, Rhode Island.

Ohbuchi, K., Kameda, M., & Agarie, N. (1989). Apology as aggression control: Its role in mediating appraisal of and response to harm. *Journal of Personality and Social Psychology, 56*, 219–227.

Regan, D. T., Williams, M., & Sparling, S. (1972). Voluntary expiation of guilt: A field experiment. *Journal of Personality and Social Psychology, 24*, 42–45.

Regan, J. W. (1971). Guilt, perceived injustice, and altruistic behavior. *Journal of Personality and Social Psychology, 18*, 124–132.

Rusbult, C., Verette, J., Whiteney, G., Slovik, L., & Lipkus, I. (1991). Accommodation processes in close relationships: Theory and preliminary empirical evidence. *Journal of Personality and Social Psychology, 60*, 53–78.

Salovey, P., Mayer, J. D., & Rosenhan, D. L. (1992). Mood and helping: Mood as a motivator of helping and helping as a regulator of mood. In M. S. Clark (Ed.), *Prosocial behavior: Review of personality and social psychology. Vol. 12* (pp. 215–237). Newbury Park: Sage.

Schlenker, B. R., & Darby, B. W. (1981). The use of apologies in social predicaments. *Social Psychology Quarterly, 44*, 271–278.

Tangney, J. P. (1990). Assessing individual differences in proneness to shame and guilt: Development of the Self-Conscious Affect and Attribution Inventory. *Journal of Personality and Social Psychology, 59*, 102–111.

Tangney, J. P. (1992). Situational determinants of shame and guilt in young adulthood. *Personality and Social Psychology Bulletin, 18*, 199–206.

Tangney, J. P. (1995). Shame and guilt in interpersonal relationships. In J. P. Tangney & K. W. Fischer (Eds.), *Self-conscious emotions: The psychology of shame, guilt, embarrassment, and pride* (pp. 114–139). New York: Guilford.

Tangney, J. P., Miller, R. S., Flicker, L., & Barlow, D. H. (1996). Are shame, guilt, and embarrassment distinct emotions? *Journal of Personality and Social Psychology, 70,* 1256–1269.

Vangelisti, A. L., & Sprague, R. J. (1998). Guilt and hurt: Similarities, distinctions, and conversational strategies. In P. A. Anderson & L. K. Guerrero (Eds.), *Handbook of communication and emotion* (pp. 123–154). San Diego, CA: Academic Press.

Williams, C., & Bybee, J. (1994). What do children feel guilty about? Developmental and gender differences. *Developmental Psychology, 30,* 617–623.

Zahn-Waxler, C., & Kochanska, G. (1990). The origins of guilt. In R. A. Thompson (Ed.), *The Nebraska symposium on motivation 1988: Socioemotional development.* Vol. 36 (pp. 182–258). Lincoln: University of Nebraska Press.

Zahn-Waxler, C., & Radke-Yarrow, M. (1990). The origins of empathic concern. *Motivation and Emotion, 14,* 107–130.

Zahn-Waxler, C., & Robinson, J. (1995). Empathy and guilt: Early origins of feelings of responsibility. In J. P. Tangney & K. W. Fischer (Eds.), *Self-conscious emotions: The psychology of shame, guilt, embarrassment, and pride* (pp. 143–173). New York: Guilford.

CHAPTER 11

Guilt in the Classroom

Christopher Williams

Institute for Prevention Research, Cornell University Medical College, New York, New York

INTRODUCTION

By all accounts, guilt is an unpleasant emotion characterized by self-blame that arises from real or imagined antisocial or immoral actions, substandard behavior, or acts that cause another to feel distress (Quiles & Bybee, 1997; Williams & Bybee, 1994). Contrary to the traditional psychoanalytic depiction of guilt as a source of mental illness and maladjustment, feelings of guilt are not necessarily concomitants of psychopathology (see Bybee & Quiles, chapter 13, this volume; Tangney, chapter 1, this volume). Guilt may reflect a healthy conscience and serve as a deterrent against future wrongdoing. Emerging evidence suggests that guilt is not invariably a useless and debilitating emotion and may often be beneficial.

With the emergence of the new Functionalist perspective, a more complex view of guilt is beginning to receive empirical attention. Functionalists suggest that the goals and utility of all emotions must be considered (e.g., Barrett, 1995; Campos, 1995; Campos, Mumme, Kermoian, & Campos, 1994). They champion a balanced view of the role of guilt in adjustment, suggesting that negativity does not in and of itself render an emotion useless or pathological. Indeed, when guilt feelings are evoked by a specific, circumscribed event and when the individual is positioned to act upon these feelings, research findings indicate the emotion may be beneficial (see Bybee & Quiles, chapter 13, this volume; Bybee & Williams, 1994; Quiles & Bybee, 1997).

Much of the early work on guilt did not include children and adolescents as participants and it is worthy to note that few guilt measures appropriate for children existed until recently (see Ferguson & Stegge, chapter 2, this volume). With the growing body of empirical literature on guilt in general and with the development of instruments appropriate for use with younger age groups, our understanding of the important role that guilt may play in academic and out-of-school settings has burgeoned. In this chapter, I begin by exploring the ways in which guilt may serve useful functions. I then explore the role guilt may play in the regulation and control of classroom conduct, in fostering academic achievement, and in determining participation in risky, unsupervised out-of-school activities. I then turn to differences observed in guilt as a function of academic track. I close by suggesting conditions under which teachers and parents may effectively use and induce guilt feelings among young people to raise scholastic and socioemotional competence.

WHY MIGHT GUILT SHOW ADAPTIVE RELATIONSHIPS WITH BEHAVIOR?

Guilt is an inherently punishing emotion that involves turning inward and against the self. Guilt may cause individuals who engage in misdeeds to experience considerable discomfort. *The emotion may, then, operate as a self-administered sanction.* As such, it may serve as a form of reprimand for a wide variety of behaviors, such as cheating, that may go undetected by teachers and others. Guilt may act as a self-imposed punishment or deterrent that serves over time to mitigate or eliminate undesirable behaviors (Baumeister, Stillwell, & Heatherton, 1994; Mosher, 1979).

Guilt may also serve punitive functions when formal punishment is inappropriate. Unlike guilt, externally imposed punishment is typically restricted to cases of failure and misbehavior. Students might, for example, be grounded by their parents for receiving poor grades or sent to detention for fighting. In contrast, guilt may arise (or be induced by authority figures) in cases when students have not committed a transgression, but have instead fallen short of an ideal. Consider a student who could have made an effort to talk with a new transfer student or invited him or her to join in a social activity, but did not. Consider another student who could have received an A by studying over the weekend, but chose instead to socialize or daydream, and subsequently received a B+. No wrongdoing has occurred and formal punishment might be out of the question. In the absence of external sanctions, the weight of their own conscience may lead students to feel guilty and hence experience internally imposed punishment. Parent and teacher expressions of disapproval and disappointment may also be directed at inducing guilt in the child in instances where formal punishment is inappropriate.

Guilt may prevent the individual from planning and imagining hedonic aspects of prohibited acts, lessening the opportunity and temptation to commit the deed (Bybee & Williams, 1994). According to folk wisdom, the thought is father to the deed. In cases where guilt results from envisioning the wrongdoing, plans to execute the act may never materialize. The seventh grader, for example, who feels guilty over merely thinking about having sex with another student may be less likely to consummate the act. Because feelings of guilt intrude, hedonic pleasures may never be fully imagined and the act may seem less tempting. The act may also be less feasible because guilt prevents the student from fully formulating how they might arrange to be alone with the object of their desire and how they might make advances.

Hoffman (1978) describes anticipatory guilt. This feeling of guilt is considered to be cognitively demanding because the person must not only conceptualize an event that has not yet occurred, but must also anticipate the outcome of the event (e.g., another's distress or letting someone else down). Some students have the ability to imagine a situation and take steps to prevent it from occurring. Students who can clearly imagine the guilt and remorse associated with earning poor grades may study earnestly to avoid disappointing their parents. Students who imagine guilt feelings over not meeting a friend for a scheduled lunch might take extra steps to honor their engagement.

Individuals may learn a lesson from past transgressions and avoid committing similar acts in the future. In our own research, we observe that students often mention guilt-producing incidents that still trouble them years later. Guilt over even one incident may convince individuals that rewards gained by wrongdoing (e.g., receiving an object without paying) are just not worth the pain of conscience that results (e.g., guilt over stealing). Reactions may prove so traumatic that the individual completely forswears or renounces the behavior. Protocols described by Bybee, Merisca, and Velasco (chapter 9, this volume) are illustrative. Students occasionally report that a single incident of shoplifting or smoking was so intensely unpleasant and guilt-rendering that they never again engaged in the behavior. Often in these cases, feelings of guilt are accompanied by an epiphany, a realization that did not exist before as to why the actions are wrong. The emotional experience may be so unpleasant and powerful that the event may be seared into long-term memory for a lifetime.

There are, of course, limits to the ability of an individual to avoid guilt-producing incidents. Many of these events involve accidents, guilt by association, and guilt over situations beyond the individual's control (Williams & Bybee, 1994) and hence are unavoidable. Even events that are under volitional control may be difficult if not impossible to consistently avoid. A high-guilt individual may, for example, succeed in avoiding major transgressions (such as hitting another student), yet may be unable to avoid more minor altercations (such as arguments).

Guilt may stop or disrupt an ongoing action sequence in midstream and redirect it (Baumeister, Stillwell, & Heatherton, 1995). Individuals may not have the time or inclination to ponder daily events and choose a principled plan of action unless forced to do by stinging or biting feelings of guilt (Merisca & Bybee, 1994). Guilt may be powerful enough to intrude upon one's stream of consciousness and change the course of behavior.

Expressions of guilt by the transgressor may communicate remorse and recognition of wrongdoing, increasing the chance that observers will make favorable attributions, react in a sympathetic manner, and feel justice has been served. Acknowledgment of culpability and expression of remorse provide a signal that the transgressor is aware that a code of conduct exists and that it has been broken (Lindsay-Hartz, 1984). Individuals who assume responsibility for their actions compared to those who try to evade blame are generally viewed more favorably by observers and are considered less likely to repeat the wrongful act (Weiner, Amirkham, Folkes, & Verette, 1987; Weiner, Figueroa-Munoz, & Kakihara, 1991). Guilt and empathy are closely related emotions, and expressions of guilt by the transgressor may, through emotional contagion, engender feelings of compassion and may prompt forgiveness by the victim (Barrett, 1995). Finally, when transgressors suffer pain from guilt, feelings of distress are redistributed from victim to perpetrator where they rightfully belong, restoring equity to interpersonal relationships (Baumeister et al., 1994).

Common methods of alleviating guilt are inherently prosocial, restorative, and reconciliatory in nature (Bybee & Williams, 1994). Unlike shame, where typical reactions include retaliation, shrinking away, and avoiding the situation, common guilt reactions serve positive functions. Individuals experiencing guilt typically report a pressing need to confess, apologize, and make reparation (Baumeister et al., 1995; Tangney, 1992), behaviors that serve relationship-mending functions. Other reactions to guilt-producing situations such as compensation and atonement may also result in achievement and prosocial behavior. Students who feel guilty about doing poorly on an earlier exam, for example, may work harder to raise their grade. Children who feel guilty about parental sacrifices may be driven to excel to make their parents proud of them.

Guilt has its origins in empathy and needs for social acceptance and love and may share temperamental antecedents with empathy and prosocial behavior (Hoffman, chapter 4, this volume; Zahn-Waxler & Kochanska, 1990; Zahn-Waxler & Robinson, 1995). The early origins of guilt may also offer insight into its role in the regulation and control of behavior. Empathy occurs early in development when an individual realizes someone else is in distress. Guilt arises when individuals become capable of realizing that they are responsible for causing another's distress (Hoffman, 1978, chapter 4, this volume). Like empathy, guilt is considered a moral or social emotion that is closely related to prosocial behavior. Zahn-Waxler and Robinson (1995) note that guilt, empathy, and prosocial actions are far from synonymous, but raise the possibility that common temperament dimensions such as sociability may underlie all three constructs.

Guilt is also said to develop alongside conscience and drives for achievement, and holds the potential for fomenting individualistic strivings (Bybee & Zigler, 1991; Hoffman, 1978). Although guilt is said to arise alongside empathy and needs for affirmation and positive regard, its later development and evolution during adolescence is affected by the internalization of ethical imperatives and societal values (Bybee & Zigler, 1991; Kochanska, 1991). According to Freud (1962), the development of guilt is intrinsically linked to the development of the superego. The superego is composed of two constituents, the conscience, which contains moral or ethical strictures, and the ego-ideal, which may contain aspirations for individualistic achievement such as career success and desires for physical fitness and attractiveness (Freud, 1962). Williams and Bybee (Merisca & Bybee, 1994; Bybee & Williams, 1994) provide empirical evidence that guilt is linked not only to prosocial behaviors, but to a wide spectrum of goal-directed behaviors. Guilt may provide an impetus for self-centered strivings or, alternatively, internalization of high standards may lead to both guilt and personal achievement.

GUILT AND CLASSROOM BEHAVIOR

Guilt is related to less aggression. Children, adolescents, and young adults who are higher on guilt are less aggressive and less likely to engage in acting-out behavior or show externalizing symptoms (Bybee & Williams, 1994; Merisca & Bybee, 1994; Quiles & Bybee, 1997; Tangney, Wagner, Fletcher, & Gramzow, 1992; Mosher, 1979). Teacher, parental, self-, and roommate reports are all in agreement. Guilt may, then, inhibit disobedient, unruly, and defiant behavior in the classroom, a setting where behavioral control and self-management are paramount. Alternatively, individuals who repeatedly commit acts of aggression may become inured to this type of behavior, exhibiting dulled emotional responses. Empirical findings indicate that individuals who are more predisposed to guilt are less likely to be juvenile delinquents, repeat serious criminal offenders, and sociopaths (Harpur, Hakstian, & Hare, 1988; Mosher, 1979). These findings not only attest to the robust nature of correlations between guilt and aggression, but suggest that the link between lack of guilt and violence is found across the life span and in deviant as well as normative samples.

Studies of children and adults alike support the view that *guilt is related to more prosocial behavior and better conduct.* Young children with a higher predisposition for guilt are less likely to play with a forbidden toy (Kochanska, DeVet, Goldman, Murray, & Putnam, 1994), more likely to aid a small animal, and more willing to help both infants and adults (Chapman, Zahn-Waxler, Cooperman, & Iannotti, 1987). Children, adolescents, and young adults who are more prone to guilt are more likely to be seen as caring and considerate by their peers (Bybee & Williams, 1994; Merisca & Bybee, 1994).

Among college students, Merisca and Bybee (1994) find that greater guilt is related to more interpersonal prosocial behavior, less aggressiveness, and fewer racist attitudes. Among college students, greater guilt is related to greater use of apologies (Baumeister et al., 1995). The relationship between guilt and prosocial behavior, then, remains robust at higher age levels. Moreover, guilt is correlated with higher rates of volunteerism for charity work and eschewal of racist attitudes among young adults. This suggests that the emotion serves not only to foment close interpersonal relationships, but to engender compassion toward members of other socioeconomic and ethnic backgrounds as well (Merisca & Bybee, 1994).

Guilt is related to greater assertiveness. Guilt does not always function to maintain smooth interpersonal relationships or to increase conformity to group or popular opinion. Students who are more prone to guilt exhibit more assertive social skills (Bybee & Williams, 1994). Specifically, individuals with a greater proclivity for guilt are more likely to defend their views under group pressure, challenge unfair rules, and take positions of leadership. As going along with the group often increases interpersonal bonding and social cohesion, the findings suggest that high guilt individuals may choose principle over popularity when pressed to choose.

GUILT AND EDUCATIONAL PERFORMANCE

The association of guilt to personal strivings and achievement outside the domain of interpersonal and moral behavior has received relatively little theoretical and empirical attention. Our own research suggests that the emotion may be produced by, and in turn regulate, self-centered strivings. Bybee and Williams (1994) examine the functions of guilt and its relationship to academic achievement. Students who score higher on guilt have fewer learning problems and better educational performance according to teacher reports (Bybee & Williams, 1994). Guilt-prone students are more diligent in their study habits according to teacher reports, exhibiting a longer attention span, heightened achievement motivation, and greater task completion. Students may exhibit conscientiousness and responsibility in their schoolwork in order to avoid painful feelings of guilt over substandard work or weak test performance.

A link between guilt and academic performance is also found by Merisca and Bybee (1994). College freshmen scoring higher on guilt have better study skills according to roommate reports. Moreover, when information on the students' grade point average was collected at the end of the academic year, data analyses indicated that freshmen who score higher on guilt receive better grades in their classes.

Guilt may play other roles as well in imposing discipline and control in the classroom. Bybee and Williams (1994) find that guilt is associated with better frustration tolerance. Higher guilt individuals are, according to teachers, better able to control their temper, check emotional outbursts, project a balanced and stable mood state, and concentrate on tasks. The ability to be patient, composed, focused, and directed may enhance school and work productivity.

GUILT AND OUT-OF-SCHOOL ACTIVITIES

Greater guilt is related to less sexually promiscuous activity. Young people who score higher on guilt are more likely to delay sexual intercourse. D'Augelli and Cross (1975) report that female college students scoring higher on sex guilt are less likely to engage in sexual foreplay and to have sexual intercourse. Similarly, in a sample of young adult men, Bybee, Zielonka, and Mayne (1997) find that men scoring higher on sex guilt report being older at the time of first sexual intercourse. These researchers also find that high scorers on predispositional guilt have more sexually conservative attitudes and are less sexually promiscuous.

Greater guilt is not related to greater contraceptive use and may interfere with sexual communication and information seeking. In fact, some studies indicate that women scoring higher on guilt may be more reluctant to seek medical advice and obtain information on contraception (Gerrard, 1987). Men scoring high on guilt express greater embarrassment over condom use and have more difficulty talking about sexual issues with their partners (Bybee et al., 1997).

Greater guilt is related to less sexually coercive activity. A study by Mosher (1971) indicates that undergraduate males who score higher on guilt are less likely to attempt to persuade or coerce their dates into having sex with them. Bybee et al. (1997) confirm that young adult men who are higher on predispositional guilt are less sexually assertive. These findings have implications for date rape in that they indicate men who score higher on guilt are less likely to be sexually aggressive. Indeed, among prison inmates, men high on guilt are less likely to be rapists or other sex offenders (Persons, 1970).

Less guilt is related to greater illegal drug usage. Individuals scoring low on guilt are more likely to have taken illicit drugs (Schill & Althoff, 1975). Lower guilt is also correlated with more frequent drug usage and use of a greater variety of illegal drugs (Schill & Althoff, 1975).

EFFECTS OF ACADEMIC TRACK ON GUILT

What effect does academic track have on guilt? Bybee and Zigler (1991) report that children in high compared to middle academic tracks score higher on guilt. One interpretation of this finding is that a greater capacity for guilt among higher track students may reflect an increased cognitive capacity to generate numerous, abstract, or rigorous ideals. Guilt over failure to attain ideals is common among adolescents (Williams & Bybee, 1994). Alternatively, greater guilt among higher academic track students may reflect the higher expectations set for them by parents, teachers, and principals. High academic track children may be held to higher scholastic, social, and conduct standards than their less intellectually gifted peers.

Another interpretation for findings of differences in guilt across academic track is that many schools continue to group gifted students together. Principled, responsible, and conscientious high achievers may set an example for other students and serve as role models and friends. They may also have little tolerance for subpar performance by themselves or others and may refuse to honor rationalizations. The classroom climate may be self-perpetuating. Students may adopt the high aspirations of high achievers and feel guilty when they do not meet these goals or match the standards set by their peers.

GUILT AND DISCIPLINE

Williams and Bybee (1994) found 5th, 8th, and 11th graders commonly report that parents are a major source of guilt. Indeed, parents are the individuals who most frequently evoke feelings of guilt in students at all grade levels. The mentioning of parents shows no sign of decline with development during adolescence. Individuals often generate feelings of guilt in others when they are victimized. Parents, however, need not be directly affected by their child's behavior to evoke guilt. As Williams and Bybee (1994) note, parents may intentionally provoke guilt feelings by lecturing, nagging, and expressing disappointment in their offspring about any number of moral and personal failings. Parents may actively use guilt induction as an effective form of discipline.

Baumeister (chapter 6, this volume) quite accurately concludes that individuals with whom one is involved in close, communal relationships are generally most capable of inducing guilt. Family members and peers are commonly mentioned by children and adolescents as sources of guilt (Williams & Bybee, 1994). Are teachers without power to induce guilt? Williams and Bybee (1994) report that approximately one-quarter of all students in their sample spontaneously mention adults who were not relatives, such as teachers and other authority figures, when describing three guilt-producing incidents. Apparently, teachers can, and commonly do, produce guilt in students.

Guilt induction may serve as a discipline technique in lieu of formal punishment when the conduct in question does not involve a transgression. Parents and teachers may use guilt induction to prod students to reach for high standards of academic and social performance. Indeed, by the 11th grade, students commonly report feeling guilty about neglecting responsibilities and failing to attain ideals (Williams & Bybee, 1994).

The work of Quiles and Bybee (1997) indicates that guilt shows the most adaptive relationships with social adjustment when the guilt is evoked by a specific, precipitating event rather than an ongoing condition. By suggesting means of alleviating guilt that are appropriate and commensurate to the lapse, parents and teachers may help ensure that guilt is channeled into constructive action, rather than lingering on, undirected and useless. Work by Baumeister (see Summary, chapter 6, this volume) suggests that guilt will be the most potent when it is evoked in the context of a warm, underlying relationship. Specific means of inducing guilt are discussed by Donenberg and Weisz (chapter 12, this volume). Various researchers point to the danger of overreliance on or misuse of guilt induction (e.g., Jones, Kugler, & Adams, 1995). Frequent or inappropriate attempts to induce guilt may be met with resentment.

SUMMARY

Traditionally, guilt is viewed as a source of psychopathology. I began this chapter by summarizing ways in which guilt may be adaptive in the classroom environment. I then reviewed empirical data indicating that guilt shows adaptive relationships with a wide range of behaviors inside and outside the classroom. Relationships appear to be robust across age level and, indeed, similar findings appear in childhood and adulthood.

Guilt is a social emotion. Greater guilt is positively correlated with healthy interpersonal relationships and with caring, considerate, honest, and trustworthy behavior. Guilt is inversely related to aggressive, acting-out behavior. Moreover, greater guilt is related to volunteerism and eschewal of racist attitudes, suggesting that individuals higher on guilt are more tolerant and accepting of others with backgrounds different from their own and more conscious of inequities. The relationship of guilt to constructive social behavior is becoming increasingly well established.

In our own work, we repeatedly find evidence that guilt may play a pervasive role in positive adjustment. Its functions may not be limited to the interpersonal domain as one might conclude from the plethora of recent articles investigating social aspects of guilt. My colleagues and I have repeatedly maintained that guilt may play a much broader role in adjustment, regulating and controlling a wide variety of goal-related and health-oriented activities (e.g., Bybee & Williams, 1994; Bybee et al., 1991; Quiles & Bybee, 1997). Findings reviewed in the present chapter indicate that individuals with greater levels of guilt show more frustration tolerance, exhibit better academic performance, and achieve higher grades in their classes. Moreover, greater guilt is inversely correlated with high-risk sexual activities and illegal activities. Taken in combination this work demonstrates the potentially far-reaching effects of guilt within and beyond the classroom.

I closed the chapter with a discussion of the role that teachers and parents may play by inducing guilt in students in order to encourage them to engage in positive behaviors. As young people make the transition from childhood to adolescence to early adulthood, the options available to caregivers seeking to discipline, inspire, and socialize may become increasingly limited. Curfews, detentions, restrictions on television watching, and grounding may no longer be feasible means of controlling and restricting the individual's behavior. Guilt induction, however, remains available as an influence technique throughout the life span. Both guilt and guilt induction have darker sides as well. Chronic guilt is linked with mental illness (see Bybee &

Quiles, chapter 13, this volume), whereas guilt induction may sometimes backfire, resulting in hostility and resentment (see Baumeister, chapter 6, this volume). Guilt and guilt induction appear to be most effective when the act or lapse is circumscribed and means of restitution are apparent. Guilt induction may work best when used sparingly and in a warm, communal atmosphere.

REFERENCES

Barrett, K. C. (1995). A functionalist approach to shame and guilt. In J. P. Tangney & K. W. Fischer (Eds.), *Self-conscious emotions: The psychology of shame, guilt, embarrassment, and pride* (pp. 25–63). New York: Guilford.

Baumeister, R. F., Stillwell, A. M., & Heatherton, T. F. (1995). Personal narratives about guilt: Role in action control and interpersonal relationships. *Basic and Applied Social Psychology, 17,* 173–198.

Baumeister, R. F., Stillwell, A. M., & Heatherton, T. F. (1994). Guilt: An interpersonal approach. *Psychological Bulletin, 115,* 243–267.

Bybee, J., Leckman, J. F., Lavietes, S., & Tamborlane, W. (1991, April). *Guilt, depressive symptoms, and the quality of diabetic adherence among adolescents with insulin-dependent diabetes mellitus.* Paper presented at the Annual Meeting of the Eastern Psychological Association.

Bybee, J., & Williams, C. (1994, April). *Does guilt show adaptive relationships with socioemotional competency and academic achievement?* Paper presented at the Biennial Conference on Human Development, Pittsburgh, Pennsylvania.

Bybee, J., Zielonka, E., & Mayne, T. (1997). *The relationship of guilt to sexually risky behavior among heterosexual and homosexual men.* Manuscript in preparation, Northeastern University, Boston, MA.

Bybee, J., & Zigler, E. (1991). The self-image and guilt: A further test of the cognitive-developmental formulation. *Journal of Personality, 59,* 733–745.

Campos, J. J. (1995). Foreword. In J. P. Tangney & K. W. Fisher (Eds.), *Self-conscious emotions: The psychology of shame, guilt, embarrassment, and pride* (pp. ix–xi). New York: Guilford.

Campos, J. J., Mumme, D. L., Kermoian, R., & Campos, R. G. (1994). A functionalist perspective on the nature of emotion. In N. A. Fox (Ed.), The development of emotion regulation: Biological and behavioral considerations. *Monographs of the Society for Research in Child Development, 59* (2-3, Serial No. 240).

Chapman, M., Zahn-Waxler, C., Cooperman, G., & Iannotti, R. (1987). Empathy and responsibility in the motivation of children's helping. *Developmental Psychology, 23,* 140–145.

D'Augelli, J. F., & Cross, H. (1975). Relationship of sex guilt and moral reasoning to premarital sex in college women and in couples. *Journal of Consulting and Clinical Psychology, 43,* 40–47.

Freud, S. (1962). *The ego and the id.* New York: Norton.

Gerrard, M. (1987). Sex, sex guilt and contraceptive use revisited: The 1980's. *Journal of Personality and Social Psychology, 52,* 975–980.

Harpur, T. J., Hakstian, A. R., & Hare, R. D. (1988). Factor structure of psychopathology checklist. *Journal of Consulting and Clinical Psychology, 56,* 741–747.

Hoffman, M. L. (1978). Toward a theory of empathic arousal and development. In M. Lewis & L. Rosenblum (Ed.), *The development of affect* (pp. 227–256). New York: Plenum.

Jones, W. H., Kugler, K., & Adams, P. (1995). You always hurt the one you love: Guilt and transgressions against relationship partners. In J. P. Tangney & K. W. Fisher (Eds.), *Self-conscious emotions: The psychology of shame, guilt, embarrassment, and pride.* New York: Guilford.

Kochanska, G. (1991). Socialization and temperament in the development of guilt and conscience. *Child Development, 62,* 1379–1392.

Kochanska, G., DeVet, K., Goldman, M., Murray, K., & Putnam, S. P. (1994). Maternal reports of conscience development and temperament in young children. *Child Development, 65,* 852–868.

Lindsay-Hartz, J. (1984). Contrasting experiences of shame and guilt. *American Behavioral Scientist, 27,* 689–704.

Merisca, R., & Bybee, J. (1994, April). *Guilt, not moral reasoning, relates to volunteerism, prosocial behavior, lowered aggressiveness, and eschewal of racism.* Poster presented at the Annual Meeting of the Eastern Psychological Association, Providence, RI.

Mosher, D. L. (1971). Sex callousness toward women. In *Technical Report of the Commission on Obscenity and Pornography. Vol. 8: Erotica and social behavior.* Washington, DC: U.S. Government Printing Office.

Mosher, D. L. (1979). The meaning and measurement of guilt. In C. E. Izard (Ed.), *Emotions in personality and psychopathology* (pp. 105–129). New York: Plenum.

Persons, R. W. (1970). Intermittent reinforcement, guilt, and crime. *Psychological Reports, 26,* 421–422.

Quiles, Z., & Bybee, J. (1997). Chronic and predispositional guilt: Relations to mental health, prosocial behavior, and religiosity. *Journal of Personality Assessment, 69,* 104–126.

Schill, T. R., & Althoff, M. (1975). Drug experiences, knowledge and attitudes of high and low guilty individuals. *Journal of Consulting and Clinical Psychology, 43,* 106–107.

Tangney, J. P. (1992). Situational determinants of shame and guilt in young adulthood. *Personality and Social Psychology Bulletin, 18,* 199–206.

Tangney, J. P., Wagner, P., Fletcher, C., & Gramzow, R. (1992). Shamed into anger? The relation of shame and guilt to anger and self-reported aggression. *Journal of Personality and Social Psychology, 62,* 669–675.

Weiner, B., Amirkham, J., Folkes, V., & Verette, J. A. (1987). An attributional analysis of excuse giving: Studies of a naive theory of emotion. *Journal of Personality and Social Psychology, 52,* 316–324.

Weiner, B., Figueroa-Munoz, A., & Kakihara, C. (1991). The goals of excuses and communication strategies related to causal perceptions. *Personality and Social Psychology Bulletin 17,* 4–13.

Williams, C., & Bybee, J. (1994). What do children feel guilty about? Developmental and gender differences. *Developmental Psychology, 5,* 617–623.

Zahn-Waxler, C., & Kochanska, G. (1990). The origins of guilt. In R. A. Thompson (Ed.), *The 36th Annual Nebraska Symposium on Motivation: Socioemotional development* (pp. 183–258). Lincoln: University of Nebraska Press.

Zahn-Waxler, C., & Robinson, J. (1995). Empathy and guilt: Early origins of feelings of responsibility. In J. P. Tangney & K. W. Fisher (Eds.), *Self-conscious emotions: The psychology of shame, guilt, embarrassment, and pride.* New York: Guilford.

CHAPTER 12

Guilt and Abnormal Aspects of Parent–Child Interactions

Geri R. Donenberg

Northwestern University Medical School, Chicago, Illinois

John R. Weisz

University of California, Los Angeles, Los Angeles, California

> *Too severe inner control [of children's impulses] can prevent any direct expression of them and can produce a quite unnecessary degree of guilt and anxiety. Too much conscience can destroy the happiness and productivity of the individual, just as too little can destroy the peace and stability of society.*
>
> —Sears, Maccoby, & Levin (1957, pp. 389–390)

INTRODUCTION

Guilt feelings may be viewed along a continuum from very high to very low with problems arising at either end. At one end of the continuum, feelings of responsibility may be so exaggerated that they overwhelm the individual, inhibit freedom of expression, and focus one's attention on the needs of others at the expense of the self. At the other end of the continuum is the absence of guilt that may result in an exclusive focus on the self, little concern for others, and potential social instability. To illustrate this point, consider the following two children referred for psychiatric treatment.

Alexis, a 13-year-old Native American Indian girl, presented to the clinic with low self-esteem, dysphoria, feelings of helplessness, and excessive guilt. She was referred for treatment by her school because she'd been absent for several weeks. Alexis was brought to the initial therapy session by her mother, a single parent with few social supports and a history of depression. Alexis's mother had recently lost her job and money was tight. According to her mother, Alexis was closing herself off in her room, refusing to attend school, ignoring her friends, and crying a lot. Alexis reported that she needed to stay home from school to take care of her mother

Guilt and Children
Copyright © 1998 by Academic Press. All rights of reproduction in any form reserved.

whom she viewed as depressed and a hypersomniac. Alexis repeatedly tried to make her mother feel better by cooking dinner, cleaning the house, and encouraging her to go out, but her efforts were usually unsuccessful. As a result, Alexis reported feeling burdened by the responsibility of caring for her mother and guilty for being unable to help her. In this case, Alexis felt an exaggerated sense of responsibility for her mother's problems, and she believed it was her job to "fix" the situation. However, each effort she made was met with failure and the repeated failures compounded her feelings of guilt. Additionally, her mother did little to discourage Alexis's distorted sense of obligation, which led to greater guilt and dysphoria.

On the other end of the guilt continuum is Jonathon, a 15-year-old Caucasian boy with a history of antisocial behavior problems. Jonathon was referred for treatment by the Department of Children and Family Services for assaulting a woman in front of a grocery store. He grabbed her purse and tried to run away when a security guard in the parking lot grabbed him and had him arrested. In order to avoid jail, Jonathon agreed to attend counseling. Jonathon lived with his father and younger brother, both of whom had been in trouble with the law. In the first therapy session, it was clear that Jonathon's father did not view his son's behavior as problematic. "You know, doctor, boys will be boys, and anyway, the cops were overreacting." Jonathon, too, expressed little remorse about the incident, and he showed no empathy for the woman whom he'd assaulted. "What's the big deal? I didn't pull out a gun or anything." As this case demonstrates, Jonathon experienced little guilt for assaulting an innocent woman. He was unable to take the woman's perspective or imagine the impact of his behavior on her. He also displayed little concern for social rules or morals. Likewise, Jonathon's father showed little capacity to teach his son empathy for the woman's experience, and instead, he blamed the police for overreacting and minimized the seriousness of Jonathon's offense.

These two vignettes illustrate the important function guilt serves for children, their caregivers, and society, and they highlight how extreme levels of guilt (i.e., excessive and deficient) have serious implications for the individual and the community. Adaptive guilt keeps children's behavior within safe and reasonable boundaries; children are less likely to engage in dangerous behaviors that might harm others, and they learn to regulate their own behavior appropriately. Guilt and empathy also enhance children's social relationships, helping children get in tune with others' feelings and experiences. Attentiveness to others facilitates considerate, caring, and helpful behavior. Guilt is also an important tool for parents, teachers, and society. Parents and teachers are responsible for helping children learn how to function in society, establish meaningful relationships with others, abide by societal laws and norms, and feel a commitment to the larger community; all of these skills are based, at least in part, on a sense of empathy, guilt, and an understanding of right and wrong. Thus, guilt is a critical part of lessons that parents and educators are asked to teach children. Finally, society depends on its members to feel a certain degree of guilt in order to maintain social order. Without guilt, people would behave as they please without regard for others or the greater good.

Unfortunately, most of the empirical literature on guilt in children focuses on guilt feelings and its adaptive functions (e.g., how these feelings develop and why) (Bybee & Williams, 1994; Hoffman, 1982). Indeed, guilt has been implicated in the development of important prosocial behaviors, including conscience, altruism, empathy, and social perspective taking, and different parenting styles have been associated with the occurrence of these behaviors (Hoffman, 1983; Sears et al., 1957; Zahn-Waxler & Robinson, 1995). Significantly less is known about the maladaptive aspects of guilt, despite evidence that extremely high or low levels of guilt are associated with depression and antisocial behavior respectively (APA, 1994; Burbach & Borduin, 1986; Harpur, Hakstian, & Hare, 1988; Miller & Eisenberg, 1988; Zahn-Waxler et al., 1990). In part, little is known because much of the research is derived from nonclinical samples. We still know relatively little about the use of guilt in families of clinically disturbed children or the linkages between guilt-inducing communication and different forms of psychopathology. That children influence parent–child interactions is widely accepted (Bell, 1968), yet most of the empirical data emphasize parent (not child) behaviors that foster or inhibit guilt.

In this chapter, we review literature on the abnormal aspects of guilt in parent–child relationships, and we speculate on the association between guilt induction and different forms of psychopathology. Preliminary findings are presented from an ongoing longitudinal study of clinic-referred youngsters on the use of guilt induction by both parents and children in observed parent–child interactions, and findings are discussed in the context of childhood depression and childhood aggression.

GUILT IN INTERPERSONAL RELATIONSHIPS

According to Hoffman (1983), guilt is aroused by feelings of empathy for another person's distress and the awareness of having caused that distress. This conceptualization of guilt as an interpersonal phenomenon has received empirical support. Studies show that guilt occurs in the context of close relationships and in response to interpersonal transgressions (Baumeister, Stillwell, & Heatherton, 1994; Baumeister, Stillwell & Heatherton, in press; Jones, Kugler, & Adams, 1995; Lewis, 1986; Tangney, 1992; Vangelisti, Daly, & Rudnick, 1991), and that guilt may have its roots in the first infant–caregiver relationship (Hoffman, 1977; Lewis, 1986). Furthermore, there is extensive evidence that child-rearing strategies play an important role in socializing guilt in children (Ferguson & Stegge, 1995; Hoffman, 1983; Potter-Efron, 1989; Zahn-Waxler & Kochanska, 1990; Zahn-Waxler et al., 1990). Child-rearing strategies that foster guilt are not "guilt-induction" techniques, per se, but it seems reasonable to assume that parenting techniques that arouse guilt in children have guilt-induction properties. We review the literature on parenting behaviors associated with the development of guilt in nondisturbed children to illuminate potential associations between parental guilt induction and the development of childhood psychopathology.

Three dimensions of child rearing—modeling, affect, and discipline—are associated with the development of guilt in children (Zahn-Waxler, Cole, & Barrett, 1991). Children model and imitate prosocial behavior in their parents (Radke-Yarrow, Zahn-Waxler, & Chapman, 1983). Helpful, empathic, and concerned parents who respect the laws that govern society and who display guilt over their own transgressions are positive role models for their children. Similarly, a positive, warm, and nurturing parent–child relationship is the foundation for future healthy relationships with others, and a strong affective bond facilitates the development of children's helping behavior (Zahn-Waxler, Radke-Yarrow, & King, 1979).

Two distinct disciplinary responses to children's transgressions have been differentially linked to high and low levels of guilt in children. One disciplinary style involves parental induction methods (i.e., providing information, offering reasons or explanations, increasing understanding, and pointing out the impact of the child's behavior on others) combined with strong verbal prohibitions against hurting others. This response has been associated with high levels of guilt and reparation in children, but only when used by an otherwise loving and affectionate parent (Ferguson & Stegge, 1995; Hoffman, 1977, 1982, 1983; Sears et al., 1957; Zahn-Waxler & Radke-Yarrow, 1983; Zahn-Waxler et al., 1979). The second response pattern entails the use of power assertive discipline methods (i.e., threats or use of physical punishment, unexplained prohibitions—"Stop that!"—deprivation of privileges or material objects, use of force to control behavior). This pattern is associated with children's fear of retaliation or punishment rather than guilt and results in little reparative behavior by children. Hoffman (1983) and others argue that power assertive messages lead children to focus on themselves (i.e., being punished or abandoned) rather than on others (Zahn-Waxler & Kochanska, 1990; Zahn-Waxler et al., 1990; Zahn-Waxler et al., 1979). Early research suggested that a third discipline strategy—parental love withdrawal (i.e., expressions of anger or disapproval in response to transgressions, ignoring the child, turning away, refusing to communicate, expressing dislike, threatening separation)—was related to children's self-criticism and reparation (Grusec, 1966; Karylowski, 1982; Zahn-Waxler et al., 1979), but more recent data are inconclusive (Hoffman, 1983).

Child-rearing techniques associated with the development of guilt in children may not reflect deliberate attempts by parents to arouse children's guilt. We reviewed the literature for reports on parents' and children's attempts to elicit guilt. We found few theoretical writings and even fewer investigations that directly examine the use and function of guilt induction in interpersonal relationships. Although Vangelisti et al. (1991) evaluate adult relationships, findings may nonetheless provide insight into the uses and functions of guilt induction in parent–child relationships. According to Vangelisti et al. (1991), guilt is invoked verbally and nonverbally by pointing out another person's misbehavior or failure and then emphasizing the person's responsibility for that lapse. Engendering guilt serves numerous purposes: (a) to maintain interpersonal relationships; (b) to alter another person's behavior; (c) to exact revenge against the transgressor; (d) to reaffirm the transgressor's concern for the victim; (e) to teach moral and ethical standards; (f) to make the transgressor feel remorseful and blameworthy for the negative event; and (g) to act as a mechanism of social control (Allen & Edwards, 1988; Baumeister et al., 1995; Christopher & Frandsen, 1990). Guilt induction is believed to be an effective control strategy because it leads to behavior change on the part of the transgressor (Ferguson, Stegge, & Damhuis, 1991; Tangney, 1992). Data from Vangelisti et al. (1991) support the notion that guilt is used to control others. They found the three most common goals that adults reported for making others feel guilty were to (a) alter their behavior; (b) establish dominance; and (c) relieve insecurity. The primary reason why adults invoke guilt appears to be interpersonal neglect.

Our review of previous research and theory revealed that people use very diverse methods to engender guilt in others and they utter guilt inducements in a variety of ways (Vangelisti et al., 1991). Vangelisti et al. (1991) identified 12 different techniques adults use to elicit guilt in each other, and some of these techniques may be applied to parent–child relationships. For example, parents and children may (a) state role obligations ("As a member of this family, you are expected to do certain chores"); (b) state relationship obligations ("Mothers are supposed to buy their daughters new shoes"); (c) make comparisons ("Your sister had the same class, and she didn't have any problem getting an A"); (d) interrogate the other (Weren't you supposed to be at your friends house last night? Why weren't you there?"; (e) state rule violations ("Going to the family reunion is more important than watching the football game with your friends"); (f) report the nature of things ("You know you're supposed to do your homework before you watch TV"); (g) confront deception ("You told me you went to school yesterday, but your teacher called and said you were absent"); (h) demand consistency ("You promised to buy me new clothes and you haven't done it"); and (i) acquiesce ("Fine. I won't go to the movies with my friends, so I can be home when Grandma comes over").

Vangelisti et al. (1991) also reported five types of speech uttered by adults to induce guilt, and these too, can be applied to parent–child relationships. Table I lists the five types of speech and the specific guilt-induction techniques that are relevant to parent–child relationships. The most common types of speech identified by Vangelisti et al. (1991) were accusations ("All you think about is yourself"), questions ("How could you do that?"), and admonishments ("Don't promise something if you can't follow through on it"). The five speech types and different guilt-induction techniques share at least three common characteristics: They are controlling (i.e., attempt to alter one's behavior), interpersonal, and negative.

Taken together, the categorization scheme outlined by Vangelisti et al. (1991) may inform the process and purpose of guilt induction in parent–child relationships. For example, parents may invoke guilt in children via induction, love withdrawal, and/or power assertive methods in order to gain children's cooperation or compliance, teach social mores, reaffirm their dominance, and develop children's capacity for empathy. Children, on the other hand, may induce guilt in their parents via accusations ("You're too overprotective!") and questions ("Why do you let Martin

TABLE I   Speech Types and Techniques Used to Elicit Guilt in Parent–Child Relationships[a]

Speech type	Guilt-induction technique
Assertives	Accusations, statements of role obligation, statements of relationship obligations, statements of rule violation
Direct directives	Suggestions, orders, demands for consistency
Indirect directives	Admonishments, requests, wishes
Interrogatives	Questions, interrogations, confrontations involving deception
Expressives	Sarcasm, comparisons to others, acquiescence, enunciations of sacrifice

[a]From Vangelisti, A., Daly, J., & Rudnick, J. (1991). Adapted with permission from the authors.

do things but not me?") in order to relieve insecurity about the parent's love, reaffirm relationship ties, and/or attempt to assert control over parents. Guilt induction tends to be used by less powerful relationship partners to influence more powerful partners (Vangelisti et al., 1991), so one might expect children to use guilt to change parent behavior.

GUILT AND PSYCHOPATHOLOGY

Like adaptive guilt, dysfunctional guilt may have its origins in early childhood and may be affected by child-rearing processes (i.e., modeling prosocial behavior, parent–child attachment, and parental discipline). Dysfunctional guilt may result when normal developmental processes have gone awry. For example, power assertive discipline methods are associated with deficiencies in guilt. The use of power assertive discipline exclusively may lead to extremely low levels of guilt, a prominent feature of sociopathy, aggression, and conduct problems. On the other hand, induction when used by supportive parents is associated with the development of adaptive guilt. However, parenting styles that overemphasize children's responsibility for transgressions may lead to exaggerated guilt, a common symptom of depression. Thus, dysfunctional guilt (i.e., deficient or excessive) may be linked to specific socialization experiences and different forms of psychopathology. Evidence linking child-rearing dimensions to dysfunctional guilt is now reviewed in the context of two forms of childhood psychopathology (i.e., aggression and depression) that represent possible outcomes corresponding to extreme levels of maladaptive guilt.

Excessive Guilt

Excessive guilt and parental guilt induction are associated with depression (APA, 1994; Burbach & Borduin, 1986; Crook, Raskin, & Eliot, 1981; Harder, Cutler &

Rockart, 1992), but less is known about the mechanisms of parent–child interaction involved in the development of high levels of guilt (Zahn-Waxler & Radke-Yarrow, 1983). Developmental models suggest that young children's cognitive limitations interfere with their capacity to differentiate harm they cause to others from harm they observe and, thus, they are prone to accept responsibility for others' distress whether they caused it or not (Zahn-Waxler & Robinson, 1995). Young children rely heavily on caregivers to distinguish for them harm they caused and harm they observed, and without appropriate caregiver guidance, young children are especially vulnerable to developing an exaggerated sense of responsibility for negative events and high levels of guilt. Feelings of intense guilt early in development may interfere with mastery of salient developmental tasks (e.g., separation-individuation) and produce deficiencies in important skills (e.g., social perspective taking) (Zahn-Waxler & Kochanska, 1990). Exaggerated guilt has also been linked to unrealistic parental expectations regarding child obedience and self-control, and parental prohibitions against "thinking about" transgressions (Potter-Efron, 1989).

Much of the empirical data linking child rearing to high levels of guilt in children stem from research on maternal depression. Parental disturbance and a negative affective climate in the family of a depressed parent may produce conditions that predispose children to excessive guilt and train children to use guilt-induction techniques (Zahn-Waxler et al., 1991). For example, children of depressed mothers are exposed to chronic and pervasive distress in their caregiver (e.g., high levels of guilt, irritability, sadness, and anxiety), and they experience more maternal rejection and criticism than children of well mothers (Downey & Coyne, 1990). These children become overinvolved in their caregiver's distress (Zahn-Waxler et al., 1991); and early involvement in others' problems is an antecedent of later depression (Block, 1987). The combination of overinvolvement and repeated failure to help the parent feel better may produce feelings of helplessness, futility, and anger resulting in enduring guilt patterns and depression. Furthermore, children whose behavior is repeatedly associated with another's distress (i.e., maternal depression) may develop a propensity to view their behavior as responsible for the distress (Zahn-Waxler et al., 1990), resulting in pervasive feelings of guilt and subsequent depression. Indeed, evidence suggests that children of affectively ill mothers show increased feelings of responsibility for others (Zahn-Waxler et al., 1990), higher levels of empathy at a young age (Radke-Yarrow, Zahn-Waxler, Richardson, Susman, & Martinez, 1994; Zahn-Waxler & Kochanska, 1990), impaired social perspective-taking ability (Zahn-Waxler et al., 1988), increased distress around others' distress, increased guilt, and suppression of frustration and other negative emotions compared to children of well mothers.

Children of depressed mothers are also at risk for developing an exaggerated sense of responsibility and for using excessive guilt induction by modeling their parents' behavior (Zahn-Waxler et al., 1979). For example, depressed mothers report more guilt in their relationships with their children than nondepressed mothers, they use more guilt induction with their children than well mothers, and these mothers display a more negative attributional style consistent with depressogenic thinking (i.e., global, stable, and internal attributions) (Susman, Trickett, Iannotti, Hollenbeck, & Zahn-Waxler, 1985; Weissman & Paykel, 1974). Evidence confirms that children model their parents' behavior; children of parents who make negative attributions employ a similar attributional style (Seligman, Peterson, Kaslow, Tanenbaum, Alloy, & Abramson, 1984).

Depressed mothers' disciplinary responses may also lead to excessive guilt in their children. Compared to well mothers, depressed parents are less available, responsive, consistent, and contingent toward their children (for a review see Downey & Coyne, 1990). Depressed mothers report more disappointment in their children, greater difficulty tolerating separation and increased autonomy, and more often emphasize their own problems and/or identify their children as the cause of their sadness (Susman et al., 1985). Children repeatedly held responsible for others' transgressions or heavily admonished for minor transgressions are likely to become chronically self-blaming and self-punishing, symptoms associated with depression.

In sum, excessive guilt feelings may develop in children of depressed mothers as a result of (a) the negative affective climate in the family that the child feels responsible for creating; (b) parental emphasis on the child's accountability for negative events; (c) parental negative attributions about the child; (d) parental use of guilt induction, love withdrawal, and disappointment as discipline strategies; and (e) very high parental expectations for child maturity (Zahn-Waxler et al., 1990). Parenting styles that induce excessive guilt in children appear to be associated with child depression.

Deficient Guilt

Sociopathy, conduct problems, and antisocial behavior are associated with low levels of empathy and guilt (APA, 1994; Harpur et al., 1988; McMahon & Forehand, 1988; Miller & Eisenberg, 1988), but scant evidence exists on the specific mechanisms of parent–child relationships responsible for the development of deficient guilt. Evidence for the role of parental modeling in the development of insufficient guilt comes from (a) the high rate of antisocial behavior in parents and siblings of children with conduct problems (Loeber, 1990; Loeber & Stouthamer-Loeber, 1986); (b) parental lack of responsibility taking (e.g., externalizing transgressions and blaming others for their misdeeds) (Rutter & Giller, 1983); (c) the absence of parental empathy toward distressed others, including their own children (Tangney, Wagner, Fletcher & Gramzow, 1992; Zahn-Waxler et al., 1979); and (d) abusive parenting styles or the use of "violence" to punish violence (Sears et al., 1957; Trickett & Kuczynski, 1983).

Abused children are believed to be at especially high risk for developing antisocial behavior and deficient empathy and guilt since they are exposed to particularly harsh and antisocial parental models (e.g., violent and unempathic) (Miller & Eisenberg, 1988). Indeed, compared to nonabusive parents, abusive parents are more coercive, negative, and punitive toward their children (Reid, 1986; Trickett & Kuczynski, 1983). As such, an evaluation of abused children's prosocial behavior may provide a unique opportunity to study the effects of modeling on the development of deficient guilt and antisocial behavior (Klimes-Dougan & Kistner, 1990; Trickett & Susman, 1988). In a study comparing abused and nonabused preschoolers, Klimes-Dougan and Kistner (1990) found that abused children displayed more aggression and withdrawal toward their distressed peers on the playground than nonabused youngsters, and they appeared to have significant prosocial skills deficits. Results from other studies are consistent with these findings. Abused toddlers show higher levels of aggressive, unempathic, and inappropriate responses to peers' distress, and they display less concern for and offer less help to distressed peers (Howes & Eldredge, 1985; Klimes-Dougan & Kistner, 1990). Thus, unempathic, aggressive role models appear to beget unempathic, aggressive offspring.

In addition to modeling, investigators propose that failures in the early parent–child attachment relationship may lead to the development of deficient guilt and antisocial behavior (Bowlby, 1988; Loeber, 1990). Children who have not bonded to their primary caregiver will be less likely to internalize important socialization messages, such as expectations for prosocial behavior. Research indicates that lack of parent–child bonding is an important risk factor for subsequent antisocial behavior (Bowlby, 1988; MacDonald, 1985).

Parental discipline techniques are also implicated in the development of deficient guilt and aggression in children (Sears et al., 1957). In a study by Knott, Lasater, and Shuman (1973), low levels of guilt were associated with strict parental guidelines, the use of physical punishment, and an atmosphere where children were discouraged from questioning their elders and rewarded for aggressing against others. More recent evidence corroborates these findings; extreme power assertive discipline methods, such as coercion and physical punishment, have strong links to aggression, antisocial behavior, and the development of low levels of guilt (Biglan, Lewin, & Hops, 1990; Dishion, Patterson, & Kavanagh, 1993; Patterson, 1982). The presence of empathy and guilt reduces and inhibits aggression, anger, and the externalization of blame (Knott et al., 1973; Miller & Eisenberg, 1988; Quiles & Bybee, in press; Tangney et al., 1992). Thus, parents who accept, endorse, or inconsistently punish their children's aggression fail to teach appropriate prosocial behavior, such as empathy, and their children, in turn, fail to internalize important social morals and values (Patterson, 1982; Richman & Harper, 1979; Sears et al., 1957).

These data suggest that guilt-induction strategies designed to invoke feelings of social responsibility in children may be deficient in families of youngsters who develop antisocial behavior problems (Richman & Harper, 1979). However, research on adult relationships contradicts this conclusion; indeed, Vangelisti et al. (1991) found that guilt induction among adults is associated with aggressiveness. Adults who attempt to engender guilt show little empathic concern for others and exhibit poor perspective-taking ability. Vangelisti et al. (1991) propose that guilt induction is an indirect method of aggressing against others and that aggression is associated with high levels of guilt induction.

GUILT INDUCTION IN PARENT–CHILD INTERACTIONS OF CLINIC-REFERRED YOUNGSTERS

In sum, much of the theoretical and empirical work to date suggests that extreme efforts to invoke guilt may be associated with depression in children, and deficient efforts to engender guilt may be associated with aggression in children. However, given the paucity of data relating guilt to psychopathology outside college student samples (see Bybee & Quiles, chapter 13, this volume), such linkages are speculative and await empirical support. In the remainder of this chapter, we present prelimi- nary findings on the use of guilt induction by parents and their clinic-referred children during a videotaped interaction conducted in our laboratory. Since most of the research on guilt has been conducted in nonclinical samples and using adults, we were curious whether parents and their clinically disturbed children would try to make each other feel guilty during discussions of conflict and whether instilling guilt would be associated with child psychopathology. Based on previous research and theory, we hypothesized that child depression would be associated with greater use of guilt induction by parents during parent–child interactions, and that aggres- sion would be associated with fewer efforts by parents to invoke guilt. We were also curious how depression and aggression might interact to influence parents' and children's guilt inducements. In addition to psychopathology effects, we were inter- ested in the impact of other potentially important factors on parents' and children's use of guilt (i.e., parent age, education, and income, and child age, gender, ethnicity, and religion).

OVERVIEW OF THE STUDY

To address these issues, we asked 82 parent–child dyads to discuss a real-life conflict while we videotaped them. Subjects were part of a larger longitudinal research project investigating treatment-seeking patterns of clinic-referred youth. Our sam- ple came from six mental health clinics in central and southern California. The children ranged in age from 7 to 16 years, with a mean age of 11 years 2 months. Two-thirds of the children were male. The sample was ethnically diverse with about 43% Caucasian, 25% Latino, 20% mixed, and 12% African-American. The religious breakdown was about 75% Christian, 9% no religion, 8% Jewish, 7% other, and 1% Muslim. About 3/4 of the families reported incomes below $30,000 per year. Children participated in the study with their primary caregivers—approximately

89% were biological mothers, 6% were biological fathers, 2% were foster parents, 1% were grandmothers, and 1% were aunts.

A subset of the larger battery of measures completed by parents, teachers, and children was examined. The measures of child adjustment were (a) parent report on the Child Behavior Checklist (CBCL; Achenbach, 1991); (b) child report on the Youth Self-Report (YSR; Achenbach & Edelbrock, 1987); (c) teacher report on the Teacher Report Form (TRF; Achenbach & Edelbrock, 1986); and (d) parent report on the Diagnostic Interview Schedule for Children (DISC; Shaffer, Fisher, Piacentini, Schwab-Stone, & Wicks, 1991 a,b). The CBCL, YSR, and TRF generate raw and T-scores for broad-band internalizing (e.g., sadness, anxiety) and externalizing (e.g., fighting, swearing) syndromes, and individual narrow-band syndromes (e.g., aggressive, depressed/anxious). The DISC is a structured diagnostic interview for children that generates an array of *DSM III-R* diagnoses. The four child adjustment measures were combined to form two standardized Likert scales. One score was created for aggression and one score was created for depression/anxiety with means of zero and standard deviations of 1.0. Each child adjustment measure received equal weight. Where the TRF and/or YSR were not available for a particular subject,[1] the remaining measures were used to derive the standard scores. The alpha reliability for the aggression scale was .68, and for the depression/anxiety scale it was .65.

The discussion topic for the videotaped interaction was derived from the Potential Parent-Child Problems (PPCP) questionnaire, a measure we adapted from two others (i.e., Christensen & Margolin, 1988; Marshall, Longwell, Goldstein, & Swanson, 1990) and modified to include topics relevant to adolescents. Parents and children independently indicated how much they disagreed with each other on 14 issues (e.g., child's grades or schoolwork, chores, friends, talking on the telephone, watching television, bedtime, curfew, privacy) using a scale from 1–5, where 1 = Do Not Disagree and 5 = Strongly Disagree. We used a procedure similar to that of Marshall et al. (1990) and Christensen and Margolin (1988) for identifying a topic for discussion; the item rated as most conflictual by both parent and child and least discrepant between the two respondents was chosen as the topic for the videotaped conflict discussion. Subjects were given 6 minutes to discuss and try to resolve the conflictual issue identified on the PPCP. Topics accounting for approximately 80% of the interactions were chores around the house (23%), schoolwork or getting into trouble at school (20%), listening to directions (15%), getting along with siblings (12%), and bedtime (9%). We coded the full 6-minute interaction.

Interactions were analyzed using a well-developed microanalytic coding system, the Structural Analysis of Social Behavior (SASB; Humphrey & Benjamin, 1989),

---

[1] A third of the teacher reports were unavailable because many children were on school vacation at the time of the assessment, and others had not been in class for the 2 months required for administration of the Teacher Report Form (Achenbach & Edelbrock, 1986). Also, 26% of the children were too young for the Youth Self-Report (Achenbach & Edelbrock, 1987), which is normed for children 11 years and older.

whose reliability and validity have been documented extensively (e.g., Humes & Humphrey, 1994; Humphrey, 1987, 1989; Humphrey, Apple, & Kirschenbaum, 1986).[2] Consistent with previous research, parents and children in our study used multiple strategies to engender guilt. Examples of parent and child communications coded as guilt inducing are provided in Table II, categorized in a manner that is consistent with the five types of speech identified by Vangelisti et al. (1991) and listed in Table I.

The SASB did not have a designated code for guilt induction, so this dimension was formed by summing together all of the codes that reflected an attempt to elicit guilt. Those codes considered to represent guilt induction were SASB code 2–6, Sulking and Appeasing, in combination with at least one of five other codes.[3] SASB code 2–6 was considered the primary guilt-induction code because it is highly interdependent, negative, and controlling (i.e., characteristics that are consistent with an interpersonal view of guilt and common across the diverse speech types and guilt-induction techniques identified by Vangelisti et al., 1991). However, SASB code 2–6 alone does not capture the full complexity of a guilt-inducing message. The codes used to form the guilt dimension in this study are consistent with previously reported methods of inducing guilt in others (Vangelisti et al., 1991).

Counts of guilt-inducing communications were aggregated for each subject. Using generalized linear models (McCullagh & Nelder, 1989), we evaluated the aggregate use of guilt induction for each parent and child while controlling for child age, gender, ethnicity, religion, parent age, education, and income. Thus, each of these factors was included as predictors in the model along with the scores for child aggression, child depression/anxiety, and the interaction term for these two scales. Results are reported in Table III.

---

[2]Videotapes of parent–child interactions were transcribed verbatim for verbal and nonverbal behavior, and the transcripts were used along with the actual tapes for coding with the SASB system (Humphrey & Benjamin, 1989). The SASB includes 16 individual codes: Eight for communications directed toward the other person and eight for communications directed toward the self. Coding is based on discrete units of communication consisting of sentences, complete thoughts, or nonverbal gestures (e.g., laughing). Coding each unit of communication requires raters to consider the meaning of the spoken words and the manner in which they are spoken, including nonverbal and contextual nuances of the communication such as tone of voice, facial expression, and body posture. Long comments may consist of several units. Each communication unit may be assigned up to three codes in order to capture the full meaning and complexity of the communication.

The videotapes were coded by an advanced undergraduate student in psychology and the first author. Coders were initially trained to use the SASB system at Northwestern University Medical School (supervised by Laura Humphrey, Ph.D.), the primary laboratory for the SASB. This was followed by practice and feedback until acceptable reliability was attained. Coders continued to meet and receive feedback through the duration of coding to prevent criterion drift. Interrater reliability was established using a subsample of 22% of the subjects. Pearson correlations for parent child behavior were $r = .81$ and $r = .75$ respectively.

[3]Combined codes including SASB code 2-6, Sulking and Appeasing, and any of the following five codes were used to form the guilt dimension: (a) SASB code 1–4, Nurturing and Protecting; (b) SASB code 1–5, Watching and Controlling; (c) SASB code 2–2, Disclosing and Expressing; (d) SASB code 1–2, Affirming and Understanding; and (e) SASB code 2–1, Asserting and Separating.

Data analyses yielded two effects related to child psychopathology. The use of guilt induction was higher among parents of more aggressive children, but parent-initiated guilt was unrelated to depression/anxiety in children. These findings contradict the hypothesis that parental guilt induction would be associated with higher levels of childhood depression/anxiety and lower levels of childhood aggression. To the contrary, parent-initiated guilt actually increased with higher levels of aggression.

There may be at least two reasons for this apparent contradiction. First, closer examination of the literature on which the hypotheses were based suggests that the discrepancy between our findings and previous writings may not be as dramatic. Indeed, Bybee and Quiles (chapter 13, this volume) point out that despite a rich theoretical literature associating guilt with clinical depression, few empirical studies have examined this relationship, particularly among children. Second, it may not be appropriate to assume that children's guilt feelings are fully accounted for by parental guilt-induction efforts. It may be possible, for example, that parents of aggressive children frequently attempt to invoke guilt in their children, but that their efforts are unsuccessful particularly if guilt is invoked in the context of a hostile, coercive, and combative parent–child relationship. Similarly, parents of aggressive children may attempt to engender guilt *in reaction to* their children's aggression with the hope of altering their children's behavior (i.e., to stop the aggression and to increase empathy and social perspective taking). This is consistent with research showing that adults use guilt to change other people's behavior (Vangelisti et al., 1991). It may be that parental guilt induction alone does not explain the high or low levels of guilt associated with depression and aggression in children respectively. Indeed, there is evidence from earlier research that guilt develops differently in children depending on the overall quality of the parent–child relationship (Ferguson & Stegge, 1995; Hoffman, 1982, 1983).

The other finding related to psychopathology revealed a significant interaction of aggression and depression/anxiety for child-initiated guilt (see Table III). To follow-up on the interaction, we examined the effect of high and low levels of depression/anxiety on aggression. Figure 1 shows that children's use of guilt induction does not change as a function of aggression at *low* levels of depression/anxiety. However, child-initiated guilt induction increases considerably as a function of aggression at *high* levels of depression/anxiety. This finding indicates that children who are both aggressive and depressed/anxious use more guilt induction than children who are only aggressive or only depressed/anxious, or children with low levels of depression/anxiety and aggression.

Increased use of guilt by aggressive and depressed/anxious children raises two potentially interesting issues. First, we know very little about the observed behavior of clinic-referred children with comorbid aggression and depression/anxiety, and we know virtually nothing about the use of guilt induction by these youth. These data suggest that the association between guilt and different types of child psychopathology is complicated, and that comorbidity may be uniquely linked to children's use of guilt induction. For example, guilt induction may be thought of as a passive-aggressive control strategy, whereby individuals are overtly submissive but covertly

TABLE II   Examples of Guilt-Inducing Comments by Parents and Children

---

Assertives

Child examples

- You didn't show me [how to read] in the first grade or second grade . . . so now I don't know how.
- Even if you drive me, you won't let me go anywhere.
- You didn't teach me what you were supposed to.
- Moms are supposed to help you with your homework.
- Dad is always at work and we [never] have time to spend with our family.
- You say how hard dad works and that he's too old to play tennis with me, but he plays tennis with his friends.

Parent examples

- Everytime we bring up the subject, you always try to find some other thing to talk about or pay attention to.
- It's not my fault that this happened.
- I told you to be in by midnight, but you were at your friend's house.
- It's the principle of the thing, John.
- Yeah, but you know what? I can't do everything. I can't cook, do the laundry, and clean, and wash the dishes, and go to school.
- [When you don't clean your room], the inspectors come [to our house] and report me for being a bad housekeeper.
- I did laundry when I was your age.

Direct directives

Child examples

- See, that's the thing. You can't treat me like a 12-year-old.
- Come on, Mom. You promised we could go.

Parent examples

- You know the responsibility. It's time for you to start carrying your share.
- You know that's not true, so stop saying it.
- Come on, Jordan, get serious.
- Don't act like that.
- You are going to break that if you don't leave it alone.
- Will you please stop doing that. You're [going to] hurt me.
- I'm talking to you. I'm asking you to tell me.
- You have to do other things besides talk on the phone with your friends.

Indirect directives

Child examples

- All you think about is yourself.
- We never get to go anywhere fun.
- I wish you and dad wouldn't fight so much in front of me.

TABLE II *(continued)*

Parent examples

- If you would listen to me the first time, we wouldn't have to argue.
- You know, all I ask [of you] is for a little help.
- Can't you just answer me without all this goofing around?
- You see? You're not paying attention to me.
- I do everything around the house without any help from you.

Interrogatives

Child examples

- Well, why do we have to do what that lady says?
- Why can't you ever listen to me?

Parent examples

- Why do you have to answer [me] that way?
- Do you think I do anything in the house at all?
- How come you didn't talk to me about that before?
- Well, what are you [going to] do about your friends?
- How could you do that to me?
- Are you going to listen to me next time?
- Why don't you ever do what I tell you to do?
- What are you going to do when you go back to school next Monday?
- Is that going to be your attitude at school?
- Doesn't it? Doesn't it bother you, huh? Doesn't it?

Expressives

Child examples

- All of my friends' parents let them stay out until 1:00 A.M.
- See-ee, lots of my friends get to go a lot of places together.
- I know that M-o-om.
- Fine, you're right!
- I know!
- He talks when he's not supposed to, but I'm the one who gets in trouble.
- That's no fai-i-r!

Parent examples

- I gave up working full-time to be home when you get home from school.
- I'm not doing it to be mean. I'm just doing it to try to help you.
- I'm supposed to have a life, too.
- You'll be 18 soon and out on your own, and I'll be stuck at home with no life because I gave in [to you] all the time.
- Whenever I get up in the morning, I clean my room and I do all kinds of stuff that you never do.
- Why can't you be more like your sister?
- My father never let me go out anywhere at all, but I'm not [going to] do that to you.

TABLE III   Guilt Induction Predicted by Child Psychopathology and Other Demographic Characteristics for 82 Parent–Child Dyads

Predictors	Logit coefficient	Corrected asymptotic standard error[a]	Corrected Z[b]	Estimated odds	p
Parent-initiated guilt					
Aggression	0.13	0.08	1.67	1.14	.05
Depression/anxiety	0.07	0.09	0.87	1.08	—
Aggression by depression/anxiety	−0.10	0.08	−1.31	0.91	—
Child age	1.34	0.40	3.38	3.81	.001
Parent age	−0.39	0.12	−3.33	0.68	.001
Jewish	0.12	0.16	0.78	1.13	—
African-American	0.41	0.20	2.08	1.51	.01
Child-initiated guilt					
Aggression	−0.09	0.06	−1.55	0.91	—
Depression/anxiety	0.06	0.06	1.12	1.07	—
Aggression by depression/anxiety	0.13	0.05	2.59	1.13	.005
Child age	−0.10	0.29	−0.34	0.91	—
Parent age	−0.07	0.09	−0.73	0.94	—
Jewish	0.31	0.11	2.78	1.37	.005
African-American	−0.20	0.15	−1.29	0.82	—
Constant (parent baseline)	−1.23	0.16	−7.86		
Child effect (deviation from parent baseline)	0.53	0.11	4.69	1.69	

[a]Standard errors were corrected for sample design using Huber's (1967) method.
[b]Corrected Z-scores asymptotically follow the normal distribution.

controlling and hostile. For instance, an adolescent may tell his/her parents, "Fine. I won't go to the concert, even though everyone else's parents are letting them go," with an inflection that implies "You don't love me as much as my friends' parents love them." The dual nature of this guilt-inducing behavior may be especially consistent with the presence of both aggression and depression/anxiety in children; the covert hostility in the guilt message may be linked to aggression, and the overt submissiveness in the guilt message may be linked to depression/anxiety. Second, some authors argue that guilt induction is an indirect, manipulative control technique designed to shape another person's behavior (Simonds & Simonds, 1981; Susman et al., 1985). Our finding, viewed from this perspective, suggests that children with comorbid depression/anxiety and aggression may be especially likely to use manipulation rather than direct attempts to influence their parents.

Several findings related to the non-psychopathology variables emerged (see Table III). Parents used more guilt induction with older children than younger chil-

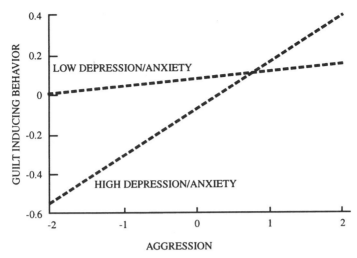

FIGURE 12.1   The interaction of aggression and depression/anxiety for children's guilt-inducing behavior.

dren, and younger parents used more guilt induction than older parents. Higher levels of parental guilt induction toward older children may be explained, in part, by evidence that guilt is used to establish dominance over others (Vangelisti et al., 1991). Parents may be more inclined to establish psychological control/dominance with a larger and more mature child than a younger child, because other methods of control or punishment (e.g., time out) are no longer feasible. Relatedly, as the age gap narrows between children and parents as children approach adulthood, parents may feel a greater need to establish their authority. Parents may also believe that adolescents will understand and be affected by guilt induction more than younger children. Finally, as parent–adolescent relationships transform into adult–adult relationships, parents may begin to use the kinds of control techniques identified in communication between adults (e.g., Vangelisti et al., 1991).

There may be at least three reasons why older parents direct less guilt toward their troubled children than younger parents. First, older parents may possess a larger repertoire of child-rearing strategies to alter their children's behavior and, thus, they may rely less on guilt induction and more on alternative methods. Second, older parents may be less controlling in general since they have had more life experience and they may be more secure and confident in their parenting skills. Third, younger parents may feel a greater need to establish their authority and dominance with their children because of the narrower age gap between themselves and their children.

Also in this study, parents of African-American children used more guilt induction than non-African-American parents, but Jewish and non-Jewish parents did not differ from each other. The only non-psychopathology effect related to child-initiated guilt was being Jewish; Jewish children directed more guilt toward their parents than non-Jewish children. Child age, parent age, and being African-American were not associated with child-initiated guilt. Child gender and parent education and income were not associated with the use of guilt by parents or children.

These findings linking guilt induction to ethnicity and religion provide interesting grist for the mill. For example, higher levels of guilt induction by Jewish than non-Jewish children may illuminate ways that these youngsters exert control in parent–child relationships, and point to difficulties these children may have using straightforward and direct methods to influence their parents. That African-American parents elicited more guilt than non-African-American parents may provide evidence of ethnic group differences in perceptions regarding the appropriateness of guilt induction as a child-rearing technique. Indeed, Pehrson (1990) reported that whites viewed guilt induction negatively while non-whites viewed it more positively. This finding offers insight into an important child-rearing style in the subset of African-Americans in this clinic-referred sample. Finally, the absence of effects related to child gender is somewhat surprising given other evidence that parents invoke guilt at different rates in boys and girls (Zahn-Waxler et al., 1991). However, these data suggest that gender may be less important for parent- or child-initiated guilt than other factors in clinic-referred children and adolescents.

SUMMARY AND FUTURE DIRECTIONS

Discipline practices alone do not show a consistent relationship to children's guilt, and as a result, several authors have begun to study links between parenting styles and the development of guilt within the broader context of parent personality, affective style, emotional problems, family cultural values, and children's temperament (Ferguson & Stegge, 1995; Zahn-Waxler & Kochanska, 1990; Zahn-Waxler & Robinson, 1995). The preliminary findings reported in this chapter support a broader context for understanding guilt induction in parent–child relationships, and they extend the research to a clinic sample of children and adolescents. We reviewed theory and empirical evidence linking guilt to normal and abnormal development in children, and we hypothesized about how guilt might be associated with childhood aggression and childhood depression/anxiety as a result of child-rearing practices and parent–child interactions. Most of the data linking guilt and psychopathology, however, are derived from studies on parental depression and not child deviance. Thus, we still know relatively little about the impact of child psychopathology on maladaptive aspects of guilt and expressions of guilt in parent–child relationships. We presented some preliminary findings from a study of clinically disturbed children and adolescents that revealed that child psychopathology, parent age, child age, religion and ethnicity influence parents and children's use of guilt in parent–child interactions.

Several directions for future research are evident from this review. First, little is known about the abnormal aspects of guilt in parent–child relationships or the role of child rearing in the development of maladaptive guilt in children. Future research is needed to examine how abnormal guilt *develops and changes* throughout childhood and adolescence in the context of individual parent and child characteristics, family relationships, peer interactions, and the school. For example, our preliminary findings suggest that ethnicity, age, and religion influence parents' and children's use of guilt, but other data are needed to fully explain the linkages between guilt and culture or guilt and religion. Replications of these findings with larger and more diverse samples of clinically disturbed children are needed. Identifying linkages between abnormal levels of guilt (i.e., excessive and deficient) and different forms of child psychopathology will enhance our understanding of important risk factors for children, and because children with excessive guilt may be at high risk for depression and children with deficient guilt may be at high risk for antisocial behavior problems, research efforts should be focused on strategies for reducing excessive guilt and teaching appropriate empathy. Finally, future models of maladaptive guilt in children need to cast a broader net to explain the multiple interacting factors that influence how guilt develops and evolves over time.

ACKNOWLEDGMENTS

The first author was supported by a National Research Service Award (#1 F31 MH10448-01A1) from the National Institute of Mental Health (NIMH) and the Warren Wright Adolescent Center endowment. The second author was supported by NIMH Research Scientist Award #1 K05 MH01161. The research project was supported by NIMH research grant #R01 MH 49522 to John Weisz. We are grateful to Marie Dennig, Susan Han, Stanley Huey, Blair Paley, and Karen Rudolph, for their assistance, and we extend special thanks to Dana Nelson for her extensive help with data coding and reduction. In addition, we thank Kenny Smith for his assistance with the computer software, Gary McClelland for his statistical consultation, and Denise Remboldt, Lisa Staab, Jennifer Weller, Terri Garcia, and Lori Matsumura for their help in transcribing videotapes and entering data. Finally, we thank the administrators and clinical staff at the following participating clinics: San Fernando Valley Child Guidance Clinic, Reiss–Davis Child Study Center, Los Angeles Child Guidance Clinic, Catholic Psychological Services, California School of Professional Psychology, Fresno, and Fresno County Mental Health Center, and the participating parents and children, without whose help this study would not have been possible.

REFERENCES

Achenbach, T. (1991). *Manual for the Child Behavior Checklist/ 4-18 and 1991 Profile.* Burlington: University of Vermont Department of Psychiatry.

Achenbach, T., & Edelbrock, C. (1986). *Manual for the Teacher's Report Form and Teacher Version of the Child Behavior Profile.* Burlington: University of Vermont, Department of Psychiatry.

Achenbach, T., & Edelbrock, C. (1987). *Manual for the Youth Self-Report and Profile.* Burlington, VT: University of Vermont, Department of Psychiatry.

Allen, T., & Edwards, R. (1988). Evaluators' perceptions of teachers' use of behavior alteration techniques. *Communication Education, 37,* 188–197.

American Psychiatric Association. (1994). *Diagnostic and statistical manual of mental disorders (4th ed.).* Washington, DC: Author.

Baumeister, R. F., Stillwell, A. M., & Heatherton, T. F. (1994). Guilt: An interpersonal approach. *Psychological Bulletin, 115,* 243–267.

Baumeister, R. F., Stillwell, A. M., & Heatherton, T. F. (1995). Personal narratives about guilt: Role in action control and interpersonal relationships. *Basic and Applied Social Psychology, 17,* 173–198.

Bell, R. (1968). A reinterpretation of the direction of effects in studies of socialization. *Psychological Reports, 75,* 81–95.

Biglan, A., Lewis, L., & Hops, H. (1990). A contextual approach to the problem of aversive practices in families. In G. Patterson (Ed.), *Aggression and depression in family interactions* (pp. 103–129). Hillsdale, NJ: Erlbaum.

Block, J. H. (1987, April). *Longitudinal antecedents of ego-control and ego-resiliency in late adolescence.* Paper presented at the Biennial Meeting of the Society for Research in Child Development, Baltimore, MD.

Bowlby, J. (1988). Developmental psychiatry comes of age. *American Journal of Psychiatry, 145,* 1–10.

Burbach, D., & Borduin, C. (1986). Parent–child relations and the etiology of depression: A review of methods and findings. *Clinical Psychology Review, 6,* 417–429.

Bybee, J., & Williams, C. (1994). *When is guilt adaptive? Relationships to prosocial behavior, academic and social strivings, and mental health.* Unpublished manuscript.

Christensen, A., & Margolin, G. (1988). Conflict and alliance in distressed and non-distressed families. In R. Hinde & J. Stevenson-Hinde (Eds.), *Relationships within families: Mutual influences* (pp. 263–282). Oxford: Oxford University Press.

Christopher, F. S., & Frandsen, M. M. (1990). Strategies of influence in sex and dating. *Journal of Social and Personal Relationships, 7,* 89–105.

Crook, T., Raskin, A., & Eliot, J. (1981). Parent–child relationships and adult depression. *Child Development, 52,* 950–957.

Dishion, T., Patterson, G., & Kavanagh, K. (1993). An experimental test of the coercion model: Linking theory, measurement, and intervention. In J. McCord & R. Tremblay (Eds.), *Preventing antisocial behavior: Interventions from birth through adolescence* (pp. 253–282). New York: Guilford.

Downey, G., & Coyne, J. (1990). Children of depressed parents: An integrative review. *Psychological Bulletin, 108,* 50–76.

Ferguson, T. J., & Stegge, H. (1995). Emotional states and traits in children: The case of guilt and shame. In J. P. Tangney & K. W. Fischer (Eds.), *Self-conscious emotions: The psychology of shame, guilt, embarrassment, and pride* (pp. 175–197). New York: Guilford.

Ferguson, T. J., Stegge, H., & Damhuis, I. (1991). Children's understanding of guilt and shame. *Child Development, 62,* 827–839.

Grusec, J. (1966). Some antecedents of self-criticism. *Journal of Personality and Social Psychology, 4,* 244–252.

Harder, D., Cutler, L., & Rockart, L. (1992). Assessment of shame and guilt and their relationships to psychopathology. *Journal of Personality Assessment, 59,* 584–604.

Harpur, T., Hakstian, A., & Hare, R. (1988). Factor structure of the psychopathy checklist. *Journal of Consulting and Clinical Psychology, 56,* 741–747.

Hoffman, M. (1977). Moral internalization: Current theory and research. In L. Berkowitz (Ed.), *Advances in experimental social psychology: Vol. 10* (pp. 86–135). New York: Academic.

Hoffman, M. (1982). *Development of prosocial behavior: Empathy and guilt.* New York: Academic Press.

Hoffman, M. (1983). Empathy, guilt, and social cognition. In W. F. Overton (Ed.), *The relationship between social and cognitive development* (pp. 1–51). Hillsdale, NJ: Erlbaum.

Howes, C., & Eldredge, R. (1985). Responses of abused, neglected, and non-maltreated children to the behaviors of their peers. *Journal of Applied Developmental Psychology, 6,* 261–270.

Huber, P. (1967). The behavior of maximum likelihood estimates under non-standard conditions. *Proceedings of the Fifth Berkeley Symposium on Mathematical Statistics and Probability, 1,* 221–233.

Humes, D., & Humphrey, L. (1994). A multimethod analysis of families with a polydrug-dependent or normal adolescent daughter. *Journal of Abnormal Psychology, 103,* 676–685.

Humphrey, L. (1987). Comparisons of bulimic-anorexic and nondistressed families using structural analysis of social behavior. *American Academy of Child and Adolescent Psychiatry, 26,* 248–255.

Humphrey, L. (1989). Observed family interactions among subtypes of eating disorders using Structural Analysis of Social Behavior. *Journal of Consulting and Clinical Psychology, 57,* 206–214.

Humphrey, L., Apple, R., & Kirschenbaum, D. (1986). Differentiating bulimic-anorexic from normal families using an interpersonal and a behavioral observation system. *Journal of Consulting and Clinical Psychology, 54,* 190–195.

Humphrey, L., & Benjamin, L. (1989). *An observational coding system for use with Structural Analysis of Social Behavior: The training manual.* Chicago: Northwestern University Medical School.

Jones, W. H., Kugler, K., & Adams, P. (1995). You always hurt the one you love: Guilt and transgressions against relationship partners. In J. P. Tangney & K. W. Fischer (Eds.), *Self-conscious emotions: The psychology of shame, guilt, embarrassment, and pride,* (pp. 301–321). New York: Guilford.

Karylowski, J. (1982). Two types of altruistic behavior: Doing good to feel good or to make the other feel good. In V. J. Derlega & J. Grzelak (Eds.), *Cooperation and helping behavior* (pp. 397–413). New York: Academic.

Klimes-Dougan, B., & Kistner, J. (1990). Physically abused preschoolers' responses to peers' distress. *Developmental Psychology, 26,* 599–602.

Knott, P. D., Lasater, L., & Schuman, R. (1973). Aggression–guilt and conditionability for aggressiveness. *Journal of Personality, 42,* 332–344.

Lewis, H. B. (1986). The role of shame in depression. In M. Rutter, C. Izard, & P. Read (Eds.), *Depression in young people,* (pp. 325–339). New York: Guilford.

Loeber, R. (1990). Development and risk factors of juvenile antisocial behavior and delinquency. *Clinical Psychology Review, 10,* 1–41.

Loeber, R., & Stouthamer-Loeber, M. (1986). Family factors as correlates and predictors of juvenile conduct problems and delinquency. In N. Morris & M. Tonry (Eds.), *Crime and Justice: An Annual Review of Research,* (Vol. 7, pp. 29–149). Chicago: University of Chicago Press.

MacDonald, K. (1985). Early experience, relative plasticity and social development. *Developmental Review, 5,* 99–121.

Marshall, V., Longwell, L., Goldstein, M., & Swanson, J. (1990). Family factors associated with aggressive symptomatology in boys with attention deficit hyperactivity disorder: A research note. *Journal of Child Psychology and Psychiatry, 31,* 629–636.

McCullagh, P., & Nelder, J. A. (1989). *Generalized linear models* (2nd ed.). London: Chapman and Hall.

McMahon, R. J., & Forehand, R. (1988). Conduct disorders. In E. J. Mash & L. G. Terdal (Eds.), *Behavioral assessment of childhood disorders (2nd ed.)* (pp. 105–153). New York: Guilford.

Miller, P. A., & Eisenberg, N. (1988). The relation of empathy to aggressive and externalizing/antisocial behavior. *Psychological Bulletin, 103,* 324–344.

Patterson, G. (1982). *A social learning approach to family intervention: Vol. 3, Coercive family process.* Eugene, OR: Castalia.

Pehrson, K. L. (1990). Parental self-assessment and behavioral problems of preschool children. *Military Medicine, 155,* 148–152.

Potter-Efron, R. T. (1989). Guilt generating messages and behavior from the family origin. In R. T. Potter-Efron (Ed.), *Shame, guilt and alcoholism: Treatment issues in clinical practice* (pp. 175–190). New York: Haworth.

Quiles, Z., & Bybee, J. (in press). Chronic and predispositional guilt: Relations to mental health, prosocial behavior, and religiosity. *Journal of Personality Assessment.*

Radke-Yarrow, M., Zahn-Waxler, C., & Chapman, M. (1983). Children's prosocial dispositions and behavior. In M. Hetherington (Ed.), *Handbook of child psychology Vol. 4* (pp. 469–545). New York: Wiley.

Radke-Yarrow, M., Zahn-Waxler, C., Richardson, D., Susman, A., & Martinez, P. (1994). Caring behavior in children of clinically depressed and well mothers. *Child Development, 65,* 1405–1414.

Reid, J. B. (1986). Social-interactional patterns in families of abused and nonabused children. In C. Zahn-Waxler, E. M. Cummings, & R. Iannotti (Eds.), *Altrusim and aggression: Biological and social origins* (pp. 238–255). Cambridge: Cambridge University Press.

Richman, L. C., & Harper, D. C. (1979). Parental child-rearing characteristics and delinquent adolescents' response to behavioral treatment. *American Journal of Orthopsychiatry, 49,* 527–529.

Rutter, M., & Giller, H. (1983). *Juvenile delinquency: Trends and perspectives.* Middlesex, UK: Penguin.

Sears, D., Maccoby, E., & Levin, H. (1957). *Patterns of child rearing.* Evanston, IL: Row, Peterson and Co.

Seligman, M. E. P., Peterson, C., Kaslow, N., Tanenbaum, R., Alloy, L., & Abramson, L. (1984). Attributional style and depressive symptoms among children. *Journal of Abnormal Psychology, 93,* 235–238.

Shaffer, P., Fisher, P., Piacentini, J., Schwab-Stone, M., Wicks, J. (1991a). *Diagnostic Interview Schedule for Children (DISC 2.3)—Parent Version.* New York: Columbia University.

Shaffer, P., Fisher, P., Piacentini, J., Schwab-Stone, M., Wicks, J. (1991b). *Diagnostic Interview Schedule for Children (DISC 2.3)—Child Version.* New York: Columbia University.

Simonds, M., & Simonds, J. (1981). Relationship of maternal parenting behaviors to preschool children's temperament. *Child Psychiatry and Human Development, 12,* 19–31.

Susman, E., Trickett, P., Iannotti, R., Hollenbeck, B., & Zahn-Waxler, C. (1985). Child rearing patterns in depressed, abusive, and normal mothers. *American Journal of Orthopsychiatry, 55,* 237–251.

Tangney, J. (1992). Situational determinants of shame and guilt in young childhood. *Personality and Social Psychology Bulletin, 18,* 199–206.

Tangney, J., Wagner, P., Fletcher, C., & Gramzow, R. (1992). Shamed into anger? The relation of shame and guilt to anger and self-reported aggression. *Journal of Personality and Social Psychology, 62,* 669–675.

Trickett, P., & Kuczynski, L. (1983, August). *Children's misbehaviors and parental discipline in abusive and nonabusive families.* Paper presented at the Annual Convention of the American Psychological Association, Anaheim, CA.

Trickett, P. K., & Susman, E. J. (1988). Parental perceptions of child-rearing practices in physically abusive and nonabusive families. *Developmental Psychology, 24,* 270–276.

Vangelisti, A. L., Daly, J. A., & Rudnick, J. R. (1991). Making people feel guilty in conversations: Techniques and correlates. *Human Communication Research, 18,* 3–39.

Weissman, M. M., & Paykel, E. S. (1974). *The depressed woman: A study of social relationships.* Chicago: University of Chicago Press.

Zahn-Waxler, C., Cole, P., & Barrett, K. (1991). *Guilt and empathy: Sex differences and implications for the development of depression.* New York: Cambridge University Press.

Zahn-Waxler, C., & Kochanska, G. (1990). The origins of guilt. In R. A. Thompson (Ed.), *Nebraska Symposium on Motivation: Socioemotional development: Vol. 36* (pp. 183–249). Lincoln, NE: University of Nebraska Press.

Zahn-Waxler, C., Kochanska, G., Krupnick, J., & McKnew, D. (1990). Patterns of guilt in children of depressed and well mothers. *Developmental Psychology, 26,* 51–59.

Zahn-Waxler, C., Mayfield, A., Radke-Yarrow, M., McKnew, D., Cytryn, L., & Davenport, Y. B. (1988). A follow-up investigation of offspring of parents with bipolar disorder. *American Journal of Psychiatry, 145,* 506–509.

Zahn-Waxler, C., & Radke-Yarrow, M. (1983). Early altruism and guilt. *Academic Psychology Bulletin, 5,* 247–259.

Zahn-Waxler, C., Radke-Yarrow, M., & King, R. A. (1979). Child rearing and children's prosocial initiations toward victims of distress. *Child Development, 50,* 319–330.

Zahn-Waxler, C., & Robinson, J. (1995). Empathy and guilt: Early origins of feelings of responsibility. In J. P. Tangney & K. W. Fischer (Eds.), *Self-conscious emotions: The psychology of shame, guilt, embarrassment, and pride* (pp. 143–173). New York, NY: Guilford.

CHAPTER 13

Guilt and Mental Health

Jane Bybee and Zandra N. Quiles

Northeastern University, Boston, Massachusetts

*This brings us to the long story of the origin or genesis of responsibility . . .
that labor man accomplished upon himself over a long period of time. . . .
How does one create a memory for the human animal? How does one go
about to impress anything on that partly dull, partly flighty human
intelligence—that incarnation of forgetfulness—so as to make it stick? . . .
Whenever man has thought it necessary to create a memory for himself, his
effort has been attended with torture, blood, sacrifice. . . . The severity of all
primitive penal codes gives us some idea how difficult it must have been
for man to overcome his forgetfulness and to drum into these slaves of
momentary whims and desires a few basic requirements of communal
living. . . . We need only recount some of our ancient forms of punishment:
stoning, breaking on the wheel, piercing with stakes, drawing and
quartering, trampling to death with horses, boiling in oil or wine, the popular
flaying alive, cutting out of flesh from the victim and leaving him in the sun,
a prey to flies. By such methods the individual was finally taught to
remember five or six "I won'ts" which entitled him to participate in the
benefits of society.*
—Frederich Nietzsche (1956/1971, pp. 30–31).

From without or within, pain, suffering, and agony may be necessary to control and constrain, to redirect and restrict, to civilize and socialize. For will to triumph over instinct, for mindfulness to win out over thoughtlessness, for prosocial actions to take precedence over selfishness, strong inducements or deterrents must be present. Fear of and scars from physical punishment provide one means of socializing. External punishment as a tool of discipline and as a means of social control is, however, inherently limited to situations in which untoward acts are detectable or may be attributed to a given individual and, used alone, is only moderately effective in controlling aversive behaviors (Baumrind, 1971). Moreover, the infliction of physical injury may itself be uncivil and even unconscionable. From corporeal punishment in school to the torture of political prisoners, the current zeitgeist reflects an increasing intolerance and abhorrence of the intentional infliction of physical harm as a method of social control.

Guilt and Children
Copyright © 1998 by Academic Press. All rights of reproduction in any form reserved.

The tension, remorse, and self-hatred that arises alongside guilt may be extremely hurtful and even unbearable. Yet internal pain and mental anguish may provide a more palatable and humane means of regulating and controlling behavior than infliction of physical injury, mutilation, and death. Indeed, the pain and harshness of guilt may be necessary to make the emotion capable of regulating and controlling behavior. Individuals may not have the time or inclination in their day-to-day dealings to reflect upon every decision in order to choose the morally principled path (Merisca & Bybee, 1994). The sudden sting of conscience in the form of guilt, however, may be strong enough to interrupt an ongoing action sequence and redirect it (Baumeister, Stillwell, & Heatherton, 1994). Nagging feelings persevering after a wrongdoing may prompt the individual to take corrective and reparative actions (Tangney, Wagner, Fletcher, & Gramzow, 1992a). Guilt may also act as a self-administered punishment that keeps memories of past transgressions alive and accessible, a deterrent that serves over time to reduce or eliminate occurrences of the triggering event (Mosher, 1979). Even a single guilt-producing event may be so traumatic that it leads the experiencing individual to foreswear or renounce the behavior (Bybee & Williams, 1994, 1996). Moreover, unpleasant guilt feelings may offset hedonistic pleasures of imagining prohibited acts. Guilt over thoughts of wrongdoing may interfere with planning the logistics of committing the deed, thereby making the act less tempting, less feasible, and less likely to occur (Bybee & Williams, 1994, 1996).

Predispositional guilt is related to empathy, greater use of apologies, and less aggressiveness (Quiles & Bybee, 1997; Tangney, 1991; Tangney et al., 1992a). The emotion may serve to regulate and control actions outside social situations as well. Individuals with a greater proclivity for guilt receive better grades in school, have increased frustration tolerance, and adhere more closely to a prescribed medical regimen (Bybee, Leckman, Lavietes, & Tamborlane, 1991; Merisca & Bybee, 1994). Guilt apparently, then, works. Individuals who are more predisposed to the emotion appear to be better socialized, exhibiting more prosocial, achievement-oriented, and healthy behavior.

IS THERE A DARKER SIDE TO GUILT?

Guilt has long been viewed as a source of psychopathology. According to psychoanalytic theory, guilt results from the development of the superego (Lewis, 1979a). The conscience inhibits the outward expression of hostility, driving anger instead inward and against the self in order to condemn and punish the self for untoward thoughts and actions. Guilt is, according to this perspective, internalized aggression. With development, as the superego becomes stronger and more exacting, attendant feelings of guilt may become harsh, powerful, irrational, and consuming. When guilt is pervasive or overwhelming, the resultant pain, self-loathing, mental anguish, and despair may become unbearable and psychopathology may ensue (Harder,

1995; Leckman et al., 1984; Zahn-Waxler & Kochanska, 1990). The dramatic escalation in the prevalence of affective and anxiety disorders (and decline in the prevalance of externalizing disorders) during adolescence is said to result in part from the processes of socialization (Zahn-Waxler, Cole, & Barrett, 1991).

Freud (1930/1961) draws analogies between the ontogeny of the individual and the phylogenesis of civilization. With both individual development and the evolution of humankind, instinctual drives are increasingly renounced as internal controls such as shame and guilt become more refined and, ultimately, overutilized. In the process, humans become socialized and capable of regulating and controlling their own behavior in the absence of externally imposed punishment. Socialization on a personal and a global level, however, bears a high cost. In *Civilization and Its Discontents,* Freud (1930/1961; p. 81) states,

> My intention [is] to represent the sense of guilt as the most important problem in the development of civilization and to show that the price we pay for our advance in civilization is the loss of happiness through the heightening of the sense of guilt.

The view of guilt as a contributing factor in the genesis of mental illness has long been accepted as a *sine qua non* of psychoanalytic theory. Guilt plays a prominent role in cognitive theories of mental illness as well (Beck, 1967, 1979; Lewis, 1979a; Prosen, Clark, Harrow, & Fawcett, 1983). Guilt has been associated with a number of internalizing disorders, but most frequently with depression (Blatt & Schichman, 1983; Harder, 1995; Harder, Cutler, & Rockart, 1992; Kugler & Jones, 1992; Lewis, 1979b; Zahn-Waxler et al., 1991). This link has become so well accepted that items assessing guilt are used as operational indices of depression in the most widely used and respected inventories (e.g., Beck's [1967] Depression Inventory; Blatt's [1979] Depressive Experiences Questionnaire; Kovacs's [1980] Childhood Depression Inventory). "Excessive or inappropriate guilt" numbers among the nine criteria used to diagnose major depression as defined by *DSM-III-R* (American Psychiatric Association, 1987). The emotion is also said to be symptomatic of obsessive-compulsive disorder, paranoia, and bulimia (e.g., Blatt & Schichman, 1983; Fairburn & Cooper, 1984; Lewis, 1979a). The view of guilt as a precursor of mental illness has spilled over into the popular literature. In one self-help book (cited by Gaylin, 1979), for example, a chapter is boldly entitled, "The Useless Emotions—Guilt and Worry."

As reviewers note (e.g., Tangney, Wagner, & Gramzow, 1992b), however, remarkably few empirical studies definitively link guilt with depression and other forms of psychopathology. Indeed, prior to the 1990s, few studies had examined the link between guilt and depression. The post-1990 studies that examine the relationship of guilt to mental illness generally do not include clinical samples, examining instead symptoms of psychopathology among student samples. Moreover, studies yield conflicting findings. Several researchers report that guilt is related to depression (Harder et al., 1992; Kugler & Jones, 1992; Leckman et al., 1984). Other researchers report that guilt does not relate to depression (e.g., Bybee et al.,

1991; Bybee & Williams, 1994, 1996; Tangney, Burggraf, & Wagner, 1995; Tangney et al., 1992b). The picture seems no less clear for other mental illnesses. In several studies, greater guilt is correlated with more severe symptoms of obsessive-compulsiveness, anxiety, somatization, and psychoticism (on the Symptom Checklist-90-Revised [SCL-90-R], Harder et al., 1992). In contrast, other researchers report that guilt is unrelated to these symptoms of psychopathology (using the SCL-90-R, when shame is controlled, from Tangney et al., 1992b).

Is guilt related to mental illness? We must begin by acknowledging that data from clinical samples is needed in order to definitively answer this question. We can, however, address whether guilt is related to mental health as indexed by the absence of psychiatric symptoms. We argue that there is a much larger consensus across studies than might appear from the preceding, brief review of the literature. We turn now to developing a theoretical perspective intended to address and elucidate relationships between guilt and symptoms of mental illness. The basic principles of our model are summarized in Table I.

PRINCIPLE 1: TWO FUNDAMENTALLY DIFFERENT FORMS OF GUILT EXIST THAT SHOW RADICALLY DIFFERENT RELATIONSHIPS TO MENTAL HEALTH

The central tenet of the present theory is that two fundamentally different variants of guilt exist: predispositional guilt, which is a personality proclivity for experiencing guilt in response to specific, circumscribed, eliciting situations, and chronic guilt, an ongoing condition of guiltiness, regret, and remorse unattached to an immediate precipitating event. We argue that these two forms of guilt display profoundly different relationships to mental health. We maintain that a predispositional readiness to experience guilt is generally adaptive. Individuals who score higher on predispositional guilt feel more intense guilt when confronted with an eliciting situation (Okel & Mosher, 1968). Experiences of sharp, short-lived feelings of guilt, however, are unlikely to undermine long-term mental health. Indeed, intense feelings of guilt may prompt prosocial behavior and inhibit the expression of symptoms of sociopathy and externalizing disorders. In contrast, we maintain that continual, ongoing feelings of guilt are damaging to mental health. Chronic feelings of guilt, unresolved and unalleviated, may become virulent, providing an ongoing source of self-degradation and an endless reminder of the failing that evoked the guilt. We argue that chronically guilty individuals are at risk for depression and other internalizing disorders as well as externalizing disorders.

Evidence that two different forms of guilt exist among adults and among children is provided by Quiles and Bybee (1997) and Ferguson (Ferguson, Stegge, Miller, & Olsen, 1996), respectively. Quiles and Bybee (1997) provide empirical evidence that extant measures of guilt designed for adults assess two types of guilt:

TABLE I Principles Guiding the Relationship of Guilt to Mental Health

Principle 1:	Two fundamentally different forms of guilt exist that show radically different relationships to mental health.
Principle 2:	Predispositional guilt, no matter how intense, is not maladaptive.
Principle 3:	Chronic, unalleviated guilt is maladaptive.
Principle 4:	Predispositional guilt is related to fewer symptoms of externalizing disorders and sociopathy.
Principle 5:	Predispositional guilt is distinguishable from knowledge and moral standards: Guilt, not moral standards, is related to prosocial behavior.
Principle 6:	Chronic, unalleviated guilt is associated with more severe symptoms of externalizing disorders.
Principle 7:	Chronic guilt is distinguishable from shame: Both are maladaptive and show distinct relationships to indices of psychopathology.
Principle 8:	Characteristics of the individual may determine whether guilt is short-lived or chronic, in turn, affecting mental health.
Principle 9:	Reactions to the precipitating situations may determine whether guilt becomes chronic (or is absent), in turn, affecting mental health.
Principle 10:	The nature of the guilt-evoking events may determine whether guilt is short-lived or chronic, in turn, affecting mental health.

chronic and predispositional. They report that measures assessing continual feelings of guilt unattached to a precipitating event (e.g., the Personal Feelings Questionnaire [PFQ-2] from Harder et al., 1992; the Guilt Inventory [GI] from Kugler & Jones, 1992) fall together on a single factor. Measures assessing a readiness to experience guilt in response to a circumscribed eliciting event (e.g., the Mosher Forced Choice Guilt Scale [MFCGS] from Mosher, 1966, 1979; the Test of Self-Conscious Affect [TOSCA] from Tangney et al., 1992b) comprise a second, distinct factor. Along these same lines, Tamara Ferguson and her colleagues report that extant measures of guilt designed for children assess two quite different forms of guilt with distinct correlates (Ferguson & Stegge, chapter 2, this volume; Ferguson et al., 1996). Canonical correlations indicate that guilt arising in reaction to circumscribed, guilt-evoking situations (the C-CARS; Stegge & Ferguson, 1990) may be distinguished from guilt assessed by semiprojective measures containing intentionally ambiguous narratives (the Children's Interpretation of Interpersonal Distress and Conflict [CIIDC]; Zahn-Waxler, Kochanska, Krupnick, & Mayfield, 1988).

Why Isn't Predispositional Guilt Harmful? A Comparison of Guilt and Shame

Insights into why predispositional guilt is not maladaptive are provided by comparing guilt with shame. Shame proneness is widely held to be much more destructive

than guilt proneness (Tangney et al., 1992b, 1995). In shame, the object of appro-
bation is the entire self. The focus of attention is on personal shortcomings, inadequacies, and pejorative qualities. The self comes under painful scrutiny, is found to
be lacking, and is condemned. Guilt, in contrast, draws attention to the wrongfulness of the precipitating event (Lindsay-Hartz, 1984; Tangney et al., 1992b). Experiences of guilt may be less painful and destructive because a positive sense of self
remains intact.

Further, as it is more difficult to remake or recast the self than to undo an isolated
deed or lapse, guilt compared to shame may more readily prompt corrective or
remedial actions (Lindsay-Hartz, 1984; Tangney et al., 1992b). Along these same
lines, shame gives rise to action tendencies such as hiding, shrinking away, and
avoidance that impede efforts to repair the situation, whereas guilt is typically accompanied by a pressing need to expiate or alleviate the emotion (Tangney et al.,
1992b). Guilt prompts confession, apologies, and reparation, responses that are
more conducive to confrontation and rectification.

Moreover, individuals experiencing shame are concerned with exposure, with
others' appraisals, and with worry that others will think poorly of them (Ferguson,
Stegge, & Damhuis, 1991). This acute self-consciousness and fear of public disapproval may be devastating and debilitating to mental well-being. Individuals experiencing guilt are more concerned with the victim and possible injury. Guilt is
closely related to empathy which, in turn, is associated with socioemotional competence (Batson, Duncan, Ackerman, Buckley, & Birch, 1981; Eisenberg, Miller,
Shell, McNalley, & Shea, 1991; Hoffman, 1982; Leith & Baumeister, 1996; Tangney, 1991).

Tangney maintains that guilt does not, and from a theoretical perspective should
not, relate to depression and other forms of mental illness (e.g., Tangney et al.,
1992b, 1995). She points out that because guilt, unlike shame, draws attention to
the behavior rather than to the self, it gives rise to internal, specific, and fairly
unstable attributions that are unlikely to have long-term adverse effects on mental
health. Tangney notes that guilt and shame often co-occur and argues that by
partialling out the effects of one emotion, the effects of the remaining "pure"
emotion may be best seen. In a series of well-crafted studies, Tangney and her
colleagues utilize measures assessing a personality proclivity for shame and a personality proclivity for guilt. They provide convincing evidence that "guilt-free" shame
is associated with hostility and poor mental health, whereas "shame-free" guilt is
associated with prosocial behavior and is unrelated to symptoms of psychopathology
(Tangney et al., 1995).

Why Is Chronic Guilt Maladaptive? A Functionalist
Perspective on Emotion Regulation

The functionalists challenge the view of emotions as inherently confusing and de-
stabilizing and the perception that negative emotions are necessarily maladaptive

(Campos, Mumme, Kermoian, & Campos, 1994; Cole, Michel, & Teti, 1994; Thompson, 1994). They argue that any emotion may be adaptive or maladaptive, depending on the circumstances. Tangney's position that shame is invariably devastating, ugly, and maladaptive is, then, at odds with the functionalist approach. Functionalists maintain that shame can serve such adaptive roles as helping the individual acquire self-knowledge by highlighting how the individual appears to others and fostering deference to standards of group conduct (Barrett, 1995; Ferguson et al., 1991). The gaze aversion, slumping of the body, and hiding of the face may communicate deference and submission, whereas withdrawal and avoidance may move the individual out of view and away from judgmental eyes (Barrett, 1995). Tangney's position that "shame-free" guilt is invariably adaptive also stands in opposition to the functionalist position that all emotions, including guilt, are potentially maladaptive.

According to the functionalist perspective, it is not negativity, but rather ineffective emotion regulation, that makes an emotion dysfunctional (Campos et al., 1994; Cole et al., 1994; Thompson, 1994). Emotion dysregulation may occur when individuals do not have access to an emotion that is typical and appropriate for the situation or when one emotion becomes dominant to the exclusion of others (Cole et al., 1994). This viewpoint parallels our position that the lack of a predisposition for guilt, as well as overdominance as indexed by chronic guilt, is maladaptive. Emotion dysregulation may also occur when the individual cannot effectively calibrate emotional states. The well-adjusted individual attenuates or amplifies the intensity of emotion, curtails or extends the duration of emotional states, and retards or hastens the onset of an emotion, as needed (Cole et al., 1994; Thompson, 1994). We maintain that (a) characteristics of the individual (such as being depressed) that interfere with the ability to manage emotion, (b) reactions (such as self-hatred and rumination) that needlessly prolong and aggravate rather than redress and alleviate guilt, and (c) types of situations that are difficult to regulate and control will all tend to make guilt chronic and, hence, maladaptive. We develop these points in later sections of the present chapter.

Why Are Chronic and Predispositional Guilt Independent? Parallels with Research on Affect Intensity and Frequency

Our position that chronic and predispositional guilt are relatively independent and show radically different relationships to mental health has parallels in the work of Diener and his colleagues (Diener & Emmons, 1985; Larsen, Diener, & Emmons, 1986). Diener maintains that affect frequency (the duration or amount of time in which the affect predominates) and intensity (the strength with which one experiences positive affect) represent separate processes that contribute independently to affective experience. The intensity of positive affect is strongly and positively correlated with the intensity of negative affect. Individuals, then, that experience powerful positive emotions are typically the same individuals who experience powerful negative emotions. The frequency of positive and negative affect are inversely correlated, that is, individuals who feel generally happy do not tend to be the same individuals as those who feel generally unhappy (Diener, Colvin, Pavot, & Allman, 1991; Diener & Emmons, 1985). Further, *affect intensity is not significantly correlated with affect frequency* (Diener, Larsen, Levine, & Emmons, 1985; Larsen et al., 1986). Findings that measures of guilt such as the PFQ-2 that assess frequency are only modestly correlated with measures of guilt that assess the intensity of one's predisposition for guilt should not then be interpreted as a sign of the poor validity of the competing scale (e.g., Harder, 1995; Tangney et al., 1995), but as evidence that for guilt—as for emotions in general—frequency and intensity are largely independent. Quiles and Bybee's (1997) finding that chronic and predispositional guilt factors are orthogonal also attests to the independence of the two dimensions.

Diener reports that the intensity and frequency of positive affect are largely independent in their relationships to mental heath (Diener et al., 1985, 1991). Intensity of emotional highs is not related to long-term happiness nor to self-esteem (Diener et al., 1991). In a similar vein, we argue that individuals with a greater predisposition to feel strong or intense feelings of guilt in response to precipitating events are not more prone to mental illness. Experiencing occasional intense bursts of emotion should not be centrally important to long-term well-being.

Diener finds that chronicity (or frequency/duration) of positive emotion is related to good mental health. A steady modicum of positive affect relates to high self-esteem, high self-confidence, and feelings of happiness (Diener et al., 1985). Along these same lines, we argue that continual, ongoing, chronic feelings of guilt are associated with poor mental health. We now provide empirical evidence to buttress our position that predispositional and chronic guilt show radically different relationships to mental health.

PRINCIPLE 2: PREDISPOSITIONAL GUILT, NO MATTER HOW INTENSE, IS NOT MALADAPTIVE

Upon review, we discover that guilt measures that require participants to react to demarcated situations (e.g., Tangney, Wagner, & Gramzow's [1989] TOSCA; Mosher's [1966] MFCGS) do not relate to symptoms of depression (Bybee, Zigler, Berliner, & Merisca, 1996; Bybee & Williams, 1994, 1996; Quiles & Bybee, 1997; when shame is held constant, from Tangney et al., 1992b). Moreover, measures of predispositional guilt are unrelated to somatic, obsessive-compulsive, anxious, paranoid, and other psychopathological symptoms (Quiles & Bybee, 1997; when shame is held constant, from Tangney et al., 1992b). When effects of sex and social desirability are held constant, the pattern of findings remains unchanged (using the SCAII-R, Harder et al., 1992; Quiles & Bybee, 1997). Finally, Bybee et al. (1996) report that predispositional guilt is unrelated to symptoms of eating disorders.

A number of researchers have suggested that increases in guilt up to a point may not be maladaptive, but when guilt becomes extreme, excessive, or exaggerated, it then holds the potential for destructiveness (Baumeister et al., 1994; Kugler & Jones, 1992; Leckman et al., 1984; Modell, 1971; Zahn-Waxler & Kochanska, 1990; Zahn-Waxler et al., 1991). Empirical studies demonstrate that emotions such as fear show curvilinear relationships with indices of adjustment, becoming counterproductive at very high levels (e.g., Leventhal, 1970). Do overly intense feelings of guilt overwhelm and paralyze the individual? Bybee and Williams (1994, 1996) assess whether an extreme predisposition for guilt is maladaptive. They find no evidence that individuals with a very strong proclivity for guilt (scores in the top 10%) are more prone to depression or are more maladjusted on indices of socioemotional well-being.

PRINCIPLE 3: CHRONIC, UNALLEVIATED GUILT IS MALADAPTIVE

When we turn away from studies using measures of predispositional guilt toward those using measures of chronic guilt that require participants to rate how often, frequently, or continually they experience guilt (e.g., the PFQ-2 from Harder et al., 1992; the GI from Kugler & Jones, 1992), a radically different pattern of findings emerges. Chronic guilt shows maladaptive relations with depression and somatic, obsessive-compulsive, anxious, paranoid, and other pathological symptoms assessed by the SCL-90-R (Jones & Kugler, 1993; Harder et al., 1992; Quiles & Bybee, 1997). Researchers report that the pattern of findings remains unchanged when effects of sex and social desirability are controlled (Harder et al., 1992; Quiles & Bybee, 1997). In addition, Quiles and Bybee (1997) demonstrate that measures of chronic guilt compared to measures of predispositional guilt, show significantly stronger correlations with symptoms of depression and other mental illnesses.

Using a very different approach, Bybee et al. (1996) provide a test of the hypothesis that unalleviated guilt is implicated in depression. They ask students to describe three guilt-producing incidents involving school. Participants then rate how guilty they felt afterward and how effective they were in alleviating their feelings of guilt. Feelings of guilt in the school domain are unrelated to symptoms of depression and eating disorders. In contrast, ineffective alleviation of guilt correlates with both depression and disordered eating.

PRINCIPLE 4: PREDISPOSITIONAL GUILT IS RELATED TO FEWER SYMPTOMS OF EXTERNALIZING DISORDERS AND SOCIOPATHY

A widespread theoretical and research tradition portrays guilt as a moral or social emotion that develops alongside empathy (Baumeister et al., 1994; Baumeister,

Stillwell, & Heatherton, 1995; Bybee & Williams, 1994, 1996; Hoffman, 1982; Merisca & Bybee, 1994; Tangney et al., 1992a; Zahn-Waxler et al., 1991). Guilt is widely held to play a crucial role in the formation and maintenance of communal relationships. Expressions of suffering and remorse restore equity to relationships by redistributing feelings of distress from the injured party to the transgressor and relegate to the victim the power to forgive (Baumeister et al., 1994). Suffering by the perpetrator also reassures the victim that the act will not be repeated (Lindsay-Hartz, 1984).

Empirical studies confirm that individuals who have a greater proclivity for guilt are seen by their peers as more caring and considerate as well as more honest and trustworthy (Bybee & Williams, 1994, 1996). Beyond fostering and fomenting close interpersonal relationships, guilt appears to play a role in more global expressions of fairness, compassion, and spirituality. A personality proclivity for guilt is related to eschewal of racist attitudes, volunteerism for charity work, and religiosity (Merisca & Bybee, 1994; Quiles & Bybee, 1997).

The absence of guilt has long been viewed as a hallmark of sociopathy (e.g., Harpur, Hakstian, & Hare, 1988). Lack of guilt or remorse is also listed in *DSM-III-R* (APA, 1987) as a defining symptom of Disruptive Behavior Disorder among children and adolescents. Empirical evidence that a lower proclivity for predispositional guilt is linked with antisocial and criminal behavior comes from a variety of quarters. Lower predispositional guilt correlates with heightened scores on indices of hostility and aggression in both adults and children (Bybee & Williams, 1994, 1996; Merisca & Bybee, 1994; Mosher, 1979; Tangney et al., 1992a). Juvenile delinquents compared to matched controls score lower on predispositional guilt (Ruma, 1967, as cited in Mosher, 1979). Among delinquents, assaultive behavior is correlated with a lower proclivity for guilt (Heyman, 1969, as cited in Mosher, 1979). Psychopathy is associated with an absence of guilt (Harpur et al., 1988). Finally, among inmates at a maximum security reformatory, the number of sex, violent, and total crimes is inversely correlated with predispositional guilt (Persons, 1970).

PRINCIPLE 5: PREDISPOSITIONAL GUILT IS DISTINGUISHABLE FROM COGNITION, KNOWLEDGE, AND MORAL STANDARDS: GUILT, NOT MORAL STANDARDS, IS RELATED TO PROSOCIAL BEHAVIOR

Do measures of predispositional guilt really tap guilt at all? Arguments have been put forth that measures of predispositional guilt do not assess guilt per se, but instead tap moral standards, knowledge, or cognition (Harder, 1995, 1996; Kugler & Jones, 1992). Kugler and Jones (1992) maintain that measures mentioning specific precipitating events, scenarios, or moral dilemmas do not tap guilt. They argue that the Mosher guilt scale, for instance, assesses, "the cognitive potential for guilt, rather than its affective manifestation" (Kugler & Jones, 1992, p. 319). They maintain that measures we label predispositional guilt scales are actually tapping moral standards or values. In order to test their hypothesis, Kugler and Jones (1992) administered a battery of questionnaires to a large sample of college students. Predispositional guilt measures used in their study were positively correlated with an inventory of moral standards (Kugler & Jones, 1992). Harder (1995, 1996) also questions whether predispositional guilt inventories are truly assessing guilt. Harder suggests that the TOSCA, for example, taps cognitions and coping reactions rather than guilt (Harder, 1995, 1996). According to this view, predispositional guilt measures that contain specific incidents assess the cognition or knowledge that the mentioned event is wrong, immoral, or undesirable.

Refuting the position that measures of predispositional guilt are tapping cognition or knowledge rather than affect are findings from two recent studies. Merisca and Bybee (1994) find that predispositional guilt and moral standards are negligibly related to one another and have distinct behavioral and attitudinal correlates. Predispositional guilt relates to greater volunteerism, more prosocial behavior, lowered aggressiveness, and lower scores on a measure of racist attitudes. In contrast, moral reasoning is unrelated to these variables. Additional support for the view that predispositional guilt is distinguishable from cognition and/or knowledge is provided by Bybee et al. (1996), who report that among diabetic adults, predispositional guilt and diabetic knowledge are unrelated. Further, they find that for diabetic adults who are free of depression, predispositional guilt (as assessed by the TOSCA) is related to better adherence to the medical regime (Bybee et al., 1996). In contrast, diabetic knowledge is not correlated with adherence to the medical regime.

Moreover, studies confirm that individuals who score higher on measures of predispositional guilt experience more intense guilty affect. In an early study, Okel and Mosher (1968) experimentally induced males to engage in verbal aggression against their unseen partner, who became distressed and disorganized as a result of the attack. They report that males who had scored higher on predispositional guilt (assessed in a pretest by the Mosher scale) reported more intense emotional responses of guilt after the aggressive act. Similarly, Bybee et al. (1996) find individuals scoring higher on predispositional guilt experience more intense feelings of guilt after self-reported incidents involving eating and exercise.

PRINCIPLE 6: CHRONIC, UNALLEVIATED GUILT IS ASSOCIATED WITH MORE SEVERE SYMPTOMS OF EXTERNALIZING DISORDERS

Given the strong and consistent evidence that predispositional guilt is related to *less* antisocial and sociopathic behavior, our position that chronic guilt is associated with *more* antisocial behavior may appear startling. Yet empirical support for this position is amassing. Greater ongoing guilt is associated with greater hostility as assessed by self-report inventories (Harder et al., 1992; Jones & Kugler, 1993; Kugler & Jones, 1992; Quiles & Bybee, 1997). Findings by Kugler and Jones (1992; see also Jones & Kugler, 1993; Jones, Kugler, & Adams, 1995) indicate that individuals with greater chronic guilt are more likely to describe themselves as angry, resentful, suspicious, lonely, and insecure. In addition, friends and relatives perceive individuals scoring higher on chronic guilt to be more angry, argumentative, conceited, detached, and contemptuous, and less friendly, affectionate, and sociable (Jones & Kugler, 1993).

Baumeister (et al., 1994, 1995) points out that attempts at guilt induction may lead the affected person to feel resentful, pressured, and manipulated. In families or relationships where members habitually and inappropriately use guilt induction, targeted individuals may feel chronically guilty and also angry and contemptuous. Moreover, guilt in individuals inured or accustomed to such feelings may not provide a call to action, but instead may be experienced as an aggravation or nuisance that is difficult to distinguish from the ongoing background noise of chronic guilt. The resultant stress and negative affect may prompt the individual to lash out at others in a hostile manner or assume a passive-aggressive stance.

Chronic guilt may also signal the presence of an underlying problem such as familial dysfunction. Children of parents with affective disorder, for example, feel chronically guilty over needing love, requiring attention, and even merely existing (Zahn-Waxler, Kochanska, Krupnick, & McKnew, 1990). Chronic guilt may result from deep-rooted interpersonal problems (such as being physically battered or living with an alcoholic parent) that may result in estrangement from and distrust of others (Jones et al., 1995). Victims may feel chronically guilty that they might somehow have caused (or stopped) the mistreatment or helped the perpetrator become well. Likewise, instigators of abuse, neglect, betrayal, or other mistreatment may experience chronic feelings of guilt over having wronged others.

PRINCIPLE 7: CHRONIC GUILT IS DISTINGUISHABLE FROM SHAME: BOTH ARE MALADAPTIVE AND SHOW DISTINCT RELATIONSHIPS TO INDICES OF PSYCHOPATHOLOGY

Tangney maintains that guilt, when chronic, becomes fused with shame (Tangney et al., 1992b, 1995). She points out that when guilt is ongoing or insoluble, attributions may become more stable, more global, more internal, and, in short, more shame-like. In Tangney's view, the pathological guilt so often described in the clinical literature is most typically guilt with an overlay of shame. She argues that once one makes the critical distinction between shame and guilt, there is little reason to expect that guilt should be associated with psychological problems. Tangney and her colleagues (Tangney et al., 1995) report that guilt shows only negligible correlations with indices of psychopathology when effects of shame are held constant. Moreover, they maintain that guilt measures such as the PFQ-2 that make no reference to precipitating events provide participants with a shame-like task, that of making global ratings about the self. Tangney's arguments have obvious implications for the present theory as they suggest that the measures we have been calling chronic guilt, because they make no reference to precipitating events, are measuring shame as well and that it is the shared variance with shame rather than "pure" chronic guilt that is maladaptive.

Without a doubt, chronic guilt and shame are closely related. Quiles and Bybee (1997) find that measures of chronic guilt fall together with shame on a single factor. Kugler and Jones (1992) report that their measure of chronic guilt shows correlations as high as .72 with indices of shame. The PFQ-2 Guilt Scale, which we also consider a measure of chronic guilt, correlates strongly ($r = .64$) with the PFQ-2 Shame Scale (Harder et al., 1992). In contrast, predispositional guilt measures show more moderate correlations with shame. (For the TOSCA guilt and shame, $r = .45$, from Tangney et al., 1992b).

Unquestionably, chronic guilt and shame often co-occur. Acts that are repeated, that are habitual, or that form a pattern may give rise to both chronic guilt and shame as the individual feels guilty over each incident and ashamed for the characterological flaw that permitted the behavior to be continued. Singular incidents may also give rise to both chronic guilt and shame. A solitary event may mar and stigmatize, leading to ongoing guilt over the event (e.g., having an accident while driving under the influence) and shame over the label (e.g., being a drunk driver). When others reject apologies or reconciliatory gestures, the guilty party may remain guilty and may experience shame over the rebuff. Furthermore, when any attempt to discharge the emotion fails, the intropunitive aspects of guilt may become more prominent, leading to greater overlap in the symptoms shared with shame.

Is chronic guilt, then, indistinguishable from shame? By reanalyzing data from Quiles and Bybee (1997), we find support for Tangney's view that "shame-free" guilt is not maladaptive when *predispositional* measures of the emotions are used. As shown in Table II, when effects of shame are partialled out, predispositional guilt (as assessed by the TOSCA [Tangney et al., 1989] and as assessed by the MFCGS [Mosher, 1966]) is generally not related to symptoms of psychopathology. In the only exceptions, we find "shame-free" guilt is related to less hostility and fewer symptoms of paranoia, that is, better adjustment. Any mal effect of predispositional guilt does appear to be attributable to the shared variance with shame.

A totally different picture emerges when indices of *chronic* guilt are considered. As shown in Table III, *chronic guilt continues to be related to psychopathology even when the shared variance with shame is partialled out.* Chronic guilt and shame, then, make independent contributions to the variance. By including two measures of chronic guilt, the PFQ-2 (Harder & Zalma, 1990) and the GI (Kugler & Jones, 1992) (and two measures of predispositional guilt), we extend the generalizability of the findings. The somewhat higher correlations of the GI compared to the PFQ-2 with

TABLE II   Partial Correlations of Predispositional Guilt and Shame Measures to Symptoms of Psychopathology[a]

Measures	TOSCA Guilt (partialled for TOSCA shame)	TOSCA Shame (partialled for TOSCA guilt)	Mosher Guilt (partialled for TOSCA shame)	TOSCA Shame (partialled for Mosher guilt)
Beck Depression Inventory	−.03	.42****	.01	.39****
SCL-90-R:				
Somatization	−.12	.19[†]	−.08	.18[†]
Obsessive-compulsive	.10	.26**	.10	.24*
Interpersonal sensitivity	−.10	.49****	−.08	.48****
Depression	.04	.34***	.07	.32**
Anxiety	.02	.29**	.04	.28**
Phobic anxiety	−.08	.34***	−.10	.35***
Paranoid ideation	−.14	.27**	−.22*	.30**
Psychoticism	−.03	.33***	.02	.30**
Hostility	−.28**	.12	−.29**	.15

[a]TOSCA, Test of Self-Conscious Affect, SCL-90-R, Sympton Checklist-90—Revised.
[†]$p < .10$.   *$p < .05$.   **$p < .01$.   ***$p < .001$.   ****$p < .0001$.

symptoms of psychopathology are also consistent with our theoretical model. In contrast to the PFQ-2, which asks participants to rate how continuously they experience symptoms of guilt—an ambiguous time frame that may extend from hours to years, the GI includes clauses such as, "for as long as I can recall," "if I could live my life over again," and, "in the past," phrases that imply a very long time perspective. As guilt becomes extremely chronic, it should become even more maladaptive.

PRINCIPLE 8: CHARACTERISTICS OF THE INDIVIDUAL MAY DETERMINE WHETHER GUILT IS SHORT-LIVED OR CHRONIC, IN TURN, AFFECTING MENTAL HEALTH

We predict that characteristics of the individual (such as depression) that interfere with the ability to effectively alleviate guilt may lead the emotion to become chronic, ineffectual in motivating behavior, and injurious to mental health (fueling further depression in a deadly downward spiral). Depressed individuals produce fewer, lower quality, and more maladaptive strategies for managing affect (Garber, Braafladt, & Zeman, 1991). They may, then, be unable to effectively discharge feelings of guilt. In addition, individuals incapacitated by depression and accompanying symptoms of indecisiveness, fatigue, and helplessness may be unable to act upon feelings of guilt. When individuals cannot engage in reparative actions or otherwise alleviate painful feelings of guilt, feelings may turn virulent (Bybee & Williams, 1994, 1996; Tangney et al., 1992a, 1992b; Zahn-Waxler & Kochanska, 1990). Guilt for individuals high on depression (or low in self-efficacy) may further fuel feelings of self-hatred and serve as an added stressor and source of negative affect.

In two separate studies, we confirm that predispositional guilt is adaptive for individuals who are not depressed, but maladaptive for individuals scoring high on depression. Among adolescents drawn from the public school system, greater guilt is related to better educational performance and positive social interactions among those with few or no signs of depression (Bybee & Williams, 1994, 1996). For students with more severe symptoms of depression, relationships become progressively weaker and finally reverse direction. Similar findings emerge in a study of diabetic adolescents (Bybee et al., 1991). Higher guilt corresponds to better socioemotional adjustment and good adherence to the medical regimen among adolescents with few or no signs of depression, but to worse socioemotional adjustment and poor adherence for adolescents with mild to severe symptoms.

TABLE III   Partial Correlations of Chronic Guilt and Shame Measures to Symptoms of Psychopathology[a]

Measures	PFQ-2 Guilt (partialled for PFQ-2 shame)	PFQ-2 Shame (partialled for PFQ-2 guilt)	GI (partialled for PFQ-2 shame)	PFQ-2 Shame (partialled for GI guilt)
Beck Depression Inventory	.18[†]	.26**	.43****	.27**
SCL-90-R:				
Somatization	.08	.12	.28**	.08
Obsessive-compulsive	.32**	.12	.34***	.23*
Interpersonal sensitivity	.27**	.26**	.25*	.37****
Depression	.30**	.15	.44****	.22*
Anxiety	.27**	.12	.36***	.18[†]
Phobic anxiety	.11	.14	.18[†]	.17[†]
Paranoid ideation	.18[†]	.23*	.28**	.28**
Psychoticism	.33***	.14	.35***	.25*
Hostility	.22*	.01	.27**	.05

[a]PFQ-2, Personal Feelings Questionnaire-2; GI, Guilt Inventory.
[†]$p < .10$.   *$p < .05$.   **$p < .01$.   ***$p < .001$.   ****$p < .0001$.

PRINCIPLE 9: REACTIONS TO THE PRECIPITATING SITUATIONS MAY DETERMINE WHETHER GUILT BECOMES CHRONIC (OR IS ABSENT), IN TURN, AFFECTING MENTAL HEALTH

Intropunitive responses involving turning inward and against the self are concomitants of guilt (Baumeister et al., 1995; Harder & Zalma, 1990; Mosher, 1979; Tangney et al., 1995). Individuals may ruminate over the precipitating event, thinking about what happened over and over again. Individuals may experience regret and remorse, chastising themselves for allowing the guilt-producing event to occur and engaging in self-condemnation and self-hatred (Kugler & Jones, 1992). Individuals may also engage in self-destructive behavior to punish themselves or to atone for the guilt-producing thought or event (Wallington, 1973). Intropunitive responses may serve an important positive role in adjustment by intensifying the pain caused by guilt in order that it might be noticed, acted upon, and remembered. We maintain that intropunitive reactions to guilt-producing events such as rumination and self-hatred are not inherently maladaptive, but may become so in cases where they needlessly aggravate and prolong feelings of guilt. Indeed, we find that intropunitive reactions are strongly correlated ($r = .72$) with chronic guilt (Quiles & Bybee, 1997).

To the extent that reconciliatory reactions such as apologies and reparation alleviate feelings of guilt and lead to positive social outcomes, they would be expected to be beneficial to mental health. Reconciliatory reactions may enable individuals to reduce feelings of guilt by turning outward and toward others through confiding, confessing, apologizing, and making reparation (Bybee, Merisca, & Velasco, chapter 9, this volume; Tangney et al., 1992a). Confiding and confessing may enable the individual to address and work through resolutions to the guilt-producing situation and may also lower emotional involvement by venting the emotion. Apologies and restitution may repair or undo the precipitating event, stopping the emotion at its source. Apologies, confession, and reparation are means of reacting to and resolving specific events. By shortening the duration of unpleasant guilt feelings and by leading to desirable outcomes, reconciliatory responses may attenuate the pain and maximize the gain. Compared to intropunitive responses, reconciliatory responses are less strongly correlated with chronic guilt and more strongly associated with predispositional guilt (Quiles & Bybee, 1997).

In three separate studies, we examine whether reconciliatory compared to intropunitive components of guilt show differential relationships to indices of socioemotional competence. When reconciliatory items such as apology, confession, and need for reparation are removed from a measure of guilt (leaving a high preponderance of intropunitive items), the abbreviated inventory is not only highly correlated with the original scale, but shows virtually identical correlations with teacher reports of classroom adjustment (Bybee & Williams, 1994, 1996). Insofar as social and goal-directed behaviors are concerned, then, reconciliatory and intropunitive aspects of guilt may serve as the carrot and the stick, exerting equally beneficial effects.

In a study by Bybee et al. (1996), women describe circumscribed times they had felt guilty at school, times they had felt guilty about eating, and what happened afterward. Women who cope with guilt by turning outward and toward others by confiding show fewer symptoms of eating disturbances and depression, whereas women who engage in self-hatred, rumination, and destructiveness are more predisposed to these disorders. When precipitated by a circumscribed event, reconciliatory aspects of guilt may be more effective in alleviating feelings of guilt and more beneficial to mental health than intropunitive components.

In a third study, Quiles and Bybee (1997) assess intropunitive and reconciliatory responses arising from both chronic and circumscribed situations. Intropunitive and reconciliatory aspects of guilt are indistinguishable in relation to symptoms of psychopathology. When the situation is insoluble, reconciliatory responses may be unable to effectively alleviate feelings of guilt and may become harmful. A pressing but unquenchable need to undo or set things right, excessive and pervasive rumination, and an unrelenting focus on the act or the field (see Lewis, 1979a) may result in compulsions, obsessions, paranoia, and an array of intropunitive symptoms.

A third main type of reaction to guilt-producing events is cognitive restructuring or rationalization. Individuals may reduce or alleviate feelings of guilt through justification, that is, denying or minimizing the seriousness of the lapse (Bybee et al., 1996; Scott & Lyman, 1968). Alternatively, individuals may acknowledge the seriousness of the lapse, but excuse themselves from blame by citing extenuating circumstances (Bybee et al., 1996; Scott & Lyman, 1968). Bybee et al. (1996) find that women who rationalize their actions through justifications and excuses show fewer problems with depression and disturbed eating. We posit that justifications and excuses render positive effects on mental health indirectly by lowering guilt and by raising self-esteem. Justifications and excuses may, however, be related to sociopathy. By constructing a web of intellectualizations and rationalizations, individuals may protect themselves from feelings of responsibility and remorse and steel themselves to commit socially undesirable and even horrific acts in cold blood.

PRINCIPLE 10: THE NATURE OF THE GUILT-EVOKING EVENTS MAY DETERMINE WHETHER GUILT IS SHORT-LIVED OR CHRONIC, IN TURN, AFFECTING MENTAL HEALTH

When guilt results from types of situations that are overly abstract or unmanageable, coping skills may be taxed to the limit as the individual valiantly strives to control the uncontrollable with chronic guilt and its attendant problems as a likely result. Indeed, when theorists speak of pathological guilt, they often underscore that it is insoluble in nature (Lewis, 1979a; Tangney et al., 1992a; Zahn-Waxler & Kochanska,

1990). What makes a guilt-producing situation unresolvable? The precipitating condition may be a conundrum that is so highly abstract and convoluted in nature that it becomes impossible to expunge. For a description of existentialist guilt, let us revisit the writings of Nietzsche (1956/1971, pp. 57–58).

> Man with his need for self-torture, his sublimated cruelty resulting from the cooping up of his animal nature within a polity, invented bad conscience in order to hurt himself, after the blocking of the more natural outlet of his cruelty. Then this guilt-ridden man seized upon religion in order to exacerbate his self-torment to the utmost . . . we see an insanity of the will that is without parallel: man's will to find himself guilty, and unredeemably so; his will to believe that he might be punished to all eternity without ever expunging his guilt; his will to poison the very foundation of things with the problem of guilt and punishment and thus to cut off once and for all his escape from this labyrinth of obsession; his will to erect an ideal (God's holiness) in order to assure himself of his own absolute unworthiness. What a mad, unhappy animal is man! What strange notions occur to him, what perversities, what paroxysms of nonsense. . . . Here, no doubt, is sickness, the most terrible sickness that has wasted man thus far.

Guilt may also become chronic when death is involved. When the victimized party is deceased, opportunities no longer exist for apology, direct reparation, and reconciliation. Individuals may blame themselves for the other person's death, for causing them unhappiness, or for not doing enough for them while they were living. Moreover, a universal stage of the bereavement process involves sanctification of the deceased (Thomas, 1992). Recently departed loved ones, neighbors, and friends are often heralded as saints and heroes. Individuals are warned not to speak ill of the dead and may have a hard time justifying or excusing any differences or run-ins they may have had by blaming the deceased. The living may place blame on themselves even for morally ambiguous situations. Moreover, they may be tortured and tormented by thoughts that they have hurt the deceased, by wishes to turn the hands of time backward, by desires to talk with the deceased a last time in order to make amends. In reviewing students' descriptions of guilt-producing incidents, we often run across mentions of guilt feelings surrounding relatives who have died (particularly among college students). Children's taunts such as, "You'll be sorry when I'm dead," or, "You'll wish you hadn't said that when I'm gone," reflect an implicit recognition that another's death may bring intolerable guilt. Indeed, suicide may sometimes be a conscious or unconscious attempt to punish others by causing them to feel guilt.

An exhaustive discussion of all forms of unresolvable and uncontrollable situations resulting in chronic guilt is beyond the scope of this chapter. Research attention, also, has been sparse, leaving us few concrete findings to review. Suffice it to say that many harmful forms of guilt—survivor guilt (see Hoffman, 1976, 1978), guilt over eating (see Bybee et al., 1996), guilt over having passed on diseases that are inherited (such as diabetes) or communicable (such as AIDS) to a child, guilt over addictions (such as alcoholism)—share a common element: the guilt-producing condition is difficult if not impossible to reverse or repair.

DO AGE OR SEX DETERMINE WHETHER GUILT IS ADAPTIVE?

Bybee and Zigler (1991) report that guilt is related to higher self-esteem among fifth graders, but the correlation becomes insignificant at higher age levels. They suggest that young children scoring high on guilt may value praise from parents and teachers given in recognition of their high academic and social standing. Self-esteem may reflect this positive feedback. With age, the importance of adult praise falls as the need for peer approval rises (Berndt, 1982; Hunter & Youniss, 1982). Peers may not place a high value on classroom competence in appraising others. Subsequent efforts to find developmental changes in the relationships of guilt to mental health, however, have found no age-related trends. Predispositional guilt is apparently adaptive at all age levels. Bybee and Williams (1994, 1996) for example, find no evidence that relationships of guilt to acting out, depression, and other indices of socioemotional well-being change with age.

Compared to males, females are less prone to externalizing disorders and more prone to internalizing disorders (Achenbach & Edelbrock, 1981). Moreover, females are more predisposed to guilt (and score higher on chronic guilt as well). Despite these strong and consistent main effects of gender, there is no indication from the literature that guilt is more adaptive for one sex compared to the other (Bybee & Williams, 1996).

CONCLUSIONS

Guilt is good: It permits individuals to live and function freely in the absence of a police state, it encourages individuals to foment close communal relationships and to behave altruistically, and it gives rise to motivated and goal-directed behavior. By providing punishment from within, punishment from without becomes less necessary. When guilt is absent, aggression, acting out, and even sociopathy may ensue.

Yet dangers arise when guilt lingers and persists over time, unchanneled, undischarged, and virulent. When guilt is chronic, it becomes closely linked with symptoms of mental illness. When the individual is too depressed or low in self-efficacy to cope with feelings of guilt, when coping responses needlessly prolong the emotion, when the guilt-evoking condition cannot be controlled or repaired, chronic guilt and symptoms of psychopathology may result. Perhaps the most important implication of the present work is the importance of alleviating guilt constructively and effectively.

How might chronic guilt be alleviated? Lewis (1979a) suggests that reaction formation or sublimation might be therapeutic for the individual experiencing chronic guilt. Even if the other person is dead, the guilty individual might provide indirect reparation by giving to charity in memory or honor of the deceased or by providing social or financial support to the deceased person's family. Religious confession and penance, participation in Yom Kippur (the Jewish Day of Atonement) services, and ministerial or rabbinical counseling may all help alleviate chronic guilt. Chronic guilt from day-to-day hassles may be lessened by participating in amnesty days for overdue library books or delinquent tickets. Individuals might be encouraged to seek forgiveness for transgressions they have committed even when these lapses occurred long ago. Indeed, if guilt feelings are still operative years later, this may provide all the more reason for individuals to work to resolve them. Moreover, parents, educators, and therapists might be encouraged to teach effective methods of guilt alleviation. Instilling guilt may be necessary to socialize, but helping others to effectively alleviate guilt may be critical to their mental well-being. In sum, the greatest challenge from a mental health perspective may not be guilt, as Freud (1930/1961) suggests, but effective and constructive guilt alleviation.

REFERENCES

Achenbach, T. M., & Edelbrock, C. S. (1981). Behavioral problems and competencies reported by parents of normal and disturbed children aged four through sixteen. *Monographs of the Society for Research in Child Development, 46* (1, Serial No. 188).

American Psychiatric Association (1987). *Diagnostic and statistical manual of mental disorders, 3rd ed., rev.* Washington, DC: American Psychiatric Association.

Barrett, K. C. (1995). A functionalist approach to shame and guilt. In J. P. Tangney & K. W. Fischer (Eds.), *Self-conscious emotions: The psychology of shame, guilt, embarrassment, and pride* (pp. 25–63). New York: Guilford.

Batson, C. D., Duncan, B. D., Ackerman, P., Buckley, T., & Birch, K. (1981). Is empathic emotion a source of altruistic motivation? *Journal of Personality and Social Psychology, 40,* 290–302.

Baumeister, R. F., Stillwell, A. M., & Heatherton, T. F. (1994). Guilt: An interpersonal approach. *Psychological Bulletin, 115,* 243–267.

Baumeister, R. F., Stillwell, A. M., & Heatherton, T. F. (1995). Personal narratives about guilt: Role in action control and interpersonal relationships. *Basic and Applied Social Psychology, 17,* 173–198.

Baumrind, D. (1971). Current patterns of parental authority. *Developmental Psychology Monograph, 4* (No. 1, Pt. 2).

Beck, A. T. (1967). *Depression: Clinical, experimental, and theoretical aspects.* New York: Harper & Row.

Beck, A. T. (1979). *Cognitive therapy and emotional disorders.* New York: Times Mirror.

Berndt, T. J. (1982). The features and effects of friendship in early adolescence. *Child Development, 53,* 1447–1460.

Blatt, S. J. (1979). *Depressive Experiences Questionnaire.* Yale University: New Haven, CT.

Blatt, S. J., & Schichman, S. (1983). Two primary configurations of psychopathology. *Psychoanalysis and Contemporary Thought, 6,* 187–255.

Bybee, J. A., Leckman, J. F., Lavietes, S., & Tamborlane, W. (1991, April). *Guilt, depressive symptoms, and the quality of diabetic adherence among adolescents with Insulin-Dependent Diabetes Mellitus.* Paper presented at the Annual Meeting of the Eastern Psychological Association.

Bybee, J. A., & Williams, C. (1994, April). *Does guilt show adaptive relationships with socioemotional competency and academic achievement?* Paper presented at the Biennial Conference on Human Development, Pittsburgh, Pennsylvania.

Bybee, J. A., & Williams, C. (1996). *When is guilt adaptive? Relationships to prosocial behavior, academic and social strivings, and mental health.* Manuscript submitted for publication, Northeastern University.

Bybee, J. A., & Zigler, E. (1991). The self-image and guilt: A further test of the cognitive-developmental formulation. *Journal of Personality, 59,* 733–745.

Bybee, J. A., Zigler, E., Berliner, D., & Merisca, R. (1996). Guilt, guilt-evoking events, depression and eating disorders. *Current Psychology: Developmental, Learning, Personality, Social, 15,* 113–127.

Campos, J. J., Mumme, D. L., Kermoian, R., & Campos, R. G. (1994). A functionalist perspective on the nature of emotion. In N. A. Fox (Ed.), The development of emotion regulation: Biological and behavioral considerations. *Monographs of the Society for Research in Child Development, 59* (2-3, Serial No. 240).

Cole, P. M., Michel, M. K., & Teti, L. O. (1994). The development of emotion regulation and dysregulation: A clinical perspective. In N. A. Fox (Ed.), The development of emotion regulation: Biological and behavioral considerations. *Monographs of the Society for Research in Child Development, 59* (2-3, Serial No. 240).

Diener, E., Colvin, C. R., Pavot, W. G., & Allman, A. (1991). The psychic costs of intense positive affect. *Journal of Personality and Social Psychology, 61,* 412–503.

Diener, E., & Emmons, R. A. (1985). The incidence of positive and negative affect. *Journal of Personality and Social Psychology, 47,* 1105–1117.

Diener, E., Larsen, R. J., Levine, S., & Emmons, R. A. (1985). Intensity and frequency: Dimensions underlying positive and negative affect. *Journal of Personality and Social Psychology, 78,* 1253–1265.

Eisenberg, N., Miller, P. A., Shell, R., McNalley, S., & Shea, C. (1991). Prosocial development in adolescence: A longitudinal study. *Developmental Psychology, 27,* 849–857.

Fairburn, C. G., & Cooper, P. J. (1984). The clinical features of bulimia nervosa. *British Journal of Psychiatry, 144,* 238–246.

Ferguson, T. J., Stegge, H., & Damhuis, I. (1991). Children's understanding of guilt and shame. *Child Development, 62,* 827–839.

Ferguson, T. J., Stegge, H., Miller, E. R., & Olsen, M. E. (1996). *Is guilt "adaptive" or not? A comparison of two measures.* Manuscript submitted for publication, Utah State University, Logan, Utah.

Freud, S. (1961). *Civilization and its discontents* (J. Strachey, Ed. and Trans.). New York: Norton. (Original work published 1930)

Garber, J., Braafladt, N., & Zeman, J. (1991). The regulation of sad affect: An information processing perspective. In J. Garber & K. A. Dodge (Eds.), *The development of emotion regulation and dysregulation.* Cambridge: Cambridge University Press.

Gaylin, W. (1979). On feeling guilty. *The Atlantic, 243,* 78–82.

Harder, D. W. (1995). Shame and guilt assessment and relationships of shame- and guilt-proneness to psychopathology. In J. P. Tangney & K. W. Fischer (Eds.), *Self-conscious emotions: The psychology of shame, guilt, embarrassment, and pride* (pp. 368–392). New York: Guilford.

Harder, D. W. (1996). *Guilt and symptoms of psychopathology.* Paper presented at the Annual Convention of the American Psychological Association, Toronto, Canada.

Harder, D. W., Cutler, L., & Rockart, L. (1992). Assessment of shame and guilt and their relationships to psychopathology. *Journal of Personality Assessment, 59,* 584–604.

Harder, D. W., & Zalma, A. (1990). Two promising shame and guilt scales: A construct validity comparison. *Journal of Personality Assessment, 55,* 729–745.

Harpur, T. J., Hakstian, A. R., & Hare, R. D. (1988). Factor structure of the psychopathy checklist. *Journal of Consulting and Clinical Psychology, 56,* 741–747.

Hoffman, M. L. (1976). Empathy, role-taking, guilt and development of altruistic motives. In T. Likona (Ed.), *Moral development: Current theory and research.* New York: Holt.

Hoffman, M. L. (1978). Toward a theory of empathic arousal and development. In M. Lewis & L. Rosenblum (Eds.), *The development of affect, Genesis of Behavior 1,* (pp. 205–226). New York: Plenum.

Hoffman, M. L. (1982). Development of prosocial motivation: Empathy and guilt. In N. Eisenberg (Ed.), *Development of prosocial behavior* (pp. 281–313). New York: Academic Press.

Hunter, F., & Youniss, J. (1982). Changes in functions of three relations during adolescence. *Developmental Psychology, 18,* 806–811.

Jones, W. H., & Kugler, K. (1993). Interpersonal correlates of the Guilt Inventory. *Journal of Personality Assessment, 61,* 246–258.

Jones, W. H., Kugler, K., & Adams, P. (1995). You always hurt the one you love: Guilt and transgressions against relationship partners. In J. P. Tangney & K. W. Fischer (Eds.), *Self-conscious emotions: The psychology of shame, guilt, embarrassment, and pride* (pp. 301–321). New York: Guilford Press.

Kovacs, M. (1980). Rating scales to assess depression in school-aged children. *Acta Paedopsychiatrica, 46,* 305–315.

Kugler, K., & Jones, W. H. (1992). On conceptualizing and assessing guilt. *Journal of Personality and Social Psychology, 62,* 318–327.

Larsen, R. J., Diener, E., & Emmons, R. A. (1986). Affect intensity and reactions to daily life events. *Journal of Personality and Social Psychology, 51,* 803–814.

Leckman, J. F., Caruso, K. A., Prusoff, B. A., Weissman, M. M., Merikangas, K. R., & Pauls, D. L. (1984). Appetite disturbance and excessive guilt in major depression. *Archives of General Psychiatry, 41,* 839–844.

Leith, P., & Baumeister, R. F. (1996). *Empathy, shame, guilt, and narratives of interpersonal conflicts: Guilt-prone people are better at perspective taking.* Manuscript submitted for publication, Case Western Reserve University, Cleveland, OH.

Leventhal, H. (1970). Findings and theory in the study of fear communications. In L. Berkowitz (Ed.), *Advances in experimental social psychology* (Vol. 5). New York: Academic.

Lewis, H. B. (1979a). Guilt in obsession and paranoia. In C. E. Izard (Ed.), *Emotions in personality and psychopathology* (pp. 399–414). New York: Plenum.

Lewis, H. B. (1979b). Shame in depression and hysteria. In C. E. Izard (Ed.), *Emotions in personality and psychopathology* (pp. 371–396). New York: Plenum.

Lindsay-Hartz, J. (1984). Contrasting experiences of shame and guilt. *American Behavioral Scientist, 27,* 689–704.

Merisca, R., & Bybee, J. A. (1994, April). *Guilt, not moral reasoning, relates to volunteerism, prosocial behavior, lowered aggressiveness, and eschewal of racism.* Poster presented at the Annual Meeting of the Eastern Psychological Association, Providence, Rhode Island.

Modell, A. H. (1971). The origin of certain forms of pre-oedipal guilt and the implications for a psychoanalytic theory of affects. *International Journal of Psychoanalysis, 52,* 337–346.

Mosher, D. L. (1966). The development and multi-trait-multi-method matrix analysis of three measures and three aspects of guilt. *Journal of Consulting Psychology, 30,* 25–29.

Mosher, D. L. (1979). The meaning and measurement of guilt. In C. E. Izard (Ed.), *Emotions and personality in psychopathology* (pp. 105–129). New York: Plenum.

Nietzsche, F. (1971). "Guilt," "bad conscience," and related matters. In R. W. Smith (Ed.), *Guilt: man and society* (pp. 27–61) (F. Golffing, Trans.). New York: Doubleday/Anchor Books. (Original work published 1956)

Okel, E., & Mosher, D. L. (1968). Changes in affective states as a function of guilt over aggressive behavior. *Journal of Consulting and Clinical Psychology, 32,* 265–270.

Persons, R. W. (1970). The Mosher Guilt Scale: Theoretical formulation, research review, and normative data. *Journal of Projective Techniques and Personality Assessment, 34,* 266–270.

Prosen, M., Clark, D. C., Harrow, M., & Fawcett, J. (1983). Guilt and conscience in major depressive disorders. *American Journal of Psychiatry, 140,* 839–844.

Quiles, Z. N., & Bybee, J. (1997). Chronic and predispositional guilt: Relations to mental health, prosocial behavior, and religiosity. *Journal of Personality Assessment, 69,* 104–126.

Scott, M. B., & Lyman, S. M. (1968). Accounts. *American Sociological Review, 33,* 46–62.

Stegge, H., & Ferguson, T. J. (1990). *Child-Child Attribution and Reaction Survey (C-CARS).* Unpublished instrument, Utah State University, Logan, Utah.

Tangney, J. P. (1991). Moral affect: The good, the bad, and the ugly. *Journal of Personality and Social Psychology, 61,* 598–607.

Tangney, J. P., Burggraf, S. A., & Wagner, P. (1995). Shame-proneness, guilt-proneness, and psychological symptoms. In J. P. Tangney & K. W. Fischer (Eds.), *Self-conscious emotions: The psychology of shame, guilt, embarrassment, and pride* (pp. 343–367). New York: Guilford.

Tangney, J. P., Wagner, P., Fletcher, C., & Gramzow, R. (1992a). Shamed into anger? The relation of shame and guilt to anger and self-reported aggression. *Journal of Personality and Social Psychology, 62*, 669–675.

Tangney, J. P., Wagner, P., & Gramzow, R. (1989). *The Test of Self-Conscious Affect.* Fairfax, VA: George Mason University.

Tangney, J. P., Wagner, P., & Gramzow, R. (1992b). Proneness to shame, proneness to guilt, and psychopathology. *Journal of Abnormal Psychology, 101*, 469–478.

Thomas, J. L. (1992). *Adulthood and aging.* Boston: Allyn & Bacon.

Thompson, R. A. (1994). Emotion regulation: A theme in search of definition. In N. A. Fox (Ed.), The development of emotion regulation: Biological and behavioral considerations. *Monographs of the Society for Research in Child Development, 59* (2-3, Serial No. 240).

Wallington, S. A. (1973). Consequences of transgression: Self-punishment and depression. *Journal of Personality and Social Psychology, 28*, 1–7.

Zahn-Waxler, C., Cole, P. M., & Barrett, K. C. (1991). Guilt and empathy: Sex differences and implications for the development of depression. In J. Garber & K. Dodge (Eds.), *The development of emotion regulation and dysregulation* (pp. 243–272). Cambridge: Cambridge University Press.

Zahn-Waxler, C., & Kochanska, G. (1990). The origins of guilt. In R. A. Thompson (Ed.), *The 36th Annual Nebraska Symposium on Motivation: Socioemotional Development* (pp. 183–258). Lincoln: University of Nebraska Press.

Zahn-Waxler, C., Kochanska, G., Krupnick, J., & Mayfield, A. (1988). *Coding manual for Children's Interpretations of Interpersonal Distress and Conflict.* Laboratory of Developmental Psychology. National Institute of Mental Health.

Zahn-Waxler, C., Kochanska, G., Krupnick, J., & McKnew, D. (1990). Patterns of guilt in children of depressed and well mothers. *Developmental Psychology, 26*, 51–59.

LANG
BF575
G8 G85
1998

LANGLE DATE DUE

MAR 1 8 2003		
FEB 0 6 2008		
GAYLORD		PRINTED IN U.S.A.